# MASTERWORKS
## OF
## CHILDREN'S
## LITERATURE

# MASTERWORKS
# OF
# CHILDREN'S
# LITERATURE

*Volume One*
c.1550 – c.1739
*The Early Years*

EDITED BY *Francelia Butler*

GENERAL EDITOR: *Jonathan Cott*

ASSISTANT EDITOR: *Charity Chang*

THE STONEHILL PUBLISHING COMPANY
IN ASSOCIATION WITH
CHELSEA HOUSE PUBLISHERS
NEW YORK

GENERAL EDITOR: Jonathan Cott
ADVISORY EDITOR: Robert G. Miner, Jr.
VOLUME EDITOR: Francelia Butler
PROJECT DIRECTOR: Esther Mitgang
DESIGNER: Paul Bacon
EDITORIAL STAFF: Philip Minges III, Claire Bottler
PRODUCTION: Coco Dupuy, Heather White, Sandra Su, Susan Lusk,
Christopher Newton

First Printing
Printed and Bound in the United States of America
ISBN: 0-87754-375-5
LC: 79-89986
Chelsea House Publishers
   Harold Steinberg, Chairman and Publisher
   Andrew E. Norman, President
   Susan Lusk, Vice President
A Division of Chelsea House Educational Communications, Inc.,
133 Christopher Street. New York, NY 10014.

ACKNOWLEDGMENTS

*The Holy Bible Done Into Verse,* London, 1698. Courtesy of The David McCandless McKell Collection, The Ross County Historical Society, Chillicothe, Ohio.

Richard Johnson, ed.: *The Seven Champions of Christendom,* London, 1616. Courtesy of The David McCandless McKell Collection, The Ross County Historical Society, Chillicothe, Ohio.

*The Roxburghe Ballads* (selections), New York, 1969. Courtesy of AMS Press (reprint edition).

*Valentine and Orson,* London, 1736. Courtesy of the Special Collections Department at The University of Connecticut Library (16th edition).

Thomas Willis: "Apples of Gold in Pictures of Silver," from *The Key of Knowledg opening the principles of religion; and the paths of life . . .,* London, 1682. Courtesy of the British Library Board.

Photography for items reproduced from the Special Collections Department, University of Connecticut Library, is by Richard Akeroyd, a member of The National Commission on Libraries and Information Science, Washington, D.C. Photography for items reproduced from The David McCandless McKell Collection, The Ross County Historical Society, Chillicothe, Ohio, is by Tomastik.

The Editors and Publisher wish to acknowledge the encouragement and assistance of Mr. Eugene D. Rigney, Director, and Mr. Charles Tomastik, President, Ross County Historical Society, Chillicothe, Ohio; Mr. Marcus A. McCorison, Director and Librarian, and Mr. Frederick E. Bauer, Jr., Assistant Librarian, and other staff of the library of The American Antiquarian Society, Worcester, Massachusetts; Miss Judith St. John, Librarian in Charge, Osborne Collection, Boys and Girls House, Toronto, Ontario, Canada; Mr. Richard Schimmelpfing, Head of Special Collections, University of Connecticut Library, Storrs, Connecticut; Mr. Richard Akeroyd, a member of The National Commission on Libraries and Information Science, Washington, D.C.; Ms. Judy Goldstein, Boston Museum of Fine Arts, Boston, Massachusetts; the Reference Department staff, University of Connecticut Library, Storrs, Connecticut; and Mrs. Carol Boardman, editorial assistant, Storrs, Connecticut. The Publisher especially acknowledges the careful and diligent work of Mr. Lloyd Foust, Jackson Typesetters, Jackson, Michigan. The General Editor gratefully acknowledges the generous encouragement and assistance of Justin Schiller, Raymond Wapner, and Jeffrey Steinberg, who helped make MASTERWORKS OF CHILDREN'S LITERATURE possible.

Credit must be given especially to Dean Hugh Clark and the Research Foundation of the University of Connecticut.

*Dedicated to the Memory of*
*Jeffrey Joshua Steinberg*
*Founder and President of*
*Stonehill Communications, Inc.*

*In Memory of Grace Ann Likes, Sister of Francelia Butler
and for Vivian Pierce, Daughter of Charity Chang*

# Contents

*Preface*

F OR MANY YEARS, interest in and study of the history of children's literature has been fostered predominantly by teachers and librarians trained in education and library science schools—the most progressive and courageous of whom have always insisted on preserving, promoting, and protecting the best of this literature from the attacks on it by censorious individuals and pressure groups.

Readers, writers, critics, and teachers of literature generally—as well as psychologists, political scientists, and historians—now realize that the study of children's literature can no longer be restricted to specialists in the field—inestimable as their contributions have been and are. For what children either have chosen or have been forced to read not only reveals much about our societal and cultural attitudes but also discloses to us a forgotten and often maligned body of literature that ultimately cannot be conceived of as separate from our most important esthetic, ethical, and spiritual concerns.

Although no one country can claim a unique status for its contributions to the field of children's literature—both written and oral—it is commonly agreed that England has produced some of the most representative, and perhaps the most influential, works for children. The many excellent histories of English children's literature currently in print have concentrated primarily on its critical and bibliographical aspects. But MASTERWORKS OF CHILDREN'S LITERATURE is the first comprehensive source book of the history of this literature, presenting complete and authoritative texts of (and, in some cases, carefully chosen selections from) scores of ballads, fables, stories, novels, plays, poems, science texts, and picture books from 1550–1900. Although this anthology has emphasized the textual aspects of English children's literature, we also have attempted, whenever possible, to reproduce all of the accompanying original illustrative materials.

Twentieth-century children's books, of course, continue for the most part to be readily available in a great variety of editions and have therefore not been included in this collection. The growing scholarly and general interest in earlier children's literature, however, has created a need for an anthology of this kind. Children's books are among the least stable of historical documents: the best are literally read to pieces. For this reason, many famous, influential, and much-discussed works for children are effectively unavailable to students of the subject.

Each of the three major periods covered in this collection is edited by a prominent scholar of children's literature who provides an extensive introduction to the period, placing the works in their literary, cultural, and historical contexts. The editors also provide background notes which discuss the importance of each selection and indicate the editions of the texts used in this anthology. Except for the few and obvious cases where we have facsimiled certain works because of their visual importance, we have set in type all the selected works in order to present clear, readable, and accurate texts based on early and mostly rare editions. In doing so, we have adhered to certain procedures concerning changes in the original spelling, punctuation, and typography that require a short explanation.

Throughout the years covered by the first four volumes of this anthology, the existence and use of dictionaries as we now know them was minimal; and many writers and printers of that time occasionally spelled the same word various ways on the same page, or even in the same line. For the sake of accuracy, and in order to keep the flavor of the original texts, we have retained the original, sometimes inconsistent spelling and punctuation, with a few exceptions. For clarity's sake, we have: regularized the letters *i* and *j*, *u* and *v*, and *w* and *vv*, often used interchangeably during the sixteenth and seventeenth centuries; substituted the letter *s* for its secondary form ( *ʃ* ), employed until the beginning of the nineteenth century; and eliminated the practice of substituting *y* for *th* which was common until the eighteenth century.

Children's literature as a specialized field and as a commercial endeavor began in the mid-eighteenth century, and there is little scholarly research material readily available on the period 1550–1739. For this reason, both an annotated bibliography of works believed to have been shared by children and adults during this period and a selected bibliography of secondary sources have been prepared for the material covering these years.

Readers interested in an extensive annotated bibliography of books, pamphlets, catalogs, lists, and periodical articles concerning children's literature of the past two hundred years should consult Virginia Haviland's *Children's Literature: A Guide to Reference Sources* (1966) and the *First Supplement* (1972) and the *Second Supplement* (1977) to this work. These three volumes, published in Washington by the Library of Congress, are the first of an envisaged series of supplementary bibliographies to be compiled under the supervision of Miss Haviland.

J. C.

**Jonathan Cott** attended Columbia College, the University of California, Berkeley, and the University of Essex, where he studied children's literature on a Fulbright fellowship. He has contributed to publications such as the *New York Times, Parabola, The New Yorker, American Review,* and *Rolling Stone,* of which he is a Contributing Editor. He is the author and editor of several books, including *Stockhausen: Conversations with the Composer; He Dreams What Is Going On Inside His Head; Beyond the Looking Glass: Victorian Fairy Tale Novels, Stories and Poems; The Roses Race Around Her Name: Poems from Fathers to Daughters;* a collection of poems entitled *City of Earthly Love;* and *Piper at the Gates of Dawn: The Wisdom of Children's Literature.*

## General Introduction

### By Jonathan Cott

*All children are by nature evil, and while*
*they have none but the natural evil principle to guide them,*
*pious and prudent parents must check their naughty passions*
*in any way that they have in their power, and*
*force them into decent and proper behaviour*
*and into what are called good habits.*
MRS. SHERWOOD

*The newborn infant appears as an energy system that*
*brings some definite cosmic laws of*
*functioning into man's realm of operation.*
WILHELM REICH

*Little rope, little rope, oh my little rope,*
*Unwind yourself from the round ball:*
*Twirl round and round and high.*
*Take me outdoors to the air and the sun.*
*Out of the room, out of the house, the narrow house;*
*Nobody can catch us!*
*Little rope, little rope, oh my little rope,*
*Unwind yourself from the ball.*
SKIPPING RHYME

THE HISTORY of children's literature is the history of the distance between the adult and the child. In her book *Nineteenth Century Children*, Gillian Avery has shrewdly pointed out that children's literature, from its inception as a specialized and recognized field in the mid-eighteenth century, has, for the most part, represented a history of "adult taste in children." Even before the eighteenth century, however, we can see in the ways adults defined and determined what children were and should be a reflection of the universal conflict between adults' perceptions of spontaneous child-like behavior and their preconceptions concerning the education of the young. Today we are discovering that medieval children, far from being considered simply as miniature adults, were frequently looked upon as creatures undeniably different from their elders and in need of admonishment and control.

"Small children often have bad habits," Bartholomæus Anglicus—after Aristotle—wrote in his thirteenth-century treatise on medieval child-rearing: "They think only of the present, caring not at all for the future. They love games and vain pursuits, refusing to concern themselves with what is profitable and useful. They consider unimportant matters important, and important matters of little or no significance. . . . They cry and weep more over the loss of an apple or pear than over the loss of an inheritance. They forget favors they have received, desire and want everything they see, and ask for it with their voices and hands. They love the conversation and counsels of children like themselves, flee and avoid the company of the aged. They keep no secrets, but repeat everything they see and hear. Suddenly they laugh, suddenly they cry, continuously shouting, chattering and laughing."

It has been suggested that before Freud, children were considered innocent; and that before Piaget, they were considered ignorant. But this idea presumes that the history of childhood had its origins only at the end of the nineteenth century in Western Europe. As Anglicus' observations suggest, the irrepressibilities of childhood have always been impossible to ignore; and the idealization or the derogation of childhood ways has served simply to define the border between childhood's and man's estate. Today we generally think of a child neither as a copy of prelapsarian Adam nor as a Brand of Hell; we tend to feel the child is less a *tabula rasa* than a being who brings eternally young life to the living. And our ideas concerning child-rearing and education have certainly advanced beyond those of medieval times. Yet we still find many persons longing for the undifferentiated communal life of that earlier period when Being and Knowledge were supposedly not yet divided, forgetting that children at that time were frequently abandoned, abused, or simply neglected.

Today, of course, children—at least of the middle class—have more time to remain children, so much so that as they get older they frequently adopt and embrace an adolescent identity that extends almost into middle age. And as the idea of maturity recedes before them and becomes invisible, they lose sight of the fact that the freedom to develop and be accepted as a *child* was a fairly recent and privileged occurrence, one that was defined by the child's remoteness from adult concerns. Coeval with the miniaturization of the family and the quarantining of young and old persons is a resulting sense of exile: the price we have paid for the gift of our awareness of and concern for childhood. As the psychologist J. H. van den Berg explains in *Metabletica* (*The Changing Nature of Man*):

In Montaigne's day no one needed a psychology of the child; he was permitted to enter the adult's world early and unhampered, and there was no gap which necessitated a scientific bridge of understanding. There were no playgrounds then; the child played in the streets, among the adults, he was part of their life. When, in 1901, Ellen Key exclaimed that the century of the child had commenced, the children might have exulted over the fact that, at last, somebody had seen what a sad state the youngsters were in because of the growing complexity of maturity; but they might just as well have burst into tears because this had become necessary. When adults are interested in the child, there is something wrong with the child—and with the adults. Growing children were never as secure as when there was no child psychology. This psychology is the result of a state of emergency.

But, as historian Lawrence Stone writes: "Most children in history have not been loved or hated, or both, by their parents; they have been neglected or ignored by them." Considering that, the question that the above quotation begs, therefore, is: When we talk to or write for a child as a *child*, are we denying or respecting his or her being, needs, and experience?

In the sixteenth century, Montaigne advised parents to educate their children by confronting them with philosophical discourses. And a hundred years later, it was John Locke who insisted that children desire "a gentle Persuasion in Reasoning. . . . They understand it as early as they do Language; and, if I misobserve not, they like to be treated as rational Creatures." Locke's great contribution to educational theory was that he re-negotiated the generally adhered to notion of the child as a creature who was to be seen but not heard. In the words of Rosalie L. Colie, Locke "brings the child . . . out of his obscurity, his invisibility, into the light, even the glare, of philosophical examination; the child become a philosophical subject." A *philosophical subject*, but not yet a child. And it remained for Rousseau to affirm that "childhood is the sleep of reason," and to admonish his readers that "the child is a child, not an adult; you are the adult."

Rousseau's progressive, sympathetic, and even reverential attitudes concerning the nature of childhood (romping, games, songs, and amusement) cannot, however, disguise the fact that, when it came to the question of what children should read, he was a benighted authoritarian. He abhorred fables and fairy tales, and forbade Émile to read any book except *Robinson Crusoe* before the age of eighteen. Yet Rousseau's self-appointed followers in France and England in fact produced and forced upon children an enormous number of ill-tempered and stifling works. "I will write you a Dialogue," Lady Fenn announces in one such work, *The Fairy Spectator*, "in which the Fairy shall converse, and I will give you a Moral for your Dream." And when the Fairy converses, she informs the child: "I am your guardian, to watch over your mind."

Although Locke, like Rousseau, condemned fairy tales, as well as ballads and chapbook romances (calling them "useless trumpery"), he not only gave his approval to *Aesop's Fables* and *Reynard the Fox* but also urged that children be provided with books other than Horn-Books, Primers, Psalters, and Bibles—books that would instruct by means of Recreation and Play. (Think of Giles Gingerbread, who learned his letters by eating them!) But we should not overlook the fact that, for Locke, amusement and delight were simply the sugar-coated ingredients of a cachet, the medicinal purpose of which was to foster an acceptance of a conservative social and economic order, to be encouraged through the promotion of virtues such as tolerance, benevolence, industry, and moderation. (See Robert Bator's introduction to Volume III of this anthology for an extended discussion of the influence of Locke and Rousseau on eighteenth-century children's books.)

In her introduction to this volume, Francelia Butler suggests that the creation of children's literature as a specialized field in the eighteenth century came about as a result of certain economic interests that aimed to control and exploit children. And in *Mrs. Sherwood and Her Books for Children*, M. Nancy Cutt has clearly confirmed and expanded on this idea by demonstrating the effect children's books had on British imperialist policy.

> Children of literate middle-class families in particular, usually given a strict and
> thorough Sunday School training, must have carried through life ingrained impres-

sions of Mrs. Sherwood's . . . India, and an emotional bias to match. They acquired a strong conviction of the rightness of missions, which, while it inculcated sincere concern for and a genuine kindness towards an alien people for whom Britain was responsible, quite destroyed any latent respect for Indian tradition. The paternalism, so marked in British policy towards India, must have been partly the result of Victorian attitudes formed in the nursery.

Far from denying van den Berg's "state of emergency," the development of the children's book industry seems to have been a primary tool in the manipulation of children's minds, making it a task of great importance to observe and analyze the means, goals, and effects of such a body of work. And in this context, I must mention the pioneering work of Mary Ørvig, director of the Swedish Institute of Children's Books, who, with immense erudition and dialectical acumen, has explored and re-evaluated the history of the generally forgotten "girls' books" of the eighteenth and nineteenth centuries. The following remarks on this subject are taken from her lecture on the relationships between children's literature and politics entitled "One World in Children's Books?" (published by the American Library Association) :

> As children's literature became sexually segregated, the roles and stations appointed for girls were meticulously dinned into them through their reading matter. But in many of these now so abhorrent girls' books one can discern an early protest against the current system of child education, against the so-called womanly virtues, against the lack of education and job opportunities. The many detractors of girls' books have been unduly monolithic in their approach and have shown too little interest in the background—the social status of girls, their educational, occupational, and economic opportunities. Behind the girls' book one can trace many features of the history and attitudes of the entire century, the background and activities of the first women writers, religious and social trends, economic conditions, the surplus of women, the women's emancipation movement and, what is perhaps most important of all, the ideal of womanly upbringing and education. Girls were deliberately excluded from the intellectual trends and social change of their times. But there were rebels among them, and many escapes were attempted. . . . People nowadays are right in rejecting the idea of books for boys or girls only. But even then girls' books were popularly smiled at. Boys' books on the other hand were seldom viewed in the same critical light, which was unfortunate. If girls' books were prudish, boys' books were no less handicapped by their emotional sterility and their adulation of beefy biceps, not to mention their preoccupation with war, otherwise known as adventure.

In this kind of analysis, children's literature does not merely reflect a specific social scene but rather becomes a kind of magnifying glass to the operations and processes of the society at large. This "magnifying" effect can easily be seen in many fairy tales, in the medieval *Reynard the Fox*, in the numerous early chap-book versions of *The World Turned Upside Down* (in which a child turns into a parent, a soldier into a nurse), in juvenile animal stories like the eighteenth-century *Biography of a Spaniel* and *Keeper's*

*Travels,* in Victorian political satires like *Petsetilla's Posy* and *The Rose and the Ring,* and, most obviously, in the distorting mirror-world of Lewis Carroll.

But even in many overtly didactic works for children—with the possible exception of the life-denying "Joyful Deaths" tradition promulgated by the Puritans and, later, by writers like Hannah More and Mrs. Sherwood—the ineradicable nature of childhood energy insists on attaining a power that no "improving" or "cautionary" force can destroy. For in the attempt to admonish and chastise reprehensibly "childish" behavior, these minatory works cannot help but evoke what Herbert Marcuse has termed "the words, the images, the music of another reality, of another order repelled by the existing one and yet alive in memory and anticipation." Just the simple depiction of scurrying little mice (*The Life and Perambulation of a Mouse*), prankster children (*Holiday House*), ill-mannered Goops (*Goops and How To Be Them*), or any of Dr. Seuss's rambunctious heroes allows the reader to fantasize the subversion of the restricting moral and social order and to envisage a reality more open and connected to the instinctual urges of childhood.

But however fascinating it may be to expose the social and psychological mechanisms existing at the heart of the cautionary school of children's literature, it is essential first to recognize the enormous distance, revealed in this literature, between the authors' notion of themselves as rational, tutelary authorities and of their readers as primitive, unformed little charges. By contrast, the greatest and most imaginative children's literature (e.g., the works of William Roscoe, George MacDonald, and Beatrix Potter) makes us aware of how little distance actually lies between its creators' sense of themselves as "adults" and as "children." As Maurice Sendak has stated in a *New Yorker* interview with Nat Hentoff:

> I don't believe, in a way, that the kid I was grew up into me. He still exists somewhere, in the most graphic, plastic, physical way. It's as if he had moved somewhere. I have a tremendous concern for him and interest in him. I communicate with him—or try to—all the time. One of my worst fears is losing contact with him. I don't want this to sound coy or schizophrenic, but at least once a day I feel I have to make a contact. The pleasures I get as an adult are heightened by the fact that I experience them as a child at the same time. Like, when autumn comes, as an adult I welcome the departure of the heat, and simultaneously, as a child would, I start anticipating the snow and the first day it will be possible to use a sled. This dual appreciation does break down occasionally. That usually happens when my work is going badly. I get a sour feeling about books in general and my own in particular. The next stage is annoyance at my dependence on this dual appreciation, and I reject it. Then I become depressed. When excitement about what I'm working on returns, so does the child. We're on happy terms again.

The importance of this kind of "contact" has been attested to throughout history: "The great man is the man who hasn't lost the heart he had when he was a little child" (Mencius); "Genius is childhood recalled at will" (Baudelaire); "Childhood is the nearest to true life" (André Breton). For "childhood" is truly that mysterious area where, in the words of the painter Joan Miró "creation takes place and from which there flows an inexplicable radiance that finally comes to be the whole man."

It is this awareness of the inseparability of what is "grown-up" from what is "child-like"—experienced at the root of all creative endeavors—that has led many persons to refuse to recognize the value of a separate literature for children. Francelia Butler points out that before the eighteenth century, children shared with adults a literature of "dual interest." (See her introduction to this volume for an extended discussion of this subject.) And Samuel Johnson, in conversation with Mrs. Thrale, expressed his disdain for the "new" writings intended specifically for children:

> "Babies do not want (said he) to hear about babies; they like to be told of giants and castles, and of somewhat which can stretch and stimulate their little minds." When in answer I would urge the numerous editions and quick sale of Tommy Prudent or Goody Two-Shoes: "Remember always (said he) that the parents buy the books, and that the children never read them."

A century later, Chekhov, in a letter to a friend, wrote:

> I don't like what is known as children's literature; I don't recognize its validity. Children should be given only what is suitable for adults as well. Children enjoy reading Andersen, *The Frigate Pallada*, and Gogol, and so do adults. One shouldn't write for children; one should learn to choose works suitable for children from among those already written for adults—in other words, from genuine works of art.

Surprisingly, this attitude is as reminiscent of pre-eighteenth-century practice as it is a prescient indication of the kind of enlightened contemporary ideas we find expressed in a work like *Bibliophile in the Nursery* by William Targ: "A good children's book strikes a vibration in the soul that lasts a lifetime. And when a reader or collector achieves maturity and a special sense of values, he may recognize that the best books are really those that children have loved for many generations of lifetimes."

The Psalms of David, the Parables of Jesus, *The Flowers of St. Francis*, *Le Morte d'Arthur*, the poetry of Blake, George MacDonald's *The Golden Key*, the works of Lewis Carroll and Beatrix Potter, *The Wind in the Willows*, *The Wizard of Oz*, *Millions of Cats*, *Babar the King*—all of these exist in one timeless and ageless universe, fulfilling the requirement, as stated by the critic of the *Quarterly Review* of 1844, that a children's book be a "union of the highest art with the simplest form."

If at one time, our special awarenesses of childhood resulted in the exile of children from the adult world (and vice versa), today's pluralistic society has made us intensely conscious of the fact that, as van den Berg himself argues, "it is simply [no longer] permissible to deny the child its inner contrasts." And this realization applies equally to our expectations concerning the possibilities of children's literature. For by allowing themselves to "contact" the child within, authors and illustrators during the past hundred years have discovered and expressed the real feelings of children (in works like Flora Shaw's *Castle Blair*, Kenneth Grahame's *The Golden Age*, and Maurice Sendak's *Where The Wild Things Are*) and have returned to and drawn inspiration from the origins of children's literature (fairy tales, ballads, street games, nursery rhymes)—as well as from the signals, gestures, and the lore and the language of children themselves which, in the words of George Steiner, represent "a night-raid on adult territory."

Today, many creators of children's literature, along with those interested in the history of this literature—which is itself a generally unknown territory—are attempting to discover and explore the needs and realities of children, as well as the intentions and motivations of the adults who have written for them. In so doing, they are not only recognizing the distance between childhood and adulthood that exists, to a greater or lesser extent, in every era and culture, but are also beginning to observe the ways in which every society is writ small in the literature it creates for its young. The art of observation, according to Walter Benjamin, is the "real genius of education" and "at the heart of unsentimental love." And the aim of MASTERWORKS OF CHILDREN'S LITERATURE is simply to encourage such observation.

Francelia Butler, a pioneer in the teaching of children's literature to university students, received her doctorate in Renaissance English from the University of Virginia. She teaches her subject at the University of Connecticut at Storrs, as well as at the Sir George Williams campus, Concordia University, Montreal, Canada. She has written books and articles in the field of the seventeenth century, including *The Strange Critical Fortunes of Timon of Athens* (Iowa State University Press), and has edited *The Doctor on the Stage: Medical Undercurrents of Seventeenth-Century Drama* (University of Tennessee Press). She is the founder and editor-in-chief of the journal *Children's Literature* (Yale University Press), the founder of the Seminar on Children's Literature of the Modern Language Association, and a member of the founding board of the Children's Literature Association. In addition to her essays in *Children's Literature,* her publications in this field include articles for the *New York Times, Signal, Virginia Quarterly Review,* and *The Antioch Review,* as well as a module on children's literature published by Empire State College, Saratoga Springs, New York. She is the author of *Sharing Literature with Children* (David McKay Co.—Longman, Inc.) and of a forthcoming adult novel on child abuse, *The Lucky Piece* (Van Vactor-Goodheart, Boston). She presided over the 1983 National Endowment for the Humanities Institute on Children's Literature in Connecticut.

## Children's Literature From The Late Sixteenth To The Early Eighteenth Century

### By Francelia Butler

CHILDREN'S LITERATURE—depending on how you define it—either was born or died in the seventeenth century.

In the narrow sense of a literature created exclusively for children, children's literature was born in the seventeenth century, in the grim tracts produced especially for children by Puritan society, and is continued today in the tasteless books subtly promoting certain values in a cute or heavy-handed way, which still flood the market. But one may have a fuller notion of children's literature as literature vibrant with human life and experience—the literature of the ballads, folk tales, the chapbooks and the plays—in short, the literature that parents and children once were lucky enough to enjoy together without self-consciousness. This literature of dual appeal began to shrivel and die in the late seventeenth century.

Up to and during much of the seventeenth century, most children were fortunate in not having a special literature designed to reflect the guilt feelings of adults and to shape their behavior in accordance with the desires of adults. They shared with their parents all books both light and heavy, from *Tom Thumb* to the lurid tales of John Foxe's *The Acts and Monuments of the Church*, popularly known as *The Book of Martyrs* (1563). Literary joys and terrors were not designed for children alone but for everybody. The solid debates between characters in the morality plays were everybody's concern, as were the raucous puppet shows and stage plays—including Shakespeare's—in which children often performed. They took part also in the elaborately staged and costumed masques such as Milton's *Comus* (1634). Like little Mamillius in Shakespeare's *Winter's Tale*, they relished old folk tales. And they participated in the mummers' plays, or masked festivals, often about St. George slaying a Turkish knight or a dragon—who always came to life again.

William Sloane, in his important volume *Children's Books in England and America in the Seventeenth Century* (Columbia University, N.Y., 1955), defines a children's book as "a book written for children only." Since over half of his book is a checklist of books for children, Sloane had to establish some way of narrowing the material to be examined. Valuable as his bibliography is, it has confused some readers about the kind of literature to which the majority of English children in the seventeenth century were exposed.

Sloane himself understands the limitations of his checklists. In speaking of "thumb" or miniature Bibles, he writes: "It was the eighteenth-century condensations, however, and not the seventeenth-century ones, which were specially prepared for children. In the seventeenth century, these works children shared with adults." His definition of children's literature necessarily forces him to leave out—as he is well aware—some of the most popular and influential books told to or read by children.

"Children then as now," he writes, "did not read *Pilgrim's Progress* as the popular guidebook to rebirth and the controversial pamphlet that it was; they read it as an exciting story of adventure." Sloane must omit *Pilgrim's Progress* from his checklist, and he must also leave out many other works interesting to children and adults alike: "It was only when the seventeenth century closed, however, that the romances and fairy tales in penny chapbooks became the pastime only of children." As Sloane says: "To a large extent children's literature in the seventeenth century paralleled adult literature, both popular and cultivated."

In ballads and chapbooks—cheap paperbound books sold by merchants or chapmen— whole families in the seventeenth century enjoyed such stories of adventure as those in *Guy of Warwick*, dating from the thirteenth century as a metrical romance and continued as extremely popular verse by Samuel Rowlands in the seventeenth century. Rowlands' version went into nine editions between 1600 and 1700. A great chapbook favorite was *Jack the Giant Killer*, probably of Indo-European origin, to which Shakespeare alludes in the most poignant part of *King Lear*, the Heath scene (Act III, scene iv), when Edgar as Mad Tom says:

> Child Rowland to the dark tower came; his word was still
> Fie, foh, and fum!
> I smell the blood of a British man.

A 1630 edition of *Tom Thumb* is in the Bodleian Library, Oxford, a gift of Robert Burton, author of *The Anatomy of Melancholy*. This small black letter book is in split Poulter's measure, or alternate rhyming lines of four and three feet. In 1686, John Dunton sold *The History of Tom Thumb* in Boston, Massachusetts. Dr. Harry B. Weiss, who made a study of this book, wrote in *The Scientific American* (34 [1932]: 157–166) that "although the coarseness of the seventeenth century would not be permitted to circulate in the nurseries of today, it should be remembered that in the seventeenth century, *Tom Thumb* was as popular with adults as with children."

The Bodleian Library has a copy of *The History of the Children in the Wood* (1687), originally a ballad, and the British Museum has a ballad account of the children dated 1640 (Rox.1.284). This early story of child abuse, shared by many adults and children, appeared in a number of editions in the seventeenth and eighteenth centuries and on into the nineteenth century. Another book shared by adults and children was *Valentine and Orson*, translated from the French by Henry Watson and printed in England by Wynkyn de Worde in the early sixteenth century. In his study of this work, Arthur Dickson (Columbia University Press, 1929) notes that "for four centuries, edition has followed edition, to a total of at least seventy-four, the latest in 1919." This is an archetypal story of twin brothers, thrust into a hostile world, who later learn who they are and achieve their rightful place.

From the time that a ballad appeared on this theme in 1588, children and adults together heard musical and dramatic versions of an early sixteenth-century German story of a man who sold his soul to the devil. The man was Dr. Faustus, a real-life alchemist. Even in the nineteenth century, the tale rang in the ears of Goethe after he saw it as a little boy when he visited a puppet show. The story of Fortunatus, a youth from Famagusta, also came from the continent—there was a Dutch version in 1509. Fortunatus was blessed by the Goddess of Fortune with a magical purse that not only furnished him with a limitless supply of money but automatically converted it to the currency of the country through which he was passing. Besides the purse, he acquired a magical hat, which enabled him to travel at will whenever he clapped it on his head. (Magical purses and hats are old folk motifs, found also in Japan and Russia and other parts of the world.) In 1599, Thomas Dekker produced a play entitled *Old Fortunatus*.

The story of the male-dominated Griselda, related by Chaucer in "The Clerkes Tale," was still interesting to seventeenth-century adult and child readers. It was published in play form in London in 1603. With the rise of the merchant class in London, people were attracted by the story of Simon Eyre, a legendary shoemaker who became Lord Mayor of London. Thomas Deloney told the story in prose in *The Gentle Craft* in 1599, and Thomas Dekker wrote a play about Eyre, *The Shoemaker's Holiday*, in 1600. In the same vein, Deloney wrote a story, *The Pleasant History of John Winchcombe, in his Younger Years called Jack of Newbury, the Famous and Worthy Clothier of England* (1597), about someone who started as an apprentice and became head of a clothing business during the reign of Henry VII and Henry VIII. This lively story was well received in the rising bourgeois climate in England. Knighthood was no longer in flower, and young men had begun to hope that possibly they, too, could break out of the rigid socioeconomic system.

Older children read Thomas Nashe's *The Unfortunate Traveler, or the Life of Jack Wilton* (1594), a picaresque story, or plotless string of adventures, of a rogue of low birth. "Quoth thee!" (Says you!) says Wilton, as he thumbs his nose at wealth, religious traditions, kingships, and the army. The teenagers of the day also relished the gossipy accounts of the affair between Queen Elizabeth and the Earl of Essex.

Besides prose, children with their elders in the seventeenth century could recite many rhymes. Iona and Peter Opie, in *The Oxford Dictionary of Nursery Rhymes* (1951), have tracked a number of these to their sources in broadsides (large sheets on which ballads or notices were printed), plays, and elsewhere. William S. and Ceil Baring-Gould, in *The Annotated Mother Goose* (1967), have tracked other rhymes to their sources, often in the seventeenth century.

Though written slightly earlier than the period with which we are concerned, some poems of interest both to children and adults were written in Scotland in the sixteenth century. C. S. Lewis, religious philosopher at Oxford and author of the Narnia series of fantasies for children, refers to this poetry in his *English Literature of the Sixteenth Century* (Oxford, 1954)—poetry which reminds him of Edward Lear and Lewis Carroll. Among the poems he mentions is *Cowkelbie Sow* (Bannatyne CCCI), to be found in *The Bannatyne Manuscript*, Vol. 4 (Blackwood, Edinburgh, 1930), published by the Scottish Text Society.

In *Cowkelbie Sow*, as Lewis points out, "the element of extravagance is supplied not so much by the events as by the preposterous connections between them." A sow is sold for three pennies. One of the pennies is lost. The finder spends it on a pig and decides to give a party (here follows a list of the guests). When the guests set about killing the pig, it flees with a yell which brings all the pigs of the neighborhood to its rescue (here follows a list of pigs). This rouses the owners of the other pigs (here follows a list of owners), and so on, "the humor depending on the inconsequences and apparent logic with which each new catalog and each new story branches out of what has gone before." Sometimes bawdy, the fantasy in this narrative poem is gentle, and occasionally "we are allowed to hear God laugh." Characters include a giantess, a King of Faerie, and elves.

Another poem, "in lines which hop and dance," (Bannatyne CLXXVI), describes the laying of a ghost—a timid but merry spirit not as big as a gnat, nevertheless a thief who has stolen from God, Abraham, and the Man in the Moon. The poem ends with the ghost marrying a flea and becoming the father of "Orpheus king and Elpha quene."

Literature in its oral form as drama was experienced by school boys in England at least from the twelfth century. By the mid-sixteenth century, children were performing such plays as *Ralph Roister Doister* by Nicholas Udall and William Stevenson's *Gammer Gurton's Needle*. John Lyly's plays were acted by boys. Before the sixteenth century, no distinction was made between drama for children and adults.

Shakespeare makes frequent reference to popular literature in his plays, and there can be little doubt that as an alert boy, he read or heard the popular anecdotes and ballads. In *Much Ado About Nothing*, he refers, for instance, to *A Hundred Merry Tales* printed by John Rastell in 1526. These tales contain considerable folk wisdom. Here is Tale 51, for example:

> A certain friar had a boy that ever was wont to bear this friar's money and on a time when the boy was far behind his master as they walked together along the way, they met a man who knew that the boy bore the friar's money and said, "How, Master Friar, shall I bid thy boy catch up with thee?" "Yea," quoth the friar.

> Then went the man to the boy and said, "Thy master biddeth thee give me forty pennies." "I will not," quoth the boy. Then called the man with a high voice to the friar and said, "Sir, he saith he will not." Then quoth the friar, "Beat him," and when the boy heard his master say so, he gave the man forty pennies.

> By this ye may see it is folly for a man to say yea or nay to a matter except he knows fully what the matter is.

Many of the jest books of the seventeenth century contain jokes that amused both young and old. In *A Nest of Ninnies* (1608), Robert Armin, a clown or comedian in Shakespeare's company of actors, tells the story of a young fellow, John, who loved to toll church bells. Getting a chance at them one day, he began to ring them, at which everyone dutifully arrived at the Church and asked who had died. "My Nurse's chicken," John told them.

Shakespeare's plays are rich with folk rhymes. In Act I of *Much Ado*, there is reference to an early version of Bluebeard, in which the heroine relates Bluebeard's murders as a dream. In *King Lear*, Edgar intones, "Pillicock sat on Pillicock hill: Halloo, halloo,

loo, loo!" Later, he chants, "Sleepest or wakest thou, jolly shepherd?/Thy sheep be in the corn;/And for one blast of thy minikin mouth,/Thy sheep shall take no harm." (Robert Graves observed that there is more poetry in Mother Goose than in *The Oxford Book of English Verse*.)

Besides the various genres of literature mentioned above, there were also other kinds of works enjoyed by children and adults, including the first picture book, the *Orbis Pictus* by John Amos Comenius, a Czech Protestant refugee who had unorthodox ideas about instruction. Comenius believed that learning should be pleasant, realistic, and down-to-earth, and that pictures helped this process. His delightful book (translated into English in 1659), similar to a primer, consists of charming woodcuts and interesting definitions in English and in Latin.

*Æsop's Fables* was a work of interest to children and adults. However, in the seventeenth century there were editions specifically for children. *Aesop* had been in England at least since the twelfth century and was among the first books printed by William Caxton in the late fifteenth century. Sir Thomas Elyot, in a book of manners for boys, *The Book Named the Governor* (1531), recommended *Aesop* as reading for children, as did John Locke in *Some Thoughts Concerning Education* (1693). Sir Roger L'Estrange published an *Aesop* specifically for children (1692 and 1699). This work contains some fables so bawdy that when republished in Paris in 1931 in a shortened version for adults, it was actually "cleaned up"—though the spicy Alexander Calder illustrations compensated for the omission of the equally spicy literary material. The Paris edition was reprinted by Dover in 1967. Locke himself brought out a soberer version of *Aesop* for children in 1703. In these fables, the humanity outweighs the didacticism. *Aesop* remains an all-time favorite.

John Bunyan's *Pilgrim's Progress* (1678) was not written for children but has had an enduring popularity with many children as well as with adults. The structure of Louisa M. Alcott's *Little Women* was determined in part by *Pilgrim's Progress*. Chapter titles in the former parallel steps of Christian's journey: "Burdens," "Beth Finds the Palace Beautiful," "Amy's Valley of Humiliation," "Jo Meets Apollyon," "Meg Goes to Vanity Fair," "The Valley of the Shadow." Meg, Jo, Beth, and Amy also act out *Pilgrim's Progress*. In Chapter 1, their mother reminds them:

"Do you remember how you used to play *Pilgrim's Progress* when you were little things? Nothing delighted you more than to have me tie my piece-bags on your backs for burdens, give you hats and sticks and rolls of paper, and let you travel through the house from the cellar, which was the City of Destruction, up, up, to the house–top, where you had all the lovely things you could collect to make a Celestial City."

"What fun it was, especially going by the lions, fighting Apollyon and passing through the valley where the hobgoblins were!" said Jo.

"We never are too old for this, my dear, because it is a play we are playing all the time in one way or another. . . ."

Huck Finn also knew *Pilgrim's Progress*, which he found "interesting but tough." What he needed was *Pilgrim's Progress in Words of one Syllable* (New York: Mc-

Loughlin Brothers, 1884), rather than one of the other editions of *Pilgrim's Progress* issued for children in the nineteenth century.

In an article on "Pilgrim's Progress as Fairy Tale" (*Children's Literature*, Vol. I, 1972), Alison White notes the close resemblance in theme between *Pilgrim's Progress* and J. R. R. Tolkien's *Lord of the Rings*. She also finds that *Pilgrim's Progress* fathered a succession of literary fantasies by such writers as Lewis Carroll, George MacDonald, and Charles Kingsley. Bunyan's allegory is, she says, "the world's greatest Cinderella story. A man in rags and with a 'magic' burden is clothed (as by a fairy godmother) in a 'broidered' coat . . . and wins a crown in a city of gold where he feasts with the greatest of princes."

A delight of the seventeenth century is the great old romance, *The Seven Champions of Christendom*, descended from a medieval romance (Bevis of Hampton). Written by an Elizabethan popular writer, Richard Johnson, and published in the late sixteenth century, this creative and lively mélange of old elements in other tales continued to be read well into the nineteenth century. As children's literature, it is important not only in itself but because it influenced the development of the English mummers' (masked) plays of St. George (see Sir E. K. Chambers, *The English Folk-Play*, Oxford, 1933). In *The Seven Champions*, St. George survives impossible odds and always wins out against infidel knights, just as he does in the mummers' plays once so common in English villages.

Chambers points out that the Turkish knight, Slasher, in the mummers' plays has armor of brass which also closely parallels the brass scales of the dragon in *The Seven Champions*. Slasher boasts:

> My head is made of iron strong,
> My body's made of steel,
> My arms and legs of beaten brass,
> No man can make me feel.

During the seventeenth century, the main champion, St. George, also appeared in ballads.

Episodic in structure, the action in *The Seven Champions* moves rapidly. Psychologically, the narrative carries interest as a small group of men works together for a common cause. Like Ulysses' men or the brothers in the *Mahabharata*, St. George has to grapple with several giants. In Jungian psychology giants are the uncontrolled passions. Sometimes, as Marie-Louise Franz of the Jung Institute suggests in her work *Shadow and Evil in Fairy Tales* (1974), the strength of giants, stupidly employed if divorced from reason, can be harnessed and put to the service of saintly persons. That is, the evil in one's nature, if recognized, can be used constructively. So it is with St. George, if one follows this psychological interpretation. In the land of the Amazons, a conquered giant agrees to be "ever after his sworn, true servant, and attend on him with all diligence."

Obviously the accepted seventeenth century and earlier custom of having children share literature with adults grew out of a general attitude toward children. John Earle expresses it well in a "character" book in which certain types of persons in society are depicted. In *Microcosmographie* (1628), his first "character" is that of a child:

A childe is a Man in a small Letter, yet the best Copie of *Adam* before hee tasted of Eve, or the Apple; and hee is happy whose small practice in the World can only write this Character. Hee is natures fresh picture newly drawne in Oyle, which time, and much handling, dimmes and defaces. His Soule is yet a white paper unscribled with observations of the world, wherewith at length it becomes a blurr'd note booke. Hee is purely happy, because he knowes no evill, nor hath made meanes by sinne to bee acquainted with misery. Hee arrives not at the mischiefe of being wise, nor endures evils to come by foreseeing them. He kisses and loves all, and when the smart of the rod is past, smiles on his beater. Nature and his parents alike dandle him, and tice him on with a bait of sugar to a draught of worme-wood. He playes yet like a young Prentice the first day, and is not come to his taske of melancholy. His hardest labour is his tongue, as if he were loath to use so deceitfull an Organ; and he is best company with it when hee can but prattle. Wee laugh at his foolish sports, but his game is our earnest: and his drums, rattles and hobby-horses but the Emblems, and mocking of man's businesse. His father hath writ him as his owne little story, wherein hee reades those dayes of his life that he cannot remember; and sighs to see what innocence hee has out-liv'd. The elder hee growes, he is a stayer lower from God; and like his first father much worse in his breeches. Hee is the Christians example, and the Old-mans fate: the one imitates his purenesse, and the other falls into his simplicitie. Could hee put off his body with his little coate, he had got eternity without a burthen, and exchang'd but one Heaven for another.

The key words here are "his game is our earnest," his toys the "emblems" (symbols) of adult life. Since children and adults were one, most children could freely read imaginative works and bawdy joke books—until the Puritans became more active and spread the idea that only serious works, often depressing and self-flagellating, were suitable for sinfully conceived children. Other people of the time, however, did not agree with the Puritan emphasis on children conceived in sin. When Ben Jonson (1573?–1637) related the death of his own little boy, his comfort lay in the fact that the child had escaped the world's and the flesh's "rage." Poignantly, he writes:

> Here doth lie
> Ben Jonson his best piece of poetry.

Similarly, Henry Vaughan (1621–1695), in "The Retreate," saw childhood as a pure time in human development:

> Happy those early dayes! when I
> Shin'd in my Angell infancy.
> Before I understood this place
> Appointed for my second race,
> Or taught my soul to fancy ought
> But a white, Celestiall thought.
> When yet I had not walkt above
> A mile, or two, from my first love,
> And looking back (at that short space,)

Could see a glimpse of his bright–face;
When on some *gilded Cloud,* or *flowre*
My gazing soul would dwell an houre,
And in those weaker glories spy
Some shadows of eternity;
Before I taught my tongue to wound
My Conscience with a sinfull sound,
Or had the black art to dispence
A sev'rall sinne to ev'ry sence,
And felt through all this fleshly dresse
Bright *shootes* of everlastingnesse.
  O how I long to travell back
And tread again that ancient track!
That I might once more reach that plaine,
Where first I left my glorious traine,
From whence th' Inlightned spirit sees
That shady City of Palme trees;
But (ah!) my soul with too much stay
Is drunk, and staggers in the way,
Some men a forward motion love,
But I by backward steps would move,
And when this dust falls to the urn
In that state I came return.
                    *—The Retreate.*

This poem has been quoted in entirety in an effort to counteract the general idea that books in the seventeenth century depicted children as sinful. The Calvinists saw them that way, but they were only part of the population.

Even the guilt-ridden Anglican priest John Donne cannot accept the view of children as guilt-ridden. Rather, he blames the difficulties of children on the new scientific concepts of the universe that were throwing into doubt old religious attitudes based on the idea of an established world order with the earth at the center. As a result, everything in society is disturbed. In *The First Anniversary,* a poem of 470 lines in memory of the dead teenager, Elizabeth Drury, Donne praises her "saintlinesse," but at the same time declares:

Wee are borne ruinous: poore mothers cry,
That children come not right, nor orderly;
Except they headlong come and fall upon
An ominous precipitation.   (lines 95–98) .

Quite possibly at that moment Donne had in mind a popular obstetrical text of the period, *The byrth of mankynde,* first translated in 1540 from a German version and published continuously in many editions through 1634. One well-known edition was printed in London by Richard Watkins in 1598. In this text, a distinction is made between "headfirst" and "headlong" birth—"headfirst" being normal, and "headlong" being "not naturall":

> When the child commeth headlong, one of the hands coming out and appearing before, as in the viii. figure, then let the birth proceed no farther [without the assistance of the midwife].

The modern attempt to suppress or control the fantasy lives of children began in the seventeenth century with the Puritans, who must bear the responsibility for the development of children's "literature" as a separate field. Originally evangelical and designed to save children, all of whom were believed to be conceived in sin, the purpose of this separate literature for children became distorted as Puritans became less religious and more mercantile. A strong affinity existed between Calvinism and capitalism, expressed in the belief that the virtuous will profit. Puritans were often the merchant class in seventeenth-century England. It was easy for them to move from Edward Hake's declaration in 1574 that "Children by nature are evil" to attempts to do something about it in a commercial way.

As an example, William Sloane describes the publishing career of Nathaniel Crouch:

> On his evangelistic *Young man's calling* (1679); his *Apprentices companion* (1678); his illustrated emblem book, *Delights for the Ingenious* (1694), to which he added fifty versified riddles; his forty-two *Delightful fables* (1691)—on these and other publications, Nathaniel Crouch grew rich. . . . It is most significant for us that Nathaniel Crouch, a shrewd businessman, ventured often on books for children.
>
> *—Children's Books in England and America*
> *in the Seventeenth Century*, p. 5.

Indeed, the marked separation of children's literature from adult literature, its emergence as a separate field, began with such "warnings to apprentices" that Crouch and other printers published, beginning in the late sixteenth century. There was John Browne's *The marchants aviso, or instructions very necessary for their sonnes and servants*, written by a Bristol merchant in 1589; a ballad entitled *A Warning to youth, shewing the lewd life of a merchant's sonne of London* (1603); *The prentises practise in godlinesse* (1608); a ballad to the tune of Dr. Faustus, entitled *Youth's warning-peace. In a true relation of the woefull death of William Rogers, of Cranbroke, in Kent, an apothecary, who, refusing all good counsell, and following lewd company, dyed miserably* . . . (1635); Abraham Jackson's *The pious prentice* (1640); *The apprentices warning-piece. Being a confession of Peter Moore . . . a warning to such leud servants who walk the same steps* (1641).

Prior to this period, in the fifteenth and sixteenth centuries, several courtesy books had been published designed to instruct elegant young men of the universities on the way of life of a nobleman. Among those that are best known is Baldassare Castiglione's *Il Cortegiano*, translated into English by Thomas Hoby as *The Courtier* (1561). The Puritan attention to the lower class set a new tone. True, the "warnings to apprentices" were interspersed with books of advice to sons and daughters, but those, too, were more evangelical than previous works of advice to children.

The trend was obvious. Toward the end of the seventeenth century, the "warnings to apprentices" were converted into warnings to still younger children, in which religion was used as a tool to force compliance with strictures on labor, either at home or elsewhere. Drinking and smoking, malingering and loitering were crimes against God because they were crimes against God's counterpart on earth's end of the chain of being—the employer. These habits reduced the time an apprentice could spend on the job and caused him to demand more money.

From the warnings to young apprentices, the Puritans moved rapidly into the "Joyful Death" books, by which they controlled the fantasies of young children. In these books of deathbed confessions, children acknowledged their deficiencies in their "duties" to employer or parent. These confessions proved so effective that they were even translated into Indian languages in America and used along with firewater and gunpowder to control the Indians.*

The grandfather of all these "Joyful Death" books was James Janeway's *A Token for Children, being an exact account of the conversion, holy and exemplary lives and joyful deaths of several young children* (1671). This work was quickly imitated by many Puritans in America, including Cotton Mather, who published a supplement in 1700 containing reports of the joyous deaths of American children. (A unique copy is at the American Antiquarian Society in Worcester, Massachusetts.) Publication of these books by printers in small New England towns continued on into the nineteenth century and can be located in the library of the Connecticut Historical Society, Hartford, the A. S. W. Rosenbach catalog of *Early American Children's Books* in the Free Library of Philadelphia, and in other libraries.

Out of these confessions grew the Sunday School movement, begun by Robert Raikes, a shipowner in Gloucester, England. The purpose of the movement, as naively revealed by Raikes's biographers, was to keep poverty-stricken children busy on Sundays so that they would not damage his ships, and by educating them on Sunday, to keep their work days free for work. Raikes even paid the children a penny or so apiece to go to Sunday School and get their weekly booster shot of guilt. (A biographer of Raikes expressed shock that the children had to be paid to go to the funeral of their "benefactor.") **

Understandably, Raikes obtained almost instant sympathy and support from other businessmen. From Raikes on, in fact, the continued course of the separation of children's literature from the main mass of literature can be clearly pursued through the efforts of the Protestant merchant class to establish Sunday Schools. The warnings to

---

* See A.S.W. Rosenbach, *Early American Children's Books* (Portland, Maine, 1933), #808: [Wright, Alfred and Byington, Cyrus,] Triumphant Deaths of Pious Children. In the Choctaw language—By Missionaries of the American Board of Commissioners of Foreign Missions (Boston: Crocker and Brewster, for the Board, 1835).

** The story of Raikes appears in several books, among them, W. F. Lloyd's *Sketch of the Life of Robert Raikes, Esq.* (New York, 1891), which was printed earlier in London; J. Henry Harris' *Robert Raikes: The Man and His Work* (New York and Bristol, England, 1899); and Guy Kendall's *Robert Raikes: A Critical Study* (London, 1939).

apprentices and their deathbed confessions in the seventeenth century are only the obvious roots of an historic development which was given impetus by the Sunday School movement and is still going on in moralizing attitudes toward current social ills, as subtly propagandized in children's books. The historic process has tended to create a literature which, in the words of P. L. Travers, author of *Mary Poppins*, often appears to be "a spurious field."

Because of the importance of the Sunday School literature in relation to the field of children's literature as a whole from its seventeenth–century beginnings to the present time, it might be well to look more closely at Raikes's activities.

In Lloyd's biography of Raikes, referred to above, a letter from Raikes is quoted that appeared in the *Gloucester Journal*, November 3, 1783, indicating his reason for beginning the Sunday School movement:

> Some of the Clergy in different parts of this country, bent upon attempting a reform among the children of the lower class, are establishing Sunday Schools for rendering the Lord's day subservient to the ends of instruction, which has hither-to been prostituted to bad purposes. Farmers, and other inhabitants of the towns and villages, complain that they receive more injury in their property on the Sabbath, than all the week besides: this in great measure proceeds from the lawless state of the younger class, who are allowed to run wild on that day, free from all restraint. To remedy this evil, persons duly qualified are employed to instruct those that cannot read; and those that may have learnt to read, are taught the catechism and conducted to church. . . . The barbarous ignorance in which they had before lived being in some degree dispelled, they begin to give proofs that those persons are mistaken, who consider the lower orders of mankind as incapable of improvement, and therefore think an attempt to reclaim them impracticable, or at least not worth the trouble.

No doubt Raikes's motives were mixed. He also had benevolent purposes, but they were clearly tied to business motives.

Another letter of Raikes's is dated November 25, 1783:

> The beginning of this scheme was entirely owing to accident. Some business leading me one morning into the suburbs of the city, where the lowest of the people (who are principally employed in the pin manufactory) chiefly reside, I was struck with concern at seeing a group of children, wretchedly ragged, at play in the street. . . . Ah! Sir, said the woman to whom I was speaking, could you take a view of this part of the town on a Sunday, you would be shocked indeed, for then the street is filled with multitudes of these wretches, who, released on that day from employment, spend their time in noise and riot, playing at chuck, and cursing and swearing in a manner so horrid, as to convey to any serious mind an idea of hell rather than any other place.

Clearly the poor were supposed to accept their wretched condition without letting off steam. In another letter Raikes then outlines his progress in beginning Sunday Schools—

"the number of children at present thus engaged on the Sabbath are between two and three hundred, and they are increasing every week." He is not concerned with improving their economic state, however: "The want of decent apparel, at first, kept great numbers at a distance, but now they begin to grow wiser." One must catch them young: "You will understand that these children are from 6 years old to 12 or 14." This letter was (appropriately) published in the *Gentleman's Magazine*, 1784 (Vol. 54, p. 410).

In 1785, a London merchant, William Fox, began to cooperate with Robert Raikes in the movement, and a society was established. More rich men soon joined the group. As Raikes wrote Fox, "Maynard Colchester and William Lane, Esqrs., two gentlemen of property in the neighbourhood, having heard the happy effects arising from an attention to the morals of the rising generation of the poor, determined to try what could be done among the little lawless rabble."

Bank directors gave their enthusiastic backing. On September 7, 1785, the society for the support and encouragement of Sunday schools issued a letter urging cooperation and explaining motives:

> In manufacturing towns, where children from their infancy are necessarily employed the whole week, no opportunity occurs for their receiving the least degree of education. To remedy this evil, some gentlemen, actuated by the most benevolent motives, have established in some of these towns, Sunday Schools, where children and others are taught to read, and are instructed in the knowledge of their duty as rational and accountable human beings.

Education was minimal—aside from instruction on duty to employer-benefactors. In a letter addressed to the Sunday School Society on October 7, 1786, Raikes delightedly reported on the success of the institution of Sunday Schools:

> After the public service, a collection, for the benefit of the institution, was made at the doors of the church. When I considered that the bulk of the congregation were persons of middling rank, husbandmen and other inhabitants of adjacent villages, I concluded that the collection, if it amounted to twenty-four or twenty-five pounds, might be deemed a good one. My astonishment was great indeed, when I found that the sum was not less than fifty-seven pounds! This may be accounted for from the security which the establishment of Sunday Schools has given to the property of every individual in the neighbourhood.

Teaching children to read was good property insurance, so long as control was kept over what they read. The publications of the American Tract Society, such as *Good Examples for Good Children* and the dozens of other tracts disseminated by the thousands by various organizations that were branches of the Sunday School movement, served a valuable socioeconomic purpose, but somehow cheated the whole human being—by controlling the child with repressive fantasies. The manipulation of the child through literature was well under way, to be followed by more sophisticated literature designed for the same purpose.

Examples from the seventeenth and early eighteenth centuries of manipulative works expressly written for children include John Bunyan's evangelical work *A Book for Boys and Girls*, published in 1686, two years before Bunyan died. Benjamin Keach's *War with the Devil* influenced generations of children. First published in 1676, numerous editions appeared in England and in America. Even more influential was Isaac Watts's *Divine Songs Attempted in Easy Language for the Use of Children*, originally printed in England in 1715. According to the Rosenbach catalogue, it ran through a hundred editions in England before the middle of the century and was equally popular in America. Another important book is Hugh Peters's catechism, *Milk for Babes, and Meat for Men* (1641). Peters was a militant Puritan who did his writing while a prisoner in the Tower of London.

The influence of the Puritans in developing separate reading for children is still felt in modern books for children, some of which are propagandistic in nature—deplored by child psychiatrists for excessive realism, unawareness of intrapsychic conflict, and unhealthy reflections of adult guilt, and despised by literary scholars for lack of aesthetic worth. Fortunately, there is now a strong trend, possibly animated by television, for literature which appeals to a dual audience.

To summarize, most children in the late sixteenth and seventeenth centuries drew their reading from the same sources as adults. Out of the literature they selected the things they enjoyed—chapbooks, plays, romances, broadsides of ballads. They relished tales of witches and fairies. As the seventeenth century went on and the Puritan merchant class became strong, this "frivolous" literature was discouraged. The seventeenth century saw the beginnings of a literature for children only. Therefore one can say that much literature enjoyed by adults and children together—children's literature in the best sense—died in the seventeenth century, and segregated literature was born during that period. Fortunately, there are exceptions. Some great books have been written which children and adults enjoy sharing and many of the old tales have been republished in beautiful editions.

*Part One*
*Ballads*

# 1

# *The Norfolke Gentleman,*
# *His Last*
# *Will and Testament:*

### *And How He Committed the Keeping of*
### *His Children to His Owne Brother, Who Dealt Most Wickedly with Them:*
### *And How God Plagued Him for It*
### *(more commonly known as* The Children in the Wood*)*

CHILD ABUSE HAS *a long history, as psychohistorians have shown. The sixteenth-century ballad about the murders of the babes in the wood was printed in various versions several times during the seventeenth century. The story is still well known to many people. At least the phrase, "they were like babes in the wood," still means "they were innocent and helpless."*

The Norfolke Gentleman *is reprinted from* The Roxburghe Ballads, *Vol. 2, nos. 4–6. (Hertford. Printed for the Ballad Society, 1872–1874. Reprinted by AMS Press, 1969).*

TO THE TUNE OF *Rogero.*

NOW PONDER WELL, you parents deare,
  The words which I shall write;
A dolefull story you shall heare,
  Which time hath brought to light.
A gentleman of good account
  In Norfolke liv'd of late,

Whose wealth and riches did surmount
  Most men of his estate.

Sore sicke he was, and like to die,
  No helpe that he could have;
His wife by him as sicke did lie,

3

And both possest one grave.
No love between these two was lost,
    Each was to other kinde;
In love they lived, in love they dide,
    And left two babes behinde.

The one a fine and pretty boy,
    Not passing three years old;
The next a girle, more young than he,
    And made of beauties' mold.
This father left his little sonne,
    As well it doth appeare,
When hee to perfect age should come,
    Three hundred pounds a yeare.

And to his little daughter Jane
    Three hundred pounds in gold
To be paid downe at marriage day,
    Which might not be contrould:
But if these children chance to die
    Ere they to age should come,
Their uncle should possess this wealth;
    And so the will did runne.

"Now, brother," said the dying man,
    "Looke to my children deare;
Be good unto my boy and girle,
    No friends I else have here.
To God and you I doe commend
    My children night and day;
But little time, be sure, wee have
    Within this world to stay.

"You must be father and mother both,
    And uncle, all in one;
God knowes what will become of them
    When wee are dead and gone!"
With that bespake their mother deare,
    "O brother mine!" quoth shee,
"You are the man must bring my babes
    To wealth or misery.

"If you do keepe them carefully,
    Then God will you reward;
If otherwise you seeme to deale,
    Your deede God will regard."
With lips as cold as any clay
    Shee kist her children small:
"God bless you both, my little lambes!"
    With that the teares did fall.

These speeches then their brother spoke
    To this sick couple there,
"The keeping of your children young,
    Sweet sister, do not feare;
God never prosper mee nor mine,
    Or aught else that I have,
If I do wrong your children small
    When you are laid in grave."

Their parents being dead and gone,
    The children home hee takes;
And brings them home unto his house,
    And much of them he makes.
Hee had not kept these pretty babes
    A twelvemonth and a day,
But, for their wealth, he did devise
    To make them both away.

Hee bargain'd with two ruffians rude,
    That were of furious mood,
That they should take the children young,
    And slay them in the wood:
And told his wife, and all the rest,
    He did the children send
To be brought up in faire London,
    With one that was his friend.

[FINIS]

## *The Second Part*

To the same tune.

Away then went these pretty babes,
  Rejoycing of that tide,
And smiling with a merry minde,
  They should on cockhorse ride.
They prate and prattle pleasantly,
  As they rode on their way,
To them that should their butchers bee,
  And worke their lives' decay.

So that the pretty speech they had,
  Made murtherers' hearts relent;
And that they tooke this deede to doe,
  Full sore they did repent.
Yet one of them more hard of heart,
  Did vow to doe his charge,
Because the wretch, that hired them,
  Had paid them very large.

The other would not 'gree thereto,
  So here they fell at strife,
With one another they did fight
  About these children's life.
And he that was of mildest mood
  Did kill the other there,

Within an unfrequented wood;
  While babes did quake for feare.

He tooke the children by the hand,
  When teares stood in their eye,
And bade them come and goe with him,
  And looke they did not cry!
And two long miles hee led them thus,
  When they for bread complaine:
"Stay here," quoth he, "Ile bring you
    bread,
  When I doe come againe."

Those pretty babes, with hand in hand,
  Went wandering up and downe;
But never more they saw the man
  Approaching from the towne.
Their pretty lips with black-berries
  Were all besmear'd and dy'd,
And when they saw the darksome night,
  They sate them downe and cry'd.

Thus wandred these two little babes
  Till death did end their griefe,

In one another's armes they dy'd
    As babes wanting reliefe:
No buriall these pretty babes
    Of any man receives,
Till Robin Redbreast, painefully,
    Did cover them with leaves.

And now the heavy wrath of God
    Upon their uncle fell;
Yea, fearefull fiends did haunt his house;
    His conscience felt an hell:
His barns were fir'd, his goods consum'd,
    His land was barren made,
His cattle dy'd within the fields,
    And nothing with him staid.

And in the voyage of Portugall,
    Two of his sonnes did die;
And to conclude, himselfe was brought
    To extreame misery:
He pawn'd and morgag'd all his land
    Ere seaven yeares went about,
And now at length this wicked act
    Did by this meanes come out.

The fellow which did take in hand
    The children for to kill,
Was for a robery judg'd to death—
    As was God's blessed will—
Who did confesse the very truth,
    The which is here exprest;
Their uncle died while he, for debt,
    In prison long did rest.

Al you that be executors made,
    And overseeers eke,
Of children that be fatherlesse,
    Of infants mild and meeke!
Take you example by the same,
    And yeeld to each their right,
Lest God with such like misery,
    Your wicked minde requite.

FINIS.

# 2

# A Most Pleasant
# Ballad of
# Patient Grissell

I<small>N</small> STRIKING CONTRAST *to the independent Dame Custance of the mid-sixteenth-century* *school play,* Ralph Roister Doister, *is the meek and patient Griselda, whose story was first told in the Middle Ages. With literary roots in Petrarch and Boccaccio, it was Englished by Chaucer and related by his Clerk in* The Canterbury Tales.

*In song, poetry, and prose the story has been told in many countries of how Griselda, a poor girl, was wedded to a rich Marquis, who tested her loyalty by pretending to murder their two children, a little boy and girl, and by turning her out penniless, only to call her back to prepare for his wedding to a second wife. Through all these cruelties, Griselda kept her silence and poise and did not rebuke her husband, her attitude being, "You are my Lord and I love you. Your wish is my command." Returning to his castle to dress the bride for his second wedding, Griselda receives a great surprise: It is she who is to have a second honeymoon. Her children are alive and well. They are teenagers now, and she is introduced to them. Her husband's behavior was merely a character investigation (of her character, supposedly) to which he had been driven by envious members of his court:*

*"And you that envied her estate,/Whom I have made my loving mate,/Now blush for shame, and honor vertuous life;/The chronicles of lasting fame,/Shall ever more extoll the name/Of Patient Grissell, my most constant wife."*

*"The chronicles of lasting fame" have indeed extolled her behavior. It is only in the twentieth century that people seem to have forgotten about her. An outrage to those fighting for women's liberation, her behavior is distasteful now to anyone.*

*What must be remembered, however, is that her story is not so much that of a real woman—though it might have been, for fidelity and purity were more important in the days of primogeniture (Claudio in Shakespeare's* Much Ado *is scarcely less savage towards his love, Hero). With the religious conviction deep in the medieval consciousness, men and women probably both saw the story more as an allegory of a human being's relationship to God. As Job continued to love and accept the cause of his trials, God, so must Griselda continue to love and accept the cause of her trials, God's corresponding figure on the chain of being, the Marquis.*

*The late sixteenth-century ballad reprinted here was copied in an eighteenth-century version (1723), the notable difference between the two versions being that in the later one, the alternate long lines were divided approximately in half at the caesura or pause in each line, so that instead of "A noble marques, as he did ride on hunting," one finds, "A Noble Marquis,/As he did ride a Hunting."*

*Patient Griselda is an example of the old folk tale which becomes a medieval romance, subsequently a ballad and seventeenth-century prose paperback, then an eighteenth-century chapbook, next a textbook story for children in the nineteenth century, and ultimately reaches the twentieth-century literary dustbin, to be rummaged through by scholars. Why does this gradual diminution occur? Perhaps because with the accumulation of knowledge, only the essence of a story can be conveniently retained. The brain has its own computer system.*

Patient Grissell *is reprinted from* The Roxburghe Ballads, *Vol. 2, nos. 4–6. (Hertford: Printed for the Ballad Society, 1872–1874. Reprinted AMS Press, 1969).*

TO THE TUNE OF *The Bride's Good-morrow.*

A NOBLE MARQUES, as he did ride on hunting,
  Hard by a forest side;
A proper mayden, as she did sit a spinning,
  His gentle eye espide:
Most faire and lovely, and of curteous grace was she,
  Although in simple attire;
She sung full sweet with pleasant voyce melodiously,
  Which set the lord's hart on fire.
The more he looked, the more he might,
Beauty bred his harte's delight;
  And to this dainty damsell then he went:
"God speede," quoth he, "thou famous flower,
Faire mistres of this homely bower,
  Where love and vertue lives with sweete content."

With comely jesture and curteous milde behaviour,
  She bade him welcome then;
She entertain'd him in faithful friendly maner,
  And all his gentlemen.

The noble marques in his hart felt such a flame,
   Which set his senses at strife;
Quoth he, "Faire maiden, shew me soone what is thy name?
   I meane to make thee my wife."

"Grissell is my name," quoth she,
"Farre unfit for your degree,
   A silly maiden, and of parents poore."
"Nay, Grissell, thou art rich," he sayd,
"A vertuous, faire, and comely maid!
   Graunt me thy love, and I wil aske no more."

At length she consented and, being both contented,
   They married were with speed;
Her contrey russet was chang'd to silk and velvet,
   As to her state agreed.
And when that she was trimly tyred in the same,
   Her beauty shined most bright,
Far staining every other brave and comly dame
   That appeare in sight.
Many envied her therefore,
Because she was of parents poore,
   And 'twixt her lord and she great strife did raise:—
Some sayd this, and some sayd that,
Some did call her begger's brat,
   And to her lord they would her soone dispraise.

"O, noble marques," quoth they, "why doe you wrong us,
   Thus bacely for to wed,
That might have gotten an honorable lady
   Into your princely bed?
Who will not now your noble issue still deride,
   Which shall hereafter be borne,
That are of blood so base by their mother's side,
   The which will bring them in[to] scorne.
Put her therefore quite away,
And take to you a lady gay,
   Whereby your linage may renowned be."
Thus every day they seemde to prate
That malis'd Grisselles good estate,
   Who tooke all this most milde and patiently.

When that the marques did see that they were bent thus
   Against his faithfull wife,
Whom he most deerely, tenderly, and entirely,
   Beloved as his life;

Minding in secret for to prove her patient hart,
   Therby her foes to disgrace,
Thinking to play a hard uncurteous part,
   That men might pittie her case.
Great with childe this lady was,
And at length it came to passe
   Two goodly children at one birth she had;
A sonne and daughter God had sent,
Which did their father well content,
   And which did make their mother's hart full glad.

Great royall feasting was at these children's christ'nings,
   And princely triumph made;
Six weekes together, al nobles that came thither
   Were entertained and staid.
And when that al those pleasant sportings quite were done,
   The marques a messenger sent
For his young daughter, and his pretty smiling son,
   Declaring his full intent;—
How that the babes must murdred be,
For so the marques did decree:
   "Come, let me have the children," then he said.
With that faire Grissell wept full sore,
She wrung her hands and sayd no more,—
   "My gracious lord must have his will obeyd."

## The Second Part

### To the same tune.

SHE TOOKE THE babies, even from their nursing ladies,
  Betweene her tender armes:
She often wishes, with many sorrowfull kisses,
  That she might helpe their harmes:
"Farewel, farewel, a thousand times, my children deere!
  Never shall I see you againe!
'Tis long of me, your sad and wofull mother heere,
  For whose sake both must be slaine.
Had I been borne of royall race,
You might have liv'd in happy case,
  But you must die for my unworthines!
Come, messenger of death," said shee,
"Take my despised babes to thee,
  And to their father my complaints expres."

He tooke the children, and to his noble maister
  He brings them both with speed:
Who secret sent them unto a noble lady,
  To be nurst up indeed.
Then to faire Grissell with a heavy heart he goes,
  Where she sate mildly alone;
A pleasant gesture and a lovely looke she shewes,
  As if this griefe she never had knowen.

Quoth he, "My children now are slaine!
What thinkes faire Grissell of the same?
  Sweet Grissell, now declare thy mind to me."
"Sith you, my lord, are pleas'd in it,
Poore Grissell thinks the action fit;
  Both I and mine at your command will be."

"My nobles murmur, faire Grissell, at thy honor,
  And I no joy can have
Til thou be banisht both from my court and presence,
  As they unjustly crave.
Thou must be stript out of thy costly garments all,
  And, as thou camest to me,
In homely gray, instead of bisse and purest pall,
  Now must all thy clothing be:
My lady thou canst be no more,

Nor I thy lord, which grieves me sore;
   The poorest life must now content thy minde;
A groat to thee I must not give,
To maintaine thee while I doe live:
   Against my Grissell such great foes I finde."

When gentle Grissell did heare these wofull tidings,
   The teares stood in her eyes;
Nothing she answered; no words of discontent
   Did from her lips arise.
Her velvet gown most patiently she slipped off,
   Her kirtle of silke the same;
Her russet gown was brought again with many a scoffe:
   To beare them all herselfe she did frame.
When she was drest in this array,
And ready was to part away,
   "God send long life unto my lord," quoth shee;
"Let no offence be found in this,
To give my lord a parting kisse."—
   With wat'ry eyes, "Farewell, my deare," quoth he.
From stately pallace, unto her father's cottage,
   Poore Grissell now is gone:
Full sixteene winters she lived there contented;
   No wrong she thought upon:
And at that time through all the land the speaches went,
   The marques should married be
Unto a lady of high and great descent;
   And to the same all parties did agree.
The marques sent for Grissell faire,
The bride's bed-chamber to prepare,
   That nothing therein should be found awrye:
The bride was with her brother come,
Which was great joy to all and some;
   And Grissell tooke all this most patiently.

And, in the morning, when they should to the wedding,
   Her patience sore was tride;
Grissell was charged, herself, in princely manner
   For to attire the bride.
Most willingly she gave consent to do the same:
   The bride in bravery was drest,
And presently the noble marques thither came,
   With all his lords, at his request.
"O Grissell, I would aske," quoth he,
"If to this match thou wilt agree?
   Methinks thy lookes are waxen wondrous coy."

With that they all began to smile,
And Grissell, she replide the while,
   "God send lord marques many yeares of joy."

The marques was moved to see his best beloved
   Thus patient in distresse;
He stept unto her, and by the hande he tooke her,—
   These words he did expresse:
"Thou art my bride, and all the brides I meane to have;
   These two thine owne children be."
The youthfull lady on her knees did blessing crave;
   Her brother as well as she.
"And you that envied her estate,
Whom I have made my loving mate,
   Now blush for shame, and honor vertuous life;
The chronicles of lasting fame,
Shall ever more extoll the name
   Of Patient Grissell, my most constant wife."

FINIS.

# Tom Thumbe, His Life and Death:

### Wherein is Declared Many
### Marvailous Acts of Manhood,
### Full of Wonder, and Strange Merriments:
### Which Little Knight Lived in King Arthurs Time,
### And Famous in the Court of Great Brittaine

D<small>R. HARRY WEISS</small> (Scientific Monthly, *Vol. 34, February 1932), who has made a study of many old chapbooks, calls* Tom Thumbe *a member of the "swallow" cycle—that is, those stories of heroes swallowed and regurgitated by various animals. (Perhaps Jonah was the first.)*

*Tales of diminutive heroes are common to many cultures. Japan, for instance, has its stories of the exploits of Momotaro, who was born out of a peach.*

*The hack writer, Richard Johnson, published a prose version in 1621. A 1630 edition, "Printed for John Wright," was owned by Robert Burton, author of* The Anatomy of Melancholy.

*In the seventeenth century, the story was popular both with children and adults in England and in America, where as early as 1686, John Dunton was selling it from his Boston warehouse.*

Tom Thumbe, His Life and Death *is reprinted from Joseph Ritson, ed.,* Ancient Popular Poetry from Authentic Manuscripts and Old Printed Copies, *revised by Edmund Goldsmid (Edinburgh: private printing, 1884).*

IN ARTHURS COURT Tom Thumbe did
    live,
  A man of mickle might,
The best of all the table round,
  And eke a doughty knight:

His stature but an inch in height,
  Or quarter of a span;
Then thinke you not this little knight,
  Was prov'd a valiant man?

His father was a plow-man plaine,
  His mother milkt the cow,
But yet the way to get a sonne
  'This' couple knew not how,

Untill such time this good old man
  To learned Merlin goes,
And there to him his deep desires
  In secret manner showes,

How in his heart he wisht to have
  A childe, in time to come,
To be his heire, though it might be
  No bigger than his Thumbe.

Of which old Merlin thus foretold,
  That he his wish should have,
And so this sonne of stature small
  The charmer to him gave.

No blood nor bones in him should be,
  In shape and being such,
That men should heare him speake,
    but not
  His wandring shadow touch:

But so unseene to go or come
  Whereas it pleasd him still;
Begot and borne in halfe an houre,
  To fit his fathers will:

And in foure minutes grew so fast,
  That he became so tall
As was the plowmans thumbe in height,
  And so they did call

Tom Thumbe, the which the Fayry-
    Queene
  There gave him to his name,
Who, with her traine of Goblins grim,
  Unto his christning came.

Whereas she cloath'd him richly brave,
  In garments fine and faire,
Which lasted him for many yeares
  In seemely sort to weare.

His hat made of an oaken leafe,
  His shirt a spiders web,
Both light and soft for those his limbes
  That were so smally bred;

His hose and doublet thistle downe,
   Together weav'd full fine;
His stockings of an apple greene,
   Made of the outward rine;

His garters were two little haires,
   Pull'd from his mothers eye,
His bootes and shooes a mouses skin,
   There tand most curiously.

Thus, like a lustie gallant, he
   Adventured forth to goe,
With other children in the streets
   His pretty trickes to show.

Where he for counters, pinns, and points
   And cherry stones did play,
Till he amongst those gamesters young
   Had loste his stock away.

Yet could he some renue the same,
   When as most nimbly he
Would dive into 'their' cherry-baggs,
   And there 'partaker' be,

Unseene or felt by any one,
   Untill a scholler shut
This nimble youth into a boxe,
   Wherein his pins he put.

Of whom to be reveng'd, he tooke
   (In mirth and pleasant game)
Black pots, and glasses, which he hung
   Upon a bright sunne-beame.

The other boyes to doe the like,
   In pieces broke them quite;
For which they were most soundly whipt,
   Whereat he laught outright.

And so Tom Thumbe restrained was
   From these his sports and play,
And by his mother after that
   Compel'd at home to stay.

Whereas about a Christmas time,
   His father a hog had kil'd
And Tom 'would' see the puddings made,
   'For fear' they should be spil'd.

He sate upon the pudding-boule,
   The candle for to hold;
Of which there is unto this day
   A pretty pastime told:

For Tom fell in, and could not be
   For ever after found,
For in the blood and batter he
   Was strangely lost and drownd.

Where searching long, but all in vaine,
   His mother after that
Into a pudding thrust her sonne,
   Instead of minced fat.

Which pudding of the largest size,
   Into the kettle throwne,
Made all the rest to fly thereout,
   As with a whirle-wind blowne.

For so it tumbled up and downe,
   Within the liquor there,
As if the devill 'had' been boyld;
   Such was his mothers feare,

That up she tooke the pudding strait;
   And gave it at the doore
Unto a tinker, which from thence
   In his blacke budget bore.

But as the tinker climb'd a stile,
   By chance he let a cracke:
Now gip, old knave, out cride Tom
     Thumbe,
   There hanging at his backe:

At which the tinker gan to run,
   And would no longer stay,
But cast both bag and pudding downe,
   And thence hyed fast away.

From which Tom Thumbe got loose at
    last
And home return'd againe:
Where he from following dangers long
    In safety did remaine.

Untill such time his mother went
    A milking of her kine,
Where Tom unto a thistle fast
    She linked with a twine.

A threade that helde him to the same,
    For feare the blustring winde
Should blow him thence, that so she
      might
    Her sonne in safety finde.

But marke the hap, a cow came by,
    And up the thistle eate.
Poore Tom withall, that, as a docke,
    Was made the red cowes meate:

Who being mist, his mother went
    Him calling every where,
Where art thou Tom? where art thou
    Tom?
    Quoth he, Here mother, here:

Within the red cowes belly here,
    Your sonne is swallowed up.
The which unto her feareful heart
    Most carefull dolours put.

Meane while the cowe was troubled much,
    In this her tumbling wombe,
And could not rest until that she
    Had backward cast Tom Thumbe:

Who all besmeared as he was,
    His mother tooke him up,
To beare him thence, the which poore lad
    She in her pocket put.

Now after this, in sowing time,
    His father would him have

Into the field to drive his plow,
    And thereupon he gave

A whip made of barly straw,
    To drive the cattle on:
Where, in a furrow'd land new sowne,
    Poor Tom was lost and gon.

Now by a raven of great strength
    Away he thence was borne,
And carried in the carrions beake
    Even like a graine of corne,

Unto a giants castle top,
    In which he let him fall,
Where soon the giant swallowed up
    His body, cloathes and all.

But in his belly did Tom Thumbe
    So great a rumbling make,
That neither day nor night he could
    The smallest quiet take,

Untill the gyant had him spewd
    Three miles into the sea,
Whereas a fish soone tooke him up
    And bore him thence away.

Which lusty fish was after caught
    And to king Arthur sent,
Where Tom was found, and made his
      dwarfe,
    Whereas his dayes he spent

Long time in lively jolloty,
    Belov'd of all the court,
And none like Tom was then esteem'd
    Among the noble sort.

Amongst his deede of courtship done,
    His highnesse did command,
That he should dance a galliard brave
    Upon his queenes left hand.

The which he did, and for the same
    The king his signet gave,

Which Tom about his middle wore
 Long time a girdle brave.

Now after this the king would not
 Abroad for pleasure goe,
But still Tom Thumbe must ride with
 him,
 Plac't on his saddle-bow.

Where on a time when as it rain'd,
 Tom Thumbe most nimbly crept
In a button hole, where he
 Within his bosome slept.

And being neere his highnesse heart,
 He crav'd a wealthy boone,
A liberall gift, the which the king
 Commanded to be done,

For to relieve his fathers wants,
 And mothers, being old;
Which was so much of silver coyne
 As well his armes could hold.

And so away goes lusty Tom
 With three pence on his backe,
A heavy burthen, which might make
 His wearied limbes to cracke.

So travelling two dayes and nights,
 With labour and great paine,
He came into the house whereas
 His parents did remaine;

Which was but halfe a mile in space
 From good king Arthurs court,
The which in eight and forty houres
 He went in weary sort.

But comming to his fathers doore,
 He there such entrance had,
As made his parents both rejoice,
 And he thereat was glad.

His mother in her apron tooke
 Her gentle sonne in haste,

And by the fier side, within
 A walnut shell him plac'd.

Whereas they feasted him three dayes
 Upon a hazell nut,
Whereon he rioted so long
 He them to charges put;

And there-upon grew wonderous sicke,
 Through eating too much meate,
Which was sufficient for a month
 For this great man to eate.

But now his business call'd him foorth,
 King Arthurs court to see,
Whereas no longer from the same
 He could a stranger be.

But yet a few small April drops,
 Which setled in the way,
His long and weary journey forth
 Did hinder and so stay.

Until his carefull father tooke
 A birding trunke in sport,
And with one blast blew this his sonne
 Into king Arthurs court.

Now he with tilts and turnaments
 Was entertained so,
That all the best of Arthurs knights
 Did him much pleasure show.

As good Sir Lancelot of the Lake,
 Sir Tristram, and sir Guy;
Yet none compar'd with brave
  Tom Thum,
 For knightly chivalry.

In honour of which noble day,
 And for his ladies sake,
A challenge in king Arthurs court
 Tom Thumbe did bravely make.

Gainst whom these noble knights did run,
 Sir Chinon, and the rest,

Yet still Tom Thumbe with matchles
   might
  Did beare away the best.

At last sir Lancelot of the Lake
  In manly sort came in,
And with this stout and hardy knight
  A battle did begin.

Which made the courtiers all agast,
  For there that valiant man
Through Lancelots steed, before them all,
  In nimble manner ran.

Yea horse and all, with speare and shield,
  As hardly he was seene,
But onely by king Arthurs selfe
  And his admired queene,

Who from her finger tooke a ring,
  Through which Tom Thumb made
    way,
Not touching it, in nimble sort,
  As it was done in play.

He likewise cleft the smallest haire
  From his faire ladies head,
Not hurting her whose even hand
  Him lasting honors bred.

Such were his deeds and noble acts
  In Arthurs court there showne,

As like in all the world beside
  Was hardly seene or knowne.

Now at these sportes he toyld himselfe
  That he a sicknesse tooke,
Through which all manly exercise
  He carelesly forsooke.

Where lying on his bed sore sicke,
  King Arthurs doctor came,
With cunning skill, by physicks art,
  To ease and care the same.

His body being so slender small,
  This cunning doctor tooke
A fine prospective glasse, with which
  He did in secret looke

Into his sickened body downe,
  And therein saw that Death
Stood ready in his wasted guts
  To sease his vitall breath.

His armes and leggs consum'd as small
  As was a spiders web,
Through which his dying houre grew on,
  For all his limbs grew dead.

His face no bigger than an ants,
  Which hardly could be seene:
The losse of which renowned knight
  Much griev'd the king and queene.

And so with peace and quietnesse
    He left this earth below;
And up into the Fayry Land
    His ghost did fading goe.

Whereas the Fayry Queene receiv'd,
    With heavy mourning cheere,
The body of this valiant knight,
    Whom she esteem'd so deere.

For with her dancing nymphes in greene,
    She fetcht him from his bed,
With musicke and sweet melody,
    So soone as life was fled:

For whom king Arthur and his knights
    Full forty daies did mourne;
And, in remembrance of his name
    That was so strangely borne,

He built a tomb of marble gray,
    And yeare by yeare did come
To celebrate the mournefull day,
    And buriall of Tom Thum.

Whose fame still lives in England here,
    Amongst the countrey sort;
Of whom our wives and children small
    Tell tales of pleasant sport.

FINIS.

$$4$$

# A Pleasant New Ballad
# To Sing both Even and Morne,
# Of the Bloody Murther of
# Sir John Barley-corne

T HIS JOLLY *seventeenth-century ballad describes symbolically the process of planting barley, watching it grow, harvesting it, stacking it, separating it from the chaff, drying it out, and preparing it in a vat to make good ale. Over one hundred versions of the song have emanated from various parts of England, beginning with the period of King James I. The ballad is still popular with young folksingers.*

A Pleasant New Ballad to Sing both Even and Morne, of the Bloody Murther of Sir John Barley-corne *is reprinted from* The Roxburghe Ballads, *Vol. 2, nos. 4–6 (Hertford: printed for the Ballad Society, 1872–1874. Reprinted by AMS Press, 1966).*

TO THE TUNE OF *Shall I Lye beyond thee.*

As I WENT through the North Countrey,
   I heard a merry greeting;
A pleasant toy and full of joy—
   two noble men were meeting:

And as they walkèd for to sport
   upon a summer's day,

Then with another nobleman
   they went to make a fray:

Whose name was Sir John Barley-corne;
   he dwelt down in a dale;
Who had a kinsman dwelt him nigh,
   they cal'd him Thomas Goodale.

21

Another namèd Richard Beere
   was ready at that time;
Another worthy knight was there,
   call'd Sir William White Wine.

Some of them fought in a Blacke-Jacke,
   some of them in a Can;
But the chiefest in a Blacke-pot,
   like a worthy noble man.

Sir John Barly-corne fought in a boule,
   who wonne the victorie,
And made them all to fume and sweare
   that Barly-corne should die.

Some said "Kill him," some said
   "Drowne,"
   others wisht to hang him hie—
For as many as follow Barley-corne
   shall surely beggers die.

Then with a plough they plow'd him up,
   and thus they did devise
To burie him quicke within the earth,
   and swore he should not rise.

With harrowes strong they combèd him,
   and burst clods on his head:
A joyfull banquet then was made
   when Barly-corne was dead.

He rested still within the earth
   till raine from skies did fall,
Then he grew up in branches greene,
   which sore amazed them all.

And so grew up till Mid-sommer,
   which made them all afeard;
For he was sprouted up on hie,
   and got a goodly beard.

Then he grew till S. James's tide,
   his countenance was wan;
For he was growne unto his strength,
   and thus became a man.

[Wherefore] with hookes and sickles
   keene
   into the field they hied;
They cut his legs off by the knees,
   and made him wounds full wide.

Thus bloodily they cut him downe
   from place where he did stand,
And, like a thiefe, for treachery,
   They bound him in a band.

So then they tooke him up againe,
   according to his kind,
And packt him up in severall stackes,
   to wither with the wind.

And with a pitch-forke that was sharpe
   they rent him to the heart;
And like a thiefe, for treason vile,
   they bound him in a cart.

And tending him with weapons strong,
   unto the towne they hie,
And straight they mowed him in a mow,
   and there they let him lie.

There he lay groning by the walls
   till all his wounds were sore;
At length they tooke him up againe,
   and cast him on the floore.

They hyrèd two with holly clubs,
   to beat on him at once;
They thwackèd so on Barly-corne
   that flesh fell from the bones.

And then they tooke him up againe
   to fulfill women's minde;
They dusted and they sifted him
   till he was almost blind.

And then they knit him in a sacke,
   which grievèd him full sore:
Then steep'd him in a Fat, God wot,
   for three dayes space and more.

Then they tooke him up againe,
  and laid him for to drie;
They cast him on a chamber floore,
  and swore that he should die.

They rubbèd and they stirrèd him,
  and still they did him turne;
The malt-man swore that he should die,
  his body he would burne.

They spightfully tooke him up againe,
  and threw him on a kill:
So dried him there with fire hot,
  and thus they wrought their will.

Then they brought him to the mill,
  and there they burst his bones;
The miller swore to murther him
  betwixt a paire of stones.

Then they tooke him up againe,
  and serv'd him worse th[a]n that;
For with hot scalding liquor store
  they washt him in a Fat.

But not content with this, God wot,
  that did him mickle harme,
With threatning words they promisèd
  to beat him into barme.

And lying in this danger deep,
  for feare that he should quarrell,
They tooke him straight out of the Fat,
  and tunn'd him in a barrell.

And then they set a tap to him,
  even thus his death begun;
They drew out every dram of blood,
  whilst any drop would run.

Some brought jacks upon their backes,
  some brought bill and bow;
And every man his weapon had
  Barly-corne to overthrow.

When Sir John Good-ale heard of this,
  he came with mickle might,
And there he tooke their tongues away,
  their legs, or else their sight.

And thus Sir John, in each respect,
  so paid them all their hire,
That some lay sleeping by the way,
  some tumbling in the mire.

Some lay groning by the wals,
  some in the streets downe right;
The best of them did scarcely know
  what they had done ore-night.

All you good wives that brew good ale,
  God turne from you all teene;
But if you put too much water in,
  The devill put out your eyne!

FINIS.

$$\boxed{5}$$

# The Seven Champions
# Of Christendom

### Being a Compendious History of
### Their Lives and Actions, &c.

TESTIMONY TO THE *importance of* The Seven Champions of Christendom *are the various ways in which the tales were told, including the ballad editions, one of which is here reproduced. The ballad necessarily excludes the rich descriptive matter which enlivens the romance. A few touches are left. As in Milton's* Paradise Lost, *bad odors denote evil—St. George kills a "dreadful Dragon" annoying everyone "with Stinks," and destroying many thousands of people. St. Dennis of France eats some mulberries which turn out to be part of a King's daughter under a spell on account of her pride. Because he has literally partaken of that pride, he is changed into a deer until his horse brings him a rose, which breaks the spell for both man and maid. (The rose, after all, is the queen of flowers, the flower of the Virgin Mary, and it has magical powers.)*

The Seven Champions of Christendom *is reprinted from* A Collection of Old Ballads *(London: printed for J. Roberts, 1723–25), Vol. 1, pp. 28–36.*

### TO THE TUNE OF *The Christean Warriors.*

In my former Argument, I refused to give the History, or rather the Fable of St. George; but lest any of my Readers should be unacquainted with it, I have inserted the following Ballad; where they'll not only find his History, but that of the other Six Champions of Christendom with it; and the Account is, I believe, as authentick as any we have extant. The only Thing I have to object to the Poet here, is his Partiality; for he has bestow'd Half the Song upon our English Hero, whilst the other Six have but one Half between them all.

NOW OF THE Seven Champions here,
  My Purpose is to write;
To shew how they with Sword and Spear
  Put many Foes to flight:

Distressed Ladies to release,
  And Captives bound in Chains;
That Christian Glory to increase,
  Which evermore remains.

First, I give you to understand,
  That Great St. *George* by Name.

Was the true Champion of our Land;
  And of his Birth and Fame;
And of his Noble Mother's Dream,
  Before that he was born,
The which to her did clearly seem
  Her Days would be forlorn.

This was her Dream: That she did bear
  A Dragon in her Womb;
Which griev'd this Noble Lady fair,
  'cause Death must be her Doom.
This Sorrow she could not conceal,

24

So dismal was her Fear;
So that she did the same reveal
   Unto her Husband dear;

Who went for to enquire straight
   Of an Inchanteress;
When knocking at her Iron Gate,
   Her Answer it was this:
'The Lady shall bring forth a Son,
   'By whom, in Tract of Time,
'Great Noble Actions shall be done;
   'He will to Honour climb:

'For he shall be in Banners wore;
   'This Truth I will maintain:
'Your Lady she shall dye before
   'You see her Face again.
His Leave he took, and Home he went;
   His Wife departed lay:
But that which did his Grief augment,
   The Child was stole way.

Then did he travel in Despair,
   Where soon with Grief he dy'd;
While the young Child, his Son and Heir,
   Did constantly abide
With the wife Lady of the Grove,
   In her inchanted Cell;
Amongst the Woods he oft did rove,
   His Beauty pleas'd her well.

Blinded with Love, she did impart,
   Upon a certain Day,
To him her cunning Magick Art,
   And where Six Champions lay,
Within a brazen Castle strong,
   By an inchanted Sleep;
And where they had continued long;
   She did the Castle keep.

She taught and shewed him ev'ry Thing,
   Thro' being free and fond;
Which did her fatal Ruin bring;
   For with a Silver Wand,
He clos'd her up into a Rock,
   By giving one small Stroke;

So took Possession of her Stock,
   And the Inchantment broke.

Those Christian Champions being freed
   From their inchanted State,
Each mounted on his prancing Steed,
   And took to Travel strait;
Where we will leave them to pursue
   Kind Fortune's Favours still,
To treat of our own Champion, who
   Did Courts with Wonders fill:

For as he came to understand,
   At an old Hermit's Cell,
How in the vast *Egyptian* Land,
   A Dragon, fierce and fell,

Threaten'd the ruin of them all
   By his devouring Jaws;
His Sword releas'd them from that Thrall,
   And soon remov'd the Cause.

This dreadful Dragon must destroy
   A Virgin ev'ry Day:
Or else with Stinks he'll them annoy,
   And many Thousands slay.
At length, the King's own Daughter dear,
   For whom the Court did mourn,
Was brought to be devour'd here;
   For she must take her Turn.

The King, by Proclamation, said,
   If any hardy Knight
Could free this fair young Royal Maid,
   And slay the Dragon quite;
Then should he have her for his Bride,
   And (after Death) likewise
His Crown and Kingdom too beside:
   St. *George* he won the Prize.

When many hardy Strokes he'd dealt,
   And could not pierce his Hide,
He run his Sword up to the Hilt,
   In at the Dragon's Side;
By which he did his Life destroy,
   Which cheer'd the drooping King;

This caus'd an universal Joy,
  Sweet Peals of Bells did ring.

The Daughter of a King, for Pride
  Transform'd into a Tree
Of Mulberries, which *Dennis* spy'd;
  And being hungery,

Of that fair Fruit he eat a Part,
  And was transform'd likewise
Into the Fashion of a Hart,
  For Seven Years precise.

At which he long bewail'd the Loss
  Of manly Shape; then goes
To him his true and trusty Horse,
  And brings a blushing Rose,
By which the Magick Spell was broke,
  And both were fairly freed
From the inchanted heavy Yoke:
  They then in Love agreed.

Now we come to St. *James* of *Spain*,
  Who slew a mighty Boar,
In hopes that he might Honour gain;
  But he must die therefore:
Who was allow'd his Death to chuse,
  Which was by Virgins Darts;
But they the same did all refuse,
  So tender were their Hearts.

The King's Daughter at length by Lot,
  Was doom'd to work his Woe;
From her fair Hands, a fatal Shot
  Out of a golden Bow,
Must put a Period to the Strife;
  At which, Grief did her seize;
She of her Father begg'd his Life,
  Upon her bended Knees:

Saying, My gracious Sovereign Lord,
  And honour'd Father dear,
He well deserves a large Reward;
  Then be not so severe;
Give me his Life. He grants the Boon;
  And then without Delay,
This *Spanish* Champion, e're 'twas Noon,
  Rid with her quite away.

Now come we to St. *Anthony*,
  A Man with Valour fraught,
The Champion of fair *Italy*,
  Who many Wonders wrought:
First, he a mighty Giant slew,
  The Terror of Mankind:
Young Ladies fair, pure Virgins too,
  This Giant kept confin'd

Within his Castle-Walls of Stone,
  And Gates of solid Brass;
Where Seven Ladies made their Moan,
  But out they could not pass.
Many brave Lords, and Knights likewise,
  To free them did engage;
Who fell a bleeding Sacrifice
  To this fierce Giant's Rage.

Fair Daughters to a Royal King!
  Yet Fortune, after all,
Did our renowned Champion bring,
  To free them from their Thrall;
Assisted by the Hand of Heav'n,
  He ventur'd Life and Limb;
Behold, the fairest of the Sev'n,
  She fell in Love with him.

That Champion good, bold St. *Andrew*,
  The famous *Scottish* Knight,
Dark gloomy Desarts travell'd through,
  Where *Phœbus* gave no Light;
Haunted with Spirits, for a while
  His weary Course he steers;
Till Fortune bless'd him with a Smile,
  And shook off all his Fears.

This Christian Champion travell'd long,
  Till at the length he came
Unto the Giant's Castle strong,
  Great *Blanderon* by Name:
Where the King's Daughters were
    transform'd
  Into the Shape of Swans;
Tho' them he freed, their Father storm'd,
  But he his Malice shuns:

For tho' Five Hundred armed Knights
   Did straight beset him round,
Our Christian Champion with them fights,
   Till on the Heathen Ground
Most of those *Pagans* bleeding lay;
   Which much perplex'd the King:
The *Scottish* Champion clears the way,
   Which was a glorious Thing.

St. *Patrick* too of *Ireland*,
   That Noble Knight of Fame,
He travell'd, as we understand,
   Till at the length he came
Into a Grove where Satyrs dwelt;
   Where Ladies he beheld,
Who had their raged Fury felt,
   And were with Sorrow fill'd:

He drew his Sword, and did maintain
   A sharp and bloody Fray,
Till the Ring-leader he had slain;
   The rest soon fled away.
This done, he ask'd the Ladies fair,
   Who were in Silks array'd,
From whence they came, and who they
     were?
   They answered him, and said;

We are all Daughters to a King,
   Whom a brave *Scottish* Knight
Did out of Tribulation bring:
   He having took his Flight,
Now after him we are in Quest:
   St. *Patrick* then replies,
He is my Friend, I cannot rest
   Till I find him likewise:

So Ladies, if you do intend
   To take your Lot with me,
This Sword of mine shall you defend
   From savage Cruelty.
The Ladies freely gave Consent
   To travel many Miles;
Thro' shady Groves and Woods they went,
   In Search of Fortune's Smiles.

The Christian Champion *David* went
   To the *Tartarian* Court;
Where, at their Tilt and Tournament,
   And such like Royal Sport,
He overthrew the only Son
   Of the Count *Palatine*;
This noble Action being done,
   His Fame began to shine.

The young Count's sad and sudden Death,
   Turn'd all their Joys to Grief;
He bleeding lay, bereav'd of Breath,
   The Father's Son in Chief:
But Lords and Ladies blaz'd the Fame
   Of our brave Champion bold;
Saying, They ought to write his Name
   In Characters of Gold.

Here have I writ a fair Account
   Of each Heroick Deed,
Done by these Knights; which will
     surmount
   All those that shall succeed.
The ancient Chronicles of Kings,
   E're since the World begun,
Can't boast of such renowned Things,
   As these brave Knights have done.

St. *George* he was for *England*,
   St. *Dennis* was for *France*;
St. *James* for *Spain*, whose valiant Hand
   Did Christian Fame advance:
St. *Anthony* for *Italy*,
   *Andrew* for *Scots* ne're fails;
*Patrick* too stands for *Ireland*,
   St. *David* was for *Wales*.

Thus have you those stout Champions
     Names
   In this renowned Song:
Young captive Ladies bound in Chains,
   Confin'd in Castles strong,
They did by Knightly Prowess free,
   True Honour to maintain;
Then let their lasting Memory
   From Age to Age remain.

# The Mad Merry Prankes
# Of Robbin Good-fellow

J UST AS PATIENT GRISELDA *once delighted centuries of singers and story tellers because of her assertion of the need for unquestioning faith, no matter how bitter the trials, so the "Puck" figure in whatever guise he has been known, has endeared himself to readers for many ages. His appeal may be more enduring because agnostics question whether faith should be unquestioned; that reaction is, in Freudian terms, more closely related to the domination of superego telling us what we must do and believe. Puck, however, is an "id" figure, something delightful growing out of our unrepressed dreams as he did in Shakespeare's* Midsummer Night's Dream. *He is not malicious, but the fun-loving part of a child. Attributed to Shakespeare's friend, Ben Jonson, the following early seventeenth-century ballad echoes lines from Shakespeare's play and will still "make good sport with ho, ho, ho!"*

The Mad Merry Prankes of Robbin Good-fellow *is reprinted from* The Roxburghe Ballads, *Vol. 2, nos. 4–6 (Hertford: printed for the Ballad Society, 1872–1874. Reprinted by AMS Press, 1966).*

TO THE TUNE OF *Dulcina.*

F ROM OBERON IN fairyland,
  the king of ghosts and shadowes there,
Mad Robbin I, at his command,
  am sent to view the night sports here:
    What revell rout

    Is kept about,
In every corner where I goe,
    I will o'er see,
    And merry be,
And make good sport with ho, ho, ho!

More swift than lightening can I flye,
  and round about this airy welkin
    soone,
And, in a minute's space, descry
  each thing that's done beneath the
    moone;
      There's not a hag
      Nor ghost shall wag,
Nor cry "goblin!" where I doe goe,
      But Rob[b]in I
      Their feats will spye,
And feare them home with ho, ho, ho!

If any wanderers I meet
  that from their night-sports doe trudge
    home,
With counterfeiting voyce I greet
  and cause them on with me to roame,
      Through woods, through lakes,
      Through bogs, through brakes,—
Ore bush and brier with them I goe;
      I call upon
      Them to come on,
And wend me, laughing ho, ho, ho!

Sometimes I meet them like a man;
  sometimes an oxe, sometimes a hound;
And to a horse I turne me can,
  to trip and trot about them round.

But, if to ride
My backe they stride,
More swift than winde away I goe;
  Ore hedge and lands,
  Through pooles and ponds,
I whirry, laughing, ho, ho, ho!

When ladds and lasses merry be
  With possets and with junkets fine,
Unseene of all the company,
  I eate their cakes and sip their wine;
      And to make sport,
      I fart and snort,
And out the candles I doe blow;
      The maides I kisse,
      They shrieke, "Who's this?"
I answer nought, but ho, ho, ho!

Yet now and then, the maids to please,
  I card at midnight up their wooll:
And while they sleep, snort,
    fart and fease,
  with wheele to threds their flax I pull:
      I grind at mill
      Their malt [up] still,
I dresse their hemp, I spin their towe;
      If any wake,
      And would me take,
I wend me, laughing, ho, ho, ho!

## *The Second Part*

### TO THE SAME TUNE.

When house or harth doth sluttish lie,
  I pinch the maids there blacke
    and blew;
And, from the bed, the bed-cloathes I
  pull off, and lay them naked to view:
      twixt sleepe and wake
      I doe them take,
And on the key-colde floore them throw;
      If out they cry,
      Then forth flye I,

And loudly laugh I, ho, ho, ho!
When any need to borrow ought,
  we lend them what they doe require;
And for the use demaund we nought,
  our owne is all we doe desire:
      If to repay
      They doe delay,
Abroad amongst them then I goe,
      And night by night
      I them affright,

With pinching, dreames, and ho, ho, ho!
When lazie queanes have nought to doe
  but study how to cogge and lie,
To make debate, and mischiefe too,
  twixt one another secretly:
      I marke their glose,
      And doe disclose
To them that they had wrongèd so;
      When I have done,
    I get me gone,
And leave them scolding, ho, ho, ho!

When men doe traps and engins set
  in loope-holes, where the vermine
    creepe,
That from their foulds and houses fet
  their ducks and geese, their lambs and
    sheepe:
      I spy the gin,
      And enter in,
And seemes a vermine taken so,
      But when they there
      Approach me neare,

I leape out, laughing, ho, ho, ho!
By wels and gils in medowes greene,
  we nightly dance our *hey-day guise,*
And to our fairy King and Queene
  wee chant our moone-light harmonies.
      When larkes 'gin sing,
      Away we fling;
And babes new borne steale as we goe;
      An elfe in bed
      We leave in stead,
And wend us, laughing, ho, ho, ho!

From hag-bred Merlin's time have I
  thus nightly reveld to and fro:
And, for my pranks, men call me by
  the name of Robin Good-fellow:
      Fiends, ghosts, and sprites
      That haunt the nights,
The hags and goblins doe me know,
      And beldames old,
      My feats have told,
So *Vale, Vale,* ho, ho, ho!
             FINIS.

*Part Two*
*Poetry*

# "August Eclogue"
## From The Shepheardes Calender

## By EDMUND SPENSER

THOUGH THE FAERIE QUEEN, *designed to fashion young men in virtuous and gentle discipline, is Spenser's most famous work, his* Shepheardes Calender, *written earlier, was very popular. The "August Eclogue," for example, in the* Calender, *shows the musical quality of Spenser's poetry. It contains a roundelay, a musical duel between two shepherds, Willye and Perigot. Another boy, Cuddye, is the judge. The prizes are a lamb and a "mazer" (a carved wooden cup). Cuddye judges that they have both won the musical battle. He awards the lamb to Willye and the cup to Perigot.*

*The tale of the Egalitarian Giant in Book V, Canto II of* The Faerie Queene, *though not reproduced here, might well have fascinated children. A giant has attracted a huge crowd by maintaining that he is in favor of dividing all things equally among the people. The giant stands high on a cliff beside the sea, and to dramatize his statements, he holds in his hands a pair of massive scales: he would all things "reduce unto equality." So the common people "did about him flocke" like "foolish flies about an hony crocke,/In Hope by him greate benefite to gaine,/And uncontrolled freedome to obtaine." When Sir Artegall, the Knight of Justice, sees what is going on, he accosts the giant, pointing out that there are many intangibles in life which cannot be equally divided. He then orders his squire, Talus, the right arm of justice, to get rid of the Giant:*

> Approaching nigh unto him cheeke by cheeke,
> He shouldered him from off the higher ground,
> And down the rock him throwing, in the sea him drownd.

*"So downe the cliffe the wretched Gyant tumbled." And so Spenser gets rid of any ideas the populace might entertain about communism—or democracy, too, for that matter. Such ideas had in fact been proposed but quickly quelled. Words unfamiliar to a reader can be checked in the Oxford English Dictionary, though most can be understood in the context in which they are found. I have explained a few in brackets opposite the lines.*

### ROUNDELAY

| | | |
|---|---|---|
| *Perigot.* | It fell upon a holly eve, | |
| *Willye.* | hey ho hollidaye, | |
| *Perigot.* | When holly fathers wont to shrieve: | [were accustomed] |
| *Willye.* | now gynneth this roundelay. | |

*Perigot.*  Sitting upon a hill so hye
*Willye.*       hey ho the high hyll,
*Perigot.*  The while my flocke did feede thereby,
*Willye.*       the while the shepheard selfe did spill:     [waste time]
*Perigot.*  I saw the bouncing Bellibone,
*Willye.*       hey ho Bonibell,
*Perigot.*  Tripping over the dale alone,
*Willye.*       she can trippe it very well:
*Perigot.*  Well decked in a frocke of gray,
*Willye.*       hey ho gray is greete,
*Perigot.*  And in a Kirtle of greene saye,              [fine cloth]
*Willye.*       the greene is for maydens meete:         [proper]
*Perigot.*  A chapelet on her head she wore,
*Willye.*       hey ho chapelet,
*Perigot.*  Of sweete violets therein was store,
*Willye.*       she sweeter than the violet.
*Perigot.*  My sheepe did leave theyr wonted foode,
*Willye.*       hey ho seely sheepe,
*Perigot.*  And gazd on her, as they were wood,          [crazy]
*Willye.*       woode as he that did them keepe.
*Perigot.*  As the bonilasse passed bye,
*Willye.*       hey ho bonilasse,
*Perigot.*  She roude at me with glauncing eye,          [darted]
*Willye.*       as cleare as the christall glasse:
*Perigot.*  All as the Sunnye beame so bright,
*Willye.*       hey ho the Sunne beame,
*Perigot.*  Glaunceth from *Phoebus* face forthright,
*Willye.*       so love into thy hart did streame:
*Perigot.*  Or as the thonder cleaves the cloudes,
*Willye.*       hey ho the Thonder,
*Perigot.*  Wherein the lightsome levin shroudes, [radiant lightning hides]
*Willye.*       so cleaves thy soule a sonder:
*Perigot.*  Or as Dame *Cynthias* silver raye
*Willye.*       hey ho the Moonelight,
*Perigot.*  Upon the glyttering wave doth playe:
*Willye.*       such play is a pitteous plight.
*Perigot.*  The glaunce into my heart did glide,
*Willye.*       hey ho the glyder,
*Perigot.*  Therewith my soule was sharply gryde,        [pierced]
*Willye.*       such woundes soone wexen wider.
*Perigot.*  Hasting to raunch the arrow out,
*Willye.*       hey ho the arrowe,
*Perigot.*  Ne can I find salve for my sore,
*Willye.*       love is a curelesse sorrowe.
*Perigot.*  And though my bale with death I bought,
*Willye.*       hey ho heavie cheere,

| | |
|---|---|
| *Perigot.* | Yet should thilk lasse not from my thought: |
| *Willye.* | so you may buye gold to deare. |
| *Perigot.* | But whether in paynefull love I pyne, |
| *Willye.* | hey ho pinching payne, |
| *Perigot.* | Or thrive in welth, she shal be mine. |
| *Willye.* | but if thou can her obteine. |
| *Perigot.* | And if for gracelesse greefe I dye, |
| *Willye.* | hey ho gracelesse griefe, |
| *Perigot.* | Witnesse, shee slewe me with her eye: |
| *Willye.* | let thy follye be the priefe. |
| *Perigot.* | And you, that sawe it, simple shepe, |
| *Willye.* | hey ho the fayre flocke, |
| *Perigot.* | For priefe thereof, my death shall weepe, |
| *Willye.* | and mone with many a mocke. |
| *Perigot.* | So learnd I love on a hollye eve, |
| *Willye.* | hey ho holidaye, |
| *Perigot.* | That ever since my hart did greve. |
| *Willye.* | now endeth our roundelay. |

*       *       *

*Cuddye.*

Fayth of my soule, I deeme ech have gayned.
For thy let the Lambe be *Willye* his owne:
And for *Perigot* so well hath hym payned.
To him be the wroughten mazer alone.

# Nymphidia, the Court of Fairy

## By MICHAEL DRAYTON

ACCORDING TO TRADITION, *Shakespeare died of a fever contracted after a drinking bout with Michael Drayton. Drayton, too, was from Warwickshire, and his poetry reveals him as a charming Elizabethan. One long poem of his,* Poly-Olbion, *attempts to capture the essence of the English spirit and its past by interweaving geography, folk tale, and history. In a mixture of prose and poetry, Rudyard Kipling attempted a somewhat similar synthesis in* Puck of Pook's Hill *(1905).*

*Nymphidia is a graceful poem, the fancy and rhythm of which might well appeal to children as well as to adults, as Professor William Wooden points out in* Children's Literature, *volume 6 (Temple University Press, 1977).*

OLD CHAUCER doth of Thopas tell,
Mad Rabelais of Pantagruel,
A latter third of Dowsabell,
With such poor trifles playing;
Others the like have labored at
Some of this thing, and some of that,
And many of they know not what,
But that they must be saying.

Another sort there be that will
Be talking of the Fairies still,
Nor ever can they have their fill,
As they were wedded to them;
No tales of them their thirst can slake,
So much delight therein they take,
And some strange thing they fain would
     make,
Knew they the way to do them.

Then since no Muse hath been so bold,
Or of the later, or the old,
Those elvish secrets to unfold
Which lie from others' reading,
My active Muse to light shall bring
The court of that proud Fairy King,
And tell there of the reveling;
Jove prosper my proceeding.

And thou, Nymphidia, gentle fay,
Which meeting me upon the way
These secrets didst to me bewray,
Which I now am in telling;
My pretty light fantastic maid,
I here invoke thee to my aid,
That I may speak what thou hast said,
In numbers smoothly swelling.

This palace standeth in the air,
By necromancy placed there,
That it no tempests needs to fear,
Which way soe'er it blow it.
And somewhat southward toward the
     noon,
Whence lies a way up to the moon,
And thence the Fairy can as soon
Pass to the earth below it.

The walls of spiders' legs are made,
Well mortised and finely laid;
He was the master of his trade
It curiously that builded;
The windows of the eyes of cats,
And for the roof, instead of slats,
Is covered with the skins of bats,
With moonshine that are gilded.

Hence Oberon him sport to make
(Their rest when weary mortals take,
And none but only fairies wake)
Descendeth for his pleasure.
And Mab his merry queen by night
Bestrides young folks that lie upright,
In elder times the Mare that hight,
Which plagues them out of measure.

Hence shadows, seeming idle shapes
Of little frisking elves and apes
To earth do make their wanton 'scapes,
As hope of pastime hastes them,
Which maids think on the hearth they see
When fires well near consumed be,
There dancing heys by two and three,
Just as their fancy casts them.

These make our girls their sluttery rue,
By pinching them both black and blue,
And put a penny in their shoe
The house for cleanly sweeping;
And in their courses make that round,
In meadows and in marshes found,
Of them so called the Fairy ground,
Of which they have the keeping.

These when a child haps to be got
Which after proves an idiot,
When folk perceive it thriveth not,
The fault therein to smother
Some silly doting brainless calf
That understands things by the half
Say that the fairy left this aufe
And took away the other.

But listen and I shall you tell
A chance in Fairy that befell,
Which certainly may please some well
In love and arms delighting;
Of Oberon that jealous grew
Of one of his own Fairy crew,
Too well, he feared, his queen that knew,
His love but ill requiting.

Pigwiggen was this Fairy knight,
One wondrous gracious in the sight
Of fair Queen Mab, which day and night
He amorously observed;
Which made King Oberon suspect
His service took too good effect,
His sauciness and often checked
And could have wished him starved.

Pigwiggen gladly would commend
Some token to Queen Mab to send,
If sea, or land, could aught him lend
Were worthy of her wearing;
At length this lover doth devise
A bracelet made of emmet's eyes,
A thing he thought that she would prize,
No whit her state impairing,

And to the queen a letter writes,
Which he most curiously endites,
Conjuring her by all the rites
Of love, she would be pleased
To meet him, her true servant, where
They might without suspect or fear
Themselves to one another clear
And have their poor hearts eased.

"At midnight the appointed hour,
And for the queen a fitting bower"
Quoth he, "is that fair cowslip flower
On Hipcut Hill that groweth;
In all your train there's not a fay
That ever went to gather May
But she hath made it in her way,
The tallest there that groweth."

When by Tom Thumb, a Fairy page,
He sent it and doth him engage
By promise of a mighty wage
It secretly to carry;
Which done, the queen her maids
    doth call
And bids them to be ready all;
She would go see her summer hall,
She could no longer tarry.

Her chariot ready straight is made,
Each thing therein is fitting laid,
That she by nothing might be stayed,
For naught must her be letting;
Four nimble gnats the horses were,
Their harnesses of gossamer,
Fly Cranion her charioteer
Upon the coach-box getting.

Her chariot of a snail's fine shell
Which for the colors did excel,
The fair Queen Mab becoming well
So lively was the limning;
The seat, the soft wool of the bee;
The cover, gallantly to see,
The wing of a pied butterfly,
I trow 'twas simple trimming.

The wheels composed of crickets' bones
And daintily made for the nonce,
For fear of rattling on the stones
With thistledown they shod it;
For all her maidens much did fear
If Oberon had chanced to hear
That Mab his queen should have been
    there
He would not have abode it.

She mounts her chariot with a trice,
Nor would she stay for no advice
Until her maids that were so nice
To wait on her were fitted,
But ran herself away alone,
Which when they heard, there was not
    one
But hasted after to be gone
As she had been diswitted.

Hop, and Mop, and Drop so clear,
Pip, and Trip, and Skip that were
To Mab their soverign ever dear,
Her special maids of honor;
Fib and Tib, and Pink and Pin,
Tick and Quick, and Jill and Jin,
Tit and Nit, and Wap and Win,
The train that wait upon her.

Upon a grasshopper they got,
And what with amble and with trot,
For hedge nor ditch they spared not
But after her they hie them.
A cobweb over them they throw
To shield the wind if it should blow;
Themselves they wisely could bestow
Lest any should espy them.

But let us leave Queen Mab a while,
Through many a gate, o'er many a stile,
That now had gotten by this wile,
Her dear Pigwiggen kissing,
And tell how Oberon doth fare,
Who grew as mad as any hare
When he had sought each place with care
And found his queen was missing.

By grisly Pluto he doth swear,
He rent his clothes and tore his hair,
And as he runneth here and there
An acorn cup he greeteth,
Which soon he taketh by the stalk,
About his head he lets it walk,
Nor doth he any creature balk,
But lays on all he meeteth.

The Tuscan poet doth advance
The frantic paladin of France,
And those more ancient do enhance
Alcides in his fury,
And others Ajax Telamon;
But to this time there hath been none
So bedlam as our Oberon,
Of which I dare assure you.

And first encountering with a wasp,
He in his arms the fly doth clasp
As though his breath he forth would
    grasp,
Him for Pigwiggen taking;
"Where is my wife, thou rogue?"
    quoth he,
"Pigwiggen, she is come to thee;
Restore her, or thou diest by me!"
Whereat, the poor wasp quaking

Cries, "Oberon, great Fairy King,
Content thee, I am no such thing;
I am a wasp, behold my sting!"
At which the Fairy started;
When soon away the wasp doth go;
Poor wretch was never frighted so,
He thought his wings were much too slow,
O'erjoyed they so were parted.

He next upon a glow-worm light,
(You must suppose it now was night)
Which, for her hinder part was bright,
He took to be a devil,
And furiously her doth assail
For carrying fire in her tail;
He thrashed her rough coat with his flail;
The mad king feared no evil.

"Oh," quoth the glow-worm, "hold thy
     hand,
Thou puissant king of Fairyland,
Thy mighty strokes who may withstand;
Hold, or of life despair I!"
Together then herself doth roll,
And tumbling down into a hole
She seemed as black as any coal
Which vexed away the Fairy.

From thence he ran into a hive;
Amongst the bees he letteth drive,
And down their combs begins to rive,
All likely to have spoiled;
Which with their wax his face besmeared
And with their honey daubed his beard;
It would have made a man afeared
To see how he was moiled.

A new adventure him betides;
He met an ant, which he bestrides
And post thereon away he rides
Which with his haste doth stumble
And came full over on her snout;
Her heels so threw the dirt about
For she by no means could get out
but over him doth tumble,

And being in this piteous case
And all beslurried, head and face,
On runs he in this wild goose chase,
As here and there he rambles,
Half blind, against a molehill hit
And for a mountain taking it
For all he was out of his wit,
Yet to the top he scrambles.

And being gotten to the top
Yet there himself he could not stop
But down on th'other side doth chop,
And to the foot came rumbling,
So that the grubs therein that bred,
Hearing such turmoil overhead,
Thought surely they had all been dead,
So fearful was the jumbling.

And falling down into a lake
Which him up to the neck doth take,
His fury somewhat it doth slake;
He calleth for a ferry;
Where you may some recovery note:
What was his club he made his boat,
And in his oaken cup doth float
As safe as in a wherry.

Men talk of the adventures strange
Of Don Quixote, and of their change,
Through which he armed oft did range,
Of Sancho Panza's travel;
But should a man tell every thing
Done by this frantic Fairy King
And them in lofty numbers sing,
It well his wits might gravel.

Scarce set on shore but therewithal
He meeteth Puck, which most men call
Hobgoblin, and on him doth fall
With words from frenzy spoken.
"Ho, Ho!" quoth Hob, "God save thy
     grace,
Who dressed thee in this piteous case?
He thus that spoiled my sovereign's face,
I would his neck were broken."

This Puck seems but a dreaming dolt,
Still walking like a ragged colt,
And oft out of a bush doth bolt
Of purpose to deceive us,
And leading us makes us to stray
Long winter's nights out of the way,
And when we stick in mire and clay,
Hob doth with laughter leave us.

"Dear Puck," quoth he, "my wife is gone;
As e'er thou lov'st King Oberon,
Let everything but this alone,
With vengeance and pursue her;
Bring her to me, alive or dead,
Or that vile thief Pigwiggen's head;
That villain hath defiled my bed;
He to this folly drew her."

Quoth Puck, "My liege, I'll never lin,
But I will thorough thick and thin,
Until at length I bring her in;
My dearest lord, ne'er doubt it;
Thorough brake, thorough brier,
Thorough muck, thorough mire,
Thorough water, thorough fire,
And thus goes Puck about it."

This thing Nymphidia overheard,
That on this mad king had a guard,
Not doubting of a great reward
For first this business broaching;
And through the air away doth go
Swift as an arrow from the bow,
To let her sovereign Mab to know
What peril was approaching.

The Queen, bound with love's powerful'st
     charm,
Sat with Pigwiggen arm in arm;
Her merry maids that thought no harm
About the room were skipping;
A humble-bee, their minstrel, played
Upon his hautboy; every maid
Fit for this revels was arrayed,
The hornpipe neatly tripping.

In comes Nymphidia and doth cry,
"My sovereign, for your safety, fly,
For there is danger but too nigh,
I posted to forewarn you;
The King hath sent Hobgoblin out
To seek you all the fields about,
And of your safety you may doubt,
If he but once discern you!"

When like an uproar in a town
Before them everything went down,
Some tore a ruff and some a gown,
'Gainst one another justling;
They flew about like chaff i'the wind;
For haste some left their masks behind;
Some could not stay their gloves to find;
There never was such bustling.

Forth ran they by a secret way
Into a brake that near them lay;
Yet much they doubted there to stay,
Lest Hob should hap to find them;
He had a sharp and piercing sight,
All one to him the day and night,
And therefore were resolved by flight
To leave this place behind them.

At length one chanced to find a nut
In th'end of which a hole was cut,
Which lay upon a hazel root,
There scattered by a squirrel
Which out the kernel gotten had,
When quoth this fay, "Dear Queen, be
     glad;
Let Oberon be ne'er so mad,
I'll set you safe from peril.

"Come all into this nut," quoth she,
"Come closely in; be ruled by me;
Each one may here a choser be;
For room ye need not wrastle,
Nor need ye be together heapt";
So one by one therein they crept
And lying down, they soundly slept,
As safe as in a castle.

Nymphidia that this while doth watch,
Perceived if Puck the queen should catch,
That he would be her over-match,
Of which she well bethought her;
Found it must be some powerful charm,
The Queen against him that must arm
Or surely he would do her harm,
For throughly he had sought her.

And listening if she aught could hear
That her might hinder or might fear,
But finding still the coast was clear,
Nor creature had descried her;
Each circumstance and having scanned,
She came thereby to understand
Puck would be with them out of hand,
When to her charms she hied her.

And first her fern seed doth bestow,
The kernel of the mistletoe,
And here and there, as Puck should go,
With terror to affright him,
She night-shade strews to work him ill,
Therewith her vervain and her dill,
That hindreth witches of their will,
Of purpose to despite him.

Then sprinkles she the juice of rue,
That groweth underneath the yew,
With nine drops of the midnight dew
From lunary distilling;
The moldwarp's brain mixed therewithal,
And with the same the pismire's gall,
For she in nothing short would fall,
The Fairy was so willing.

Then thrice under a briar doth creep,
Which at both ends was rooted deep,
And over it three times she leap,
Her magic much availing;
Then on Proserpina doth call,
And so upon her spell doth fall
Which here to you repeat I shall,
Not in one tittle failing:

By the croaking of the frog,
By the howling of the dog,
By the crying of the hog,
Against the storm arising;
By the evening curfew bell,
By the doleful dying knell,
Oh, let this my direful spell,
Hob, hinder thy surprising.

By the mandrake's dreadful groans,
By the lubrican's sad moans,
By the noise of dead men's bones
In charnel houses rattling;
By the hissing of the snake,
The rustling of the fire-drake,
I charge thee thou this place forsake,
Nor of Queen Mab be prattling.

By the whirlwind's hollow sound,
By the thunder's dreadful stound,
Yells of spirits underground,
I charge thee not to fear us;
By the screech-owl's dismal note,
By the black night-raven's throat,
I charge thee, Hob, to tear thy coat
With thorns if thou come near us.

Her spell thus spoke, she stepped aside
And in a chink herself doth hide
To see thereof what would betide,
For she doth only mind him;
When presently she Puck espies,
And well she marked his gloating eyes
How under every leaf he pries
In seeking still to find them.

But once the circle got within,
The charms to work do straight begin,
And he was caught as in a gin;
For as he thus was busy,
A pain he in his headpiece feels,
Against a stubbed tree he reels
And up went poor Hobgoblin's heels,
Alas, his brain was dizzy.

At length upon his feet he gets;
Hobgoblin fumes, Hobgoblin frets,
And, as again he forward sets
And through the bushes scrambles,
A stump doth trip him in his pace,
Down comes poor Hob upon his face
And lamentably tore his case
Amongst the briars and brambles.

"A plague upon Queen Mab," quoth he,
And all her maids, wheree'er they be!
I think the devil guided me
To see her so provoked."
Where, stumbling at a piece of wood,
He fell into a ditch of mud,
Where to the very chin he stood
In danger to be choked.

Now, worse than e'er he was before,
Poor Puck doth yell, poor Puck doth roar;
That waked Queen Mab, who doubted
    sore
Some treason hath been wrought her,
Until Nymphidia told the queen
What she had done, what she had seen,
Who then had well-near cracked her
    spleen
With very extreme laughter.

But leave we Hob to clamber out,
Queen Mab and all her Fairy rout,
And come again to have a bout
With Oberon yet madding;
And with Pigwiggen now distraught,
Who was much troubled in his thought,
That he so long the queen had sought
And through the fields was gadding.

And as he runs he still doth cry,
"King Oberon, I thee defy
And dare thee here in arms to try
For my dear Lady's honor,
For that she is a queen right good,
In whose defense I'll shed my blood,
And that thou in this jealous mood
Hast layed this slander on her."

And quickly arms him for the field,
A little cockle-shell his shield,
Which he could very bravely wield
Yet could it not be pierced;
His spear, a bent both stiff and strong
And well-near of two inches long;
The pile was of a horse-fly's tongue,
Whose sharpness naught reversed.

And puts him on a coat of mail,
Which was of a fish's scale,
That when his foe should him assail,
No point should be prevailing;
His rapier was a hornet's sting;
It was a very dangerous thing,
For, if he chanced to hurt the King,
It would be long in healing.

His helmet was a beetle's head,
Most horrible and full of dread,
That able was to strike one dead,
Yet did it well become him;
And, for a plume, a horse's hair,
Which, being tossed with the air
Had force to strike his foe with fear
And turn his weapon from him.

Himself he on an earwig set,
Yet scarce he on his back could get,
So oft and high he did corvet
Ere he himself could settle;
He made him turn and stop and bound,
To gallop, and to trot the round;
He scarce could stand on any ground
He was so full of mettle.

When soon he met with Thomalin,
One that a valiant knight had been,
And to King Oberon of kin.
Quoth he, "Thou manly Fairy,
Tell Oberon I come prepared,
Then bid him stand upon his guard;
This hand his baseness shall reward,
Let him be ne'er so wary.

"Say to him thus, that I defy
His slanders and his infamy,
And, as a mortal enemy
Do publicly proclaim him;
Withal, that if I had mine own,
He should not wear the Fairy crown,
But with a vengeance should come down,
Nor we a king should name him."

This Thomalin could not abide,
To hear his sovereign vilified,
But to the Fairy court him hied;
Full furiously he posted
With everything Pigwiggen said,
How title to the crown he laid
And in what arms he was arrayed,
As how himself he boasted.

'Twixt head and foot, from point to point
He told th'arming of each joint,
In every piece, how neat and quaint,
For Thomalin could do it;
How fair he sat, how sure he rid,
As of the courser he bestrid,
How managed and how well he did;
The king, which listened to it,

Quoth he, "Go, Thomalin, with speed,
Provide me arms, provide my steed
And everything that I shall need;
By thee I will be guided;
To straight account call thou thy wit,
See there be wanting not a whit
In everything see thou me fit,
Just as my foe's provided."

Soon flew this news through Fairyland,
Which gave Queen Mab to understand
The combat that was then in hand
Betwixt those men so mighty;
Which greatly she began to rue,
Perceiving that all Fairy knew
The first occasion from her grew
Of these affairs so weighty.

Wherefore, attended with her maids,
Through fogs and mists and damps she
    wades
To Proserpine, the Queen of Shades
To treat that it would please her
The cause into her hands to take
For ancient love and friendship's sake,
And soon thereof an end to make,
Which of much care would ease her.

A while there let we Mab alone,
And come we to King Oberon,
Who, armed to meet his foe, is gone
For proud Pigwiggen crying;
Who sought the Fairy king as fast,
And had so well his journies cast,
That he arrived at the last,
His puissant foe espying.

Stout Thomalin came with the king;
Tom Thumb doth on Pigwiggen bring,
That perfect were in everything
To single fights belonging;
And therefore they themselves engage
To see them exercise their rage
With fair and comely equipage,
Not one the other wronging.

So like in arms these champions were
As they had been a very pair,
So that a man would almost swear
That either had been either;
Their furious steeds began to neigh
That they were heard a mighty way;
Their staves upon their rests they lay;
Yet, e'er they flew together,

Their seconds minister an oath
Which was indifferent to them both
That on their knightly faith and troth
No magic them supplied,
And sought them that they had no charms
Wherewith to work each other's harms,
But came with simple open arms
To have their causes tried.

Together furiously they ran,
That to the ground came horse and man;
The blood out of their helmets span,
So sharp were their encounters.
And though they to the earth were
     thrown,
Yet quickly they regained their own;
Such nimbleness was never shown,
They were two gallant mounters.


When in a second course again
They forward came with might and main,
Yet which had better of the twain
The seconds could not judge yet;
Their shields were into pieces cleft,
Their helmets from their heads were reft,
And to defend them nothing left
These champions would not budge yet.


Away from them their staves they threw;
Their cruel swords they quickly drew,
And freshly they the fight renew,
That every stroke redoubled;
Which made Proserpina take heed
And make to them the greater speed,
For fear lest they too much should bleed,
Which wondrously her troubled.


When to th'infernal Styx she goes,
She takes the fogs from thence that rose,
And in a bag doth them enclose;
When well she had them blended,
She hies her then to Lethe spring,
A bottle and thereof doth bring
Wherewith she meant to work the thing
Which only she intended.


Now Proserpine with Mab is gone
Unto the place where Oberon
And proud Pigwiggen, one to one,
Both to be slain were likely;
And there themselves they closely hide
Because they would not be espied,
For Proserpine meant to decide
The matter very quickly,


And suddenly unties the poke
Which out of it sent such a smoke
As ready was them all to choke,
So grievous was the pother;
So that the knights each other lost
And stood as still as any post,
Tom Thumb nor Thomalin could boast
Themselves of any other.


But when the mist gan somewhat cease,
Proserpina commandeth peace,
And that a while they should release
Each other of their peril;
"Which here," quoth she, "I do proclaim
To all, in dreadful Pluto's name,
That, as ye will eschew his blame,
You let me hear the quarrel.


"But here yourselves you must engage
Somewhat to cool your spleenish rage;
Your grievous thirst and to assuage
That first you drink this liquor,
Which shall your understanding clear,
As plainly shall to you appear,
Those things from me that you shall hear,
Conceiving much the quicker."


This Lethe water, you must know,
The memory destroyeth so
That of our weal or of our woe
It all remembrance blotted;
Of it nor can you ever think;
For they no sooner took this drink
But naught into their brains could sink
Of what had them besotted.


King Oberon forgotten had
That he for jealousy ran mad,
But of his queen was wondrous glad
And asked how they came thither;
Pigwiggen likewise doth forget
That he Queen Mab had ever met,
Or that they were so hard beset
When they were found together.

Nor neither of them both had thought
That e'er they had each other sought,
Much less that they a combat fought,
But such a dream were loathing;
Tom Thumb had got a little sup,
And Thomalin scarce kissed the cup,
Yet had their brains so sure locked up,
That they remembered nothing.

Queen Mab and her light maids the while
Among themselves do closely smile
To see the king caught with this wile,
With one another jesting;
And to the Fairy court they went
With mickle joy and merriment,
Which thing was done with good intent,
And thus I left them feasting.

[FINIS]

( 9 )

# The Mower's Song
## By ANDREW MARVELL

ONE OF THE MOST *charming metaphysical poets was Andrew Marvell. His poems, many of which have to do with nature and love, are often very musical. Marvell was a friend of John Milton and assistant to Milton in the Latin Secretaryship for Oliver Cromwell. For the young or the young at heart are meant such poems as* The Mower's Song.

MY MIND WAS ONCE the true survey
Of all these meadows fresh and gay,
And in the greenness of the grass
Did see its hopes as in a glass;
When Juliana came, and she,
What I do to the grass, does to my thoughts and me.

But these, while I with sorrow pine,
Grew more luxuriant still and fine,
That not one blade of grass you spied,
But had a flower on either side;
When Juliana came, and she,
What I do to the grass, does to my thoughts and me.

Unthankful meadows, could you so
A fellowship so true forgo,
And in your gaudy May–games meet,
While I lay trodden under feet?
When Juliana came, and she,
What I do to the grass, does to my thoughts and me.

But what you in compassion ought,
Shall now by my revenge be wrought;
And flowers, and grass, and I, and all
Will in one common ruin fall;
For Juliana comes, and she,
What I do to the grass, does to my thoughts and me.

And thus, ye meadows, which have been
Companions of my thoughts more green,
Shall now the heraldry become
With which I shall adorn my tomb;
For Juliana comes, and she,
What I do to the grass, does to my thoughts and me.

46

## 10

# *Nursery Rhymes*
# *Of the Seventeenth Century*

THE BEST COLLECTION *of nursery rhymes of the seventeenth century may be found in the* Oxford Dictionary of Nursery Rhymes *by Iona and Peter Opie. These rhymes have been drawn from many sources, including riddles, ballads, songbooks, and plays. Though such rhymes have probably always existed and fragments can be traced to Roman sources, "it is, we feel," write the Opies, "from the beginning of the seventeenth century onwards that the majority of the rhymes must be dated" (p. 6, Introduction). About seventy rhymes in this category can be found in their volume.*

*Beyond their research, there is very little to be added. Two rhymes of French origin which date to the seventeenth century and earlier are now sometimes skipped in English. One of them was collected by Angela Tietolman of Montreal, Canada in July, 1974 from a ninety-year old Frenchman. Though he associated it with the Napoleonic Wars, actually it is much earlier. It seems to refer to La Palice, Grand Marshal of the French army, who was killed at Pavie in 1525. The original rhyme went:*

> Monsieur d'la Palice est mort
> Mort devant Pavie;
> Un quart d'heure avant sa mort,
> Il était encore en vie.

*Later, another stanza was added:*

> Il c'est fait faire un habit
> De quatre ou cinq planches.
> Le tailleur qui lui a fait
> Il n'avait pas mis de manches.

*Originally, the rhyme was flattering to the Marshal, who fought up to a quarter of an hour before his death. Later, the rhyme became distorted in various ways in English translation:*

> Mr. Policeman is dead
> Dead before Paris
> A quarter-hour before he died,
> He was still alive.

> They made him a suit
> Of four or five boards.
> The tailor who made it
> Forgot to make the sleeves.

47

*And:*

> May you have six sons
> In fancy uniforms
> And when they're shot
> Let them rot
> In wooden uniforms with no sleeves!

*So a hideous spell can be cast on an enemy. The wooden uniform with no sleeves is a coffin, of course.*

*Another French rhyme sometimes heard in English is certainly very old and may date originally from Rabelais'* Gargantua *in the sixteenth century. In English it goes:*

> I ate an egg
> And a ton of bread
> Forty cows
> And as many hens
> And still I was hungry!

*A beautiful rhyme with ancestors in the seventeenth century is more often associated with the eighteenth-century ballad. "O no, John." As William Cabell Bruce's biography indicates, it was known to an American colonial patriot, John Randolph of Roanoke, but its archetypal concept of a lady on a hilltop suggests an earlier origin:*

> On the hilltop stands a lady
> Who she is I do not know
> All she wears is gold and silver
> And she needs a nice young man.

*The vision of a lady on a hilltop is found in the myth about the Greek goddess of Justice, who three times visited earth seeking justice—in the gold age, the bronze age, and finally in the iron age—and each time, in rage and disappointment, fled back to her mountain top, the last time never to return.*

*Edmund Spenser pictures Sapience, or Wisdom, high on the lap of God; John Donne sees Truth as alone on a hill, craggy and steep; Shakespeare, in* Timon *of Athens, finds Fortune "upon a high and pleasant hill," and Tennyson sees Freedom alone on the heights. I heard the rhyme chanted in the 1940s on the playground of a Black school in Ball's Hill, Virginia. The concept is a lasting one.*

*"Who killed Cock Robin?" is another ancient rhyme often chanted or sung. There is a possibility that it is medieval in origin and refers to the death of spring. One contemporary riddle-rhyme has relatives in the seventeenth century. Now it goes:*

> What are you doing here, Sir?
> Drinking up the beer, Sir!
> Where did you get the beer, Sir?

It wasn't far nor near, Sir.
    Yes, Sir, no, Sir,
    I must be on my way, Sir.

Have you a horse to ride, Sir?
    I'm sitting on its hide, Sir.
But no mount I see, Sir.
    Its hide is sewn on me, sir.
    Yes, Sir, no, Sir,
    I must be on my way, Sir.
Pray, what is your name, Sir?
    My name is—

*(and it is jumped to or a ball is bounced to the letters)*

*The old folksong and rhyme about "The Grand Old Duke of York" who went up a hill with forty thousand men and didn't come down again had its historic counterpart in the seventeenth century, when the King of France was the tragic victim of an unsuccessful military move. (Or it may have other connotations—see Game Rhymes)*

*Though it cannot be traced to the sixteenth century, one enduring rhyme which may well go back that far is:*

I had a little nut tree
    Nothing would it bear
But a silver nutmeg
    And a golden pear
The King of Spain's daughter
    Came to visit me
And all because of
    My little nut tree.

*The sexual innuendoes fit very well with the relationship both of Henry VIII and of Charles I with Spanish princesses. The silver nutmeg was an elegant thing to carry to suppers, for it contained a nutmeg and a small grater convenient in spicing meats or drinks. Congreve mentions a nutmeg carried this way in* Way of the World *(Act III).*

*Variants of many nursery rhymes are found in Shakespeare, often in the most poignant scenes. In this connection, mention was made in the introduction of variants of Little Boy Blue, Fee Fie Foh Fum, and the forgotten old woman who lived under the hill.*

# 11

# *Ring A Ring O' Roses and Other Game Rhymes*

FOR RING-A-RING O' ROSES, *there is no evidence of age, as it lies until recently in the oral tradition. Possibly the game of dancing in a circle is related to the May Pole dances and other remote rituals, including those of the Druids. (Druid worshippers still may be found in various places and still occasionally hang garlands on the great trees in the forest of Meudon, France.) Some scholars have conjectured, without evidence, that the "roses" are the blotches that appeared on bodies during the periodic plagues which endured well into the seventeenth century. Death was sudden: "All fall down." The tune most associated with it is the ancient, typical pentatonic teasing sound, such as in the taunt, "Mary's got a boy friend." Curiously, this sound has been used for teasing in many parts of the world.*

Ring-a-ring o' roses,
A pocketful of posies
A-tisha! A-tisha!
We all fall down!

*Many conjectures have been made about the identity of the duke or king in the dance rhyme about the leader marching up the hill and down again. Some scholars think it was a king of France, while others think it was a Duke of York who was commander in chief of the English army at the end of the eighteenth century. However, when I was in Ireland, a taxi driver pointed to the site of the famous Battle of the Boyne, near Drogheda north of Dublin, and said: "This is where the brave old Duke of York marched up the hill and down again, like in the nursery rhyme." It is a matter of history that a great battle did take place between the former Duke of York, James II, and the Protestant, William of Orange, near the Boyne River in 1690. James was soundly defeated and gave up any serious attempt to regain his throne. Whether he marched up a hill or not, symbolically, at least, he fell from high estate.*

Oh, the brave old Duke of York
He had ten thousand men.

50

He marched them up to the top of the hill
And he marched them down again.
And when they were up they were up.
And when they were down they were down,
And when they were only half-way up,
They were neither up nor down.

*Another famous game rhyme is "London Bridge," which comes in many versions, one of which appears below. Its origins lie somewhere long ago in the oral tradition. Conjecture has it that it was bad luck to span a bridge and that the rhyme suggests human sacrifice—it can only be built after a fair lady has been flung into its waters.*

London Bridge is falling down, falling down, falling down
London Bridge is falling down
My fair Lady!
Iron and wood will build it up, build it up, build it up
Iron and wood will build it up
And a fair Lady!
Here comes a chopper to chop off her head, chop off her
        head, chop off her head
Here comes a chopper to chop off the head
Of my fair Lady!

*It is possible that some folktales arose out of primitive games in which the players were participating, in a sense, in the unfolding of a dramatic story. We know that, often, the reverse process took place—stories led·to games, as they sometimes do now: a Cinderella game board, for example. Northrop Frye sees riddles as a somewhat sadistic game which may have spawned more extended forms of communication, such as detective stories, which keep children or adults guessing up to the last minute. One of the best known riddles is "Humpty Dumpty":*

Humpty Dumpty sat on a wall
Humpty Dumpty had a great fall
All the king's horses and
All the king's men
Couldn't put Humpty together again!
(An egg)

*Not only do many rhymes and folktales have a game origin, but also some plays— including the Japanese* Kyogen, *the comic interludes in* no *drama, which often end with a chase, suggesting their game origin.*

*It is a curious thing that whereas we forget more sophisticated poetry, we never forget the simple nursery rhymes or the games that sometimes accompany them. Perhaps Professor Leonard Mendelsohn of Concordia University, Montreal, is correct in relating this phenomenon to the game of life: the discord often contained within the rhyme is held together by the jog-trot framework of the rhyme itself, and we find comfort in this process. That is, the rhymes seem to tell us: Yes, the world is a discordant, terrible place in many respects, but there is nevertheless an overall structure or pattern.*

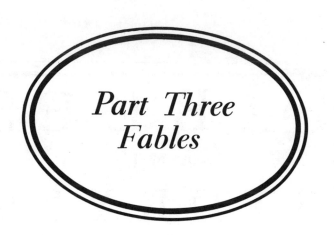

*Part Three*
*Fables*

# FABLES

## AND

# STORYES

## MORALIZED.

Being a

## SECOND PART

### OF THE

# Fables of ÆSOP,

## AND

## Other Eminent Mythologists, &c.

By Sir *Roger L'Estrange*, Kt.

*L*ONDON:

Printed for *R. Sare* at *Grayes-Inn-gate* in *Holborn*,

MDCXCIX.

$$\widehat{12}$$

# Aesop's Fables

## By SIR ROGER L'ESTRANGE

SELECTIONS

T HE INTRODUCTION REPRODUCED HERE *and the selection of fables intended especially for children are interesting because they reveal how different the definition of the word "bawdy" must have been from the way it would be defined now. Sex and violence, the two taboos in many current books, were manifestly present in favorite reading of children of the seventeenth century. Foxe's* Book of Martyrs, *popular with youngsters then, was exceedingly violent, sadistic, and cruel; and many of L'Estrange's fables are the kind of smutty story that might circulate now at some office parties. Recently there has been a trend—commercially instigated, some think—to introduce salacious material to children. The problem as to whether children should be introduced to sexually oriented and violent material, or whether they should be introduced to some of it under certain conditions, seems to be a perennial and undecided one, or at least one on which there is great disagreement. Perhaps L'Estrange will afford an historical perspective.*

*L'Estrange himself is an interesting kind of person to have written fables for children. An ardent royalist in the service of Charles I, he was imprisoned several times in his long life (1616–1704). He even came near to being executed—sentence of death was pronounced on December 26, 1644 by a judge for the Puritan government. Even when offered a pardon if he would become a Puritan, he steadfastly refused. Carrying out the sentence was delayed, and he was eventually allowed to escape from prison in 1648 because he was believed to be dying of consumption. He immediately began actively plotting for a return of the royalists and was forced to flee to Holland. In 1653, he came back to England and somehow established a truce with the Puritan government (some say he distributed bribes). L'Estrange was a prolific writer of various tracts of a political nature, including several urging a rigid censorship of the press. During the last great plague in London, that of 1665, he stayed bravely on in the city publishing his periodical,* The Public Intelligencer. *On occasion, he interviewed Samuel Pepys to obtain news.*

*Again in 1677, his political activities got him in trouble, and he was forced to flee to Scotland and from there to Holland. Four years later, he came back to London and published a weekly called* The Observator. *A supporter of James II, L'Estrange was knighted in 1685. On the arrival of William and Mary, however, and the "Glorious Revolution," his fortunes changed and he was put in prison, but later released on bail. In 1692 he had a stroke, got better, and again became actively involved in politics, enough so that he was arrested and committed to Newgate prison for four years.*

*Beside all his political problems, he had to put up with a gambling wife, a recalcitrant daughter, and the worry of a sick son. Still, along with his political pamphlets and periodicals, he managed to turn out the most extensive collection of fables in existence.*

*He also wrote a few bawdy books and did some translations from the classics. Pepys found him a good conversationalist and Dr. Johnson described him as being the first man to write for a political party for pay and fight for that party, right or wrong. His inner drive seemed to keep him going. He died five days before his eighty-eighth birthday.*

*To those interested in seventeenth century politics, some of his political views can be ascertained from his fables.*

*The following selections from L'Estrange's* Aesop's Fables *are reprinted from a 1699 edition, printed for R. Sare at Grayes-Inn-Gate in Holbern, London.*

*The selections from L'Estrange's* Fables and Storyes Moralized. Being a Second Part of the Fables of Aesop, *and* Other Eminent Mythologists, &c. *are reprinted from the 1699 edition in the Guildhall Library, London. Since there are no illustrations in the L'Estrange edition, we are providing a random but representative selection of wood-cuts from the Caxton edition of 1484.*

# TO THE READER

T HE MAN THAT PUTS Pen to Paper on the Wrong side of *Fourscore*, might every jot with as good a Grace, set up for a *Beau*, as for an *Author*. But it is with some *Writers*, and *Readers*, as it is with the *Indians*, and their *Idols*; the People *Worship* the *Devil*, they say, for fear he should hurt them. Under This Awe, I am now to tell the *Gentle Reader*, that a Phancy took me in the Head some years since, to write a kind of a *Paraphrase* upon *Æsop*; under the Title of [*Fables of Æsop*, and *Other Eminent Mythologists*, with *Morals*, and *Reflexions:*] which amounted to little more than the Turning of an *Old School-Book* into a *New* one, by casting out some *Nauseous*, and *Pedantick Fopperyes* that had been Foisted into't, and putting the Whole into somewhat a more *Fashionable Air*, and *Dress*.

This I propounded to digest into a *Compendious Abstract* of *Instructive Precepts* and *Councels*, to be still ready at hand, for the Use and Edification of *Children:* which I look'd upon as a Work highly Necessary for a *Common Good*, and not more *Wanted* neither, than *Desir'd*. For as the *Foundations* of a *Virtuous* and a *Happy Life*, are all laid in the very Arms of our *Nurses*, so 'tis but *Natural*, and *Reasonable*, that our *Cares*, and *Applications* toward the Forming, and Cultivating of our *Manners*, should *Begin* There too. And in Order to Those Ends, I thought I could not do better, than to Advance That Service under the Veyle of *Emblem*, and *Figure*, after the *Practice*, and *Methods* of the *Antients*.

But it will be a Hard Matter however yet, for a *Sober Man* that undertakes this Province, to *Carry his Point*, and at the same time, to Preserve his *Credit:* For *Children* must be Ply'd with *Idle Tales*, and *Twittle-Twattles*; and betwixt *Jeast* and *Earnest*, *Flatter'd*, and *Cajol'd*, into a *Sense*, and *Love* of their *Duty*. A *Childs Lesson*, must be fitted to a *Childs Talent* and *Humour*; and there are so many *Little Arts*, and *Mimical Fooleries*, that fall in by the way, toward the Discharging of *This Function*, that a Man of *Worth* and *Character*, will hardly come off a *Saver* by the *Office*: For he must *Act One Part* under the *Masque* of *Another*, to acquit himself. But I have spoken at Large to These Heads already elsewhere, and particularly in my *Preface* to the *Former Volume*; to which I refer myself.

Upon the turning of These Things over and over in my Thoughts, the Matter swell'd insensibly under my Hand, and instead of a *Pocket-Manual*, according to my *First Project*, it came in the end to a *Folio*, of *more than double That Bulk*. But This *misreckoning* was no Disappointment to my *Design:* nay, on the Contrary; it answer'd all the *Parts*, and *Pretences*, of the *Undertaking*, as well *Publique*, as *Private:* That is to say; It did the Part of a *School-Book*, with a respect to the *Training up of Children*, and the Office of a *Political* Discourse, with a Regard to the *Government of Life*, Both in One. Now within the Compass of This Division, may be comprehended *all Practical Duties whatsoever:* whether the Persons concern'd be *Noble*, or *Ignoble*; *Men*, *Women*, or *Children*, it Matters not: for *Princes Themselves are made of the same Clay with Other Men, and Subjected, by Providence to the Ordinary Rules and Measures of* Mankind.

I am now to tell the *Reader* once again, that, in pursuance of my First Proposal, I have here follow'd it with [*a Second Part*] of *Select Fables*, and *Stories*, to the very same Purpose and Intent with the *Other*. Let me be understood, as to the *Manner* of the *Operation* and the *Drift* of *Applying* it: wherein I have also consulted the *Best Authorities* I could meet withal, in the *Choyce* of the *Collection*, without Streyning any Thing all This while, beyond the Strictest *Equity* of a *Fair*, and an *Innocent Meaning*; or making a Spiteful Use of *Wire-drawn Inferences*, and *Intimations*, to the *Wrong*, or *Scandal* of my Neighbour, which would be much the same Thing with Turning one of the most *Useful Duties* of a *Sociable* Life, into the Worst of *Libells*. But there's a Great Difference, betwixt carrying the *Image* to the *Man*, and bringing the *Man* to the *Image*; Or I might as well have said, betwixt Pointing at the *Vice*, or at the *Person*.

Now as it has been my Care in the First place to suit my *Materials* to my *Business*: so have I really made a *Scruple* of keeping close to my Text, without Lashing out into any *Extravagant Excesses*, of what sort soever, either *Personal*, or *Publick*. And as I have not taken upon me to *Amplify*, or *Expatiate* upon the Subject of any *Immoral Liberties* that fell in my Way, to the Prejudice of *Candor*, and *Good Faith*; so neither have I *Encourag'd* any, by Forcing the *Figure* beyond the Plain Sense and Reason of the *Thing*. But still, after the doing of a Common Justice to the Nature and Quality of the *Case*, and *Occasion*, I have a Word or Two yet more to say upon the *First Motive* that led me to *This Undertaking*: provided only, by way of Precaution, that the *Reader* is not to expect *Order* out of Confusion; or that such a *Rhapsody* as This is, of *Independent Tales*, and *Whimsies*; *Broken Thoughts*, and *Scatter'd Fragments*, should be *all of a Piece*: neither is it *Necessary*, or *Expedient* that they *should* be so, if in This *Diversity* of *Prospect*, every *Part* does but Agree with it *Self*. Wherefore let it Suffice, *Method*, and *Connexion* apart, that there is nothing wanting yet toward the Perfecting of the Work, according to the *Scheme* of the *First Model:* for there is not a Case perhaps in Nature, that does not some way or other fall within the Reach of These *Innuendos*, and serve to Instruct us abundantly, in all the Offices of *Piety*, and *Good Manners*, by drawing *Good* out of *every* Thing, even out of *Evil it self*.

After the *Settling* of This Provision, and carrying That Point as far as it would go; the Thing was as yet but *half-done*, methought, without a Further Regulation, in Matter of *Speech*, for the purpose, *Ornament*, and the like, as well as in *Manners:* by which Word, [ M A N N E R S , ] may be understood, *the Command of our* Passions, *under the Direction of a* Consummated Virtue. This Consideration brought me back again to my *First General Proposition*, toward the Institution of *Youth:* and *That Thought* Prompted me as naturally *forward*, to a *further Enquiry*, by what Means I might best Advance my Design. Upon the Agitation of *This Question*, I came, in fine, to *This Result within my Self*, that *nothing spoils Young People, like Ill Example*; and that the very *Sufferance* of it, within the Reach of *Their Ken*, or *Imitation*, is but a more Artificial way of *Teaching* them to do *Amiss:* So that there remains little more to be done upon *This Article*, then to keep a *Guard* upon my *Words*, and *Thoughts*, and to Distinguish *Good* from *Evil*; especially, where the Doctrine, indifferently speaking, may be either *Nourishment*, or *Poyson*. Now *This Medly*, (such as it is) of *Salutary Hints*, and *Councels*, being Dedicated to the *Use*, and *Benefit* of *Children*, the Innocence of it must be preserv'd *Sacred* too, without the least Mixture of any Thing that's *Prophane*, *Loose*, or *Scurrilous*, or but so much as *Bordering* That way. This is the *Caution* I have prescrib'd to my Self, as the *Rule* I am to *Walk* by: and I am in hope that the Course I have taken in the Conduct of *This Affair*, will stand the *Test:* or however, that the *Good Will* may serve at worst, to *Attone* for the *Failings:* to say nothing of a *Final Appeal to the Register of the Parish where I was Born:* which will bring me off at last.

Having now spoken more than enough, to the *Morality*, and *Usefulness* of *This Tract*, (if I have not spoil'd it in the *Making*,) I am once more to *tell the Reader*, before we part, that *I* have now Consulted the *Virtue*, and the *Conscience* of the *Office I* have here taken upon me, as *I* ought to do. Over and above that *I* have render'd the *Figures* as *Clear*, and *Instructive*, as *I* could; in *Easy Words*, and *Plain Honest English*. And, to wrap up all in a Little; *I* have so order'd it, that *Children*, *I* hope, will be the *Better* for't, and *Men* never the *Worse:* which will be but *Fair Quarter betwixt Man and Man, to all Intents and Purposes.*

## The Asses made Justices.

A DOCTOR OF Divinity, and a Justice of Peace, met upon the Road; the Former excellently well mounted, and the other upon the Merry Pin it seems, and in Humour to make Sport with him. *Doctor*, says he; *your great Master had the Humility to ride upon an Ass, and one would think that an Ass might have e'en contented you too.* Alas alas! Sir says the Doctor; the *Asses*, they say, are all made *Justices*, and there are none to be gotten.

### THE MORAL.

THIS Encounter happen'd upon a Great Change in the Bench, and the Justice here in the Story was a Commissioner of the Last Edition. The Justice, in short, would needs be meddling, and the Doctor was too Hard for him; which may serve for a Caution to all People, not to lash out into Intemperances of Scomme, and Banter, without understanding their Men, and their Measures.

## An Ant and a Lyon.

T HERE WAS A Time when a Pittifull *Pismire* had the confidence to read a Lecture of Good Advice to a *Lyon*. I do not set-up, says the *Ant*, for a *Politician*, but if you'll take my Councel upon the Point of *menage*, and *Good Husbandry*, my Life for yours, you shall never Repent it. Alas! I am but a Diminutive Creature, you see, and a small Matter you'll say will maintain me; and yet I have enough to do, let me tell you, with hard Labour one part of the year, to keep my self from Starving the other. Now, to my thinking, you should do well to go the same way to work and lay up somewhat in store for a Rainy-Day. *Soft and fair, my little Fool*, says the Other; *This may do well enough for a* Pismire, *but not for a* Lyon: *for the Rules of* Providence and Thrift, *were never made for* Princes, *but for* Beggars.

## An Ant and a Mouse.

THE *Pismire* was no sooner turn'd off by the *Lyon*, but away she trudges to a *Mouse*, upon the same Errand. How comes it, says she, that you that are a kind of a Corn-Merchant your self, with a Pair of Good Shoulders to bear a Burden that you, I say, should lye idling all the Harvest-Time, without making any Provision for a Hard Year, as we do, you see, and I thank my Starrs for't, our Stores are never empty. Well well! says the *Mouse*, but That's none of my Bus'ness; for I am under another way of Government. There is a Certain Person of Quality that joyns with me, and we Two keep House together. We have a matter of Thirty Servants for the getting-in of our Harvest: beside those that stow it up afterwards in our Granaryes and Barns. Now This is all for the Service of the *Mice* in the first place. And were not we a Company of fine Fools do you think, to drudge out a Livelyhood by our own Labour, when we may have it better Cheap by the Sweat of other People's Brows!

### THE MORAL.

WE may gather from These Two Phancies, that it is but lost Labour for People to inculcate Good Husbandry to Those that live upon the Spoil, where the Servile Industry of the One, serves only to support the Pomp and Luxury of the Other: beside that it does not become Private Persons to break-in upon the Functions of Publique Ministers, which is the same Thing with an *Ant* prescribing to a *Lyon*.

And the same *Pismire* again, to the *Mouse*, is the Case of many a Well-meaning Officious Wretch, that is more Bold as we say, then Welcome, out of a Publique-spirited Zeal to the Common Good. And what comes on't at last, but the turning of him off from one to another, with his Labour for his Pains: and assigning him a Reward for his Services in other World? unless he had rather content himself with the Empty Character in This, of an officious Consciencious Fool.

## Asses to Jupiter.

As *Jupiter* was upon the Bench hearing of Causes, up comes a Troup of *Representative Asses* to him, in the Name of their Companions, with a Long Story of their Grievances. They set forth in their Petition, that the World had taken up a Lewd Custom, whenever People had a mind to mark any one for an Egregious Coxcomb, This or That Blockhead, they'd say, was a very *Ass*, and so cast a Scandal upon the whole *Arcadian Brotherhood*. Why might not an *Oxe*, or a *Hog* have done every jot as well as an *Ass?* Not that they pretended to set-up for *Philosophers* neither; but they took it ill to be branded with a particular Reproche, when the Common Appellation of a *Beast* would have done as well. *Jupiter* took the Matter into Consideration, and gave the Deputies This Answer. *Gentlemen-Commissioners*, says he, *you come to me for Redress, and I do not find you have any Wrong done you: but it sticks in your Stomach, I perceive, that the Rest of your Fellow-Brutes, are not Branded for Company.*

THE MORAL.

'TIS a Common Thing for Men to Complain without a Cause, and to find themselves uneasy in what Condition soever they are: without understanding, either what they Would have, or what they Aile. Now what's the Grievance all This while here! but the *Asses* takes it ill to be call'd by their *Name*, and to be distinguished by their *Nature*? It is no Crime, or Shame, for any thing to *Be*, what Providence hath *Made* it, or consequently to be Rated, or Understood, for what it Is. But the *Asses* here in the Fable, have a mind to Cover their Ears under the Foxe's Skin, and Appear Wiser, and Better, then, in Truth they Are. *Why should not all Beasts fare alike* they cry? Now That's not so much an Argument, as the Caprice of an Ill natur'd Envy and Recrimination, as if we were ever the Better for being in Ill Company.

## A Boy Leading a Calfe.

As a *Boy* was leading a *Calfe*, with both Hands, a Nobleman happening to pass by upon the High-way, the Boy it seems minded the *Calfe* more than the *Lord*, and went drudging on still, without moving his Hat. *Why Sirrah*, says the Man of Dignity; *have you no more Manners then to stand staring me in the Face with your Cap on?* Alas! says the Boy, I'll put off my Hat with all my Heart, if your Lordship will but Light, and hold my Calfe in the mean time.

THE MORAL.

THERE is nothing well done that is done out of Season; and there is a Time for the doing of all Things: neither is there any Duty so binding upon us, as not to give way to a Superior Obligation: insomuch that the Best, and the Thing most necessary to be done, in one Case, falls out many times to be the Worst in Another: Provided always, that nothing that is Evil in it self, be admitted, in any Case whatsoever. Nay we are bound to leave our very Prayers, to save the Life of a Good Man in the same Instant. *Bus'ness*, in time, must give Place to *Devotion*, *Ceremony* to *Bus'ness*; and so it runs on in a Gradual Subordination of one Thing to Another, throughout the whole *Series* of our Lives.

## A Burgher and a Pear-Tree.

A SHATTER-BRAIN'D Rich *Burgher*, but a Man Curious enough in his Gardens, Pluck'd a *Pear*, and Tasted it: but the *Pear* it seems was stark Naught: He took This so Heynously, that he order'd the Tree immediately to be digg'd up by the Roots. Alas Master! says the Tree, if the Fruit be not good, it has not been a kindly Year, you know, and pray'e do not make me answerable for the Iniquityes of the Seasons? Beside, that the Burden of Sound, and Pleasant Fruit I have upon me, might have compounded, methinks, for here and there One Rotten Piece.

### THE MORAL.

THE *Three Phancys above* are much upon the same Turn. But shall we call it *Anger* now, or *Madness*, for a Man to Pick a Quarrel with the *Bushes*, and the *Brambles*, for *Scratching* him; the *Bees*, for *Stinging* him; a *Pear-Tree* for putting his Mouth out of *Tast?* and when all is done, for wreaking a Revenge upon himself. This may seem to be an Extraordinary Case, but in truth all Passions in Excess have the same Effect upon us, in Proportion to that of a Furious Choler, only they work several ways.

But the most Glorious Exployt of This kind, was the *Countryman's Revenge* upon his *Landlord*. He was the Last Life in the Lease of an Estate, in his Patron's Possession. He took somewhat ill of his Landlord, and immediately Poyson'd himself, to defeat the other of the Estate.

*Montagne* tells a Horrid Story of a Certain King, that Renounc'd God Himself upon the Loss of a Battle, and Prohibited his People, either to *Worship*, or so much as to *Name* him, for such a certain Time, in his Dominions. An Execrable Blasphemous Out-rage, and not to be thought of without Horrour.

## Books Sold by the Foot.

A COUNTRY GENTLEMAN, with more Mony than Brains, that had a mind to be taken for a Man of *Letters*, built himself a Fair Spacious Room for a Library: and when he had shelv'd and fitted it up for his Turn, he contracted with a Bookseller to furnish it with Books, from Top to Bottom, at so much a Foot; the Books to be Bound, Guilt, and Letter'd after the Best Fashion, and the Choyce of them left to the Stationers Honesty and Discretion.

### THE MORAL.

HE that Buyes *Books* by the *Foot*, may as well pretend to purchase Learning by the Pound, but he that's Master of a Fair Study of Books, values himself upon being Master also of all that's Good in't. This Freak has somewhat in it of the Humour of Another Person that I knew. (For This is all *History*) He had a Great Mind to get himself the Reputation of a Hard Student, and so kept a Candle burning in his Study all Night still, and He himself fast a sleep in his Bed all the while.

This Whimsy, of Vanity, and Ostentation, is no more then what we meet with every

Day of our Lives, in all Shapes, and Places. In one Word for all, 'tis but the same Thing over and over again in a Thousand other Instances; and the whole Bus'ness of our Lives is Semblance and Disguise.

## The Churches are Full.

As PEOPLE WERE talking together of the Hardness of the Times, why truly, says one of the Company, *the Times are pretty Difficult, but, the Lord be praised for it, the Churches are Full still.* Now This Spark was a Common *Pick-pocket*, that, for Brevity-sake, said his Prayers, and follow'd his Trade, both under one.

### THE MORAL.

THERE is not That Roguery in Nature that has not a Mask of Honesty and Religion to Cover it: and the same Pretence holds good from the Prime *Minister* to the *Mounte-bank*; and from the *Sharper* here in the *Gallery*, to the more Notorious *Pick-pockets* that we have seen, in the very Pulpits Themselves. This is an Impious, and an Execrable Imposture, 'tis true, but it will do well to Qualify the Censure however, with a Great deal of Charitable Caution, for fear of taking the *Saint* for the *Hypocrite*, instead of the *Hypocrite* for the *Saint*; and so to *set the Saddle*, as we say, *upon the Right Horse.*

## A Country-man to Jupiter.

A *Country Fellow* ran Bawling to *Jupiter* with an Out-cry, that *the Sheep eat-up all his Grass. Jupiter* gave them a Check for't, and bad 'em take that Rebuke for a Warning. But they went Gutting-on still nevertheless: and upon a *Second Complaint, Jupiter* order'd the *Wolves* to look after them. The *Wolves* were no sooner in Office, but up comes the *Bumpkin* again, with *Another* Dismal Story, what Havock they were a making, just at That Instant, with the Whole Flock. Why then, says *Jupiter*, we must e'en get *Huntsmen* to take Care of the *Wolves*. Well, says the *Countryman* again; but what if the *Huntsmen* at last should prove *Mutton-mongers Themselves* too? Where shall we be next?

### THE MORAL.

LEVITY is a Restless Sickness of the Mind, that makes a Man Uneasy whatever he does, and which way soever he turns himself. He shifts, only for Variety, and One Change is as Irksom to him, as Another. He governs his Life by Humour, not by Consideration, Choyce, or Judgment; and acts, not only *Without Reason*, but *Against* it: for he passes as well from Good to Bad, from Bad to Worse, and still Weary of the *Present*, whatever it is.

If the *Sheep* must Eat no *Grass*, the *Master* must Eat no *Mutton*: so that for a Revenge upon his *Flock*, he goes the ready way to starve *himself*. But Nature must not be put out of her Course, to gratify the Caprice, or the Avarice, of a Phantastical

Churle; who had rather the Bounties of Providence should be Perverted, or Lost, then Employ'd upon the Ends they were intended for. But so it is, that the very Granting of our Prayers, generally Speaking, would be one of the Heaviest Judgments could befall us.

Grudge the *Sheep* their *Grass*, and the next Work will be to turn them over to the *Wolves* to look after them; and then from the *Wolves* at last, to the *Hunstmen*, to secure the main Chance: that is to say, we Pray our selves out of a Happy Condition into a Miserable, and from That, into a Worse; and so Proceed till we are undone past Recovery: so that upon the whole Matter, we are Ungrateful to Providence, Enemys to our Selves, and Malevolent one toward another.

Now This is for want of Searching into, and understanding the Nature of Things, and the True Measures of Humane Affairs. It is the Great Art, and Philosophy of Life, to make the Best of the *Present*, whether it be Good or Bad; and to *Bear* the One, with *Resignation*, and Patience, and to *Enjoy* the Other, with Thankfulness, and Moderation.

## A Cuckow and a Nightingal.

IT WAS A Doleful Story that a *Cuckow* told a *Nightingal*; how Barbarously she was us'd in the World. People would stand Staring and Gaping at her, like an Owl she said; and Twitting her for bringing up other People's Brats at her Fireside. Nay if I do but happen to perch my self over any Body's Head, 'tis as much, they say, as if I call'd him *Cuckold*. Now, says the *Cuckow*, if I were but put into your Dress a little, and into your way of Singing, I phancy, I might redeem my Credit. Alas for thee, thou poor Ignorant Creature, says the *Nightingal*; there goes more to the making of a Songster then thou art aware of: The *Cuckows Pipe*, I tell thee, was never made to bear a Part in a *Consort of Nightingals*.

### THE MORAL.

ALL Creatures are uneasy, for want of somewhat or other; and we find them still as Uneasy when they have Compass'd it, as they were before: for in truth, it does not prove to be the Thing they took it for. Now This comes of indulging our selves in Extravagant Appetites. The *Cuckow* would be a *Nightingal*; that is to say, *Heaven has made us One Thing, and we had rather be another.* Now This Restlessness is not only Vexatious, but Vain, and Impious, to the Highest Degree: There's no prescribing Rules and Measures to the Doings of the Allmighty; but the Laws of God, and Nature, are Firm, and Unchangeable.

## Two Dogs and a Wolfe.

IN THE HEAT of the *Civil Wars* of *Rome*, the Neighbouring Nations were so intent upon That Opportunity of breaking in upon the *Romans*, that their Governours had the most to do in the world to keep them in order, and within the Bounds of their Duty.

But when they found that nothing was to be done by Fair Reasoning, they had recourse to Invention, and Embleme; and the Phancy was This.

They took a Couple of Hardy great *Dogs*, and set them together by the Ears, as a *Spectacle* to the People; and then in the Height of their Rage, and Fury, while they were Tearing, and Worrying one another, they order'd a *Wolfe* to be turn'd loose upon them; the *Two Dogs* were immediately *reconcil'd*, and by consent fell upon the *Common Enemy*.

THE MORAL.

THIS is no more than daily Practice and Experience. Quarrels Abroad, keep People Quiet at Home: especially where Liberty, or Ambition, is the Question; so that a *Forreign War* many times diverts a *Civil*. This was effectually the Case of *Charles the First*, the *King* was made the *Common Enemy*, and all the Popular Factions united against him under That Notion; but so soon as ever the *Royal Party* was run down, up started *Another Common Enemy*, and the *Republican Confederates* fell to work one upon another.

When a Family is divided, in, and against it self, That's the Time for a Common Enemy to make their Advantage; and no such way to make them Friends again, as the Dread of That Opposition; but we are directed how to behave our selves, both by Policy, and by Nature; or I might have said, by Prudence and Necessity.

## Two Old Dogs and Two Young.

A COUNTRY FELLOW had Four Dogs to look to his House and Flocks; Two of them Old, and the Other Two, Young. The Two Young ones were Hardy, and Forward, and perpetually Teizing the *Wolves*. The Other Two were now past Hunting, and could only Bark, and Encourage the Chase. The Two Latter advis'd their Companions not to be too Eager in their Bus'ness, but rather to spare themselves, and Husband the Game: for 'tis only for the *Wolves*-sake, they cry'd, that we are Entertain'd; so that whenever we destroy *Them*, we destroy *our selves*; for what will our Master care for us, when he has no longer any need of us?

THE MORAL.

THE *Dogs* Husbanding the *Chase*, is the same Thing with *Soldiers* Husbanding the *Warr*: every Creature has the Wit to look to one: nay the very Dogs as well as their Masters: and let the Servants be never so Bold, Faithfull, and Industrious, there runs a Vein of Private Interest, yet along with it: so that it is but Common Prudence, even in the Ordinary Affairs of This World, for Men to make themselves *Necessary* one to another, though it were but for the sake of *Civil Society*. For These Reciprocal Advantages are no other, then the Links of That Mighty Chain, that tyes the World, and the several Parts of it, together.

## A Dog and a Crocodile.

THE *Doggs*, they say, about the River *Nile*, are fain to Drink running, and to take here and there a Lap, for fear of the *Crocodiles*. A Certain *Crocodile*, taking notice of a *Dog* that kept himself upon That Guard, gave him a Rebuke for't. Had not you better, says the *Crocodile*, take a Hearty Soup once for all, than run squirting up and down Thus, as if you were afraid somebody would do you a Mischief? Why truly, says the *Dog*, I had rather go That way to work, but that I am not willing to venture my Carcass for a Mornings-Draught.

### THE MORAL.

WE should do by the *World*, in some respects, as the *Dog* does by the *River*; that is to say, we should content our selves with a Tast of sensual Refreshments, without making a Meal of them; and so to use them for a Rellish, not for a Diet. *Too much* of the World, and dwelling too long upon it, are Both Equally Dangerous, and nothing but a Mad Man, will venture Body and Soul, for the Gratifying of a Liquorish Palate, *Flesh and Bloud*, says the very same Thing to a *Man*, that the *Crocodile* does to the *Dog*; and in Cases too, of the most Desperate Extremities. [*What are you afraed off? Here's nothing will Hurt you*] This Fable, upon the Main, preaches Temperance, in the Gratifying of our Appetites: and it strikes also at the Unsteady, Cursory Humour of Tasting Things, and then leaving them: and so Skipping from This to That, without suffering any Thing to Digest.

## The Contempt of Death.

'TIS TO NO PURPOSE to *Fear*, what it is impossible to *Avoid*: beside that upon the whole Matter, *Death* is the very same Thing still, whether we *dread* it or *not*. There goes a Story of a Brave Man, that was threaten'd with an Infamous, a Lingring, and a Tormenting Death, unless he would submit to the doing of a Base thing, below the Dignity of a Man of Honour, and Justice. *You shall do well*, says he, *to frighten your* Courtiers *with These* Bugbears: *for Death is but Death at last, and for the* Manner *of it, 'tis the same Thing to me, whether I Rot in the Earth, or upon a* Gibbet.

### THE MORAL.

No Man was ever yet so Mad, as to think he should never Die; or perhaps so unreasonable, as but so much as secretly to *Wish* it, or to *Hope* for it, in Contradiction to the manifest Decrees of *Providence*, and the unalterable *Fate* of all *Created Beings*. So that if the *Mortality* be *Certain*, and the *Period* of Life *Uncertain*, what have we more to do, then to make every Hour of our Lives a Preparatory toward That Inevitable End! especially considering, that when we have once master'd *That Terrour*, we have nothing left us in This World to *Fear*.

But we are now to Distinguish betwixt the *Resolution* of a *Hero*, and the *Resignation* of a *Christian:* or, I might have said, betwixt the Motions of *Philosophy*, and the

Impulses of *Religion*; for That's the Point in Question; betwixt the *Morality* of the *Case*, and the *Christian Prospect* of a *Future State*.

## An Eagle and Other Birds.

A COMPANY OF BIRDS were got chattering together in a Congregation, and every one of them severally setting up for it self, and its own Kind, some in one way, and some in another. The *Hawk* valu'd her self upon a *Rank Wing*; the *Crow* put in for her Skill in *Augury*; the *Nightingale*, for a delicate Mellow *Pipe*; the *Peacock* for a *Beauty*, the *Partridge* for *Craft*; the *Wren* for his *Mettle*; the *Duck* for her Faculty in *Paddling*; and the *Heron* for the Credit of being reputed *Weather-wise*. Well! says the *Eagle*, and what is all This now to a Sharp Piercing *Eye*; which, without Vanity, is my Talent in Perfection: or if any of you make a Doubt on't, let but me carry him up into the Air and he shall see the Experiment.

The *Wren*, upon This, Mounts the *Eagle*, and the *Eagle* with the *Wren* upon her Back, works her self up to her Pitch; and when she was now at Lessening, she call'd to the *Wren* to look down and tell her what she saw Below? Alas! says the *Wren*, I have much ado to discern the very Earth, at This Distance: but yet at the same time, says the *Eagle*, do I see a *Black Sheep* yonder *without a Tayle*, and you shall see me immediately make a Stoop at it, and Seize it. And what was This Black Sheep at last, but a Fowler's Bait for some Bird of Prey. The *Eagle* push'd at it, and fell into the Snare her self. *Ah!* says the *Wren, if you had been but as Quick-sighted to Discover the Danger, as you were to spye out the Quarry, you would much more easily have found out the* Man *with his* Birding-Tackle, *on the one side, then the* Sheep without a Tayle, *on the Other.*

### THE MORAL.

CHRISTIANITY bids us *love our Neighbours as our Selves*, but *Nature*, at the same time, whispers us to Begin our *Charity at Home*, and that *every Man is his own Next Neighbour*. This is the Case in Common Practice, and the Instinct works more upon us then the Precept. We are all Partial to our Selves, and there is no Creature so Despicable, but it has somewhat or other to value it self upon. The *Common People* of the *Birds* set up for *Sharers* in the *Government*, which is no more then the same Thing in the *Woods*, that we find in the Common Course of *Humane Life*.

*Perspicacity*, or *Clearness of Sight*, is a Necessary Qualification, 'tis true, for *Rulers*; as it enables them to see thorough Men, and Things: But let them have a Care however of being misled by their Affections, and Hamper'd in Vain Imaginations: for in These Cases we are apt to mistake *Slavery* for *Liberty*; *Judgments*, for *Blessings*, and *Death* for *Life*; as the *Eagle* here was so intent upon the *Prey*, that she never dreamt of the *Snare*. But This is the Fate of Inconsiderate Actions, when Men give themselves up to Phancies, and Prepossessions, without looking into Consequences, and Events.

### Foxes and Rabbets.

THE *Foxes* and the *Rabbets* had been a long time at Variance, but coming at last to a Better Disposition, they appointed Commissioners to advise upon some middle Expedient toward an Accommodation, that might please Both Partys. There were several Proposals set a-foot, but they were still, either too Large, or too Narrow, till at length they call'd a great Council of *Coneys* to manage the Debate. It was there mov'd by a Grave Member of That Body, that an Application might be made to the *Foxes*, to accept of some Reasonable Composition; if it were but a matter of *Ten Rabbets a Quarter*, for the pu.ᵣ ᵉ, and the *Publique Faith* engag'd for the Performance of *Covenants.* The Project was highly approv'd, but when they were just upon the Point of naming a Committee to draw up the Address, up rises a Pert young Blade, and throws a Blunder in the way that spoil'd the Jest. Mr. *Chair-man,* says he, *I am very well pleased with This Motion; and provided the worthy Member that first started it, will make One of the Ten, himself, I'll make Another.* The Proposer had not one word more to say, and so the Question fell to the Ground.

#### THE MORAL.

THIS Fable of the *Rabbets* and the *Foxes,* has much in it of That of the *Mice,* and the *Bell* that was to be ty'd about the *Cat's Neck,* There was a Thing to be done, and no body at last to do it. This Phancy has some Affinity also with That of the *Ape's* drawing the *Chessenuts* out of the Fire with the *Cat's-Foot.* But the World, generally speaking, is made up of *Fools* and *Knaves,* and the One works for the Other. *The* Fool *Burns his Fingers, and the* Knave *Eats the Nut:* the one runs the Hazzard, and the other reaps the Benefit.

### A Gardner and a Dog.

A WIDOW-WOMAN, that had nothing to live upon but the Profit of her Orchards and Garden-stuff, was forc'd abroad once, and mightily at a Loss whom to entrust, with the Care of her Fruits and Plants in her Absence. She had in the House, a Tame *Fox,* a *Hog,* an *Ape,* and a *Goat*; and they all offer'd their Services to look to the Yards, and keep all Safe when she was away.

For my Part, says the *Ape,* there can be no Danger of Mee; for a Handfull of *Nuts,* and an *Apple a Day,* is enough to do my Bus'ness. And then for my Particular, says the *Hog,* I am no Climber of Trees, but a little Rotten Fruit, and a Few Wind-falls will serve my Turn. Well! says the *Fox,* and no body will Tax me, I am sure, for a Ravener of Roots, and Apples. No nor me neither, says the *Goat,* I am no *Costard-monger*; I rob no Orchards; but a Handful of Herbs is as good to me as a Feast.

The Widow thank'd them all for their Good Will, but says she to the *Fox,* you'll be too Crafty I fear, for a Poor Country-Wench; beside that you are so False and Sly, there is no Trusting of you: and then for the *Ape,* says she, he'll be too Lavish and Expensive; the *Goat,* I must confess, is no *Pippin-Merchant*; but then he'll do more Hurt with

Knabbing, and spoiling the *Trees*, then he could do otherwise with Eating the *Apples*; but now in the last place, the *Hog* is utterly intolerable, for he shall Rub more Plants to Death in one Day, than a whole Herd of Swine is worth. So that I must e'en leave the Care of all to my Dog: for he is no Guttler of Fruit, He kills no Plants, but keeps Thieves at a Distance, and finally for his Honesty, the whole Earth is not able to Corrupt him.

### THE MORAL.

THERE's no Danger in trusting a Servant that lies under the Double Tye of Honesty and Interest, to be True to his Master: that is to say, when a Justice of Inclination is supported and encouraged by the Advantage he reaps from the doing his Duty, and nothing to be gotten on the other hand, by abusing his Patron. Take Notice further, that the Woman's All was at stake here, and she did well to deliberate, before she came to a Resolution.

## The Force of Jealousy and Revenge.

MANY A GOOD WOMAN leads the Life almost of Hell it self, under the Implacable and Incurable Jealousyes of a Barbarous Husband; and commonly, the Better she deserves, the Worse she is treated.

*Boccace* gives an Instance of This, in the Case of the Fair Wife of one *Arimino*, a Rich Merchant. She was neither to *see*, nor to be *seen*; but close kept up, with hardly the Benefit of Common Air. This Usage set her Wits at Work, either for Ease, or for Revenge; and she bethought her self at last of one *Philippo*, a Proper Young Fellow, the very Next Door to her, and only a Wall betwixt them: so that if she could but open a Way of Communication thorough that Partition, the Work she thought would be as good as half done. She took her Time once, in her Husband's Absence, to examin every Inch of This Wall, where she spy'd at last the Glimmering of a Light, that struck thorough a Chink in a Dark Corner, into a Fair Chamber in the Next House; and the Place cover'd with a Hanging. Upon This Discovery, she made her Maid her Confident, who, upon further Enquiry, found That Appartment to be *Philippo's Quarter*. Upon This Intimation, her Mistress quickly made the Crack wide enough for a *Whispering-Hole*, and there began the *Intrigue*.

*Christmas* being now at hand, the Woman desir'd leave of her Husband to go to *Confession*, as other People did. *Very Good*, says he, *and what have you to Confess, I beseech you?* Why my Dear, *says she*, your Wife is Flesh and Bloud as well as her Neighbours; but you are no *Priest*, to take her *Confession*. The Man was Nettled at This, but told her however, that she might go, provided she went early in the Morning, and to his own Chaplain, or to some other Priest at least of his Recommendation; and upon Condition to come back immediately so soon as the Work was done.

She went to Chappel at the Time appointed; though not so early neither, but her Husband was there before her. She went first to the *Chaplain*, but he was busy, it seems, and recommended her to *Another Holy Man*; (as he call'd him) which was, in Truth, her *Husband*, in a *Priest's-Habit*, and a *Confession seat*. In the Course of her

*Confession*, she declar'd, that having been tempted, and provok'd to Lewdness, beyond her Strength, by an Unmercyfull *Husband*, she had a *Frier* that lay with her every Night, and her Husband at the same time in Bed with her himself. This Story would have made her Husband stark Mad, if his Curiosity to hear it out, had not restrain'd him. *Well!* says she, *how it is I know not, but This* Frier *does his Bus'ness certainly by the* Black Art; *for all the Doors of the House fly open to him whenever he comes: and 'tis but muttering a Few Words before he enters; and my Husband falls presently into so Profound a Sleep, as if he lay under some* Enchantment. But Daughter, says the pretended Confessor, I do not find any *Repentance* in you for what you have done, or the least *Christian Resolution* never to do it again. *No, no Sir;* says she, *I must not tell you a Lye, when I am upon so Holy a Duty. I neither* Do Repent, *nor ever* Can Repent, *of any Thing I ever did with That* Frier; *I love him so dearly*. Why then says he, your Case is Desperate, and you can have no Absolution. But you shall have my Prayers however, for the Grace of a True Penitent; and yet let me see—I could send one to you— *No no Sir*, says she, (cutting him short at That Word) *let there be no sending to our House*, I beseech you, *for my Good Man has a Phancy that the very Ratts behind the Hangings, are all* Cuckold-makers; *and that his own* Shadow *makes* Horns *at him*.

After *Confession*, she goes to Mass, and so Home again according to Covenants; and there did she find her Husband in his own Shape, and most confoundedly Musty, but he put it off with a Flamm as well as he could. *He was to go abroad by and by*, he said, *and see her no more till next Morning, wherefore praye*, says he, *let the Doors be well Lockt, and Bolted, for fear of Thieves*. She told him every Thing should be done, and so he went away for That Night.

The Husband was no sooner out of the Door, but up goes the Wife to the *Whispering place*, with a Particular History of the whole Affair; and hinting, as by the By, how easily any Man that had a Mind to't, might slip out of the Gutter of the Next House into their Garret Window while the Husband stood watching below at the Street Door; which was certainly his Design; as it appear'd by the Sequel.

*Philip* took the matter right, and by That Light found a Way to his *Mistresses Chamber,* where he entertain'd the Wife *Above-Stairs,* while the *Cuckold* was waiting Below for the *Frier* at the *Street-Door*. When they had been at This Lock several Nights successively, and no Tidings of the *Frier*, the Man call'd out to his Wife in a Rage of Impatience, to tell him every Article of her late Secret *Confession*, with the very *Name* of her *Minion* the *Frier*, or he would have her Hearts Bloud else. The Woman refus'd to do the One, and Disclaim'd the Other. Why you Impudent Brute, says he, did not you own This very Thing to your *Confessor*? Well! then says she, I did own it, and it is all True. You your self are That *Frier*, and That *Confessor* that lyes with me every Night: the *Frier* I am in Love withall, and the *Frier* to whom all your Doors fly open. Alas! I knew you as well in your *Cowle*, and in the *Confessionary*, as if I had been in your Arms. I saw the Juggle all the way thorough and thorough, and Laugh'd at the Foppish Formal Story of your Lying abroad That Night. But I hope you'll take This for a warning, without giving your self or me any further Trouble. You cannot but see how Cheap This Beastly Jealousy has made you, wherefore, prethee let it be so no more: and know, that if I had a mind to put a Slippery Trick upon you, all the Caution in the World should never hinder me. The Man was so Convinc'd of his Wives Virtue, and Innocence, that there needed no more *Cats-play* to bring her and her Lover together, and from That Time forward, he stood up for his Wives Honesty to his Lives End.

## The Punishment of Ingratitude.

A COMMON SOLDIER that had the Honour to be known to *Philip of Macedon*, for a Brave Fellow, gave the King an Account of a Storm he had been in at Sea; the Loss of the Vessel, and how narrowly he himself came off, with his Life. He begg'd at the same time, a certain Farm for his Subsistence; which the King granted him, and ordered him to be put into Possession of the Estate.

The *Proprietor*, perceiving that he was now to be undone by a Man that he had preserv'd; apply'd himself immediately to *Philip*, with the Naked Truth of the Fact. Sir *says he*, my Dwelling is in such a place by the Sea-side; where I heard an Out-cry one Night of some body in Distress: and upon going out to see what it was, there did I find the Ruins of a Wrack, and a Man Paddling in the Sea, half starv'd, and Labouring for Life. I took him up, and carry'd him Home with me, where he was Tended and Treated like a Child of the Family. At the end of Three Days, finding himself in a Travelling-Condition; he would needs be gone: so that I gave him a *Viaticum*, and he went away, with a Thousand Protestations that my Kindness should never be forgotten. And who should This be now out of the whole World, but *the very Man that Begs my Estate*! The King was so transported at This Barbarous Story (for the Soldier told him only of his Danger, and not one Word of his Benefactor) that he order'd *Pausanias* to put the Poor Creature into his Estate again, and the *Souldier* to be *Cashier'd*, and *Stigmatiz'd*, with These Words upon his Forehead. T H E U N G R A T E F U L   G U E S T.

### THE MORAL.

THERE is an *Ingratitude*, in the Concealing of Benefits; in the Forgetting of them, and likewise in *not returning Good for Good*: but the Highest Pitch of all, is the Repaying *Good* with *Evil*, especially where *Conscience, Policy,* and *Humanity* fall in over and above.

The Ungratefull Man is the *Common Enemy* of *Mankind*, and therefore nothing less then a Mark of Infamy to make him known to all People, will reach the heynousness of his Crime. So that This Inscription, is as much as publishing him by a Proclamation, to be the *Worst* of *Monsters*. It would be a Blessing to the World, if all *Court-Beggars* of This sort might be *Branded*, for an *Example*, and a *Terrour* to all *Insinuating Parasites*, and for the *Honour* of their *Masters*.

## A Lady and a Looking-glass.

THERE WAS A Certain Hard-Favour'd Lady, that Pickt a Quarrel with all sorts of *Looking-glasses*, from the very Bed-chamber to the Dairy: And there was no getting the Freak out of her Head, but that the whole Brother-hood of the *Glass-makers* were in a Plot to make her Ridiculous. This Phancy made her so Sick of the World, that she utterly quitted it, and betook her self to the *Groves*, and the *Rivers*, for Relief. But still so long as she carry'd the same Face about with her, though it were but to the *Springs*, and the *Fountains*, she was sure to be still haunted by the same Image: which honestly convinc'd her, in the Conclusion, of what she would give no Credit to before.

### THE MORAL.

THERE is nothing in This World that a *Hard favour'd Old Woman* Dreads more then a *Plain-dealing Looking Glass*, and the *Register* of the Parish where she was born. And what is it now that gives Countenance to This Unnatural Pretence of an *Everlasting Youth*, and *Beauty*; but *Pride*, and *Vanity*, on the one hand, and *Flattery*, on the other. In This Uneasiness, she makes her appeal, to the *Brooks*, and the *Rivers*; which gave her plainly to understand, that the Fault was in the *Face*, not in the *Mirrour*. This way of Reasoning brought her in the end to a Course of Sobriety, and Virtue: which was no more, upon the whole Matter, then the doing of the *same Good Thing*, upon *Differing Inducements*. Now This passes for *Vanity*, in *some* Cases, and for *Philosophy*, in *Others*: But it is the Intent that Qualifies the Action.

## A Lyon in a Sheep skin.

THERE WAS A *Wolfe*, that, by Bribery and Corruption, had made such an Interest about the Person of the *Lyon*, that let him do what he would, he was sure to be brought off. As This *Wolfe* was worrying Lambs one Day in the Absence of the Shepherd, a *Sheep* slipt away to the *Lyon*, with Tears, and Supplications for Protection, and Justice, a *Tyger*, and a *Leopard* that were of the *Wolves Cabal*, Banter'd the *Sheep* out of Countenance, and so it went off for a Jest. Soon after This, came the Shepherd's Dog Limping to the *Lyon*, with Another Complaint, that the same *Wolfe* had Bitten *him* too. *A Likely Matter, in truth, says the* Tyger, *that the* Wolfe *should begin the Quarrel. Why That* Dog *is the Churlishest Curr that ever look'd out of a Head, and the* Wolfe *as Easy a Poor Fool, as a Body would wish.* The *Lyon* swallow'd it whole, and in a Violent Heat, told the *Dog* he was a Contentious, Malapert Rascal, and, says he, if you do not mend your Manners, I'll Hang you up at your own Door. Thus was the *Lyon* misled with Evil Councel, and the Poor *Dog* turn'd away without any Hope of Redress. But it fell out, some short time after, that as the *Lyon* was taking a *Tour* in the Forrest, he heard a *Doe*, a *Fox*, and a *Deer* spending their Opinion upon the Character of This *Wolfe*, and the *Tyger's* being of the Cabal; which made him a little Sensible of the Hazzard of taking Storyes upon Trust: so that he bethought himself what to do, and the Project he had in his Head was This; to dress himself up in a *Sheep-Skin*, and to go

Sauntring toward the *Wolve's* Haunt, like a Sorry Creature that was Bewilder'd, and wanted some body to shew it the way home again. This Succeeded so well, and the Voice was so nicely Dissembled, that the *Wolfe* came out presently upon the First Bleating, to offer his Service; blessing the *Mutton* at the same time for the Providence of falling into so good Hands. With These Words, he gave a Leap at the Throat of the *Sheep-Skin*, and no sooner had he the Prey betwixt his Teeth, but the *Lyon* cast off the Disguise, and discover'd Himself. *Ah thou Traytor!* says he; *is This thy Boasted Friendship then? But I shall make you know, Sirrah, that you have now to do with a Lyon, not with a Mutton*; and so he Tore him one Bit from Another, for an Example to all Glozing Hypocrites.

### THE MORAL.

THE *Wolfe*, the *Tyger*, and the *Leopard*, are the Perfect Image of Three *Court-Parasites*, that have gotten the Ear of an Easy Prince. The Poor *Sheep* carryes the first Intelligence of the Outrage, and instead of a Redress, was Laught at for his Pains. The *Dog* seconds the First Intelligence with a Sensible Evidence in Confirmation of the Truth of it: while the Lyon Himself joyns with his Enemyes against his Friends, and without any Regard, either to the Innocency of the One, or the Fidelity of the Other. But the *Lyon*, at last, when he found his own Life and Estate in Danger, came to a just Sense of his Mistake, Confounded that Glozing Treacherous Cabal, and brought the Wolfe to Justice upon the very Spot: So that This Story may serve for a President to Posterity upon all such Occasions.

## Love and Madness.

THE POETS have a Tradition, that *Venus had Two Children at a Birth*; *Love*, and *Madness*; and they were so strangely alike too, in *Make, Countenance, Humour,* and *Manners*, that it was hard to say which was which. Give the *Girl* a *Bow* and a *Quiver*, and one would have Sworn it to be *Cupid*: and then it was but dressing up the *Boy* with a *Bib* and a *Bawble*, to make him as like his Sister again, as ever he could stare. As they grew up, they were Inseparable Companions in their Little Playes, Freaks, and Gamboles: and they had Both the very same way of Frolique, in putting Tricks upon one another. They would be *Teachy, sputtering,* and *Violent*, in one Breath, and then *Kiss and Friends* in the Next. From *Biting* and *Scratching*, they would fall to *Catter-wawling*, and *Hugging*, and never fail in the Conclusion to Brawl themselves asleep. *Venus* her self would sit Muzzling and Gazing them in the Eyes, one after the other, by the whole Hour together; till she fell in Love with her own Image, in the very Face of her Hopefull Brats.

It fell out once, upon a Particular Occasion, that *Jupiter*, with his *Lady-Sister*, and some *Gods of Quality*, had a *Merry-Meeting at Cythœra*; where the Niece and Nephew were immediately sent for to give a Relish to the Entertainment. The Word was no sooner given, but into the Parler they came, in a kind of Triumph, with their Mothers *Coach*, and *Pigeons*; and a Train of Pleasant Drolls at their Heels, like so many Lacquays to attend the Chariot. *Cupid*, upon his First Entry into the Room, made Proclamation, for all the Gods at their uttermost Peril, to pay True Faith and Allegiance to the Sovereign Deity of *Love*. Upon These Words, he mounted his *Eagle*, made his *Bow* ready, and Nicking his *Arrow*, threaten'd *Jupiter* himself with his own Thunder: while his *Mad Sister* Quoiff'd her self in a *Fool's-Cap*, with a Puppet in her Right Hand, and a Rattle in her Left.

The Gods could not forbear Laughing at the Spectacle, though they saw well enough, that they Themselves were Ridicul'd. *Apollo's Quiver* was to seek; *Mars* miss'd his *Launce*; *Nereus* his *Trident*; *Mercury's Wings* were gone; nay the very *Mother her self* did not come-off scot-free; only *Pallas*, under the Protection of her Honour, and Prudence, scap'd untouch'd. *Jupiter* was well enough pleas'd, however, with the *Farce*, and after a Thousand Busles and Fair Words, a Toy took him in the Head to throw a Plate of Kissing Comfits betwixt them. This put them presently upon the Scramble, and so from Scuffling they fell to Strokes. As *Cupid* was looking about for Arms, his Sister took a Needle, and at Two Pushes struck both her Brother's *Eyes* out. This Disaster put all into a Confusion. *Venus* fell to tearing her Hair, Beating her Breasts, and washing the Bloud from the Childs Eyes with her Tears; trying over and over if Kissing would bring him to himself again. But the Wounds were so Desperate, that *Phœbus* himself gave to understand, that it was not in the Power of Herbs to Cure them.

The *Sister* was so transported with This Accident, that she could hardly believe what she saw; and in This Passionate Consternation, she snatch'd up the Little Instrument with her Brothers Bloud yet reeking upon it; and as she was just upon the Point of putting out her own Eyes, in Revenge of her Brother's, *Jupiter* held her Hand, and bad her preserve Those Eyes for the Service of her Brother, who now stood in need of a Leader. *Madness* (or *Folly*) undertook the Office, and did as she was Commanded, and has ever since serv'd *Cupid* for one *Guide*, though *she her self wanted Another.*

THE MORAL.

HE that call'd *Anger* a *Short Madness*, might have call'd *Love* so too: for they are not nearer akin in the Fable, then they are in the World, and in the Dayly Practice of Humane Life. In short; the whole Affair of *Love* is a *Mystery*, from one end to the Other. The *Bow*, the *Arrows*, the *Quiver*, and the *Ensigns* of *Cupid's Divinity*, have all of them their Allegorical Meanings: but to run thorough the whole *Mythology*, would be *Pedantick*, and *Tedious*.

The True Intent of This Phancy is to expose the Wild and the Ridiculous Transports of This Ungovernable Passion; and to Forewarn People of the Calamitous Consequences that attend it: for it spares neither *Friend* nor *Foe*; neither Things *Sacred*, nor *Prophane*: but presses forward at a venture in the Dark, without either Fear or Wit, committing the *Conduct* of *Love* to *Folly* that *Blinded* it.

## Love and Death.

As *Love* and *Death* were Travelling the World, they happen'd to take-up in the same Inn together. Next Morning they Posted away in a Hurry, and by Mistake chang'd

Arrows, so that *Love* kill'd the *Young* People, and *Death* made the *Old* Men in *Love*. The Fable tells us, that ever since This Unlucky Adventure, *Love* and *Death* have shot at Random.

THE MORAL.

*Love* and *Death* are the Great Bus'ness of the World; which is all but *doing* and *undoing,* and the One finds work for the Other. But there's a Time for all Things, and nothing can be either Natural, or Graceful, but as it answers That *Crisis.*

## A Lyon and an Ape.

A CERTAIN Lyon, when the Good Humour was upon him, sent for an *Ape* to entertain him with a Lecture of *Morals;* and the First Point he read upon, was the Subject of *Self-Love*: which, says he, is the Root of all Evil: and neither Prince nor Peasant can acquit himself of his Duty, either Publique, or Private, till he has master'd This Weakness. But it must be the Work of Time, for *Rome was not Built in a Day.* The Advantage of it will be This, that whoever is once in Possession of This Habit, he shall never do any Thing afterwards, that is Ridiculous, or Unjust. And now, says the *Ape* again, for a further Explanation; what is it that makes any Creature Ridiculous, but Unreasonable Actions, and False Opinions! which arise effectually, from no other Ground then a natural Propension to the indulging of our own Infirmities and Errours? And what is it again, but the same Vanity, that transports us to the Approving of Those Failings in others, which we Practice, and allow of in our Selves? When at the same time, we reckon all People to be little better then Fools, that do not Act, and Think, just as we do? At This rate, we are link'd into a kind of Confederacy against Sobriety, Truth, and Virtue: out of an over-weening Partiality in Favour of our own Imperfections and Mistakes. One Fool, in fine, crys up Another, only for what he finds, and values in Himself: as there's no *Musick* in the Ear of *One Ass* like the *Braying of Another.* What is it, in fine, but *Self-Love*, that has been the Foundation of all the Iniquities that ever were committed? Whether out of Ambition, Cruelty, Pride, Malice, Revenge, Avarice; or in short out of any other Affection whatsoever? For it comes all to a Case, when we Sacrifice a Virtue for the Gratifying of a Lust. This Reasoning of the *Ape* brought him off with a whole Skin at last; for it imprinted in the very *Lyon Himself*, a kind of Reverence for the morality of the Discourse.

THE MORAL.

THIS is not the First Prince that has ask'd Councel of an *Ape;* but This is the First *Ape* perhaps that gave his Master any Advice he was the Better for. Not but that *Balaam's Ass*, in some Extraordinary Cases may be allowed to Rebuke the Prophet. But be it as it will, we may gather This Doctrine from what is before us: *there is nothing so Ridiculous in Nature, but a Good use may be made on't: for Truth and Reason carry an Awe with them under what Shape soever they appear, and from what Hand soever they come.*

## The Mad Men too many for the Sober.

ACERTAIN PERSON that was upon a Visit once to the Mad Folks, took notice of one Particular Man among the rest, that look'd a little Soberer then his Fellows: and ask'd him in a Grave way, what he was In for? *Why*, says he, *we live in a* Mad World *and the* Mad Men *are too many for us*: that is to say, they have put all the *Sober People* in *Bedlam*.

### THE MORAL.

WE are all *Mad*, more or less, and in some respect or other, every Man of us; and the Best Quarter we can pretend to in This World, is, according to *Horace's Advice*, for the *Greater Madmen to bear with the Less*. Men of Sense and Virtue lie equally at the Mercy of the Stronger Party: that is to say; at the Mercy of Sharpers and Coxcombs; and under This Division, we do but suffer the Common Lot of Humane Nature.

## No Misery like an Unsettled Mind.

AWOMAN THAT WAS as Happy in every Body's Opinion, as the Blessings of This World could make her, fell into Desperate Melancholy all on a sodain, and no Mortal could imagin the Reason of it. Now her Misfortune was This. Her Husband, in a kind Fit, bad her ask him any One Thing in This World, what was in his Power, and she should have it, provided she came to a Resolution in *Twelve Hours* what it should be. *Eleven* of the *Twelve* were already gone, and This Miserable Wretch directly at her Wits End what to pitch upon.

### THE MORAL.

IF an Angel from Heaven should offer us the Choice of any One Thing, (One and but One) out of the whole Creation, it would almost break our Brains to be so Confin'd. And yet at the same time we find our selves Uneasy under the Dispensations of Providence, without so much as Knowing what we would be at; only the Present does not please us, and we are consequently never to be pleas'd; beside that the *Compassing* of what we Wish, is not more Difficult then the *Resolving* upon it.

## No Medlers in Other People's Matters.

AGENTLEMAN'S SERVANT was taken Notice of to be sauntring up and down the Garden, one time, with his Hands in his Pocket, when his Master's House was a Fire. The People of the House call'd out to him for Help, and his Answer was, that *he never car'd for Meddling in Other People's Matters*. It was the Answer of a Girl too, upon the Burying of her Mother Alive, She confess'd indeed that she saw the Body Heave when it was laid into the Grave, but it was none of her Bus'ness; and truly for her part she was loth to make any Words on't.

THERE's no Rule that is not lyable to some Exception or other, saving That very Rule it self. A Man has Room enough to Avoid being Pragmatical and Troublesome, without being Inhumane. But in all These Cases, Reason has a Distinguishing, and a Dispensing Power; and we are left to the Government of Ordinary Prudence, in Agreement with Common Honesty, and Good Manners.

## A Man and his Wife Parted.

A MAN AND HIS WIFE were parted, and the whole World could not prevail with the Husband to take the Woman Home again: so good a Creature, they said; so Modest, so well Humour'd, so Agreeable a Companion, and the Mother of so many Pretty Children, &c. The Husband said nothing to the contrary, but gave them This Short Answer. *Look ye,* says he; holding out his Foot. *Here's a Clever, well-made Shoe, and a Pretty Thing it is to look upon; but all This while I am very uneasy in it: Pray'e good People,* says he, *do but lay your Heads together now, and tell me where it wrings me.*

THE MORAL.

'TIS a Nice Office, That of a *Match-maker,* unless a Man has the Spirit of a Prophet to Foresee all Events, or the Gift of Intuition to read the very Souls of People through their Bodys. It is not *Virtue, Fortune, Beauty, Quality, Good Wit, Good Nature, Good Humour,* and a Thousand Good Things beside, joyntly or severally, that makes the *Happy Couple,* but the *Woman* must be FIT, to be *Easy,* and of That *Fitness,* the Partys concern'd are the only Competent Judges. Now there's a Great Difference in This Case, betwixt the *Comforts* of a *Happy Life,* and the *Prudentials* of *making the best of a Bad Game;* over and above, that at the best, *Levity,* and *Satiety,* spoyls all.

## A Murder Strangely Discover'd.

*Plutarch* has a Remarkable Story of one *Bessus,* that Murder'd his own Father, and kept it a long while Secret: but being one time in Company with some Friends at supper, he spy'd a Swallow's Nest, and starting immediately upon it, struck it down with his Launce, and so destroy'd the whole Brood. This was so ill-natur'd a Thing that every Body cry'd shame on't. Well then! says *Bessus*, why should These Birds Bely me, and say that I murder'd my Father? This Surprize created such a Suspicion, that upon sifting the Matter, it was discover'd to be so indeed, and the Parricide was brought to Justice for it.

### THE MORAL.

INNOCENT Bloud cryes aloud for Vengeance, and the Bloud of a Father is yet a further Aggravation of the Crime. This is the Short of the Case. And it tells us moreover, that in Cases of This Quality, a Guilty Conscience seldom fails to cooperate with Divine Justice, in the Punishing of the Criminal.

## *Partridges and a Setting-Dog.*

A covey of *Partridges*, that went in Fear of the *Pochers*, made an Interest in a *Setting-Dog* for a Good Word to his Companions to be easy to them. The *Spaniell* undertook upon Honour, that not a *Dog* should touch them: for *we are resolv'd*, says he, *so soon as ever we have any of your People in the Wind, to fall down flat upon the Ground, and look another way, without advancing one Step further.*

This Covey of *Partridges* had the hap some few Days after, to see This very *Spaniell* abroad with his Master a *Setting*. The Dog *stopt*, all on a Sodain, and made his Point; and the Birds were over joy'd to see the Curr so True to his Articles. But the *Intrigue* was *double*, it seems, for the same Signal serv'd the *Faulconer*, as well as the *Patridges*: so that upon drawing his Net over them, the whole Covey was taken.

### THE MORAL.

THIS is the Way of the World, and a Great Part of the Bus'ness of it, too: The *Knaves* impose upon the *Fools*, and the *Weaker* are a Prey to the *Stronger*. The very same way of Manage holds in all Publique Bodyes, and Stations; in *Courts*, *Camps*, and *Palaces*, as well as in *Fields*, *Cottages*, and *Forrests*, and with the same pretence of Honesty and Good Will. The *Master-piece* is the doing of the Trick with *a Good Grace*, as the *Setter* plays his Game here under the Countenance of a Friend, and a Plain-dealer.

If the *Spaniell* could have deliver'd himself in any Other Words then what the Moralist put in his Mouth, his Civility should have been accompany'd with all the Protestations of Good Faith, and *Kindness*, that we our selves make use of in Decoying and Trepanning one another. What's the Correspondence here betwixt the *Faulconer*, and the *Setter*, but (in the Language of the *Sharpers*) a Direct *Cross-Bite*, as they call it, carry'd on against a Bubble by a Brace of Rooks. All Men, in short, would Live, though it were but like Wild Beasts, one upon another, and make advantage of the Treason without Betraying, even the very Traytor. This is it in fine, that passes for the Wisdom of the World; which is no more, in few Words, then the Knack of Wheedling one another, and the very Case here in the Question of the *Dog* and *Partridge*.

## A Pike and Little Fishes.

THE *Roches, Daces, Gudgeons,* and the whole Fry of *Little Fishes* met in Councel once, how to deliver themselves from the Tyranny of the *Pike*; with a Protestation, at the same time, *one and all,* to give over Spawning, and utterly to extinguish the whole Race: unless their Posterity might be better Secur'd against the Out-rage of That Un-natural Monster.

The Substance of This Complaint was digested into a Petition to *Jupiter,* who divided his Answer into Two Articles. First, says he, as to your Fancy of a Total Failure, Nature has made it absolutely Impossible: Beside that your Consumption is in some sort Necessary, for if there were not *Destroying* on the *One* hand, as well as *Encreasing,* on the *Other,* the Whole World would be too Little for any one Species of Creatures.

And then again for the Voracious Humour of the Pike, there is no Room left for Reasoning in the Case: for it is a Resolution founded in the Laws of Providence and Nature, that the Stronger shall Govern: over and above, that tyranny is no New Thing in This World, and whoever shall pass by *Transmigration* into a *Pike,* will go the same way to work Himself too.

### THE MORAL.

WE have here the Lively Image of a Popular *League,* and *Complaint* against *Arbitrary Power;* that is to say; against Government it self, under the Scandal of That Odious Imputation; though but in the Exercise of an Authority according to the very Order and Instinct of Nature: And what's the Grievance at last? The *Pike* devours the *Little Fishes,* and the *Fry* have a Mind to *starve* the *Pike:* the One being but the Humour of the Multitude; and the Other the Ordinance and Appointment of an Almighty Creator.

It is but natural to follow This Expostulation with a Menace; and the One just as Reasonable as the Other. And what does all This amount to now, but a Threat rather to Destroy the whole Race of *Little Fishes* at a Blow, then to lay them at the Mercy of the *Pike,* to be eaten-up Piece-meal? Now the *Pike* has not only Reason on his side, but Prescription also, and Authority, against the Clamorous Envy of an Impetuous Rabble. And at worst, where Arguments cannot prevail, he does himself right by Force, which is a Remedy that holds among Men, as well as among Fishes.

## A Peacock and a Swan.

As a *Peacock* was strutting along the Bank of a Delicate smooth River, and Priding himself in the Beauty of his Plumes, all the Swans thereabouts came sailing up towards him, in Admiration at the Majesty of his March, and the Gracefulness of his Person. When they had spoken a World of Fine Things of him, in *Their way,* one of the Company, in the Name of the rest, pronounced him the most Glorious Creature under the Canopy of Heaven. The *Peacock* answer'd vainly enough, that Nature had done her part, but yet upon the Comparison, that a *Peacock* was not to be nam'd the same Day with a *Swan.* Alas! says the *Swan,* if you speak of the Whiteness of our Feathers, there are Hundreds of other Creatures that may vye Beauty with us upon That Account: but for the Curiosity and Enamel of your Colours, 'tis an Excellence Peculiar to your Selves; beside that if you saw us Under Water, as you do Above, I am persuaded you would change your Opinion. At That Word, the *Swan* stept ashore, and shew'd the *Peacock*, an Ill favour'd Pair of Black Leggs, enough to turn his Stomach. The *Peacock*, that was Conscious to himself of the same Blemish, turn'd it off in a Blunt Careless way, that he was as Free to shew his Black Leggs, and his Feet, as his very Train.

THE MORAL.

WE have all of us a Mixture of Good and Bad, as well in our Manners, as in our Shape, Colours, Conditions, &c. which may serve to keep us from being either Vain, on the One hand, or desponding on the Other. People do naturally think well of themselves, and as naturally desire to be thought well of by others: but still every Man has his Defects, and there is as much Art shew'd in the Exposing of them on some Occasions, as there is in Covering, and Disguising them in others: but in what Cases, and in what Manner, must be left to the Direction of Ordinary Prudence.

## A Religious Intrigue.

THERE WAS A Haughty High-spirited Dame, and an Honest Wealthy Tradesman, that, as Luck and Friends would have it, came to be Man and Wife. The Woman was Handsome and Agreeable enough, but one that valu'd her self more upon her Family than upon her Beauty. She did vouchsafe however, now and then for Fashion-sake, to keep her Husband Company; but upon such Terms, he might have had a Mistress better Cheap. While This Wambling and Uneasy Humour was upon her, she took a Phancy for a Man that fell in her way by Chance, and rested neither Day nor Night for the Thought of him, but how to come at him was the Question; Letters or Messages, she durst not venture upon, but chose rather to observe his Haunts, and Walks, and so, by Tracing him from place to place, to get some Knowledge of his Wonts, and Acquaintance. While she was upon This Train of Discovery, she found no Man so great with him, as a Certain *Capuchin Frier*, a well-meaning Creature, and consequently the fitter for her purpose; as a Person, by his very Character, the best qualify'd Agent for a Goer-between. The First Thing she did, was to find him out in his *Convent*, where she desir'd him to receive her Confession: and after Absolution, she told him, that, with his Leave, she had somewhat further to say.

*Sir*, says she, *there is a Certain Person, such a kind of a Man, and he goes commonly in such and such Clothes,* (marking him so to the Life, that the Frier knew him by the Description.) *This Gentleman*, says she, *as I understand, comes often to your Reverence. He has the Look, I must confess, of a Sober, Virtuous Man; but I could wish he would leave Dogging me up and down as he does. I cannot so much as stand at my own Door, or Window, or hardly walk the Streets, but he's putting his Tricks upon me. Alas Sir, a Lady's Honour is sooner Lost then Recover'd; and a Modest Woman cannot be too tender of it. I was thinking to have told him my Mind another way, but upon Second Thoughts, one Word of yours, I phancy, will do the Work: at least if you can guess at the Man, as perhaps you may. If he deny the Thing, pray'e let him know that I am ready to Justify it, and I beseech you Sir, rattle him severely. I have Friends in a Condition, I thank Heaven for it, to acknowledge the Good Office:* with That Word, she dropt Two Pieces of Gold into his Hand, and so with the Holy Father's Blessing for That time, she departed.

It was not long before the *Frier* had an Opportunity of Schooling the Gentleman upon This Lady's Account, who was so Transported at the Story, that the *Frier* was forc'd to stop his Mouth, for fear he should lash out into Oaths, and Imprecations. Hold, says the Religious, let us have no denying of Things, for I have it from the Lady her self, who is certainly one of the most excellent Women under the Sun: wherefore Repent in Time for what's past, and mend your Manners for the future. The *Cavalier*, that saw further into a Millstone then the *Religious*, put-on a face of Confusion upon This Reproof, and, promising to do so no more, away he went according to the Direction of the Hint, and found the Lady at her Window, waiting for his coming, which was a Circumstance that expounded the Riddle.

Soon after This, away goes the Woman to her Ghostly Father with a Fresh Complaint, that This Wicked Man would be the Undoing of her. Alas! Sir, says she, where he came once before he comes Thrice now: nay and for a further Instance of his Shameless Impudence, This Gallantery, (shewing him a Purse and a Girdle) was brought me yesterday by one of his Bawds for a Present. I could have torn the Slut's Eyes out. Away you Jade you, said I, do you come to me with your Trumpery, go your ways with it back again to the Beast that sent it. In This Rage I was just about to throw it at the Head of her; but then, said I to my self, what if This Carrion should keep it now, and say I have accepted of it? So that, upon Second Thoughts, I beseech you Sir, give him his Fooleryes again, and pray'e tell him, if you please, that I want for no such Things, and how much he is mistaken in his Woman. He'll never leave, till he forces me to Complain to my Husband. But I'll do nothing rashly, and therefore pray'e advise me Sir, what Course I am to steer. Daughter, says he, have Patience, and not one Word to any Mortal of This Unlucky Affair; your Honour is in Safe Hands, and pray'e leave it to me to menage with This Gentleman. The Lady took Heart at This Encouragement, and so slipt *Ten Ducats* more into the Hand of the Holy Man, for a Farewell. He sent immediately upon This, and gave the Gentleman another Scouring.

Why what's all This for? says the *Frier*. Cannot an Honest Woman be Quiet in her own House, but you must be teizing of her with Messages? How long have you been a Dealer in *Purses*, and *Girdles*, I beseech you? The Gentleman not being instructed in This Mystery, was fain to fish it out, with Doubts, and put-offs. As for his Part, he said, he knew nothing of any *Purses* and *Girdles*. What then, says the Frier, in a Passion, False Wretch as thou art; This is the very *Purse*, and This the *Girdle*, shewing him Both. You know your own Trinkets again sure when you see them. The Man took the Matter now by the Right Handle, and looking extremely out of Countenance, own'd the Presents, submitted, and begg'd Pardon, with a Solemn Oath, that he would never Trouble the Lady again in That Kind. The Frier took his Word; gave him his Bawbles again, as he call'd them, bed him be Wiser hereafter, and so dismiss'd him for That Bout.

Away goes the Gentleman once again, as before, finds the Lady at her Window, and in his Passage gives her a Sight of the *Purse*, and the *Girdle*, as by Chance, to the Full Satisfaction of them Both.

The Husband of This Persecuted Lady being call'd out of Town about Bus'ness, some Short time after, away goes the *Wife* to the *Frier* again, in a more Forlorn Plight than before. Sir says she, This Devil has heard of my Husband's being gone out of Town, and what does He, but over the Garden-Wall This Morning by Break of Day, mounts a Tree that leads to my Window, opens the Casement, and had certainly got into my Chamber, if I had not wak'd that very Moment, and threaten'd to call out [*Thieves*] Why there's no living for a Virtuous Woman, at This Lewd rate. Good Dear Daughter, says the Religious, make no more Words of what's past, but leave him yet once again to my ordering, and if ever he troubles you any more make an Example of him. Well! Father, says she, I am all Obedience, and so she went her way.

It was not long before the *Frier* gave the Gentleman another Schooling, and he laid it on to some Tune too. Art not Thou asham'd, says he, thou Beastly Man, that a Woman's Husband cannot be out of the way a little, but thou art presently ramping over the Garden-wall, Climbing of Trees, and creeping in at Windows, like a Common House-breaker. Nay you are discovered, let me tell you, in every Step you set: wherefore out of my Sight once for all, and never look me in the Face again. He might as well have said nothing: for This was the Last Scene of the Fryer's Part in the Story. So that the Other had no more now to do, but to follow the Instructions, and to go about his Bus'ness.

THE MORAL.

THIS Story points at the Danger of *Unequal Matches*, whether in Respect of *Age*, *Birth*, or *Fortune:* for instead of creating an *Union*, it establishes a *Faction*; that sets People's Heads at work in a Phantastical Emulation how they may Out-Trick one another, under the Countenance and Privilege of that *Holy Masque*. When People find themselves uneasy once, upon This Account, and that what is *once Done* cannot be *Undone*; it is but Natural to try if they can mend themselves *Abroad*, when they find there's no Quiet to be had at *Home*.

In the Manage of *Constance* with the *Frier*, is excellently well set forth, the *Mercurial Humour* of a *Witty Woman*, when that wandring *Maggot* has once taken Possession of her Brain. And it was then Another Piece of Art, to pitch upon a *Religious* to go between, and assist in the Good Office: for there's no such *Pimp*, as a *Reverend Fool*, where That which is arrant *Bawdery* on the *one* side, is pure Matter of *Conscience* on the *other*.

In one Word more; This *Romantick* way of *Shuffling and Cutting*, has *Two Handles* to't: for it both *Teaches* Villany, and *Detects* it, and at the same time, serves both for a *Caution*, and a *Lesson*.

## A Rat retires into a Holland Cheese.

A *Rat* that had been at Rack and Manger upon his Neighbours Cheese and Bacon, till he could live no longer upon the Spoil, took-up a Fit of Mortification; renounc'd the

Vanities of the World, said his Prayers, and so retir'd into a *Holland Cheese*, that serv'd him both for a Cell, and a Castle; and supply'd him with Necessaries for Back and Belly, all in one. He was no sooner in his New *Hermitage*, but up comes a Troup of *Begging-Deputies* to him, in the Name of his Distressed Brethren, for a *Charity, let it be never so small*. They were so pester'd, they said, with *Cats*, and *Trapps*, that they were e'en perishing for want of Sustenance. *Alas for you!* says the Recluse, *My Bus'ness is of Another World you see; but give them my* Prayers *however, and my* Blessing; and with That word, he shut the Door upon the Commissioners, and left the Brotherhood to shift for Themselves.

### THE MORAL.

'Tis a Common Thing for People, when they are Old, and Uneasy, to turn *Religious*; and then call it *a Forsaking of the World*, when they are past the Gusto, and the Pleasures of it. But they have commonly the Wit at the same time to provide Necessaries, without troubling their Heads about Things Superfluous. Let This be understood with all Due Reverence, to the Right use, or Intent of a *Mortify'd*, and a *Monastique* Life: and with This, that *Christan Charity* is as much a Duty on the one Side of the Grate, as it is on the other; and that the bare *Benediction* will do little in such a Case as This, without the *Relief*.

## A Man Quarrelling with his Shadow.

A PEEVISH FELLOW, for want of other Matter to work upon, pickt a Quarrel with his Own Shadow, for dogging him up and down wherever he went. He *Kickd, Cuff'd*, and *Struck* at it, and the Shadow *Kick'd, Cuff'd*, and *Struck* again. This Freak turn'd his Brain to such a Degree, that he durst not so much as stir abroad with the Sun on his Face, for fear of the *Shadow*, at the Back of him; which, in a kind of Mimical Mockery, did the same Thing too. This put the Man to his Wits end, and so they enter'd into an Expostulation upon the Bus'ness. *You and I*, says the ʻShadow *are Inseparable Companions; and Providence it self hath predetermined us to Live and Dye Together.*

### THE MORAL.

ALL the Wrangles and Controversies of This World, are but Morals of This Fable;

whether it be Wealth, Dominion, or whatever else we contend for; and the Thing is not only Trivial but in a Great Measure Phantastical: that is to say; we Quarrel for somewhat that is not to be had; and we are displeas'd with Things that cannot be otherwise then they are. We are, in fine, for Parting Things Inseparable, and for Joyning Things Incompatible, and so unreasonably Cross, as if Nature her self were to go out of her Course to gratify our Humours.

## Sounder Sleep in a Cottage then in a Palace.

A CERTAIN GREAT MAN, that had the World at will to all Manner of purposes, for the Delight and Service of Humane Life: as Glorious Palaces, Rich Furniture and Equipage, a Splendid Train of Servants, the Best of every Thing to Eat and Drink; Delicious, well-order'd Gardens, Waterworks, Plants, Walks; and a Revenue to answer all This Pomp and Expence; a Healthful State of Body, with a Wife that was a Woman of a Thousand, and a Hopeful Stock of Children to crown the Blessing.

This Man, I say, though in the Full Possession of all that Fortune could bestow upon him, found himself yet uneasy in his Condition, to the Degree of envying, even *Drudges*, and *Slaves*. He took no Rest Night nor Day; one while the Fault was in his Chamber, another while in his Pillow; his Posture or some such other Foolery, never reflecting all This while, upon the *Cares*, and *Anxieties*, that attend *Invidious Fortunes*, and *Ill gotten Estates*.

With This Whimsy in his Head, he sends up and down among his Subjects and Tenants, to try who and who Sleeps best, and to take an account of the Ordinary Means of their Repose. At This rate, he went on, Trying, Shifting, and Enquiring from one Thing to another, till he came to be sensible in the Conclusion, that the *Fault* was not in his *Lodging*, but in his *Mind*.

### THE MORAL.

'TIS not *Treasure*, or *Power*, that lays, either the *Head*, or the *Heart* at *Rest*; but a *Quiet Conscience*, and the Candid Simplicity of a *Tender Mind*. He's the only Happy Man, that neither Desires *more*, nor Fears the Loss of what he *has*. Men are distracted. Restless, and Uneasy, betwixt an Insatiable Thirst after what they have *Not*, and a Sollicitous Apprehension for what they *Have*.

He's in a Great mistake that looks for Those Blessings in a *Court*, that are only to be found in a *Hutt*, or a *Cell*. How fast asleep was *Amiclas* (the Boat-man) upon a Bed of Bull-rushes, and Sea-weeds; and how Quiet in his Miserable Cottage, when the whole World was in a Tumult about him, and *Julius Cæsar*, at the same time, knocking at his Door; and (to Crown the Blessing,) That great Man's Fortune depending yet upon the Service of This Wretched Creature.

Nature and Providence have lodg'd the Happyness of Humane Life within our Selves, and within our Reach, and There it is we are to *look* for't; and There it is we may be sure to *find* it: without squandering our Time upon searching where it is not to be had. Beside that we set our Hearts, not only upon what we have *not*, but upon That which in truth is *not to be Compass'd:* for our Appetites, like Waves, do but make way one for another, and there's no end of Rolling: so that This Levity deprives us, not only of the *Relish*, but the *Use* also of what we have in our own Possession.

## A Turtle and a Ring-Dove.

No no, says the Inconsolable *Turtle, my Dear is Dead, and so is the whole World to me, and all that's Good in't*. In This Transport of Sorrow, away she flyes to an Old Ruinous Tower, among the Owls, and the Bats, and with a full Resolution never to move out of her Hole again. But it so fell out, that a Beautifull *Wood-Pigeon* had taken-up his Quarter in the same Retreat: and as he was not altogether a Stranger to the Art of working upon the Passions; so he made use of the Occasion to give the Comfortless Widow a Tast of his Skill That way, though, for any Thing that she minded him as yet, he might as well have Preach'd to the Dead.

When he had made his Approaches by Degrees, and came to amplify upon the Subject of the Defunct, in the Loss of such a Blessing, and the Misery of so Unsupportable an Affliction, the Widow began by little, and little, to lend an Ear to the Discourse; and, of her own accord, with Sobbs and Tears, to enter upon the History of their *Amours*, with the Charming Virtues, and Tendernesses of the Person that was now gone: never considering that while she was enlarging upon her own Calamity, on the One hand, she taught the *Pigeon* to manage his Pretence on the Other. The *Ring-Dove*, in a word, acted his Part so well, that the Turtle was by Degrees prevail'd upon, to try if she could Recover Those Satisfactions in the One, which She had Lost in the Other.

### THE MORAL.

THERE was never any such Thing under the Sun, as an *Inconsolable Widow*. Grief is no Incurable Disease, but Time, Patience, and a little Philosophy, with the Help of Humane Frailty, and Address, will do the Bus'ness. Lamentations and Out-cryes, are but matter of Course, and Good Manners, and the Pudder that is made all This while for the Death of *one* Husband, is but a Turn of Art toward the Inveigling of Another: especially when the Passion is regulated according to the Methods of Skill and Good Nature. But let it go as it will in other respects, the same Providence that hath made the Separation of Friends Necessary, hath order'd it so likewise, that the Wound shall not be Mortal. Life and Death are but according to the Course of Nature. The Loss of Friends, and Relations, may be Grievous, but not Deadly. Thus it is, and it is the Will of God that it should be so; and consequently our Duty to Submit, and Resign: over and above that it is to no purpose to Contend.

## A Traveller alights to kill Grass-hoppers.

Boccalini's *Traveller* was so Disorder'd in the Heat of the Dog-Days with the Noise of *Grass-hoppers* in his Ears, that he alighted from his Horse in great Wrath to kill them all. Now This, says the Author, was only playing the Fool to no Manner of Purpose:

for if he had but kept on, his Way, without minding them, they would e'en have gone Sputtering-on till they Burst, and the Man never the Worse for't.

THE MORAL.

THIS is to shew us how small a Matter puts us beside our Bus'ness and our Duty. For what is Humane Life but a Passage toward Eternity, and all we have to do in This World, is only to lay a Foundation for the Blessings we hope for in the next, without either Wandring, or Loytring, upon the way. We meet with This *Horse-man*, and These *Grass-hoppers*, more or less in all Conditions of Life. Every Trifle diverts us from the Offices of the Great Work; and when we should be attending the Duties of our Reasonable Being, we are carry'd away by Vanities and Pleasures, like Spaniels that run out at Check, after *Dawes*, and *Crowes*, without ever heeding their Game.

*Part Four*
*Fiction*

# 13

# Maroccus Extaticus:
## or,
# Bankes' Bay Horse In a Trance

**A Discourse Set Downe in a Merry Dialogue
Between Bankes and His Beast:
Anatomizing Some Abuses and
Bad Trickes of this Age**

Written And Intituled To
Mine Host Of The Belsavage, And All His Honest Guests

By John Dando, the Wier-Drawer of Hadley,
And Harrie Runt, Head Ostler of Besomes Inne

Published In *1595, this chapbook by "John Dando, the wier-drawer of Hadley, and Harrie Runt, head ostler of Besomes Inne," is purportedly a conversation between Bankes and his horse, which was overheard by John and Harry while lying up in a hayloft. A wire-drawer is a man who makes wire by drawing metal through a series of holes of diminishing diameter in a steel plate, called a draw-plate; an ostler, a man who attends to horses at an inn.*

*The conversation gives fascinating insights into plebeian attitudes of the day toward landlords and tenants, tricky shopkeepers, loose girls, and fashionable young men, who walk up and down at St. Paul's to see and be seen.*

*Human foibles have always been easier to accept when masked in animal exteriors. Though Bankes and his trained horse actually existed, they have entered the great world of animal fiction, of which Aesop's tales, the Panchatantra and Jataka tales, and even* Black Beauty *and* Animal Farm *are members. Although Aesop's fables differ from the following tale in having an acknowledged moral purpose, implicit moral values may be found in the dialogue between Bankes and his horse. Indeed, recorded conversations in all these tales bear a resemblance to philosophical dialogues and have more depth than is generally attributed to them.*

Maroccus Extaticus: or, Bankes' Bay Horse in a Trance *is reprinted from Percy Society's Publications, Vol. 9 (London, 1843).*

## TO THE READER

Gentle readers, or gentlemen readers, which you will, though it past manners in us to stand like a couple of eaves-dropping knaves, and steale awaie a discourse betwixt Banks and his bay horse, from Belsavage, without Ludgate, which in our conscience we must confesse is a kinde of coosning, and in a maner such as matter as if we should have gone into a cooks shop in Fleet lane, and with the smell of roast meat filled our bellies, not emptying our purses, a flat robberie, and by a figure such a peece of filching is as punishable with riboast among the turnespits at Pie Corner, where, a man of an ill minde may breake his fast with the sent of a peece of beefe puld piping hot out of the furnace. Yet considering the case as it concernes the commonwealth, and the nature of the subject handled betwixt this horse and his master, which not anie in the world, I promise yee, heard or understoode but ourselves that came hether upon other busines, wee could not choose but doo as wee have done: verie pure love to our contrie leading us to lay our wits together, and present the worlde with this pamphlet, which if it bee not mistaken, may as well serve to drive away pastime and good companie, as the finest philosophical discourse you can light upon. If it hang not wel together, thinke the fault is ours that carryed it not well awaie, for truly there was never horse in this world aunswered man with more reason, nor never man in this world reasoned more sensibly with a horse than this man and this horse in this matter, as for example, and so committing you, (not to prison) no,—but to the reading of this dialogue, we end our Epistle to the Reader.

## INTERLOCUTORES

### *Bankes and his Horse.*

BANKES.

Holla, Marocco, whose mare is dead, that you are thus melancoly? up I saie, and let you and me conferre a little uppon the cause, wherby matters and dealings may seeme to be so; you know my meaning.

HORSE.

Whereby matters and dealinges may seeme for to be? Verie good sir, spoke like a wholesome haberdasher, and as wisely, by Lady, master, as he that was sworne to his wives friends, not to credit out his wares to anie man for the first fifteene yeeres he was married.

BANKES.

And therewith mee thinkes I see him hang the hat upon the pin againe. Wast not so, Marocco? I am glad, sir, to heare you so pleasant in the threshold of my discourse, for I am come in purpose to debate a while and dialogue with you, and therefore have at you after your watering; laie out your lips and sweep your manger cleane, and summon your wits together, for I meane (by mine host leave), to recreate my selfe awhile with your horsemanship.

HORSE.

And I am as like, master, to shew you some horse plaie as ere a nag in this parish; for tis a jade can neither whinie nor wag his taile, and you have brought me up to both, I thanke you, and made me an understanding horse, and a horse of service, master, and that you know.

BANKES.

I, Marocco, I know it, and acknowledge it; and so must thou, if thou have so much ingenuitie, confesse my kindnes, thou art not onely but also bound to honest Bankes, for teaching thee so many odde prankes. I have brought thee up right tenderly, as a baker's daughter would bring up a cosset by hand, and allow it bread and milke by the eie.

HORSE.

*Majus peccatum habes;* master, you have the more to answere, God help you; for I warrant you (though I saie it that should not saie it), I eat more provender in foure and twentie houres, than two of the best geldings that Robin Snibor keeps, that a hires for two shillings a daie a peece.

BANKES.

Two shillings, Marocco, nay, what saist thou by halfe a crowne and ten groats?

HORSE.

Marie, I say, three daies hire is worth four such horses, saddles and all; for a buyes them for ten pence a saddle at S. Giles, one with another, and those accoutrements are sutable to his steeds.

BANKES.

Me thinkes such steedes should stand a man in small stead, by that he had ridde some five miles out of towne.

**HORSE.**

Yea, be sure, or halfe five miles either. And commonly the saddle fals asunder and splits in two peeces at the towns end, and one side takes his journey towards Uxbridge, and the other towards Stanes, to stop mine hosts cushions of the George.

**BANKES.**

Why thats *Suum cuique*, boye, for the waine-men of the West countrie and the carryers of Gloucestershire commonlye barter awaye their broken ware with the hostlers for pease and horsebread, and they returne them a horsebacke to Peter Pympe the patch pannel. Marocco, thou knowest where I am now.

**HORSE.**

Not I, truely, master, unlesse you meane that shrewde sadler that served you so ill the last tearme, and as I trowe his name was not Peter, his name was John Indifferent, for a wrought, me thought, as if a had not cared whether a had earned your money or no.

**BANKES.**

Beshrew him, Marocco, a deceived my hope, in a good part, of purple velvet hose that I purposde should have made mee a seemely saddle.

**HORSE.**

O maister, you are to purpose and he to dispose of those hose, then were your breeches in his hands, and sweetely he handled them as you know; here mee thinkes had you supde up but a quarter of sacke, a quart of sacke I should have said; see how my minde was, Master Patinis, upon the bagge of otes, &c., or had you come in but reasonably loded from the taverne, or taken some of the excellent muscadine at the Horne; why what an occupation might you apprehend to rayle horribly against the mechanicall fellowes of the Towne, that so they have it, care not howe they come by it. Twas but a veneriall sinne in this sadler to nycoll you, or nicke you rather of an old peece of velvet hose. But what thinke you by him that had the conscience to aske fourteen yeardes of satten for a sute of apparell, and not to put in nine of them.

**BANKES.**

Yea, Marocco, as well as of him that sold it for eighteene shillings a yearde, being not worth ten.

**HORSE.**

O he gave time, master, and then take heed of that while you live. In space growes grace, and in prosperitie of the satten, will swell wonderfully.

**BANKES.**

I am full as fast in a cunning stealers hand.

**HORSE.**

A hard harte hath hee that hath such a hande to cut such larges thongs of another mans lether, and lappe him selfe in a gentleman's livery.

BANKES.

Tush, this is a pettye matter to stand upon. And yet, Marocco, I dare saie it, and sweare it to thee, because thou art no talker; this petty matter hath pyncht neerer than every man weenes for. I am undone nowe, young gentleman. Well, *Motos præstat componere fluctus.*

HORSE.

Why, maister, of whom should you bee afraide? I am able to justifye as much as you say. Indeed those be the young men that never sawe the lyons. Young maisters and gentlemen of the carelesse cut, such as care not how they bee cut, or of what cut they bee like, so they may have to follow al fashions; and then they are cut indeed: no force, so they fall into a fashion, and walke but twentie-foure turnes in Paules, let it packe the next daye for the third peny. Maister M. *Nemo ceditur nisi a seipso.* Byrch and greene holly, and thou be beaten, boy, thank thine owne follie; he that will thrust his necke into the yoke, is worthy to be used like a jade. He that hath been a gentleman of faire demeanes, and will so demeane him selfe to let landes and lordshippes flie for a little bravery, *Luat pœnas et in pistrino,* let him crye, and let him lye, yea, and dye to, for any pittie he is like to have at my hands.

BANKES.

Why how now, Marocco? O ye are too sowre. Dare you tell me of my splene agaynst the sadler? and be so bitter against the young gallantes of our age; what man, nay horse rather, nay asse as thou art, to become odious to the flower of Englande with thy foule manners. It is as naturell for young men to be brave and amorous, as for olde men to be grave and serious. Why, colte, then youle take uppon you, I see? Doo you not heare what they saie that scarse vouchsafe you an answere?—*Patres æquum esse censent nos jam a pueris illico nasci senes, neque illarum affines esse rerum quas fert adolescentia.*

HORSE.

Maister, you mistake me, I am no such severe horse nor sullen asse, but I can allowe a yong gentleman his madde trickes, yea, and his merrie tricks too for a need. But master, this Latine I learned when I gambolde at Oxford, *Est modus in rebus, sunt certi denique fines.* This is it urgeth me thus farre, and I speake it in passion too, and wyth the action of my heade and heeles, that a mercadore, naye a mechanicall fellowe shall go so farre out of himselfe and all a has, that for one or two tearmes arraie, a shall for his lives tearme and tearme of life, become beggeries, bondmen, and usuries vassall, *O tempora, O mores, O poetarum flores,*—you shall find in an old tracte printed by Winkin de Woorde, this olde sayde sawe: Whats a gentleman but his pleasure, O pleasure, what a treasure it is to take pleasure with measure.

BANKES.

Measure, Marocco, nay, nay, they that take up commodities make no difference for measure betweene a Flemishe ell and an English yard.

HORSE.

I knowe an ell Flemish cost English Anthonie halfe a yard of the best ware he had.

BANKES.

That ware shall never see ware againe, in so good sorte as it hath done, nor sit in a shower of raine on the top of Amwell hill.

HORSE.

Go to, master, hum drum is sauce for a cunnie; you and I will doo verie ill to speake in private, we are so plaine.

BANKES.

Plaine, Marocco, nay and I were as plaine as I will bee, I should crie out-right, for in this I agree with thee, and with thee the world agrees; and besides teares and com- miseration on the state of gentlemen that have ungentlefied, why I might saie, dishonored themselves by buying and selling.

HORSE.

Have they so, master? Why would hee bee a buyer then? why would hee bee a seller?

> This buying and selling,
> By all mens telling,
> Is gaine without swelling
> To him that sells his dwelling,
> Nor his bonds cancelling.

BANKES.

Ho, ho, good Marocco, I see now a dozen of bread does as much with you, as three pipes of tobacco taken in an odde alehouse, to a weake braine.

HORSE.

I am not dronke, master, after my watering, that you need to challenge me thus: I know what I saie, and saie what I knowe.

> To buy this measure,
> And this momentarie pleasure,
> With so much treasure
> To sell seate and seizure,
>     And repent at leasure.

Go to, master, he is a bad waster, that consumes his daies and houres, and reapes *pour un plaisure, nulle,* Cambridge and Oxford can record: and the foule dolorous fortune of many a faire boorde, what it is?

What is it to come into the clouches,
   For aglets or brouches,
Of these pure appearing asses,
That like simple glasses,
Seeme what they are not,
Let them storm, I care not:
   Unpittied might he bee
   That imbases his degree
   With this indignitie.

I tell you, master, for a truth I tell you too, I knowe a man that in this towne had a bible lying on his shoppe-boorde and solde but three yardes of satten unto a gentleman, and forswore himself at leaste three times in the coping, and yet the booke laie open before him, and hee came newe from reading of Solomon's Proverbes.

BANKES.

That had beene somewhat grosse in him if he had beene reading the twentith of Exodus.

HORSE.

No, no, his minde was on the twentith daie of the moneth following, when his money was due.

BANKES.

Tis good to have an eie to the maine; house-keeping is chargeable, and rent must bee paide, the landlord will have his due: *caveat emptor*, let the tenant looke to it.

HORSE.

The landlord will leade to the divell, and the tenant will follow after.

BANKES.

What else? they be relatives: landlord and tenant are as *Pater* and *Filius*.

HORSE.

O master, I could relate to you of these relatives, if it became me to speake like a common-wealths man, what an abuse is ingendered twixte the landlord and tenant.

BANKES.

Occasion of what, Marocco.

HORSE.

Of more amisse, by gis, than easily amended is, of bauderie, and beggerie, and such lyke matters, master. *Ambubaiarum collegia, pharmacopolæ, mendici, mimi, balatrones, hoc genus omne* crie out and complaine for the loss of this good landlordes worship, God rest his soule, sayes J. B. wee could have had no wrong while hee lived. So hee had had his rent at the daie, the devill and John of Comber should not have fetcht Kate L. to Bridewell, no nor all the court whipt C. F. at the cart, Ile tell you master, come what complaint coulde have come against Petticoate-lane, Smocke-alley, Shordich, or Rotton-rowe, there were champions and spokesmen for this crue, other manner of felowes I wis, than you thinke for, such as sit in their sattens and riche furres, and wyth a dash of a penne in a counting house, coulde doo more than the proudest plaintiefe that com-meneth anie matter or sute against this sisterhoode, yea and seale up his letter and their lyps both at once, that murmure anie thing against the inhabitantes of this holy corner. Master I coulde have shewed you the coppie of a letter that was lost in this yarde by chaunce, written by a man of some account, so favourably to the treasurer of Bridewell, in the behalfe of an honest tenaunt of his, such a tenant, master, as had her name a *tenendo*, and would holde so fast betweene the thigh, that shame it was for him that had anie shame, to be so shamelesse to use anie meanes to keep her from open shame.

### BANKES.

Thou speakest of mallice against some or other, Marocco and perhappes thou meanest that drabbe that the last daie when shee sawe thee heere doe thy trickes, sayd thou wert a devill, and I a conjurer.

### HORSE.

Against her, master, no of mine honestie! she is but a poore whoore, to her I meane. Tush, she that I talke of can entertaine you with a duzen of tiffite taffetie girles in a morning, I, and the worst of them, when she is at the worst, shall have a wrought wast-coate on her backe, and a bockram smocke worth three pence, as well rent behind as before, I warrant you.

### BANKES.

Those rents, by your leave Marocco, helpe to paie the landlords rent at the quarter's end.

### HORSE.

I, master, and the landlorde by your leave helpes to rent some of them betweene the quarters.

### BANKES.

Thats but a tricke of youth, lad, *omnis homo menda*, everie man may amend.

### HORSE.

True master, *Et ut hora sic vita*, a loves a whoore as his life. For hee will forbeare as long as shee will beare, and thats ka mee and ka thee, knave he and queene she.

### BANKES.

Had neede bee of exceeding patience, Marocco, to forbeare as long as sheele beare, for a better bearing beast is not in all Shordich, nor Houndsdich neither than this beastly beast that I thinke thou meanest. But speake not so loude, for and if her landlord heard you, he would annswere for her.

HORSE.

I thinke so, has answered so long for her that a can scarce answere for himselfe; and I speake not so loude that I feare him *Male audit ubique*, master, a heares verie badlye everie where: and worse a will heare, and a holde on, yea master, and loose hearing and seeing to, and a vie it and see it, as a has done these duzen yeres.

BANKES.

Well, whats that to the purpose? these wrongs are private, and touch himself, and wrack not the commonwealth, as thou exclaymest.

HORSE.

O master, then you know nothing: for understand you as of nownes, some be substantives, some be adjectives: so of landlords, some of them bee covetous, and some bee lecherous, and hee is both.

BANKES.

Sayest me so. Well then, Marocco, whether does more harme in the commonwealth, the covetous, or the lecherous landlord.

HORSE.

Tush, master, that question is no question.—For though it bee a question, betweene the covetous and the prodigall, yet it is no question betwixt the covetous and the lecherous. The lecherous landlord hath his wench at his commandment, and is content to take ware for his money, his private scutcherie wounds not the commonwealth farther than that his whoore shall have a house rent free, when his honest neighbour's wife and children shall neither have a peece of a house or household loafe for him. Let him passe for a farting churle, and weare his mistres favors, viz. rubies and precious stones on his nose, &c. And this *et cetera*, shall, if you will, bee the perfectest poxe that ever grewe in Shordich or Southwarke.

BANKES.

And these have been bigge inflamations, and more unquenchable than the great fire that burnt so much blew threed on the toppe of Fish-street Hill.

HORSE.

But the covetous landlord is the caterpiller of the commonwealth; hee neither feares God nor the divell, nor so hee may racke it out, cares not what tenant he receives: he is no wencher (praie God he be no bencher) hee sits warme at home, and sets downe his accounts, and saies to himselfe, my houses goe nowe but for twentie poundes for the yeare, Ile make them all baudie houses, and they will yeeld me twice as much. Uppon the Exchange comes to him one or two honest men to take them at his hands, the poore artificer or his lyke, of what trade soever, offers him the rent it hath gone for, and sureties perhaps. Yea, saie so, good securitie, and foure pounds a yere for a house: comes Pierce Pandor, and baudie Bettrice his wife, two that I warrant you were knowen well enough what they were; I, two that had beene as well carted and whipt, and covered with dust over head and eares, and they forsooth will begin the world anue again, having a fresh wench or two that came but from the carryers that morning, though shee had tapt many a canne in Long-lane, at Barthelmew tide. With this stocke of wenches will this trustie Roger and his Bettrice set up forsooth with their pamphlet pots, and stewed prunes, nine for a tester, in a sinfull saucer, and they will offer this covetous and wretched landlorde five poundes by the yere, yea, sixe pounds to have his house and his countenance wythal. But hee that will go to the divill for money, will admit them with favour, and so let them have his house, with promise of anie thing, so there bee anie mcanc to do it, and hee to be sure of his rent. God is his judge hee does it for no fleshy respect, but even of a mere worldly motion, to beare sinne out with sinne, and lecherie with covetousnesse. Let the parish complaine, why (says hee) what should I doo? I have my rent paid at my day, I must make money of my lande, and so let them doo their heartes out, thinkes hee, I shall have my rent the readier. This cormorant is hee that cares not how he get it, so hee have it. This stymphalist is hee, that with five or six tenements, and the retinue thereunto belonging, infectes the aire with stench, and poisons that parish, yea, and twentie parishes off with the contagion of such carrion as lies there in their bumble baths, and stinke at bothe ends like filthie greene elder pipes. For him and them, master, such landlordes and such tenants, good master, wish as I wish.

BANKES.
What's thy wish, Marocco?

HORSE.
That at the quarter daie, the parish would of their owne devotion to the common wealth, bestow a banket upon them of ale and cakes in the cage, and a hundred or two of good faggots to consume the bodies and bones of them all and everie mother's child, such landlords and such tenants as so much against conscience receive and deceive, and daie by daie and house by house, cheat, coosen, catch, and devour in pillage from gentlemen, prentises, and the good fellowes, *ab usque ad mille*, even from the outside to the inside, from the cloak to the shirt, leaving Nichol Neverthrive never a wench in the chamber, or penie in the purse.

BANKES.
Marocco, praie thy wish take effect, I wish for everie parish so pestered with such tenants and tenements, God put into their mindes to be but at cost and charges for the faggots, for ale and cakes I were mearst if it cost five markes. But how does this landlord fall into this *Præmunire?* Why is thy malice so great against them, when tis the baude and the whoore that make all this stirre?

HORSE.
O master, miserable landlords are cause of all this mischiefe. Tis he that because he will have an unreasonable rent, will upholde anie villanie in his tenant: a slave to

monie, a pandor to the baud, a piller, nay a pillow and a bolster to all the roguerie commited in his houses. And yet will this filthie felow sit at his doore on a Sonday in the High street, and my mistres his wife by him, and then forsooth talke so saint-like of the sermon that day, and what a good peece of worke the young man made, and what a goodly gift of utterance he had, but not the value of a pound of beefe wil a give him were his gift of utterance comparable to S. Augustines, or Chrisostomes eloquence. Sweare a will and forsweare upon the worke day, as well as anie. And if percase a sit in place of authoritie, O howe severe will he be in all his proceedings against a yong or good fellow in anie trifling matter. Then a takes upon him not a little. Sir (sayes hee) what did you in such an house? wherefore came you thether? And laie the lawe and the Prophetes too, and so rate a gentleman well descended, meerely priviledged with a furd gowne and a nightcap; when indeede his bringing up hath beene in beggerie and slaverie illiberally, having spent his time in conference with the water tankard at the conduit, lying miserably, and for sparing of wood, loding his gowne sleeve with fuell from the haberdashers, and wearing his handes in a frostie morning by the fugitive flames of a few wast papers, a natural enemie to all learning and liberalitie. O master, such a churle as you and I sawe heere last daie talke with two souldiers in the yard and put his hand in his pouch and gave them nere a penny.

BANKES.

Didst thou see that, Marocco? well, there be too many such as he, yet there is a choice number of sober citizens that have golden mindes, and golden purses withall.

HORSE.

That I know well, master, and to them that have such golden mindes, I wish golden mines: master, I protest to you I speake it not to flatter, but in reproach of those money-mongers, those lease-mongers, those canibals, that dishonour the citie wherein they dwell, but uprightly I speeke it, that you may not thinke I raile upon mallice against any private man, for anie private quarrel: there are many that beautifie London for their good parts, who being civily, and well brought up, are afable to straungers, charitable to the poore, liberal to schollers, and, such as citizens should be, duitiful to their prince, and devout to their citie. But as cockle is ever among corne, and drosse among gold, so wil those foule churles cumber the best corners, and march cheek by joul among the better many, with as great shew of devotion and charitie as the best. From such dissembling holynesse, such double wickednesse, good Lord delyver us.

BANKES.

'Tis almost supper time, Marocco; I heare mine host call: you have done pretily well for two pointes, referre the rest till another time.

HORSE.

As you please, master, and let this be our first lecture of the Anatomy of the world. If the trance holde me but till the next tearme, where now I have but with a drie foote overleapt these matters, I may chance of these and more leave a deeper print; and having handled a case of commodities, will saie somewhat further of their discommodities and differences, even as the bit of reason shall leade mee. And so I commit you to your supper, and myselfe to my litter; for I promise you I am not a little weary with gambolling this afternoone.

FINIS.

# THE AUTHORS TO THE READER

So Marocco dyd lye him downe, and *Laurence Holden* cald in his guest unto a shoulder of mutton of the best in the market, piping hot from the spit. We like two lazie fellowes laie trembling in the hay loft, and heard this that we have set down *verbatim* as wel as we could; and will watch narrowly but we wil seize the rest to our use, gentle Reader, whensoever it comes upon them. For *Marocco's* conclusion, this dialog shoulde seeme but an Induction to another discourse, which, how unpleasant so ever it prove to a great many, we know, that have beene wrong on the withers, and strong with the marchants booke, it will be reasonably friendly and welcome.

*Finis, quoth John Dando, and Harry Runt.*

## 14

# Robin Good-fellow;
# His Mad Prankes, and Merry Jests

### Full of Honest Mirth,
### And is a Fit Medicine for Melancholy

*T*HAT ROBIN GOOD-FELLOW *is "a fit medicine for melancholy" was meant literally in 1628, when this tract was published, for "melancholy" was regarded as an actual disease caused by an imbalance of the humours of blood, phlegm, yellow, and black bile. (Similarly, in the twentieth century, studies are made of how disease can be caused by an imbalance of hormones.) Someone with melancholy had too much black bile—the name for the disease said as much in Greek, in fact. The book was one antidote to the symptoms described in Robert Burton's great work,* The Anatomy of Melancholy, *an edition of which was published the same year.*

*Thus, Robin, as you can read for yourself, frightened a hateful old rich man into goodness and generosity, just as Scrooge, later, was frightened into reform by Marley's ghost. Half human, half fairy, he could look at the world more objectively than all-humans and change himself into whatever form seemed most effective for handling a given situation. A girl about to be raped is screaming for help. Robin hears and changes himself into a horse so that he can gallop away with her attacker. His life is full of music and dance and laughter—all known medicines for melancholy.*

Robin Good-fellow; His Mad Prankes and Merry Jests *is reprinted from Percy Society* Publications, *Vol. 2 (London, 1841).*

*N*OT OMITTING that antient forme of beginning tales, *Once upon a time* it was my chance to travaile into that noble county of Kent. The weather beeing wet, and my two-leg'd horse being almost tyred (for indeede my owne leggs were all the supporters that my body had) I went dropping into an alehouse: there found I, first a kinde wellcome, next good lyquor, then kinde strangers (which made good company), then an honest hoast, whose love to good liquor was written in red characters both in his nose, cheekes and forehead: an hoastesse I found there too, a woman of very good carriage; and though she had not so much colour (for what she had done) as her rich husband had, yet all beholders might perceive by the roundness of her belly, that she was able to draw a pot dry at a draught, and ne're unlace for the matter.

Well, to the fire I went, where I dryed my outside and wet my inside. The ale being good, and I in good company, I lapt in so much of this nappy liquor, that it begot in mee a boldnesse to talke, and desire of them to know what was the reason that the people of that country were called Long-tayles. The hoast sayd, all the reason that ever he could heare was, because the people of that country formerly did use to goe in side skirted coates. There is (sayd an old man that sat by) another reason that I have heard: that is this. In the time of the Saxons conquest of England there were divers of our country-men slaine by treachery, which made those that survived more carefull in dealing with their enemies, as you shall heare.

After many overthrowes that our countrymen had received by the Saxons, they dispersed themselves into divers companies into the woods, and so did much damage by their suddaine assaults to the Saxons, that Hengist, their king, hearing the damage that they did (and not knowing how to subdue them by force), used this policy. Hee sent to a company of them, and gave them his word for their liberty and safe returne, if they would come unarmed and speake with him. This they seemed to grant unto, but for their more security (knowing how little hee esteemed oathes or promises) they went every one of them armed with a shorte sword, hanging just behind under their garments, so that the Saxons thought not of any weapons they had: but it proved otherwise; for when Hengist his men (that were placed to cut them off) fell all upon them, they found such unlooked a resistance, that most of the Saxons were slaine, and they that escaped, wond'ring how they could doe that hurt, having no weapons (as they saw), reported that they strucke downe men like lyons with their tayles; and so they ever after were called Kentish Long-tayles.

I told him this was strange, if true, and that their countries honor bound them more to believe in this, then it did me.

Truly, sir, sayd my hoastesse, I thinke we are called Long-tayles, by reason our tales are long, that we use to passe the time withall, and make our selves merry. Now, good hoastesse, sayd I, let me entreat from you one of those tales. You shall (sayd shee), and that shall not be a common one neither, for it is a long tale, a merry tale, and a sweete tale; and thus it beginnes.

## The Hoastesse Tale of The Birth of Robin Good-fellow.

ONCE UPON A TIME, a great while agoe, when men did eate more and drinke lesse,— then men were more honest, that knew no knavery then some now are, that confesse the knowledge and deny the practise—about that time (when so ere it was) there was wont to walke many harmlesse spirits called fayries, dancing in brave order in fayry rings on greene hills with sweete musicke (sometime invisible) in divers shapes: many mad prankes would they play, as pinching of sluts black and blue, and misplacing things in ill-ordered houses; but lovingly would they use wenches that cleanly were, giving them silver and other pretty toyes, which they would leave for them, sometimes in their shooes, other times in their pockets, sometimes in bright basons and other cleane vessels.

Amongst these fayries was there a hee fayrie: whether he was their king or no I know not, but surely he had great government and commaund in that country, as you shall heare. This same hee fayry did love a proper young wench, for every night would hee with other fayries come to the house, and there dance in her chamber; and oftentimes shee was forced to dance with him, and at his departure would hee leave her silver and jewels, to express his love unto her. At last this mayde was with childe, and being asked who was the father of it, she answered a man that nightly came to visit her, but earely in the morning he would go his way, whither she knew not, he went so suddainly.

Many old women, that then had more wit than those that are now living and have lesse, sayd that a fayry had gotten her with childe; and they bid her be of good comfort, for the childe must needes be fortunate that had so noble a father as a fayry was, and should worke many strange wonders. To be short, her time grew on, and she was delivered of a man childe, who (it should seeme) so rejoyced his father's heart, that every night his mother was supplied with necessary things that are befitting a woman in child-birth, so that in no meane manner neither; for there had shee rich imbroidered cushions, stooles, carpits, coverlets, delicate linnen: then for meate shee had capons, chickins, mutton, lambe, phesant, snite, woodcocke, partridge, quaile. The gossips liked this fare so well, that she never wanted company: wine had shee of all sorts, as muska-dine, sacke, malmsie, clarret, white and bastard: this pleased her neighbours' well, so that few that came to see her, but they had home with them a medicine for the fleaes. Sweet meates too had they in such aboundance, that some of their teeth are rotten to this day; and for musicke shee wanted not, or any other thing she desired.

All praysed this honest fayry for his care, and the childe for his beauty, and the mother for a happy woman. In briefe, christened hee was, at the which all this good cheare was doubled, which made most of the women so wise, that they forgot to make themselves unready, and so lay in their cloathes; and none of them next day could remember the child's name, but the clarke, and hee may thanke his booke for it, or else it had been utterly lost. So much for the birth of little Robin.

## Of Robin Good-fellowe's Behaviour When He Was Young.

WHEN ROBIN was growne to six yeares of age, hee was so knavish that all the neighbours did complaine of him; for no sooner was his mother's backe turned, but hee was in one knavish action or other, so that his mother was constrayned (to avoyde the complaints) to take him with her to market, or wheresoever shee went or rid. But this helped little or nothing, for if hee rid before her, then would he make mouthes and ill-favoured faces at those hee met: if he rid behind her, then would hee clap his hand on his tayle; so that his mother was weary of the many complaints that came against him, yet knew she not how to beat him justly for it, because she never saw him doe that which was worthy blowes. The complaints were daily so renewed that his mother promised him a whipping. Robin did not like that cheere, and therefore, to avoyde it, hee ranne away, and left his mother a heavy woman for him.

## How Robin Good-fellow Dwelt With A Taylor.

AFTER THAT Robin Good-fellow had gone a great way from his mother's house hee began to bee a hungry, and going to a taylor's house, hee asked something for God's

sake. The taylor gave him meate, and understanding that he was masterlesse, hee tooke
him for his man, and Robin so plyed his worke that he got his master's love.

On a time his master had a gowne to make for a woman, and it was to bee done that
night: they both sate up late so that they had done all but setting on the sleeves by
twelve a clocke. This master then being sleepy sayd, Robin whip thou on the sleeves,
and then come thou to bed: I will goe to bed before. I will, sayd Robin. So, soone as
his master was gone, Robin hung up the gowne, and taking both sleeves in his handes,
hee whipt and lashed them on the gowne. So stood he till the morning that his master
came downe: his master seeing him stand in that fashion, asked him what he did? Why,
quoth hee, as you bid mee, whip on the sleeves. Thou rogue, sayd his master, I did
meane that thou shouldest have set them on quickly and slightly. I would you had sayd
so, sayd Robin, for then had I not lost all this sleepe. To bee shorte, his master was
faine to do the worke, but ere hee had made an end of it, the woman came for it, and
with a loud voyce chafed for her gowne. The taylor, thinking to please her, bid Robin
fetch the remnants that they left yesterday (meaning thereby meate that was left) ; but
Robin, to crosse his master the more, brought downe the remnants of the cloath that
was left of the gowne. At the sight of this, his master looked pale, but the woman was
glad, saying, I like this breakfast so well, that I will give you a pint of wine to it. She
sent Robin for the wine, but he never returned againe to his master.

## What Hapned to Robin Good-fellow After He Went From The Taylor.

AFTER ROBIN had travailed a good dayes journy from his masters house hee sate downe,
and beeing weary hee fell a sleepe. No sooner had slumber tooken full possession of him,
and closed his long opened eye-lids, but hee thought he saw many goodly proper personages in anticke measures tripping about him, and withall hee heard such musicke,
as he thought that Orpheus, that famous Greeke fidler (had hee beene alive) , compared
to one of these had beene as infamous as a Welch-harper that playes for cheese and
onions. As delights commonly last not long, so did those end sooner then hee would
willingly they should have done; and for very griefe he awaked, and found by him
lying a scroule, wherein was written these lines following in golden letters.

> Robin, my only sonne and heire,
> How to live take thou no care:
> By nature thou hast cunning shifts,
> Which Ile increase with other gifts.
> Wish what thou wilt, thou shalt it have;
> And for to vex both foole and knave,
> Thou hast the power to change thy shape,
> To horse, to hog, to dog, to ape.
> Transformed thus, by any meanes
> Seen none thou harm'st but knaves and queanes;
> But love thou those that honest be,

And helpe them in necessity.
Doe thus, and all the world shall know
The prankes of Robin Good-fellow;
For by that name thou cald shalt be
To ages last posterity.
If thou observe my just command,
One day thou shalt see Fayry Land.
This more I give: who tels thy prankes
From those that heare them shall have thankes.

Robin having read this was very joyfull, yet longed he to know whether he had this power or not, and to trye it hee wished for some meate: presently it was before him. Then wished hee for beere and wine: he straightway had it. This liked him well, and because he was weary, he wished himselfe a horse: no sooner was his wish ended, but he was transformed, and seemed a horse of twenty pound price, and leaped and curveted as nimble as if he had beene in stable at racke and manger a full moneth. Then wished he himselfe a dog, and was so: then a tree, and was so: so from one thing to another, till hee was certaine and well assured that hee could change himselfe to any thing whatsoever.

## How Robin Good-fellow Served A Clownish Fellow.

ROBIN GOOD-FELLOW going over a field met with a clownish fellow, to whom he spake in this manner: Friend (quoth he) what is a clocke? A thing (answered the clowne) that shewes the time of the day. Why then (sayd Robin Good-fellow) bee thou a clocke, and tell me what time of the day it is. I owe thee not so much service (answered hee againe), but because thou shalt thinke thy selfe beholding to mee, know that it is the same time of the day, as it was yesterday at this time.

These crosse answeres vext Robin Good-fellow, so that in himselfe hee vowed to be revenged of him, which he did in this manner.

Robin Good-fellow turned himselfe into a bird, and followed this fellow, who was going into a field a little from that place to catch a horse that was at grasse. The horse being wilde ran over dike and hedge, and the fellow after, but to little purpose, for the horse was too swift for him. Robin was glad of this occasion, for now or never was the time to put his revenge in action.

Presently Robin shaped himselfe like to the horse that the fellow followed, and so stood before the fellow: presently the fellow tooke hold of him and got on his backe, but long had he not rid, but with a stumble he hurld this churlish clowne to the ground, that he almost broke his necke; yet tooke he not this for a sufficient revenge for the crosse answers he had received, but stood still and let the fellow mount him once more.

In the way the fellow was to ride was a great plash of water of a good depth: thorow this must he of necessity ride. No sooner was hee in the middest of it, but Robin Good-fellow left him with nothing but a pack-saddle betwixt his leggs, and in the shape of a fish swomme to the shore, and ran away laughing, *ho, ho, hoh!* leaving the poore fellow almost drowned.

### How Robin Good-fellow Helped Two Lovers And Deceived An Old Man.

ROBIN GOING BY a woode heard two lovers make great lamentation, because they were hindred from injoying each other by a cruell old leacher, who would not suffer this loving couple to marry. Robin, pittying them, went to them and sayd: I have heard your complaints, and do pitty you: be ruled by me, and I will see that you shall have both your hearts content, and that suddainly if you please. After some amazement the maiden sayd, Alas! sir, how can that be? my uncle, because I will not grant to his lust, is so streight over me, and so oppresseth me with worke night and day, that I have not so much time as to drinke or speake with this young man, whom I love above all men living. If your worke bee all that hindreth you (sayd Robin), I will see that done: aske mee not how, nor make any doubt of the performance; I will doe it. Go with your love: for 24 houres I will free you. In that time marry or doe what you will. If you refuse my proffered kindnesse never looke to enjoy your wished for happinesse. I love true lovers, honest men, good fellows, good huswives, good meate, good drinke, and all things that good is, but nothing that is ill; for my name is Robin Good-fellow, and that you shall see that I have power to performe what I have undertooke, see what I can do. Presently he turned himselfe into a horse, and away he ran: at the sight of which they were both amazed, but better considering with themselves, they both determined to make good use of their time, and presently they went to an old fryer, who presently married them. They payd him, and went their way. Where they supped and lay, I know not, but surely they liked their lodging well the next day.

Robin, when that he came neare the old man's house, turned himselfe into the shape of the young maide, and entred the house, where, after much chiding, he fell to the worke that the mayde had to do, which hee did in halfe the time that another could do it in. The old man, seeing the speede he made, thought that she had some meeting that night (for he tooke Robin Good-fellow for his neece): therefore he gave him order for other worke, that was too much for any one to do in one night: Robin did that in a trise, and playd many mad prankes beside ere the day appeared.

In the morning hee went to the two lovers to their bed-side, and bid God give them joy, and told them all things went well, and that ere night he would bring them 10 pounds of her uncles to beginne the world with. They both thanked him, which was all the requital that he looked for, and beeing therewith well contented hee went his way laughing.

Home went he to the old man, who then was by, and marveiled how the worke was done so soone. Robin, seeing that, sayd: Sir, I pray marvaile not, for a greater wonder then that this night hath happened to me. Good neece, what is that? (sayd the old man) This, Sir; but I shame to speake it, yet I will: weary with worke, I slept, and did dreame that I consented to that which you have so often desired of me (you know what it is I meane), and me thought you gave me as a reward 10 pounds, with your consent to marry that young man that I have loved so long. Diddest thou dreame so? thy dreame I will make good, for under my hand wrighting I give my free consent to marry him, or whom thou doest please to marry (and withall writ) and for the 10 pounds, goe but into the out barne, and I will bring it thee presently. How sayst thou (sayd the old leacher), wilt thou? Robin with silence did seeme to grant, and went toward the barne. The old man made haste, told out his money, and followed.

Being come thither, he hurled the money on the ground, saying, This is the most pleasing bargaine that ever I made; and going to embrace Robin, Robin tooke him up in has armes and carried him foorth; first drew him thorow a pond to coole his hot blood, then did he carry him where the young married couple were, and said, Here is your uncle's consent under his hand; then, here is the 10 pounds he gave you and there is your uncle: let him deny it if hee can.

The old man, for feare of worse usage, said all was true. Then am I as good as my word, said Robin, and so went away laughing. The old man knew himselfe duly punished, and turned his hatred into love, and thought afterward as well of them, as if shee had beene his owne. The second part shall shew many incredible things done by Robin Good-fellow (or otherwise called Hob-goblin) and, his campanions, by turning himselfe into divers sundry shapes.

## The Second Part Of
## Robin Good-fellow,
## Commonly Called Hob-Goblin.

### How Robin Good-fellow Helped A Mayde To Worke.

ROBIN GOOD-FELLOW oftentimes would in the night visite farmers houses, and helpe the maydes to breake hempe, to bowlt, to dress flaxe, and to spin and do other workes, for he was excellent in every thing. One night hee comes to a farmers house, where there was a goode handsome mayde: this mayde having much work to do, Robin one night did helpe her, and in six houres did bowlt more than she could have done in twelve houres. The mayde wondred the next day how her worke came, and to know the doer, shee watched the next night that did follow. About twelve of the clocke in came Robin, and fell to breaking of hempe, and for to delight himselfe he sung this mad song.

> And can the physitian make sicke men well?
> And can the magician a fortune devine?
> Without lilly, germander and sops in wine?
>     With sweet-bryer
>     And bon-fire,
>     And straw-berry wyer,
>     And collumbine.

Within and out, in and out, round as a ball,
With hither and thither, as straight as a line,
With lilly, germander and sops in wine.
              With sweet-bryer,
              And bon-fire,
              And straw-berry wyer,
              And collumbine.

When Saturne did live, there lived no poore,
The king and the beggare with rootes did dine,
With lilly, germander, and sops in wine.
              With sweet-bryer,
              And bon-fire,
              And straw-berry wyer,
              And collumbine.

The mayde, seeing him bare in clothes, pittied him, and against the next night provided him a wast-coate. Robin comming the next night to worke, as he did before, espied
the wast-coate, whereat he started and said:—

Because thou lay'st me himpen, hampen,
I will neither bolt nor stampen:
'Tis not your garments new or old
That Robin loves: I feele no cold.
Had you left me milke or creame,
You should have had a pleasing dreame:
Because you left no drop or crum,
Robin never more will come.

So went hee away laughing *ho, ho, hoh!* The mayde was much grieved and discontented
at his anger: for ever after she was faine to do her worke herselfe without the helpe of
Robin Good-fellow.

### How Robin Good-fellow Led A Company Of Fellowes Out Of Their Way.

A COMPANY of young men having beene making merry with their sweet hearts, were
at their comming home to come over a heath. Robin Good-fellow, knowing of it, met
them, and to make some pastime, hee led them up and downe the heath a whole night,
so that they could not get out of it; for hee went before them in the shape of a walking
fire, which they all saw and followed till the day did appeare: then Robin left them, and
at his departure spake these words:—

Get you home, you merry lads:

Tell your mammies and your dads,
And all those that newes desire,
How you saw a walking fire.
Wenches, that doe smile and lispe
Use to call me Willy Wispe.
If that you but weary be,
It is sport alone for me.
Away: unto your houses goe
And I'le goe laughing *ho, ho, hoh!*

The fellowes were glad that he was gone, for they were all in a great feare that hee would have done them some mischiefe.

## How Robin Good-fellow Served
## A Leacherous Gallant.

ROBIN ALWAYES DID helpe those that suffered wrong, and never would hurt any but those that did wrong to others. It was his chance one day to goe thorow a field where he heard one call for helpe: hee, going neere where he heard the cry, saw a lusty gallant that would have forced a young maiden to his lust; but the mayden in no wise would yeelde, which made her cry for helpe. Robin Good-fellow, seeing of this, turned himselfe into the shape of a hare, and so ranne between the lustfull gallants legges. This gallant, thinking to have taken him, he presently turned himselfe into a horse, and so perforce carried away this gallant on his backe. The gentleman cryed out for helpe, for he thought that the devill had bin come to fetch him for his wickednesse; but his crying was in vaine, for Robin did carry him into a thicke hedge, and there left him so prickt and scratched, that hee more desired a playster for his paine, than a wench for his pleasure. Thus the poore mayde was freed from this ruffin, and Robin Good-fellow, to see this gallant so tame, went away laughing, *ho, ho, hoh!*

## How Robin Good-fellow Turned A Miserable
## Usurer To A Good House-Keeper.

IN THIS COUNTRY of ours there was a rich man dwelled, who to get wealth together was so sparing that hee could not find in his heart to give his belly foode enough. In the winter hee never would make so much fire as would roast a blacke-pudding, for hee found it more profitable to sit by other meanes. His apparell was of the fashion that none did weare; for it was such as did hang at a brokers stall, till it was as weather-beaten as an old signe. This man for his covetousnesse was so hated of all his neighbours, that there was not one that gave him a good word. Robin Good-fellow grieved to see a man of such wealth doe so little good, and therefore practised to better him in this manner.

One night the usurer being in bed, Robin in the shape of a night-raven came to the window, and there did beate with his wings, and croaked in such manner that this old usurer thought hee should have presently dyed for feare. This was but a preparation to what he did intend; for presently after hee appeared before him at his bed's feete, in the shape of a ghost, with a torch in his hand. At the sight of this the old usurer would have risen out of his bed, and have leaped out of the window, but he was stayed by Robin Good-fellow, who spake to him thus.

> If thou dost stirre out of thy bed,
> I doo vow to strike thee dead.
> I doe come to doe thee good;
> Recall thy wits and starkled blood.
> The mony which thou up dost store
> In soule and body makes thee poore.
> Doe good with mony while you may;
> Thou hast not long on earth to stay.
> Doe good, I say, or day and night
> I hourely thus will thee afright.
> Thinke on my words, and so farewell,
> For being bad I live in hell.

Having said thus he vanished away and left this usurer in great terror of mind; and for feare of being frighted againe with this ghost, hee turned very liberall, and lived amongst his neighbours as an honest man should doe.

## How Robin Good-fellow Loved A Weaver's Wife, And How The Weaver Would Have Drowned Him.

ONE DAY Robin Good-fellow walking thorow the streete found at a doore sitting a pretty woman: this woman was wife to the weaver, and was a winding of quils for her husband. Robin liked her so well, that for her sake he became servant to her husband, and did daily worke at the loome; but all the kindnesse that hee shewed was but lost, for his mistress would shew him no favour, which made him many times to exclame against the whole sex in satyricall songs; and one day being at worke he sung this, to the tune of *Rejoyce Bag-pipes*.

> Why should my love now waxe
>     Unconstant, wavering, fickle, unstayd?
> With nought can she me taxe:
>     I ne're recanted what I once said.
> I now doe see, as nature fades,
>     And all her workes decay,
> So women all, wives, widdowes, maydes,
>     From bad to worse doe stray.

As hearbs, trees, rootes, and plants
   In strength and growth are daily lesse,
So all things have their wants:
   The heavenly signes moove and digresse;
And honesty in womens hearts
   Hath not her former being:
Their thoughts are ill, like other parts,
   Nought else in them's agreeing.

I sooner thought thunder
   Had power o're the laurell wreath,
Then shee, women's wonder,
   Such perjurd thoughts should live to breathe.
They all hyena-like will weepe,
   When that they would deceive:
Deceit in them doth lurke and sleepe,
   Which makes me thus to grieve.

Young mans delight, farewell;
   Wine, women, game, pleasure, adieu:
Content with me shall dwell;
   I'le nothing trust but what is true.
Though she were false, for her I'le pray;
   Her false-hood made me blest:
I will renew from this good day
   My life by sinne opprest.

Moved with this song and other complaints of his, shee at last did fancy him, so that the weaver did not like that Robin should bee so saucy with his wife, and therefore gave him warning to be gone, for hee would keepe him no longer. This grieved this loving couple to parte one from the other, which made them to make use of the time that they had. The weaver one day comming in, found them a kissing: at this hee said [nothing] but vowed in himselfe to bee revenged of his man that night following. Night being come, the weaver went to Robin's bed, and tooke him out of it (as hee then thought) and ran apace to the river side to hurle Robin in; but the weaver was deceived, for Robin, instead of himselfe, had laid in his bed a sack full of yarne: it was that that the weaver carried to drowne. The weaver standing by the river side said:— Now will I coole your hot blood, Master Robert, and if you cannot swimme the better; you shall sincke and drowne. With that he hurled the sack in, thinking that it had bin Robin Good-fellow. Robin, standing behind him, said:—

For this your kindnesse, master, I you thanke:
Go swimme yourselfe; I'le stay upon the banke.

With that Robin pushed him in, and went laughing away, *ho, ho, hoh!*

*How Robin Good-fellow Went In The Shape Of A*
*Fidler To A Wedding, And Of The Sport*
*That He Had There.*

ON A TIME there was a great wedding, to which there went many young lusty lads and pretty lasses. Robin Good-fellow longing not to be out of action, shaped himselfe like unto a fidler, and with his crowd under his arme went amongst them, and was a very welcome man. There played hee whilst they danced, and tooke as much delight in seeing them, as they did in hearing him. At dinner he was desired to sing a song, which hee did, to the tune of *Watton Towne's End.*

## THE SONG

IT WAS a country lad
   That fashions strange would see,
And he came to a valting schoole,
   Where tumblers use to be:
He lik't his sport so well,
   That from it he'd not part:
His doxey to him still did cry,
   Come, busse thine owne sweet heart.

They lik't his gold so well,
   That they were both content,
That he that night with his sweet heart
   Should passe in merry-ment.
To bed they then did goe;
   Full well he knew his part,
Where he with words, and eke with
     deedes,
   Did busse his owne sweet heart.

Long were they not in bed,
   But one knockt at the doore,
And said, Up, rise, and let me in:
   This vext both knave and whore.
He being sore perplext
   From bed did lightly start;
No longer then could he indure
   To busse his owne sweet heart.

With tender steps he trod,
  To see if he could spye
The man that did him so molest;
  Which he with heavy eye
Had soone beheld, and said,
  Alas! my owne sweet heart,
I now doe doubt, if e're we busse,
  It must be in a cart.


At last the bawd arose,
  And opened the doore,
And saw Discretion cloth'd in rug,
  Whose office hates a whore.
He mounted up the stayres,
  Being cunning in his arte:
With little search at last he found
  My youth and his sweete heart.


He having wit at will,
  Unto them both did say,
I will not heare them speake one word;
  Watchmen, with them away!
And cause they lov'd so well,
  'Tis pitty they should part.
Away with them to new Bride-well;
  There busse your own sweet heart.


His will it was fulfild,
  And there they had the law;
And whilst that they did nimbly spin,
  The hempe he needs must taw.
He grownd, he thump't, he grew
  So cunning in his arte,
He learnt the trade of beating hempe
  By bussing his sweet heart.


But yet, he still would say,
  If I could get release
To see strange fashions I'le give o're,
  And henceforth live in peace,
The towne where I was bred,
  And thinke by my desert
To come no more into this place
  For bussing my sweet heart.

They all liked his song very well, and said that the young man had but ill lucke. Thus continued hee playing and singing songs till candle-light: then hee beganne to play his merry trickes in this manner. First, hee put out the candles, and then beeing darke, hee strucke the men good boxes on the ears: they, thinking it had beene those that did sit next them, fell a fighting one with the other; so that there was not one of them but had either a broken head or a bloody nose. At this Robin laughed heartily. The women did not scape him, for the handsomest he kissed; the other he pinched, and made them scratch one the other, as if they had beene cats. Candles being lighted againe, they all were friends, and fell againe to dancing, and after to supper.

Supper beeing ended, a great posset was brought forth: at this Robin Good-fellowes teeth did water, for it looked so lovely that hee could not keepe from it. To attaine to his wish, he did turne himselfe into a beare: both men and women (seeing a beare amongst them) ranne away, and left the whole posset to Robin Good-fellow. He quickly made an end of it, and went away without his money; for the sport hee had was better to him than any money whatsoever. The feare that the guests were in did cause such a smell, that the Bride-groome did call for perfumes; and in stead of a posset, he was faine to make use of cold beere.

## How Robin Good-fellow Served A Tapster For Nicking His Pots.

Tʜᴇʀᴇ ᴡᴀs ᴀ ᴛᴀᴘsᴛᴇʀ, that with his pots smalnesse, and with frothing of his drinke, had a good summe of money together. This nicking of the pots he would never leave, yet divers times he had been under the hand of authority, but what money soever hee had [to pay] for his abuses, hee would be sure (as they all doe) to get it out of the poore mans pot againe. Robin Goodfellow, hating such knavery, put a tricke upon him in this manner.

Robin shaped himselfe like to the tapsters brewer, and came and demaunded twenty pounds which was due to him from the tapster. The tapster, thinking it had beene his brewer, payd him the money, which money Robin gave to the poore of that parish before the tapster's face. The tapster praysed his charity very much, and sayd that God would blesse him the better for such good deedes: so, after they had drank one with the other, they parted.

Some foure dayes after the brewer himselfe came for his money: the tapster told him that it was payd, and that he had a quittance from him to shew. Hereat the brewer did wonder, and desired to see the quittance. The tapster fetched him a writing, which Robin Good-fellow had given him in stead of a quittance, wherein was written as followeth, which the brewer read to him.

I, Robin Good-fellow, true man and honest man, doe acknowledge to have received of Nicke and Froth, the cheating tapster, the summe of twenty pound, which money I have bestowed (to the tapsters content) amongst the poore of the parish, out of whose pockets this aforesayd tapster had picked the aforesaid summe, not after the manner of foisting, but after his excellent skill of bombasting, or a pint for a peny.

> If now thou wilt goe hang thy selfe,
> Then take thy apron-strings.
> It doth me good when such foule birds
> Upon the gallowes sings.
>
> *Per me* ROBIN GOOD-FELLOW.

At this the tapster swore Walsingham; but for all his swearing, the brewer made him pay him his twenty pound.

## How King Obreon Called Robin Good-fellow To Dance.

KING OBREON, seeing Robin Good-fellow doe so many honest and merry trickes, called him one night out of his bed with these words, saying:

> Robin, my sonne, come quickly, rise:
> First stretch, then yawne, and rub your eyes;
> For thou must goe with me to night,
> To see, and taste of my delight.
> Quickly come, my wanton sonne;
> Twere time our sports were now begunne.

Robin, hearing this, rose and went to him. There were with King Obreon a many fayries, all attyred in greene silke: all these, with King Obreon, did welcome Robin Good-fellow into their company. Obreon tooke Robin by the hand and led him a dance: their musician was little Tom Thumb; for hee had an excellent bag-pipe made of a wrens quill, and the skin of a Greenland louse: this pipe was so shrill, and so sweete, that a Scottish pipe compared to it, it would no more come neere it, than a Jewes-trump doth to an Irish harpe. After they had danced, King Obreon spake to his sonne, Robin Good-fellow, in this manner:

> When ere you heare my piper blow,
> From thy bed see that thou goe;
> For nightly you must with us dance,
> When we in circles round doe prance.
> I love thee, sonne, and by the hand
> I carry thee to Fairy Land,
> Where thou shalt see what no man knowes:
> Such love thee King Obreon owes.

So marched they in good manner (with their piper before) to the Fairy Land: there did King Obreon shew Robin Good-fellow many secrets, which hee never did open to the world.

### How Robin Good-fellow Was Wont To Walke In The Night.

ROBIN GOOD-FELLOW would many times walke in the night with a broome on his shoulder, and cry chimney sweepe, but when any one did call him, then would he runne away laughing, *ho, ho, hoh!* Sometime hee would counterfeit a begger, begging very pitifully, but when they came to give him an almes, he would runne away, laughing as his manner was. Sometimes would hee knocke at mens doores, and when the servants came, he would blow out the candle, if they were men; but if they were women, hee would not onely put out their light, but kisse them full sweetly, and then go away as his fashion was, *ho, ho, hoh!* Oftentimes would he sing at a doore like a singing man, and when they did come to give him his reward, he would turne his backe and laugh. In these humors of his hee had many pretty songs, which I will sing as perfect as I can. For his chimney-sweepers humors he had these songs: THE FIRST IS TO THE TUNE OF, *I have beene a fiddler these fifteene yeeres.*

> Blacke I am from head to foote,
> And all doth come by chimney soote:
> Then, maydens, come and cherrish him
> That makes your chimnies neat and trim.
>
> Hornes have I store, but all at my backe;
> My head no ornament doth lacke:
> I give my hornes to other men,
> And ne're require them againe.
>
> Then come away, you wanton wives,
> That love your pleasures as your lives:
> To each good woman Ile give two,
> Or more, if she thinke them too few.

Then would he change his note and sing the following, TO THE TUNE OF *What care I how faire she be?*

> Be she blacker then the stocke,
>   If that thou wilt make her faire,
> Put her in a cambricke smocke,
>   Buy her painte and flaxen haire.
>
> One your carrier brings to towne
>   Will put downe your city bred;
> Put her on a brokers gowne,
>   That will sell her mayden-head.

Comes your Spaniard, proud in minde,
  Heele have the first cut, or else none:
The meeke Italian comes behind,
  And your French-man pickes the bone.

Still she trades with Dutch and Scot,
  Irish, and the Germaine tall,
Till she get the thing you wot;
  Then her ends an hospitall.


A SONG TO THE TUNE OF *The Spanish Pavin.*

When Vertue was a country maide,
And had no skill to set up trade,
She came up with a carriers jade,
  And lay at racke and manger.
She whift her pipe, she drunke her can,
The pot was nere out of her span;
She married a tobacco man,
  A stranger, a stranger.

They set up shop in Hunney Lane,
And thither flayes did swarme amaine,
Some from France, some from Spaine,
  Traind in by scurvy panders.
At last this hunney pot grew dry,
Then both were forced for to fly
  To Flanders, to Flanders.


ANOTHER TO THE TUNE OF *The Coranto.*

I peeped in at the Wool sacke,
O, what a goodly sight did I
Behold at midnight-chyme!
The wenches were drinking of muld sacke;
Each youth on his knee, that then did want
A yeere and a halfe of his time.
    They leaped and skipped,
    They kissed and they clipped,
    And yet it was counted no crime.

The grocers chiefe servant brought sugar,
And out of his leather pocket he puld,
And kuld some pound and a halfe;
For which he was sufferd to smacke her
That was his sweet-heart, and would not depart,
But turn'd and lickt the calfe.
    He rung her, and he flung her,
    He kist her, and he swung her,
    And yet she did nothing but laugh.

Thus would he sing about cities and townes, and when any one called him, he would change his shape, and go laughing, *ho, ho, hoh!* For his humors of begging he used this song, TO THE TUNE OF *The Jovial Tinker.*

Good people of this mansion,
    Unto the poore be pleased
To doe some good, and give some food,
    That hunger may be eased.
My limbes with fire are burned,
    My goods and lands defaced;
Of wife and child I am beguild,
    So much am I debased.
Oh, give the poore some bread, cheese, or butter,
    Bacon, hempe, or flaxe;
Some pudding bring, or other thing:
    My need doth make me aske.

I am no common begger,
    Nor am I skild in canting:
You nere shall see a wench with me,
    Such trickes in me are wanting.
I curse not if you give not,
    But still I pray and blesse you,
Still wishing joy, and that annoy
    May never more possesse you.
Oh, give the poore some bread, cheese, or butter,
    Bacon, hempe, or flaxe;
Some pudding bring, or other thing:
    My need doth make me aske.

When any came to releeve him, then would he change himselfe into some other shape, and runne laughing, *ho, ho, hoh!* Then would hee shape himselfe like to a singing man; and at mens windowes and doores sing civil and vertuous songs, one of which I will sing TO THE TUNE OF *Broome.*

If thou wilt lead a blest and happy life,
I will describe the perfect way:
First must thou shun all cause of mortall strife,
Against thy lusts continually to pray.
Attend unto Gods word:
Great comfort 'twill afford;
'Twill keepe thee from discord.
Then trust in God, the Lord,
for ever,
for ever;
And see in this thou persever.

So soone as day appeareth in the east
Give thanks to him, and mercy crave;
So in this life thou shalt be surely blest,
And mercy shalt thou find in grave.
The conscience that is cleere
No horror doth it feare;
'Tis voyd of mortall care,
And never doth despaire;
but ever,
but ever
Doth in the word of God persever.

Thus living, when thou drawest to thy end
Thy joyes they shall much more encrease,
For then thy soule, thy true and loving friend,
By death shall find a wisht release
From all that caused sinne,
In which it lived in;
For then it doth beginne
Those blessed joyes to win,
for ever,
for ever,
For there is nothing can them sever.

Those blessed joyes which then thou shalt possesse,
No mortall tongue can them declare:
All earthly joyes, compar'd with this, are lesse
Then smallest mote to the world so faire.
Then is not that man blest
That must injoy this rest?
Full happy is that guest
Invited to this feast,
that ever,
that ever
Indureth, and is ended never.

When they opened the window or doore, then would he runne away laughing *ho, ho, hoh!* Sometimes would he goe like a Belman in the night, and with many pretty verses delight the eares of those that waked at his bell ringing: his verses were these.

> Maydes in your smockes,
> Looke well to your lockes,
> And your tinder boxe,
> Your wheeles and your rockes,
> Your hens and your cockes,
> Your cowes and your oxe,
> And beware of the foxe.
> When the Bell-man knocks,
> Put out your fire and candle light,
> So they shall not you affright:
> May you dreame of your delights,
> In your sleeps see pleasing sights.
> Good rest to all, both old and young:
> The Bell-man now hath done his song.

Then would he goe laughing *ho, ho, hoh!* as his use was. Thus would he continually practise himselfe in honest mirth, never doing hurt to any that were cleanly and honest minded.

## *How The Fairyes Called Robin Good-fellow To Dance With Them, And How They Shewed Him Their Severall Conditions.*

ROBIN GOOD-FELLOW being walking one night heard the excellent musicke of Tom Thumbs brave bag-pipe: he, remembering the sound (according to the command of King Obreon) went toward them. They, for joy that he was come, did circle him in, and in a ring did dance round about him. Robin Good-fellow, seeing their love to him, danced in the midst of them, and sung them this song TO THE TUNE OF *To him Bun.*

### THE SONG.

> Round about, little ones, quick and nimble,
> In and out wheele about, run, hop, or amble.
> Joyne your hands lovingly: well done, musition!
> Mirth keepeth man in health like a phisition.
> Elves, urchins, goblins all, and little fairyes
> That doe fillch, blacke, and pinch mayds of the dairyes;
> Make a ring on the grasse with your quicke measures,
> Tom shall play, and Ile sing for all your pleasures.

Pinch and Patch, Gull and Grim,
 Goe you together,
For you can change your shapes
 Like to the weather.
Sib and Tib, Licke and Lull,
 You all have trickes, too;
Little Tom Thumb that pipes
 Shall goe betwixt you.
Tom, tickle up thy pipes
 Till they be weary:
I will laugh, *ho, ho, hoh!*
 And make me merry.
Make a ring on this grasse
 With your quicke measures:
Tom shall play, I will sing
 For all your pleasures.

The moone shines faire and bright,
 And the owle hollows,
Mortals now take their rests
 Upon their pillows:
The bats abroad likewise,
 And the night raven,
Which doth use for to call
 Men to Deaths haven.
Now the mice peepe abroad,
 And the cats take them,
Now doe young wenches sleepe,
 Till their dreames wake them.
Make a ring on the grasse
 With your quicke measures:
Tom shall play, I will sing
 For all your pleasures.

 Thus danced they a good space: at last they left and sat downe upon the grasse; and to requite Robin Good-fellowes kindnesse, they promised to tell to him all the exploits that they were accustomed to doe: Robin thanked them and listned to them, and one begun to tell his trickes in this manner.

## The Trickes Of The Fayry Called Pinch.

AFTER THAT WEE have danced in this manner as you have beheld, I, that am called Pinch, do goe about from house to house: sometimes I find the dores of the house open; that negligent servant that left them so, I doe so nip him or her, that with my pinches their bodyes are as many colors as a mackrels backe. Then take I them, and lay I them in the doore, naked or unnaked I care not whether: there they lye, many times till broad day, ere they waken; and many times, against their wills, they shew some parts about them, that they would not have openly seene.

Sometimes I find a slut sleeping in the chimney corner, when she should be washing of her dishes, or doing something else which she hath left undone: her I pinch about the armes, for not laying her armes to her labor. Some I find in their bed snorting and sleeping, and their houses lying as cleane as a nasty doggs kennell; in one corner bones, in another eg-shells, behind the doore a heap of dust, the dishes under feet, and the cat in the cubbord: all these sluttish trickes I doe reward with blue legges, and blue armes. I find some slovens too, as well as sluts: they pay for their beastlinesse too, as well as the women-kind; for if they uncase a sloven and not unty their points, I so pay their armes that they cannot sometimes untye them, if they would. Those that leave foule shooes, or goe into their beds with their stockings on, I use them as I did the former, and never leave them till they have left their beastlinesse.

> But to the good I doe no harme,
> But cover them, and keepe them warme:
> Sluts and slovens I doe pinch,
> And make them in their beds to winch.
> This is my practice, and my trade;
> Many have I cleanely made.

## The Trickes Of The Fayry Called Pach.

ABOUT MID-NIGHT do I walke, and for the trickes I play they call me Pach. When I find a slut asleepe, I smuch her face if it be cleane; but if it be durty, I wash it in the next pisse-pot that I can finde: the balls I use to wash such sluts withal is a sows pancake, or a pilgrimes salve. Those that I find with their heads nitty and scabby, for want of combing, I am their barbers, and cut their hayre as close as an apes tayle; or else clap so much pitch on it, that they must cut it off themselves to their great shame. Slovens also that neglect their masters businesse, they doe not escape. Some I find that spoyle their masters horses for want of currying: those I doe daube with grease and soote, that they are faine to curry themselves ere they can get cleane. Others that for laysinesse will give the poore beasts no meate, I oftentimes so punish them with blowes, that they cannot feed themselves they are so sore.

> Thus many trickes I, Pach, can doe,
> But to the good I ne'ere was foe:
> The bad I hate and will doe ever,
> Till they from ill themselves doe sever.
> To helpe the good Ile run and goe,
> The bad no good from me shall know.

### The Tricks Of The Fairy Called Gull.

WHEN MORTALS keep their beds I walke abroad, and for my prankes am called by the name of Gull. I with a fayned voyce doe often deceive many men, to their great amazement. Many times I get on men and women, and so lye on their stomackes, that I cause their great paine, for which they call me by the name of Hagge, or Night-mare. Tis I that doe steale children, and in the place of them leave changelings. Sometime I also steale milke and creame, and then with my brothers Patch, Pinch, and Grim, and sisters Sib, Tib, Licke, and Lull, I feast with my stolne goods: our little piper hath his share in all our spoyles, but hee nor our women fayries doe ever put themselves in danger to doe any great exploit.

> What Gull can doe, I have you showne;
> I am inferior unto none.
> Command me, Robin, thou shalt know,
> That I for thee will ride or goe;
> I can doe greater things than these
> Upon the land, and on the seas.

### The Trickes Of The Fairy Cald Grim.

I WALKE with the owle, and make many to cry as loud as she doth hollow. Sometimes I doe affright many simple people, for which some have termed me the Blacke Dog of New-gate. At the meetings of young men and maydes I many times am, and when they are in the midst of all their good cheare, I come in, in some fearful shape, and affright them, and then carry away their good cheare, and eate it with my fellow fayries. Tis I that do, like a skritch-owle, cry at sicke mens windowes, which makes the hearers so fearefull, that they say, that the sicke person cannot live. Many other wayes have I to fright the simple, but the understanding man I cannot moove to feare, because he knowes I have no power to do hurt.

> My nightly business I have told,
> To play these trickes I use of old:
> When candles burne both blue and dim,
> Old folkes will say, Here's fairy Grim.
> More trickes then these I use to doe:
> Hereat cry'd Robin, *Ho, ho, hoh!*

### The Trickes Of The Women Fayries Told By Sib.

TO WALKE NIGHTLY, as do the men fayries, we use not; but now and then we goe to-gether, and at good huswives fires we warme and dresse our fayry children. If wee find cleane water and cleane towels, wee leave them money, either in their basons or in their shooes; but if wee find no clean water in their houses, we wash our children in their pottage, milke, or beere, what-ere we finde: for the sluts that leave not such things fitting, wee wash their faces and hands with a gilded childs clout, or els carry them to some river, and ducke them over head and eares. We often use to dwell in some great hill, and from thence we doe lend money to any poore man, or woman that hath need; but if they bring it not againe at the day appointed, we doe not only punish them with pinching, but also in their goods, so that they never thrive till they have payd us.

> Tib and I the chiefest are,
> And for all things doe take care.
> Licke is cooke and dresseth meate,
> And fetcheth all things that we eat:
> Lull is nurse and tends the cradle,
> And the babes doth dresse and swadle.
> This little fellow, cald Tom Thumb,
> That is no bigger than a plumb,
> He is the porter to our gate,
> For he doth let all in thereat,
> And makes us merry with his play,
> And merrily we spend the day.

Shee having spoken, Tom Thumb stood up on tip-toe and shewed himselfe, saying,

> My actions all in volumes two are wrote,
> The least of which will never be forgot.

He had no sooner ended his two lines, but a shepheard (that was watching in the field all night) blew up a bag-pipe: this so frighted Tom, that he could not tell what to doe for the present time. The fayries seeing Tom Thumbe in such a feare, punisht the shepheard with his pipes losse, so that the shepherds pipe presently brake in his hand, to his great amazement. Hereat did Robin Good-fellow laugh, *ho, ho, hoh!* Morning beeing come, they all hasted to Fayry Land, where I thinke they yet remaine.

> My hostesse asked me how I liked this tale? I said,
> it was long enough, and good enough to passe time
> that might be worser spent. I seeing her dry, called for
> two pots: she emptied one of them at a draught, and
> never breathed for the matter: I emptied the
> other at leisure; and being late I went
> to bed, and did dreame of this
> which I had heard.

FINIS.

$$15$$

# The Ancient True And Admirable History of Patient Grisel,

### A Poore Man's Daughter in France: Shewing How Maides, By Her Example, in their Good Behaviour May Marrie Rich Husbands; and Likewise Wives By their Patience and Obedience May Gaine Much Glorie

Written First in French,
And Therefore to French I Speake and Give Direction,
For English Dames will Live in no Subjection

But Now Translated into English,
And therefore Say Not So, for English Maids and Wives
Surpass the French in Goodnesse of Their Lives

RELATED IN ENGLISH BY *Chaucer's Clerk, this medieval tale was told earlier by Boccaccio and Petrarch. It is interesting because it teaches a moral value of obedience to a "superior" which is no longer considered valid for two reasons. First, the "superior" —a husband—is no longer considered necessarily a superior. A human being is judged, ideally at least, on merit, not on sex or economic status. The husband, unlike the wife, is rich and titled. Second, the story teaches obedience even if the superior is committing crimes. Presumably, he asks his wife to surrender their children for slaughter. Nowadays, if she complied, she would be judged as guilty as he. The story is a fascinating one to present to older children—or for adults to debate—on changes in moral values.*

*In the sixteenth and seventeenth centuries, it appeared several times as a ballad, a few times as a play, and also as a puppet show—Pepys reports that he saw it at Bartholomew Fair on August 30, 1667. Because of its long popularity in literary and oral tradition, it is included here.*

*Patient Grisel (version of 1619) is reprinted from* Chap-Books and Folk-Lore Tracts, *printed for the Villon Society, London, 1885.*

*The Historie of Patient Grisel,*
*made Marchionesse of Saluss,*
*in which is Exemplified the true Obedience and*
*Noble Behaviour of Vertuous Women*
*towards their Husbands.*

# CHAPTER I

*How the Marquesse of Saluss passed the time of his youth*
*without any desire of marriage, till he was requested by*
*the faire entreatie of a favorite, and other gentlemen, to*
*affect a wife, both for the good of the country and the*
*honour of himselfe; with his answer to the same.*

BETWEENE THE mountaines of Italy and France, towards the south, lyes the territory of Salus, a country flourishing with excellent townes and castles, and peopled with the best sort of gentles and peasants: amongst whom there lived not long since a nobleman of great hope and expectation, lord of the country, by name Gualter, Marquesse of Saluss; to whom, as the government appertained by right of inheritance, so their obedience attended by desert of his worthinesse.

He was young in yeeres, noble of lineage, and such attractive demeanour, that the best thought it a pleasure to bee commanded by him, and the worst grew more tractable by his good example: his delight was in hunting and hawking, and the pleasure of the time present extinguished the care of the time to come; for he thought not of mariage, nor to entangle himselfe with the inconveniences of a wife; till at last the people and noblemen of his country projected the contrary, as discontented to see him indisposed that way, and presaging a kind of prosperity to themselves, if by his mariage posteritie might arise to assure them the better how they might bestow their obedience hereafter. Whereupon they assembled together, and made one day amongst the rest a determiner of their resolutions, choosing out for their speaker a noble knight of great authority, faire demeanor, eloquent speech, and more inward with the Marquesse then any of the rest; who, thus acquainted with all their mindes, and prepared to utter his owne minde, took an opportunity to acquaint the renowned Marquesse with the matter.

Most honourable Sir, the great humanity extended towards us, of which I most especially have participated, hath thus emboldened me above others, to make a further triall of your patience, and forbearing my rudeness: not that there is any sufficiency or singularity in me above others, but in that heretofore I have found you so generous toward all, I make no question to finde you as gratious toward my selfe; and in that it hath pleased you to accept of our love, wee are proud againe to be under your obedience; wherein we shall rejoice the more, if you now accord to our request the sooner, which is, to marry without delay. The time passeth, and will not be recalled, your youth intreats it, and must not be denied; your country importunes it, and would not bee opposed; your neighbours desire it, and hope to bee satisfied; and all sorts request it, and wish it for your honour; for when age approacheth, death attends it at the heeles, and no man can tell when, or how it will fall upon him. Therefore wee humbly request you to accept our supplications, and accord to this importunity, that we may provide by your appointment a lady worthy of your honour and our subjection. In this wee are the more suppliant, because it will rebound so much to the good of your countrey, and the enlarging your renowne; for if it should so fall out (which God forbid) that you die without issue, we may lament the losse of our lord, but not redresse the complaints of the people: we shall want you that was al our comfort, but are sure of distresse to our everlasting trouble. If then you either love your selfe, or pity us, frame a heart to this impression, and leave not us to further feare and disquiet.

When the noble lord had thus apprehended the petition of his loving subjects, he resolved to answer them as gratiously as they had propounded the businesse with regard of duty, and so replied: My dearest friends, you have urged mee to a matter, in which as yet I have beene a mere stranger; for by nature I delight in liberty, and by custome continued my pleasures, both which must needs bee curbed by mariage, and restrained by taking a wife: notwithstanding, I cast awaie all doubts to pleasure you, and will thinke of no incombrances so you be satisfied. For though mariage hath many difficulties attending; especially, the feare of legitimation in our children, and suspicion of that honour which lies on our wives honesty, yet all shall be overcome with this resolution, that I shall please you in the same; for I am resolved, if anie good come for man's contentment by mariage, it is from God, to whom I submit this cause, and pray for the good successe of your wishes, that I may live to maintaine your peace, as well as my owne pleasure: and look wherein my contentment shall enlarge mine honour, your welfare shall be respected above my life; so that (beleeve it) I will satisfie your demands, and apply my selfe to the purpose. Only one thing I request at your hands; to take in worth my choice, and neither insult if she be a princesse of greatnes, nor repine if she be of meane estate; but love her because I have loved you, and regard her howsoever in that she is my wife; neither being curious nor inquisitive whom I will chuse, nor disaffected when it is past remedy.

When the company heard him out, and found him so willing to their satisfaction, they gave him thankes with one heart for his kinde admission, and answered with one tongue, he should not find them repugnant; but they would honor his wife as the princesse of the world, and be morigerous to him as the commander of their soules. Thus did this new report (like a messenger of glad tidings) fill all the marquisate with joy, and the palace with delight, when they understood their lord would marry, and in a manner heard the time appointed; for presently it was proclaimed through the countrey, and a day assigned for all commers to come to the court. The nobles prepared themselves in the best manner: the ladies spared no cost, either for ornaments of their bodies, or setting out their beauties; the gentles flocked to please their lord, and were brave to set out their owne greatnes: the citisens were rich in their neatnes, and handsome in their attire: the officers were formall in their showes, and sumptuous in their attendants; the countryman had his variety, and the verie peasant his bravery; in a word, al sorts gloried in the hope of that festivall, and every man's expectation attended the day of triumph. For never was such a preparation in Saluss before, nor such a confluence of people seene in that countrey; for besides the novelty, many forraine princes came to celebrate this mariage, and to shew their owne greatnes. Savoy was neare, and sent some from her snowie hills: France as neare, and sent others from her fruitful vines: Italy not far off, and sent many from her pleasant fields; and the ilands round about kept none at home that would come. Thus were his kinred invited, strangers admitted, his owne people entertained, and all sorts welcommed; but as yet no bride was seene, no woman named, no lady designed, no maid published, no wife knowne: onely the preparation was much, and the expectation greater.

All this while the Marquesse continued his hunting, and as he had accustomed, resorted much to a poore country village not farre from Salusse, where there dwelt as poore a countriman, named Janicole, overworne in yeares, and overcomne with distresse. But as it happens many times that inward graces doe moderate outward discommodities, and that God seasoneth poverty with contentment and their sufficient supportation, so had this poore man all his defects supplied in the admirable comfort of one onely daughter, so composed, as if nature determined a worke of ostentation. For such was her beauty in appearance, and vertue in operation, that it put judicious men to an extasie in the choice by comparison; but both united did heere grace each other, and when they pretended an action, it was all to go forward to perfection. And whereas in others this temporary blessing gave wings to desire to bee seene and knowne abroad, in her those innated vertues allaied the heat of all manner of passion, and breakings out of frailty. The viands they had were but meane, and the diet they kept was to satisfie nature: the time was over-ruled by their stomachs, and the ceremonies they used were thanks to God, and moderation in their repasts. The utensiles of the house were homely, yet hand-some in regard of their cleanlinesse: that bed which they had the ould man lay in, and the sweet daughter made shift with the ground. No day passed without prayers and praises to God (for was it not praiseworthy to have such grace in this disgrace), nor any night without taking account of the day passed.

Her exercise was to helpe her father in the morning, and drive forth her sheep in the day time: hee was at home making of nets, and shee abroad looking to her lambs: she was never heard to wish for any better, but to thank God it was no worse. No word of repining ever came from her mouth, or the least grudge from her heart: at night she folded her sheep and dressed her father's supper, then lay they downe to rest, and rested as well as in a bed of downe indeed. This was the glory of their poverty, and memory of their contentment.

But as fire will not be hid where there is matter combustible, so vertue will not be obscured where there be tongues and eares: nor could the Marquesse so hallow after his hawks and hounds, but report hallowed in his eare as fast this wonderment; inso-much that when it was confirmed by judicious relation he made it not dainty to be beholding to his owne experience: which when he saw concurring with fame, the miracle brought a kinde of astonishment; which continuing, the properties of such novelties, increased to meditation: and so comparing the rest with this rarity, he thought her a fit woman to make his wife, supposing that if she were vertuous by nature, she would not prove vicious by education; but rather as a diamond is a stone of the same value whether set in lead or horne, it must needs be of more excellency embellished with gold and enamell. In which resolution hee prepared his heart, and went forward with his businesse.

In the meane time the Court was daintily furnished, the plate prepared, the apparell magnificent, the coronet rich, the jewels precious, the ornaments exceeding, and all things befitting the magnificence of a prince and the dignities of a queen: only the nobles wondred, the ladies were amazed, the damsells marvelled, the gentles disputed, the people flocked, and all sorts attended to see who should possesse this wealth and bee adorned with these robes. Till at last the nuptial day came indeed: honour prepared the sumptuousness; fame divulged the glory; hymen invited the guests; magnificence adorned the roomes; the officers marshald the state, and all looked for a bride; but who she was the next chapter must discover.

## CHAPTER II

*How, after all this great preparation, the Marquesse of Saluss demanded Grisell of her poore father Janicola; and, espousing her, made her Marchionesse of Saluss.*

WHEN ALL THINGS were extended to this glorious shew, the Marquesse (as if he went to fetch his wife indeed) tooke with him a great company of earls, lords, knights, squires, and gentlemen, ladies, and attendants, and went from the palace into the countrey toward Janicolas house; where the faire mayd Grisel, knowing nothing of that which hapned, nor once dreaming of that which was to come, had made her house and selfe somewhat handsome, determining (with the rest of her neighbour virgins) to see this solemnity: at which instant arrived the Marquesse with all his gracious company, meeting with Grisel as shee was carrying two pitchers of water to her poore fathers house. Of whom (calling her by her name) he asked where her father was? She humbly answered, in the house. Goe then, said hee, and tell him I would speak with him. So the poore old man (made the poorer by this astonishment) came forth to the lord somewhat appauled, till the Marquesse, taking him by the hand, with an extraordinary chearefulnesse said, that he had a secret to impart unto him, and so, sequestering him from the company, spake these words:—Janicola, I know that you alwaies loved me, and am resolved that you doe not now hate me. You have been glad when I have been pleased, and will not now bee sorrowful if I bee satisfied: nay, I am sure, if it lie in your power, you will further my delight, and not bee a contrary to my request. For I intend to begge your daughter for my wife, and bee your sonne in lawe for your advancement. What saiest thou, man? wilt thou accept mee for a friend, as I have appointed thee for a father?

The poore ould man was so astonished, that he could not looke up for teares, nor speak a word for joy; but when the extasie had end, hee thus faintly replied:—My gracious soueraigne, you are my lord, and therefore I must accord to your will; but you are generous, and therefore I presume on your vertue; take her a Gods name, and make mee a glad father; and let that God, which raiseth the humble and meek, make her a befitting wife, and fruitful mother. Why then, replied the Marquesse, let us enter your house, for I must ask her a question before you. So hee went in, the company tarrying without in great astonishment: the faire maid was busied to make it as handsome as she could, and proud againe to have such a guest under her roofe; amazed at nothing but why hee should come so accompanied, and little conjecturing of so great a blessing approaching. But, at last, the Marquesse took her by the hand, and used these speeches: —To tell you this blush becomes you, it were but a folly; and that your modesty hath graced your comlines, may prove the deceit of words, and unbefitting my greatnes; but in a word, your father and I have agreed to make you my wife, and I hope you will not disagree to take me to your husband. For delay shall not intangle you with suspicion, nor two daies longer protract the kindnes; onely I must be satisfied in this, if your heart afford a willing entertainement to the motion, and your vertue a constancy to this resolution, not to repine at my pleasure in any thing, nor presume on contradiction, when I determine to command. For as amongst good souldiers, they must simply obey without disputing the businesse: so must vertuous wives dutifully consent withoute reproofe, or the least contraction of a brow. Therefore be advised how you answer, and I charge you take heed, that the tongue utter no more than the heart conceits. All this while Grisel was wondring at the miracle, had not religion told her that nothing was impossible to the commander of all things; which reduced her to a better consideration and thus brought forth an answere.

My gracious lord, I am not ignorant of your greatnesse, and know mine owne basenesse: there is no worth in me to be your servant, therefore there can be no desert to be your wife: notwithstanding, because God will be the author of miraculous accidents, I yeeld to your pleasure, and praise him for the fortune; onely this I will be bold to say, that your will shall be my delight, and death shall be more welcome unto mee then a word of displeasure against you.

This is sufficient, answered the great lord, and so most lovingly he took her by the hand, and brought her to the company, even before all his peeres and great ladies, and told them she should bee his wife, so that wherein they extended their love, reverence, and obedience toward her, he could exemplifie his regard, care, and diligence toward them. And because outward shewes doe sometimes grace befitting actions (lest her poverty and basenes might too much daunt their expectation, and seeme disgratious to their noblenes), he commanded them with a morall livelinesse to adorne her with the richest robes they had; so that it was a pleasure to see how the ladies bestird themselves, a delight to behould the severall services performed, the many hands about her, the jewels and pendants, the robes and mantles, the ornaments and coronets, the collanaes and chaines, with all other particulars and accoustrements, but when she was apparelled indeed, it was a ravishment exceeding report, and they which stomached her preferment were now delighted with her glory. Such a benefit hath beauty by nature, and gratiousnesse by nurture.

# CHAPTER III

## *How the Marquesse and Grisel were married together.*

AFTER THE LADIES had thus adorned poore Grisel with robes befitting her estate, the Marquesse and all the noble company returned to Saluss, and in the Cathedrall Church, in sight of the people, according to the fulnesse of religious ceremonies, they were espoused together, and with great solemnitie returned to the palace. Herein yet consisted the admiration, that no word of reproach was murmured, nor eie looked unpleasantly upon her; for by her wonderfull demeanour shee had gained so much of opinion that the basenes of her birth was not thought upon, and all her graces concurring made them verely beleeve shee was extracted of princely lineage: no man once supposed that shee could be Grisel, daughter to poore Janicola, but rather some creature metamorphosed by the powers of heaven: for besides the outward statelinesse and majesticall carriage of herselfe, the wonderfull modestie and exact symmetry of her countenance, the admirable beauty and extraordinary favor of her visage, her faire demeanour had a kinde of attraction, and her gratious words a sweet delivery; so that all that came to her were glad of their accesse, and they which went from her triumphed for their good speed: yea, report extended so far, that she was not onely visited by her owne lords and ladies with reverence, but attended on with strangers, who came from all quarters to see her and to bee beholding to their owne judgements; so that if the Marquesse loved her before for her own worth, he now reverenced her for others respect; the rather, because he found a blessing attending her presence, and all people pleased in the contract? For when any controversie hapned betweene himselfe and his nobles, she was so nobly minded, that what she could not obtaine by fair intreaty she yet mitigated by sweet perswasion. When any unkindnes hapned of forraine prince, shee urged those blessings of peace, and reasoned the matter with delightsom enforcement; and when the people were either complained of, or against, he marvelled from whence she had those pretty reasons to asswage his anger, and they verely beleeved shee was sent from heaven for their releefe. Thus was shee amiable to her lord, acceptable to her people, profitable to her country, a mirror of her sexe, a person priviledged by nature, and a wonder of the time, in which she did nothing out of time; so that the Marquesse was rather ravished than loving, and all his subjects resolved to obedience from her good example.

## CHAPTER IV

*How the lady Grisel was proved by her husband, who thus made triall of her patience.*

To OTHER BLESSINGS, in processe of time, there was added the birth of a sweet infant, a daughter, that rejoiced the mother, and gladded the father: the country triumphed, and the people clapped their hands for joy; for the Marquesse still loved her more and more, and they thought their lives not deere for her, if occasion served. Notwithstanding all this, Fortune hath still a tricke to checke the pride of life, and prosperity must be seasoned with some crosses, or eke it would taint and corrupt us too much: whereupon, the Marquesse determined now to prove his wife, and make triall of her vertues indeed; and so taking a convenient season, after the childe was fully weaned, he one day repaired secretly to her chamber, and (seeming halfe angry) thus imparted his mind.

Although, Grisel, this your present fortune hath made you forget your former estate, and that the jollity of your life overswayeth the remembrance of your birth, yet neither is it so with me, nor my nobles; for I have some occasion of distasting, and they great cause of repining, in that they must be subject to one so base, and have still before their eyes our children of such low degree; so that though (for my sake) they make good semblance of the present, yet are they resolved never to suffer any of our posterity to rule over them; of which, as they have disputed with mee, I cannot chuse but forewarne you. Therefore, to prevent this discontentment betweene us, and to maintaine that peace which must corroborate my estate, I must needes yeelde to their judgements, and take away your daughter from you, to preserve their amity: the thing I know must be displeasing to nature, and a mother cannot well indure such a losse; but there is now no remedy: only make use of your first resolutions, and remember what you promised me at the beginning of our contract.

The lady, hearing this sorrowfull preamble, and apprehending the Marquesse resolution, to her griefe, (although every word might have beene as arrowes in her sides) yet admitting of the temptation, and disputing with herselfe to what end the vertues of patience, modesty, forbearance, fortitude, and magnanimity were ordained, if they had not subjects to worke upon, and objects to looke after, thus replyed.

My lord, you are my soveraigne, and all earthly pleasures and contentments of my life come from you, as the fountaine of my happinesse, and therefore please your selfe, and (beleeve it) it is my pleasure you are pleased; as for the child, it is the gift of God, and yours. Now he that gives may take away, and as wee receive blessings from heaven, so must we not dote on them on earth, lest by setting our minds too much upon them, wee cannot set off our hearts when they are taken from us; only one thing I desire, that you remember I am a mother; and if I burst not out into passion for her losse, it is for your sake I am no more perplexed, and so you shall ever find mee a wife befitting your desires.

When the Marquesse saw her constancy, and was in a manner pleased with her modest answere, hee replied not at all at that time; for his heart was full, and what betweene joy and feare he departed: joy that so great vertue had the increase of goodnesse, feare that he had presumed too farre on such a trial. But resolved in his businesse, hee went to put it to the adventure.

# CHAPTER V

*The Marquesse sent a varlet for his daughter; but privately disposed of her with his sister, the Dutchesse of Bologna de Grace, who brought her up in all things befitting the childe of so great a person.*

Nᴏᴛ ʟᴏɴɢ ᴀꜰᴛᴇʀ this sad conference between the Marquesse and his lady, hee called a faithfull servant unto him; such a one as the poet talks of, *propter fidem et taciturnitatem dilectum*, to whom hee imparts this secrecy, and with severall instructions, what hee truly meant to do with the child, sent him to his wife with an unsavory message, which yet hee delivered in this manner.

I had not now come to you, most noble lady, though that power commanded me which hath my life in subjection, if I had not more relied upon your wisdome and vertue, than feared death it selfe. Therefore I crave pardon if I am displeasing in my message, and seeme cruell (as it were) in tearing your flesh from your sides, by bereaving you of this your daughter: for hee hath appointed it that must not bee gainsaid, and I am a messenger that cannot bee denied. But yet with what unwillingnes (God knowes my soule) in regard that you are so respected amongst us, that wee think of nothing but what may delight you, and talk not a word but of your merit and worthinesse.

When she had heard him out, remembring the conference the Marquesse had with her, and apprehending there was no disputing in a matter remedilesse, especially with a messenger, shee resolved it was ordained to dy; and although shee must now (as it were) commit it to a slaughter-house, whereby any woman in the world might with good becomming have burst out into some passion, and well enough shewed a distracted extasie, yet recollecting her spirits, and reclaiming those motives of nature already striving in her bowels, shee the tooke childe in her armes, and with a mothers blessing and sweetned kisses, the countenance somewhat sad, and the gesture without any violent excruciation, delivered it unto the fellow, not once amazed or distempred, because her lord would have it so, and shee knew not how to have it otherwise: only she said, I must, my friend, intreat one thing at your hands, that out of humanity and Christian observation, you leave not the body to bee devoured of beasts or birds, for it is worthy of a grave in her innocency, and Christian buriall, though shee were but my daughter alone.

The fellow having received the childe, durst not tarry for feare of discovery (such impression had her words made already), but returned with it to his maister, not leaving out the least circumstance of her answer, nor any thing that might enlarge her renown and constancy.

The Marquesse, considering the great vertue of his wife, and looking on the beauty of his daughter, began to enter into a kinde of compassion, and to retract his wilfulnesse; but at last resolution won the field of pity, and having (as he thought) so well begunne, would not so soone give over, but with the same secrecy hee had taken her from his wife, hee sent it away to his sister, the Dutchess of Bologna, with presents of worth, and letters of gratification, containing in them the nature of the businesse, and the manner of her bringing up, which she accordingly put in practice, receiving her neece with joy, and instructing her with diligence; so that it soone appeared under what a tutelage shee was, and whose daughter shee might be. For her pregnancy learned whatsoever they taught her, and the grace she added, quickly discovered that honour had confederated with nature to make her the offspring of such a mother.

# CHAPTER VI

*The Marquesse, not contented with this proofe, tooke away also
her sonne, in which adversity (with other additions)
she shewed an extraordinary patience.*

AFTER THIS TEMPEST was overpast, the rage whereof might easily have broken the tender sides of poore Grisels barke (for shee verely beleeved that her daughter was slaine), the Marquesse still lay in waite for the trial of his wife, watching every opportunity which might acquaint him with her discontentments; especially if he might understand whether she complained of his rigorousnesse and unkindnesse, or no: but when he not only was advertised of her constancy and faire demeanour, but saw (by experience) that shee was neither elated in prosperity nor dejected in adversity; when hee perceiued so great a temperature betweene the joy of her advancement and the sorrow for her trouble, he wondred at her constancy; and the rather, because her love and observation toward him continued with that sweetnes, and had such delectable passages, that his heart was set on fire againe, and hee knew not how to allay the extreamities of his joy. In this manner passed foure yeeres, wherein she overpassed all of her kinde, and he thought it a donative from heaven to have such a wife. At last nature bestird herselfe againe, and made her a happy mother of a faire sonne; the joy whereof led the whole country into the house of praier and thanksgiving, and brought them home againe by cresset-light and bonfires, so that she well perceived how acceptable she was to her people and beloved of her husband. Notwithstanding, with the same water that drave the mill hee drowned it, and made her still beleeve the contrary; for after two yeeres, that the childe was past the danger of a cradle, and the trouble of infancy, he tooke occasion once again to inflict upon the vertuous Grisel a new punishment, erecting his building upon the old foundation.

You knowe, saith hee, what former contentions I have had with my nobility about our marriage; not that they can lay any imputation on you or your worthy behavior, but on my fortune and disasterous affection to match myselfe so meanly: wherein yet their forward exprobation was rebated, all the while we either had no children, or that they supposed that which we had to be taken from us; all which ariseth out of the error of ambition (which in a manner is carelesse of vertue) respecting nothing but a high progeny. So that ever since this child was borne there hath passed many secret grudgings, and unkinde speeches against it, as if it were a disparagement to their greatnesse to have a lord of so meane parentage, and the country to be subject to the grand child of Janicola, whom you see never since our marriage they would admit to place of honor, or to overtop them by way of association, nor will suffer this my Gualter, though it carry the fathers name, to rule over them. Therefore, to allay the heat of these present fires, and to preserve the peace of my estate (by preventing the mischief of future troubles), I am resolved to settle my contentment, and to deale with your sonne as I have dealt with your daughter. And of this I thought it good to advertise you, as a preparative for patience, lest sorrow should distract you with oversuddennesse.

Now you ladies and dames of these times, that stand upon tearmes of spirit and greatnesse of heart (some will have it courage and magnanimity of minde), that are affrighted at the character of a foole, and silly poore soule; I speake not of strumpets, or of such as are willing to brand themselves with the impurity of uncleannesse, and dare out of impudency or cunning tell their husbands to their faces they will go where they list, and do what they please, but of such that under that impregnable target of honestie are yet so impatient at every distemperature, that they dare answer taunt for taunt: yea, like viragoes indeed, offer the first blow, though a horrible confusion follow, what would you have answered this lord? or with what fire-works would you have made your approaches unto him? I will not tarry for your answere, lest I pull the old house in peeces, and so, though I scape the timber, I may be crushed with the rubbish; but I will now anticipate (or prevent) all objections by telling you what faire Grisel said; and if there bee hope of reformation, insert it as a caution to divert you from your naturall fiercenes.

When shee had heard him out, though to the griefe of her soule, she conceived the murther of her childe, and that the apprehension renewed the sorrow of her daughters losse; yet would she give no way to such distemperature, that either hee should have cause to suspect her patience, or shee herselfe the temptation of disquiet, and therefore thus replied:—My lord, I have many times told you, that my soule rejoiceth in nothing but in your reposednes, for you are the lord of me and this infant; and though I could bee contented to shew myselfe a mother in his education, and bring him now and then unto you as the pledge of our loves, yet are you the commander of my vowes, and I will rectifie all disordered appetites by the rule of your pleasure. Take him then, a Gods name, and if hee be marked for death, it is but the common brand of all creatures; nay, if the mother may be a sacrifice of propitiation to appease your disquiet, never was lamb so meek, nor holocaust so willing to bee offred. For, what may bee comprehended under the titles of father, kinred, children, friends, life, pleasure, honours, and contentment, are all comprised under your love, and the society of a husband. Do with mee, then, what you please: the body shall serve your turne while it lives, and the soule attend you after death.

Here was an answer to pacifie the tyrants of Sicilie, and put a man quite out of his tract of proving such a wife! Yet the Marquesse onely made use of it to rejoice in the assurance of her goodness, and went the rather forward in his dangerous course of temptation.

# CHAPTER VII

*The Marquesse, resolute to prove his wife further, sendeth for*
*his son, and disposeth of him*
*as he had done of his daughter.*

As THIS PATIENT and wonderfull lady was one day sporting with her infant, like an untimely tempest (spoiling the beauty of some new rooted plants) did this messenger of death interpose himselfe between her recreation, making the hollow demand of her sonne worse than the noise of a schrich-owle over a sick mans bed: yet (as if there were a conscience in disquieting her greatnes, or if you will, her goodnes) he came forward with preambles and apologies, insinuating, with craving pardon, the authority of a lord, the duty of a servant, the terrour of death, the circumstance of obedience, and all other enforcements which might either excuse a messenger, or make the message of it selfe without blame. What should I enlarge a discourse of terrour? it is a curtesie to conclude a mischiefe with quicknes. Hee was not so sudden in his demand, as shee was ready in her dispatch, for she presently blest the child, kissed it, crossed it, adorned it, and delivered it to the executioner: onely with the same enforcement shee pleaded, as shee had spoken of in the behalfe of her daughter, not to see it perish for lack of a buriall, or devoured for want of a grave.

In this manner, and with this report, hee returned to his lord, who had still more cause of amazement, and lesse reason to trouble such a creature, had not his wilfulnes put him forward to make an end of his businesse, and taught him still variety of trying this gold in the fire. But for the time hee sent likewise this childe to his sister, the Duchesse of Bologna (yet some will have her but Countesse of Paniche), who, understanding her brothers minde, brought up both these children in such a fashion, that though no man knew whose children they were, yet they imagined whose they might bee; that is, the son and daughter of some prince, or other potentate, willing to have his children brought up to the best purpose, and befitting their birth and honour.

The ordering of this businesse in this sort made the Marquesse once againe settle himselfe in Saluss, where he kept open house to all comers, and was proud of nothing so much as the honour of his wife, and the love of his people: for although he had thus tried her patience and constancy, giving her more than sufficient cause of anguish and perturbation, yet coulde he not finde fault, or had the least demonstration of offence, but still she loved him more and more, and was so observingly dutifull and cautelous of displeasure, that many times he grew enamored of that he might command, and seemed passionate in the distractions of over-joy. Nor could the length of time make this love wearisome, for all they had lived thus a dozen years together; onely shee got the hand of him in the opinion of the people, who by this beganne to whisper against his unkindnes, that had married so vertuous a woman, and bereaved her of two children; so that if they were slaine, it was a murther, if otherwise, it was unkindnesse. For though shee were poore Janicolas daughter by birth, yet she might come from heaven for her vertue, and was sure to go thither for her piety. Notwithstanding these breakings out, which came often to the eares of his honour, such was her moderation and his government, that they only whisperd the same on her behalfe, and contented themselves with the expectation of future good, as they had the fruition of present happinesse, not meddling with the same further, than in the commiseration of her, and still acknowledging their duty to him; so that although hee knew shee might this way understand his former reasons of taking away her children, that it was but a devise, and that there were some other motives, which procured this unkindnes, yet was he still obstinate to exercise her patience, and conceit beat out another plot of offence on the anvill of a loving, yet most hardned heart.

# CHAPTER IX

### The Marquesse, to try his lady further, made her beleeve hee would marry another wife.

SOME DOZEN YEARS were passed since the Marquesse of Saluss had sent his daughter to Bologna, to his sister (as you have heard), who was by this time growne to that beautie, comelinesse, and perfection, that her fame busied all Europe; and the lady Grisel, her mother, was made acquainted with her excellency, whereupon, he very strangely sent to Rome, by a messenger of trust, for counterfeit letters to marrie [t]his paragon, and to bee dispensed from his first wife. Which was so effectually dispatched, that the messenger soone returned with the approbation of his request, and hee himselfe had many allegations in readinesse to excuse the matter, intimating the good of the countrie, and the continual desire of his people for the alteration; which, although it was far from probability, because they pitied their ladies distresse, and rather repined against their lords inconstancy, yet it served his turne for the time, and he thereupon erected the frame of this second marriage. By this time is the faire Grisel acquainted with the businesse, and troubled at the misfortune; but having many times plaied the wanton with affliction, she resettled herself to endure whatsoever should be imposed; so that when she came to the proofe, indeed, nothing affronted her constancy nor humbled her lower then her owne vertue had taught her the way.

In the mean while, the Marquesse had under hand sent to the Count of Paniche and his sister, to bring him his children with all the pompe and glory they could prepare, with caution not to discover their names, and to be at a day appointed at Saluss: so that it passed for current all over the country that a lady, a yong, brave, and gallant lady, of great lineage, and greater worth, of high renown and mighty affinity, was comming into Saluss to be espoused to the Marquesse, and that they were already come out of Bologna de Grace, a whole dayes journey forward, with such a troope and company that it was a shew of magnificence, and a spectacle of delight. For amongst the rest there was a young lord, not fully eight yeere old, whose bravery and gallantnesse drewe all mens eyes with admiration toward him, had not the lady divided the gazing, and shared with their opinion. For, besides her riches and outward ornaments, her youth (as not fully thirteene) and upright comelinesse, her bewty and gracious behauiour, she was of extraordinary stature, and majestike presence.

These things thus disposed and handsomely carried, the Marquesse tooke an opportunity thus to speak to the disconsolate Grisel before all his people. In times past, I confesse, you deserved my love, and notwithstanding the disparity betweene us, I thought it well bestowed upon you; nay, I cannot now impute any ill desert unto you: notwithstanding, for some reasons to myselfe best knowne, of which I have made the holy father acquainted, I am resolved to take another wife; who, as you heare, is on the way hitherward already: wherefore I would advise you to retire to your fathers cotage, till you heare further from me.

Alas! my lord, replied the sweet soule, I ever disputed the matter with reason, that there was no equality betweene so great magnificence and my humiliation, and in the greatest assurance of my prosperity, reputed my selfe a vassaile and handmaid, proud of nothing but my owne readinesse to be at your command, and your willingnes to employ mee in your affaires; so that, I take God to my witnes, I scarce trusted my selfe with the name of a wife, when I was in the best assurance. Therefore, I must acknowledge what you have heretofore vouchsafed as a part of great bounty, and the very fruits of your generousnes. As for returning to my poore fathers house, I am most willing; and there, as you please, like a forlorne widow will spend the rest of my dayes; yet remember I was your wife, espoused orderly, and you have had children by mee, so that if I there dye, I must yet dye the widow of such a lord, and for honors sake be so reputed. As for your new spouse, God grant her many daies of comfort, and you many yeeres of joy, that you may live in reciprocall delight one with another, and intertaine no worse contentment than poore Grisel accustomed. As for my dowry I brought, I brought only my selfe, and will have no more back againe, which was faith, love, reverence, poverty and virginity; for, as I came naked from my fathers house, I am contented to return so againe. Your jewels are in the wardrobe, and even the ring you married me withal, in the chamber: of this I weare, I shall quickly be disrobed, and if there be any further misery appointed, my patience can endure it, if your pleasure impose it; onely in recompence of my virginitie, I request a poore smocke to hide that wombe from public overlooking that was once so private to so great a prince; and because it was the bed of your infants, let it not bee the scorne of your people, but give mee leave thus to goe out of the palace, that hereafter times may wonder how quietly a woman yeelded to so great a change. Nay, let no man shed a teare, I must bee more naked than so; for though the wife of a Marquesse while I lived, and the widow when I died, yet am I not too good for a grave, but in despight of pride must return to dust and ashes.

Did I say before, they began to weep? I can assure you, when she had done, they roared out-right; yea, the Marquesse himselfe shed so many teares that he was faine to retire, and commanded the smock she had begged to be sent unto her, that shee might prosecute the enterprise, and he determine his businesse, as he had constantly projected.

# CHAPTER VIII

### How the patient Grisel was disrobed of her apparell, and restored all she had (except one poore smocke) to the Marquesse.

BEFORE I PROCEED any further in this wonderfull discovery, I am sure two things will bee objected against mee: first, the impossibility of the story; secondly, the absurdity of the example. For the story I answer, that therefore it was thus published and connected together, for the rarity of the businesse, and the sweetnes of the successe, nor is it any way stranger than many Roman passages, and Grecian discourses. For the application, it is both necessary and befitting; for whereas in the condition of women, amongst many other, there bee two especiall errours against the modesty of their sex, and quietnes of their husbands, videlicet, superiority and desire of liberty (I name not irregular behaviour, household inconveniences, and domesticks strife), this one example (as Hercules did the serpents) strangles them both in the cradle, and though it cannot prevent, yet will it exprobate the fault. First concerning superiority. I hope the instances of scripture are not made canonicall to no purpose, and out of reason and naturall inforcement: what a filthinesse is it to a generous spirit, to have a woman so presumptuous as to take an account of her husband's actions and businesse? Wherein many times they are so peremptory, that I have seene them enter the rooms of privacy, where secret businesses of strangers have been imparted, and were to be discussed, nor hath this been done with a lovely insinuation, or cunning excuse of longing, or willingness to be instructed, or other pretty inducements to permission, but with a high commanding voice, and impudent assurances of their owne worth: yea, I have knowne them breake open letters before they came to their husbands' overlooking, and have wondred even at souldiers themselves, that would give way to such indecency. Againe, to be counter checked in this wilfulnes, what clamours have beene raised! what tumults and discomforts occasioned! that instead of awful obedience and delightsome affability, they have burst out into outragiousnes, commanded teares of mischeife, and threatned suspicious revenges. But let them soile themselves in the filthinesse of this humour never so much. I say plainely, that though their husbands were fooles by nature, yet is it not befitting for a wife to discover the same, or over-rule in forren affaires, I meane matters which concerne them not: for there is no great man so weake but hath councell and supportation of inferior officers, nor mean man so sottish but hath friends or servants in the dispatch of his businesse. Secondly, concerning the desire of liberty: oh, hellish device of the divell, and fearefull custome both of France and England! I hope he that knowes the fashions of the East, of Muscovy, Spain, Italy, and the Mores, understands that no married wife goes abroad but to honorable purposes; and it is an introduction to death to salute any stranger, or be seene in private conference. For, in true understanding, what businesse should any man have with my wife three houres together in private? or why, without my leave, and that upon good grounds, should shee wander in publike? I speake not to overthrow noble societies, generous entertainment, familiar invitations, curteous behaviour, charitable welcomes, honest recreations, or peradventure, the imparting of private businesse; but meerly against foppish wantonesse, idle talke, suspicious meetings, damnable play-hunting, disorderly gaming, unbefitting exercises, and in a word, all such things as tend to obscenity and wickednes; in which (say what women can), if there be not a moderation by nature, there must be an inforcement by judgement; and that woman that will not be ruled by good councell must be over-ruled by better example,—of which, this now in hand (of Lady Grisel) is a mirror, and transparent chrystall to manifest true vertue, and wifely duty indeed; and so I come to the wonder of her obedience.

After the Marquesse was resolved to the last act of her tryall, and had sent her the smocke shee demanded, amongst all the lords, knights, ladies, and other company, she presently disrobed her selfe, and went, so accompanied, from the palace to her father's cottage, who, as you have heard (for divers reasons), was only kept from want, but never advanced out of the same.

The company could not choose but weepe and deplore the alteration of fortune; she could not choose but smile, that her vertue was predominant over passion: they exclaimed against the cruelty of her lord, she disclaimed the least invective against him: they wondred at so great vertue and patience, she resolved them they were exercises befitting a modest woman: they followed her with true love and desire to doe her good, she thanked them with a true heart, and request to desist from any further deploring of her estate.

By this time they approached the house, and the poore old man, Janicola, acquainted with the hurli-burly, came out to see what the matter was. And finding it was his daughter in her smocke, and in so honourable a company, bemoaning her distresse, he quickly left them all unspoke unto, and ran in for those poore robes, which were formerly left in the house; with which hee quickly arayed her, and told her before them all, that now shee was in her right element, and, kissing her, bad her welcom. The company was as much astonished at his moderation as at her constancie, wondring how nature could bee so restrained from passion, and that any woman had such grace to be so gracious; in which amaze, not without some reprehension of fortune, and their lord's cruelty, they left her to the poverty of the cell, and returned themselves to the glory of the palace, where they recounted to the Marquesse the strangenesse of the businesse, and the manner of the accidents, and shee continued in her first moderation and indefatigable patience, the poore father onely laughing to scorne the miseries and sodaine mutabilitie of humane condition, and comforting his daughter in her well-begun courses of modesty and reposednesse.

Not long after approched the Countesse of Paniche, or, if you will, Duchesse of Bologna, with her glorious company and beautifull lady, sending word before hand that she would be at Saluss such a day: whereupon the Marquesse sent a troope to welcome her, and prepared the court for her intertainment; the bruit of which yet had not so equall a passage, but divers contrarious opinions thus bandied themselves; some absolutely condemnied the inconstancie of the lord, others deplored the misfortune of the lady, some repined to see a man so cruell against so great worthinesse, others exemplified her praises to all eternitie; some were transported with the gallant youth and comelinesse of this new bewtifull virgine, others presumed to parallell the faire Grisel, but that shee had stepped a little before her in yeeres; some harped upon her great nobilitie and high lineage, others compared the former wife's vertue and true wisdome; some excused their lord, by the love to his countrey, others excused the lady by the nature of the adversitie, untill the approach of the faire virgine and the young noble man in her company extinguished all former conceits, and set them to a new worke, concerning this spectacle, wherein the young lady and her brave brother had such pre-eminence. Nor knewe the Earle of Paniche himselfe, or any of the company on either side, that they were his owne children by Grisel, but meerly strangers, and designed for this new mariage. So the great Marquesse made good semblance, and with his accustomed courtlinesse welcomed them all to the palace.

The very next morning (or, if you will, the day before), he sent a messenger for Grisel to come unto him in the very same manner as shee was; who protracted no time, but presently attended her lord: at her approach he was somewhat appalled, but yet setting (as wee say) the best foot forward, hee thus proceeded:

The lady, Grisel, with whom I must marrie, will bee here to-morrow by this time, and the feast is prepared accordingly: now, because there is none so well acquainted with the secrets of my palace, and disposition of my selfe as you, I would have you, for all this base attire, addresse your wisdome to the ordering of the businesse, appointing such officers as is befitting, and disposing the roomes according to the degrees and estate of the persons. Let the lady have the priviledge of the mariage chamber, and the young lord the pleasure of the gallery: let the rest be lodged in the courts, and the better sort upon the sides of the garden: let the viands be plentifull, and the ceremonies maintained: let the showes bee sumptuous, and the pastimes as it becommeth; in a word, let nothing be wanting, which may set forth my honour, and delight the people.

My lord, saith shee, I ever told you I took pleasure in nothing but your contentment, and whatsoever might consort to your delight, therein consisted my joy and happinesse: therefore, make no question of my diligence and duty in this, or any other thing which it shal please you to impose upon me. And so like a poore servant shee presently addressed herselfe to the businesse of the house, performing all things with such a quicknes and grace that each one wondred at her goodnesse and faire demeanour, and many murmured to see her put to such a triall. But the day of entertainement is now comme, and when the faire lady approached, her very presence had almost extinguished the impression of Grisels worthinesse; for some inconstant humourists gave way to the alteration, not blaming the Marquesse for such a change. But when the strangers were made acquainted with the fortune of Grisel, and saw her faire demeanour, they could not but esteeme her a woman of great vertue and honour, being more amased at her patience then at the mutability of mans conditions; till at last shee approached the lady, and taking her by the hand, used this speech.

Lady, if it were not his pleasure, that may command to bid you welcome, yet me thinks there is a kinde of over-ruling grace from nature in you, that must exact a respect unto you. And as for you, young lord, I can say no more, but if I might have my desires satisfied in this world, they should be imploied to wish you well, and to endeavour all things for your entertainement indeed. To the rest I afford what is befitting, desiring them, that if any deficiency abate their expectation, they would impute it either to my ignorance, or negligence; for it is the pleasure of him, in whose will is all my pleasure, that in all sufficiency you should have regard and suppliment. And so shee conducted them to their severall chambers, where they reposed themselves awhile, till the time of dinner invited them to repast. When all things were prepared, and the solemnity of placing the guests finished, the Marquesse sent for Grisel, and rising on his feet, took her by the hand before them all, erecting his body, and elating his voice in this manner: You see the lady is heere I meane to marry, and the company gloriously prepared to witnes the same; are you therefore contented that I shall thus dispose of my selfe, and do quietly yeeld to the alteration?

My lord, replied she before them all, wherein as a woman I might be faulty, I will not now dispute; but because I am your wife, and have devoted my selfe to obedience, I am resolved to delight in nothing but your pleasure; so that if this match be designed for your good, and determined by your appointment, I am much satisfied, and more than much contented. And for you, lady, I wish you the delights of your marriage and the honour of your husband, many yeares of happinesse, and the fruits of a chaste wedlock: only, gracious lord, take heed of one thing; that you trie not this new bride as you have done your ould wife; for she is yong, and peradventure of another straine, and so may want of that patience and government which I, poore I, have endured.

Till this he held out bravely; but nature overcomming resolution, and considering with what strange variety his unkindnesse had passed, hee could not answere a word for teares, and all the company stood confounded at the matter, wondring what would be the end of the businesse, and the successe of the extasie. But to draw them out of their doubts, the next chapter shall determine the controversie.

# CHAPTER X

*The oration of the Marquesse to his wife, and the discovery of her children, to her great joy, and the contentment of all the company.*

AFTER A LITTLE reducement of his passion, and that time and further meditation had disposed his senses to their perfect estate, the Marquesse graciously answered:—

Thou wonder of women, and champion of true vertue! I am ashamed of my imperfections, and tyred with abusing thee. I have tryed thee beyond reason, and thou hast forborne mee beyond modestie: beleeve it, therefore, I will have no wife but thy selfe, and when God hath thought thee too good for the earth, I will (if it bee not too much superstition) pray to thee in heaven. Oh! 'tis a pleasure to be acquainted with thy worth, and to come neere thy goodnes maketh a man better than himselfe. For without controversie, except thou hadst beene sent from above, thou couldst never have acted a goddesses part belowe: and therefore, seeing I have used thee so unkindly heeretofore, I protest never to disquiet thee heereafter: and wherein my cruelty extended against thee in bereaving thee of thy children, my love shall now make amends in restoring thy daughter. For this new bride is shee; and this wanton her brother. Thank this great lady (my sister) for their bringing up, and this man (you knowe him well enough) for his secrecy. Bee not amased at the matter: I have related a truth, and will confirme it on my honour; only sit downe till the dinner is done, and bid the company welcome in this poore attire; for the sun will break through slender clouds, and vertue shine in base array. I could much dilate the matter, but it is time to end, lest the circumstances will never end.

This device of the Marquesses, of kissing her so lovingly, and setting her downe by him so discreetly, did much good; for the company had time to dispute of the miracle, and the yong lady reason to prepare her obedience; which, no sooner was the dinner finished, but shee as soone performed, nothing thought upon but joy at the matter, and wonder at the accident; every one pleased to see such a unity of goodnes, and all delighted to have a businesse so well concluded. But seeing time had unclasped a booke of such jollity, there was now no further disputing, for the ladies flocked about her to attend her into the chamber, where the yong princesse her daughter was as ready as the best to apparell her, so that when shee came amongst them againe she shined like the sun after a tempest, and seemed more glorious, because her continued modesty kept her from all insulting and vaine-glorious bravery.

Thus was the Marquesse invested, as it were, with a new blessednes, and she continued in her ould constancy; onely admired by every one for her patience and sufferings, and all aplauding their reconcilement, blessing her, and the people proud they had such a lord to obey: especially satisfied when the poore Janicola was advanced to the councell, and made governor of his palace; wherein he behaved himselfe so well that for ten yeares hee still lived as he had been bred, a courtier, and did with the memory of a good report. Grisel lasted thirty yeares after him, and all went to their graves in good time, the country renowned over the world for their admirable government, and famosed for their extraordinary wonder.

*Non est ulla difficultas (ut ita dicam) neque passio, neque calamitas dira, cujus non sufferre queat pondus hominis natura.*—Euripides Orestei.

FINIS.

# 16

# The Famous History
# Of the Seven Champions
# of Christendom

## SELECTIONS

THE SEVEN CHAMPIONS, *part of the quest literature, is descended from a medieval romance,* Bevis of Hampton. *Both yarns, with their giants, dragons, satyrs, witches, enchanted gardens, magicians, and miracles—and an overall purpose of saving the world for Goodness—belong to the realm of Faerie. Though Richard Johnson gives his version seven protagonists, they really are all aspects of the leading figure, St. George. George is Everyman questing after a full life, loving a beautiful maiden, performing his duties, and finally, laying down his burdens: returning to his home town, Coventry, he "presented them with the dragon's head, then from the abundance of blood that issued from his deep wounds, and their continuous bleeding, he was forced to yield up his breath." One is reminded of the end of other English heroes, including Arthur and Robin Hood.*

*The action moves with the same racy quality as its ancient model. Descriptions are vivid and detailed. George, a direct descendant of Aeneus, has three nurses. At the age of fourteen, he is guarded by twelve Satyrs. An enchantress shows him six imprisoned knights, who turn out to be the champions with whom he will be associated in exploits in England, and the Middle and Far East. A dragon killed by St. George has been eating virgins each day for twenty-four years until "there is not now one virgin left throughout Egypt but the King's daughter." The dragon which George fights is fifty feet long. (Bevis had only a thirty-foot dragon to contend with.) George is almost vanquished by the dragon until he eats an orange. His horse, Bayard, is also revived with orange juice. A jealous suitor of the King's daughter, auburn-haired Sabra, attacks George with twelve knights, and George kills them all. George and Sabra get nosebleeds as an extrasensory warning of coming dangers. They first plight their love under a bower of jasmine trees.*

*Imprisoned in Persia, George wraps his amber-colored hair around his arms to protect them and sticks them down the throats of two hungry lions, pulling out their hearts. In the country of the Amazons, George rescues the girls from a deformed monster thirty feet tall, his head three times larger than the head of an ox, and his eyes bigger than two pewter dishes. His teeth "stand out of his mouth more than a foot." He then goes to sleep on a bed framed with ebony-wood, overhung with many pendants of gold. The tick is stuffed with the down of turtle doves, the sheets are of Median silk over which is thrown a rich quilt stuffed with cotton, covered with damask, and stitched with threads of gold.*

*The novel contains constant echoes of thoughts characteristic of the Renaissance and familiar to readers of Shakespeare and Donne. A bed of violets is the scene for a love* episode as in Donne's "Extasie." Babes have their brains dashed out (the image recalls Lady Macbeth). Eyes are "the twinkling lamps of heaven," a Petrarchan conceit remindful of Romeo's description of the eyes of Juliet. Homer's Circe image, found in Spenser's Faerie Queene, and elsewhere, appears when a Persian necromancer causes the champions, except George, to be enchanted with evil spirits in the likeness of enticing damsels. Defeated, the necromancer prefaces his suicide by an eloquent warning to all those who would control the lives of others.

The novel breathes the spirit of centuries of English history. With its rapid action and lively descriptions and bright and positive approach to problems, it still is appealing. It was published several times in America in various editions: in Amherst, New Hampshire in 1799; in Wilmington, Delaware in 1804; and in a chapbook edition in New York in 1830.

In order to make it possible for the reader to make a scholarly comparison of a seventeenth-century edition and a more modern text, we are including the first chapter of a Black Letter copy published in London in 1616 and preserved in The David McCandless McKell Collection, The Ross County Historical Society, Chillicothe, Ohio. Together with this text, we are including the first four chapters from a mid-nineteenth-century text published in London by James Blackwood & Co. Aside from some modernization of words or phraseology and minor changes in chapter divisions, the more recent work, separated from the earlier by over two hundred years, is very much the same as its predecessor, as those readers who can puzzle out the Black Letter type of the first will see. ("Black Letter" type, with heavy face and angular outlines, was used by the earliest printers.)

For those who are curious as to how the story ends, the seven champions all die, but they die with the inner knowledge of eternal glory on earth and in heaven. The champions are: St. George of England, champion of champions (as one would expect, since the author is English); St. Denis of France; St. Anthony of Italy; St. James of Spain; St. Andrew of Scotland; St. Patrick of Ireland; and St. David of Wales.

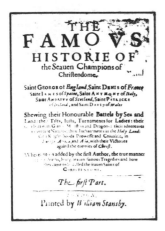

# THE HONORABLE HISTORIE OF THE
## seauen Champions of
### CHRISTENDOME.

#### Chap. I.

# The Seven Champions of Christendom

## CHAPTER I

*The strange and wonderful birth of St George of England. His being*
*stolen from his nurse, by Kalyb, the Lady of the Woods. Her love*
*to him, and her gifts. He encloses her in a rock of stone,*
*and redeems six Christian knights out of prison.*

AFTER THE ANGRY GODS had ruined the capital city of Phrygia, and turned king Priam's glorious buildings to a waste and desolate wilderness, duke Æneas, driven from his native habitation, with many of his distressed countrymen, wandered about the world, like pilgrims, to find some happy region, where they might erect the Palladium, or image of their subverted Troy; but before that labour could be accomplished, Æneas ended his days in the confines of Italy, and left his son Ascanius to govern in his stead. Ascanius dying, left the sovereign power to Sylvius; from whom it descended to the noble and adventurous Brute, who being the fourth in lineal descent from Æneas, first conquered this island of Britain, then inhabited with monsters, giants, and a kind of wild people, without any form of government.

Thus began the island of Britain to flourish, not only in magnificent and sumptuous buildings, but in courageous and valiant knights, whose most noble and adventurous attempts in the truly heroic feats of chivalry, Fame shall draw forth, and rescue from the dark and gloomy mansions of oblivion.

The land was now replenished with cities, and divided into shires or counties; dukedoms, earldoms, and lordships were the rewards of merit and noble services performed in martial fields, and not bestowed as bribes to enslave the state, or given to indulge the slothful pride and effeminacy of the flatterers of the prince.

The ancient city of Coventry gave birth to the first Christian hero of England, and the first who ever sought adventures in a foreign land; whose name is to this day held in high esteem through all parts of Europe, and whose bold and magnanimous deeds in arms gave him the title of "The valiant knight, St George of England," whose golden garter is not only worn by nobles, but by kings, and in memory of whose victories the kings of England fight under his banner. It is the history of this worthy champion of our native country, that, by the assistance of the heavenly muse, divine Calliope, I have undertaken to write.

Before his birth, his mother dreamed that she had conceived a dragon, which should cause her death. This frightful dream she long kept secret, till the painful thought grew so heavy, that she was scarce able to endure it; so taking an opportunity to disclose it to her lord and husband, then lord high steward of England, she struck such terror to his heart, that for a time he stood speechless; but having recovered his lost senses, he answered in this sort:—"My dearest and most beloved lady, what art and science can perform, with all convenient speed shall be essayed; for never will I close my eyes till

I have found some skilful person, who will undertake to unfold the mystic meaning of these terrific dreams."

This noble lord, leaving his delightful partner in company with other ladies, who came to comfort her in her melancholy condition, took his journey to the solitary walks of Kalyb, the wise lady of the woods, attended only by a single knight, who bore under his arm a white lamb, which they intended to offer as a sacrifice to the enchantress. Thus travelling, for the space of two days, they came to a thicket beset about with old withered and hollow trees, wherein they were terrified by such dismal croakings of the night raven, hissing of serpents, bellowing of bulls, and roaring of monsters, that it seemed to be rather the habitation of furies than a mortal dwelling; here was the dark and dreary mansion of the enchantress, Kalyb, lady of the woods, in the midst of which she took up her abode, in a lonely cave, which had a strong iron gate at its entrance, whereon there hung a brazen trumpet for those to sound who wanted audience.

The lord and knight, first offering their lamb with all humility before the postern of the cave, then casting off all fear, blew the trumpet, the sound of which seemed to shake the very foundation of the earth. After which, they heard a loud and hollow voice utter the following words:

"Sir Knight, from whence thou cam'st return;
Thou hast a son most strangely born;
A champion bold, from thee shall spring,
Who'll practise many a wondrous thing;
Return, therefore, make no delay,
For all is true that here I say."

This dark riddle, or rather mystic oracle, being thrice repeated in this order, so much amazed them, that they stood in doubt whether it were best to return, or sound the brazen trumpet a second time; but the lord high steward, being persuaded by the knight not to move the impatience of Kalyb, rested content with the answer she had given them, and, quitting the enchanted cave, made all the speed he could to his native habitation. In the mean time, his lady, being over-anxious with extreme pain and anguish, gave up her own life, to save that of her infant. On his breast Nature had pictured the lively image of a dragon; upon his right hand a blood-red cross, and a gold garter on his left leg. He was named George, and three nurses were provided for him; one to nurse him, another to lull and rock him asleep, and the third to prepare his food. But not many days after his birth, the fell enchantress Kalyb, being an utter enemy to all true nobility, by the help of charms and witchcraft, found means to steal away the infant from his careless nurses.

The lord high steward of England at this time returning, how were his expectations frustrated! He found his wife in her cold grave, and his son carried he knew not whither. The news of these disasters for a while bereaved him of his wits, and he stood senseless.

He mourned many months for his loss, and sent messengers into every corner of the land to make inquiry after his son; but no man was fortunate enough to return with happy tidings. He, therefore, storing himself with gold and many precious jewels, re-solved to travel the world over, to find what he wanted, or to leave his bones in some remote region. So leaving his native country, he wandered from place to place, without success, till, through care and age, his locks were turned to silver grey, and his venerable beard became like down upon a thistle: at length, quite wearied out with grief and fruitless toil, he laid himself down close by the ruined walls of a decayed monastery in the kingdom of Bohemia, and there finished his inquiry and his life together. The common people of the country, coming to the knowledge of his name by a jewel he wore in his bosom, caused it to be engraven on a marble stone, right over the place where he was buried. And there we will leave him to sleep in peace, and return to his son, still kept by Kalyb, the lady of the woods, in her enchanted cave.

And now twice seven times the sun had run his annual course since Kalyb had first in keeping the noble St George of England, whose mind often thirsted after honourable adventures, and who many times attempted to set himself at liberty; but the fell enchantress, regarding him as the apple of her eye, appointed twelve sturdy Satyrs to attend his person, so that neither force nor policy could further his intent. She kept him not to insult over as a slave, nor triumph in his wretchedness, but daily fed his fancy with all the delights that art or nature could afford; for she placed her whole felicity in him, and loved him for his beauty. But he, seeking glory from martial discipline and knightly achievements, utterly refused her proffered love, and highly disdained so wicked a creature. Whereupon she, seeing how much he neglected her, drawing him to a private part of the cave, began thus to court him:

"Thou knowest, divine youth, how eagerly I have sought thy love, and how I doat upon thy manly charms; yet thou, more cruel than the Lybian tiger, dost reject my sighs and tears. But now, my dear knight, if thou wilt but love me, for thy sake I will show all the power of my magic charms, move heaven, if thou requestest it, to rain down stones in showers upon thy enemies: I will convert the sun and moon to fire and blood, depopulate whole regions, and lay the face of nature waste."

Our noble knight St George, considering that love might blind the wisest, and guessing, by these fair promises, that he might find an opportunity to obtain his liberty, made her this answer:

"Most wise and learned Kalyb, thou wonder of the world, I will condescend to all thy heart desires upon these conditions: That I may be sole governor and protector of this enchanted cave, and that thou discoverest to me my birth, my name, and parentage."

She very willing consented to these terms, and began to answer his demands as follows: "Thou art by birth," said she, "son of the lord Albert, high steward of England; and from thy birth to this day have I kept thee, as my own child, within these solitary woods." So taking him by the hand, she led him into a brazen castle, wherein were imprisoned six of the bravest knights of the whole world. "These," said she, "are six worthy champions of Christendom: the first is St Denis of France, the second St James of Spain, the third St Anthony of Italy, the fourth St Andrew of Scotland, the fifth St Patrick of Ireland, the sixth St David of Wales; and thou art born to be the seventh, thy name St George of England, for so shalt thou be named in times to come."

Then leading him a little farther, she brought him into a magnificent building, where stood seven of the most beautiful steeds that ever eye beheld. "Six of these," said she, "belong to the six champions, and the seventh, whose name is Bayard, will I bestow on thee." Then she led him to another apartment, where hung the richest armour in the world; there choosing out the strongest corslet from her armoury, she with her own hands buckled it upon his breast, laced on his helmet, and dressed him in the armour: afterwards bringing forth a mighty falchion, she likewise put it in his hand, and said to him: "Thou art now clothed in richer armour than Ninus the first monarch of the world. Thy steed is of such force and invincible power, that whilst thou art mounted on his back, no knight in the world shall be able to conquer thee. Thy armour is of the purest Lybian steel, that no battle-axe can bruise, nor any weapon can pierce. Thy sword, which is called Ascalon, was made by the Cyclops; it will hew in sunder the hardest flint, or cut the strongest steel; and in its pummel there lies such magic virtue, that neither treason, witchcraft, nor any other violence can be offered to thee so long as thou wearest it.

Thus the enchantress, Kalyb, was so blinded by the love she had for him, that she not only bestowed all the riches of her cave upon him, but gave him power and authority, by putting a silver wand in his hand, to work her own destruction. For coming by a huge rock of stone, he struck it with this enchanted wand, whereupon it immediately opened, and exposed to view a vast number of young infants, whom the enchantress had murdered by her witchcraft and sorceries. "This," said she, "is a place of horror, where nought is heard but shrieks and groans of dying men and babes: but if your ears can endure to hear, and eyes behold them, I will lead you that way." So the lady of the woods, boldly stepping in before, and little suspecting any danger from the secret policy of St George, was deceived in her own practices; for no sooner had she entered the rock, but he struck the silver wand thereon, and it closed in an instant; and there confined her to bellow forth her lamentable complaints to senseless stones, without any hope of being released.

Thus this noble knight punished the wicked enchantress, Kalyb, and likewise set the other six champions at liberty, who rendered him all knightly courtesies, and gave him thanks for their safe deliverance. So providing themselves with all things suiting their generous purposes, they took their journey from the enchanted grove. Their proceedings, fortunes, and heroical adventures, shall be shown in the chapters following.

## CHAPTER II

*St George slays the burning dragon in Egypt, and redeems Sabra, the king's daughter, from death. Is betrayed by Almidor, the black king of Morocco, and sent to the Soldan of Persia, where he slew two lions, and remained seven years in prison.*

AFTER THE seven champions departed from the enchanted cave of Kalyb, they made their abode in the city of Coventry for the space of nine months; in which time they erected a sumptuous monument over the remains of St George's mother. And at that time of the year when Flora had embroidered the green mantle of the spring, they armed themselves like knights-errant, and took their journey to seek for foreign adventures, accounting nothing more dishonourable than to spend their time in idleness, and not achieve somewhat that might make their names memorable to posterity. So travelling thirty days without any adventures worth noting, at length they came to a broad plain, where stood a brazen pillar, and where seven several ways met, which the worthy knights thought a proper place to take leave of each other, and every one went a contrary road; we will, for this time, likewise take leave of six, that we may accompany the fortunes of our English knight, who, after many months' travel by sea and land, happily arrived within the territories of Egypt, which country was then greatly annoyed by a dangerous dragon. But before he had journeyed far in that kingdom, the silent night outspread her sable wings, and a still horror seemed to cover every part of nature. At length, he came to a poor old hermitage, wherein he proposed to seek some repose for himself and horse, till the rosy-fingered morning should again reluminate the vault of heaven, and light him on his destined course. On entering the cottage, he found an ancient hermit, bowing under the weight of age, and almost consumed with holy watching and religious tears, to whom he thus addressed himself:

"Father, may a traveller, for this night, crave shelter with you for himself and horse; or can you direct me to any town or village to which I may proceed on my journey with safety."

The old man, starting at the sudden approach of St George, made him answer:

"That he need not to inquire of his country, for he knew it by his burgonet," (for indeed thereon were engraved the arms of England.) "But I sorrow," continued he, "for thy hard fortune, and that it is thy destiny to arrive in this our country of Egypt, wherein those alive are scarce sufficient to bury the dead; such cruel devastation is made through the land by a most terrible and dangerous dragon, now ranging up and down the country; the raging appetite of which must every day be appeased with the body of a virgin, whom he swalloweth down his envenomed throat; and whenever this horrid sacrifice is omitted, he breathes such a pestiferous stench as occasions a mortal plague. And this having been practised for twenty-four years, there is not now one virgin left throughout all Egypt but the king's daughter; and she, to-morrow, is to be made an offering to the dragon, unless there can be any brave knight found who shall have courage enough to encounter him, and kill him; and then, the king hath promised to give such a knight his daughter, whose life he shall have saved, in marriage, with the crown of Egypt after his decease."

This royal reward so animated the English knight, that he vowed he would either save the king's daughter, or lose his own life in so glorious an enterprise. So taking his repose that night in the old man's hermitage, till the cheerful cock, the true messenger of day, gave him notice of the sun's uprise, which caused him to buckle on his armour, and harness his steed with all the strong caparisons of war, he took his journey, guided only by the hermit, to the valley, where the king's daughter was to be offered up in sacrifice. When he approached within sight of the valley, he saw at a distance the most amiable and beautiful virgin that ever eyes beheld, arrayed in a pure white Arabian silk, being led to the place of death, accompanied by many sage and modest matrons. The courage of the brave English knight was so stimulated by this melancholy scene that he thought every minute a whole day till he could rescue her from the threatened danger, and save her from the insatiable jaws of the fiery dragon; so advancing towards the lady, he gave her hopes that her deliverance was at hand, and begged her to return to her father's court.

The noble knight, like a bold and daring hero, then entered the valley where the dragon had his abode, who no sooner had sight of him, than his leathern throat sent forth a sound more terrible than thunder. The size of this fell dragon was fearful to behold, for, from his shoulders to his tail, the length was fifty feet; the glittering scales upon his body were as bright as silver, but harder than brass; his belly was of the colour of gold, and larger than a tun. Thus weltered he from his hideous den, and so fiercely assailed the gallant champion with his burning wings, that at the first encounter he had almost felled him to the ground; but the knight, nimbly recovering himself, gave the dragon such a thrust with his spear, that it shivered in a thousand pieces! upon which, the furious dragon smote him so violently with his venomous tail, that he brought both man and horse to the ground, and sorely bruised two of St George's ribs in the fall; but he, stepping backwards, chanced to get under an orange-tree, which had that rare virtue in it, that no venomous creature durst come within the compass of its branches; and here the valiant knight rested himself, till he had recovered his former strength. But he no sooner felt his spirits revive, than, with an eager courage, he smote the burning dragon under his yellow burnished belly, with his trusty sword Ascalon; and from the wound there came such an abundance of black venom, that it spouted on the armour of the knight, which, by the mere force of the poison, burst in two, and he himself fell on the ground, where he lay for some time quite senseless, but had luckily rolled himself under the orange-tree, where the dragon had not power to offer him any farther violence. The fruit of this tree was of that excellence, that whoever tasted it was immediately cured of all manner of wounds and diseases.

Now it was the noble champion's good fortune to recover himself a little by the pure aroma of the tree, and then he chanced to espy an orange which had lately dropped from it, by tasting of which he was so refreshed, that in a short time he was as sound as when he began the encounter. Then knelt he down and made his humble supplication, that heaven would send him such strength and agility of body as might enable him to slay the fell monster; which being done, with a bold and courageous heart, he smote the dragon under the wing, where it was tender and without scale, whereby his good sword Ascalon, with an easy passage, went to the very hilt, through the dragon's liver and heart; from whence there issued such an abundance of reeking gore, as turned all the grass in the valley to a crimson hue; and the ground, which was before parched up by the burning breath of the dragon, was now drenched in the moisture that proceeded from his venomous bowels, the loss of which forced him to yield his vital spirit to the champion's conquering sword.

The noble knight, St George of England, having performed this, first paid due honour to the Almighty for his victory; and then, with his sword, cut off the dragon's head, and fixed it on a truncheon made of that spear which, at the beginning of the battle, shivered in pieces against the dragon's scaly back. During this long and dangerous combat, his trusty steed lay, as it were, in a swoon, without any motion; but the English champion now squeezing the juice of one of the oranges in his mouth, the virtue of it immediately expelled the venom of the poison, and he recovered his former strength.

There was then in the Egyptian court, and had been for some time, Almidor, the black king of Morocco, who had long sought the love of Sabra, the king's daughter; but by no policy or means could he accomplish what his heart desired. And now, having less hope than ever, by the successful combat of St George with the dragon, he resolved to try the utmost power of art, and treacherously despoil the victor of his laurels, with which he falsely designed to crown his own temples, and thereby obtain the grace of the lady, who loathed his company, and more detested his person than the crocodile of the Nile. But even as the wolf barks in vain against the moon, so shall this fantastical and cowardly Almidor attempt in vain to seize the glory won by the English knight; although he had hired, by gifts and promises, twelve Egyptian knights to beset the valley where St George slew the burning dragon, who were to deprive him by force of the spoils of his conquest. Thus, when the magnanimous champion came riding in triumph from the valley, expecting to have been received as a conqueror, with drums and trumpets, or to have heard the bells throughout the kingdom ringing with the joyful peals of victory, and every street illuminated with bonfires and blazing tapers; contrary to his expectation, he was met with a troop of armed knights, not to conduct him in triumph to the Egyptian court, but, by insidious baseness and treachery, to deprive him of his life, and the glory he had that day so nobly acquired by his invincible arms: for no sooner had he passed the entrance of the valley, than he saw the Egyptian knights brandishing their weapons, and dividing themselves, to intercept him in his journey to the court. So, tying his horse to a tree, he resolved to try his fortune on foot, there being twelve to one; yet did St George, at the first onset, so valiantly behave himself with his trusty sword Ascalon, that, at one stroke, he slew three of the Egyptian knights, and before the golden chariot of the sun had gone another hour in its diurnal course, some he had dismembered of their heads and limbs, and some he had cut in two, so that their entrails fell to the earth, and not one was left alive to carry home the news of their defeat. Almidor, the black king, stood the whole time of the battle on the top of a mountain, to behold the success of his hired champions; but when he saw the dismal catastrophe of these mercenary knights, and how the good fortune of the English champion had carried the honour of the day, he cursed his destiny, and accused blind chance of cruelty in thus disappointing the hopes of his treacherous enterprise: but having a heart full fraught with malice and envy, he secretly vowed to himself that he would practise some other treachery to bring St George to destruction. So running before to the court of king Ptolemy, and without relating what had happened to the twelve Egyptian knights, he cried out, "Victoria, Victoria, the enemy of Egypt is slain!" Upon which, Ptolemy ordered every street of the city of Memphis to be hung with rich arras and embroidered tapestry, and likewise provided a sumptuous chariot of massive gold, the wheels and other timberwork whereof were of the purest ebony; the covering, rich silk embossed with gold; this, with a hundred of the noblest peers of Egypt, attired in crimson velvet, mounted on milk-white coursers, richly caparisoned, attended the arrival of St George, who was conducted in the most solemn manner into the city, all the loftiest as well as the sweetest instruments of music both going before and following after the resplendent chariot in which he was drawn to the court of king Ptolemy; where he surrendered up the trophies of his conquest into the hands of the beauteous Sabra, who was so ravished with the noble person and princely presence of the English knight, that, for a time, she was scarcely able to speak; but having recovered herself, she took him by the hand, and led him to a rich pavillion, where she unbuckled his armour, and with the most precious salves soothed his wounds, and with fine linen cloths wiped off the blood; after which, she conducted him to a rich repast, furnished with all manner of delicate meats, where the king her father was present, who inquired of his country, parentage, and name. After the banquet was over, he conferred on him the honour of knighthood, and put upon his feet a pair of golden spurs. But the lovely princess, his daughter, could feast on nothing but the hopes of the champion's love; and, having attended him to his night's repose, she sat near his bed, and striking the melodious strings of her lute, lulled him to rest with the sweetest harmony that ever was heard.

No sooner had the morn displayed her beauties in the east, and gilded with her radiant beams the mountain tops, than Sabra repaired to the English champion's lodgings, and presented him with a diamond of inestimable value, which she prayed him to wear on his finger, not only as an ornament, but as it was endued with many most excellent and occult virtues. The next who entered the room was Almidor, the treacherous black king of Morocco, having a bowl of Greek wine in his hand, which he offered to the noble champion St George of England; but when he stretched forth his arm to accept the same, the diamond, which the fair Sabra had made him a present of, waxed pale, and from his nose fell three drops of blood, which the king's daughter observing, suspected some secret poison to be infused in the wine; whereupon she shrieked out so loudly, and so suddenly, that it alarmed the whole court, and carried her suspicions to the ears of her father; but so great was his love for the black king, that he would not give credit to any thing which could be suggested against him.

Thus was Almidor a second time prevented in his evil designs, which made him more enraged than a chased boar; yet, resolving the third attempt should pay for all, he impatiently expected another opportunity to put his fiendish purposes in execution.

St George remained many days at the Egyptian court, sometimes revelling among the gentlemen, dancing and sporting among the ladies, at other times in tilts, tournaments, and other noble and heroic exercises; and all that time was the breast of the beauteous Sabra inflamed with the most ardent love for him, of which the treacherous Almidor had intelligence from many secret sources, and many times his own ears were witnesses to their meetings. One evening in particular, after sunset, it was his fortune to wander near a garden wall to taste the cooling air, where the two lovers, without seeing him, were seated in a bower of jessamine, and after much talk, he heard the lovesick Sabra thus complain:—

"My soul's delight, my noble George of England, dearer than all the world beside, why art thou more obdurate than the flint, since all my falling tears can never mollify thy heart? Not all the sighs, the many thousand sighs, I have sent as messengers of my true love, were ever yet requited with a smile. Refuse not her, my dear-loved lord of England, refuse not her, that, for thy sake, would leave her parents, country, and inheritance, although that inheritance be the crown of Egypt, and would follow thee as a pilgrim through the wide world. The sun shall sooner lose his splendour, the pale moon drop from her orb, the sea forget to ebb and flow, and all things change the course ordained by nature, than Sabra, heiress of Egypt, prove inconstant to St George of England; let then, the priests of Hymen knit that gordian knot, the knot of wedlock, which death alone has power to untie."

These words so fired the champion's heart, that he who before had never given way to any passion but the love of arms, was almost entangled in the snares of love. Yet, to try her patience a little more, he made her this answer:

"Lady of Egypt, art thou not content that I have risked my own life to preserve yours, but you would have me also sacrifice my honour, give over the chase of dazzling glory, lay all my warlike trophies in a woman's lap, and change my truncheon for a distaff.— No! Sabra; George of England is a knight, born in a country where true chivalry is nourished, and hath sworn to see the world, as far as the lamp of heaven can lend him light, before he is fettered in the chains of wedlock. Therefore, think no more of one that is a stranger, a wanderer from place to place, but cast your eyes on one more worthy of your own high rank. Why do you decline the suit of Almidor, who is a king, and would think no task too arduous to obtain your love?"

At which words, she instantly replied:

"The fell king of Morocco is more blood-minded than a serpent, but thou as gentle as a lamb; his tongue more ominous than the screeching night owl, but thine sweeter than the morning lark; his touch more odious than the biting snake, but thine more pleasant than the curling vine. What if thou art a stranger to our land, thou art more precious to my heart, and more delightful to my eyes, than crowns and diadems."

"But stay," replied the English champion: "I am a Christian, madam; thou a Pagan. I honour God in heaven; you, a vile impostor here below. Therefore, if you would obtain my love, you must forsake your Mohammed, and be baptized into the Christian faith." "With all my soul," replied the Egyptian lady; "I will forsake my country's gods, and for thy love become a Christian." And thereupon she broke a ring, and gave him one half as a pledge of her love, and kept the other half herself; and so, for that time went out of the garden.

The treacherous Almidor, who had listened during all this discourse, was galled to the very heart to hear how much his mistress despised him and his proffered love; but was now resolved to strike a bold stroke with the king her father, to separate her from his too successful rival; and, accordingly, hastened away to the Egyptian king, and, prostrating himself before him, declared that he had overheard a deep-concerted plan of treason, laid between his daughter and the English knight; that she had given him a solemn pledge of love, and with that pledge a promise to forsake the faith of Egypt, set the great prophet at defiance, and embrace the Christian doctrine.

"Now, by our holy prophet," replied the king, "this hated Christian shall not reap the harvest of our daughter's love, for he shall lose his head, though not in our court, where we have heaped such honours on him. But, Almidor, be secret, and I will acquaint you with my purpose: I will send him to my kinsman, the Soldan of Persia; from whom he shall never more return to Egypt, except his ghost bring tidings of his fate in that country." And to answer this purpose they contrived between them the following letter:

'To the Soldan of Persia,

'I, Ptolemy, king of Egypt, and the eastern territories, send greeting to thee, the mighty Soldan of Persia, great emperor of the provinces of the larger Asia. I make this my request, trusting to the league of friendship between us, that thou put the bearer hereof, thy slave, to death; for he is an utter enemy to all Asia and Africa, and a proud contemner of our religion. Therefore fail not hereof, as thou tenderest our mutual friendship. So we bid thee, farewell.

'Thy kinsman,
'PTOLEMY, King of Egypt.'

As soon as this letter was signed and sealed with the great seal of Egypt, St George was sent in embassy with the bloody sentence of his own destruction; and was sworn, by the honour of knighthood, to deliver it safe; leaving behind him, as a pledge of his fidelity, his good steed, and trusty sword Ascalon, in the keeping of Ptolemy, taking with him only one of the king's horses, for his easy travelling.

On the day that St George reached the Soldan's court, there was a solemn procession in honour of the false prophet Mohammed, with which the English champion was so moved, that he tore down their ensigns and streamers, and trampled them under his feet: upon which the infidels presently fled to the Soldan for succour, and showed him how a strange knight had despised their prophet, and trod their banners in the dust. Whereupon he sent a hundred of his armed knights to know the cause of that sudden uproar, and to bring the Christian champion bound into his presence; but he entertained these Persian knights with such a bloody banquet, that most of their heads were tumbled in the dirty streets, and the channels overflowed with streams of their blood; the pavement before the palace was almost covered with slaughtered men, and the walls were besprinkled with purple gore. At last the alarm-bell was rung, and the beacons set on fire; upon which the populace rose in arms, and came flocking about the English champion, like swarms of bees; whereat, through his long fatigue, and the multitude of his enemies, his undaunted courage was forced to yield, and his resistless arm, wearied with the fight, constrained to let his weapon fall to the ground. And thus he, whose valour had sent thousands to wander on the banks of Acheron, stood now obedient to the mercy of his enemies, who, with their brandished weapons and sharp-edged falchions, environed him about.

"Now, bloody-minded monster," said the Soldan, "what countryman soe'er thou art, Jew, Pagan, or misbelieving Christian, look for a sentence of severe punishment for every drop of blood thy unhappy hand hath here shed; first, thy skin shall be flayed from off thy flesh alive; next, thy flesh shall be torn with red-hot pincers from thy bones: and lastly, thy limbs parted from each other by wild horses." This bloody sentence being pronounced by the Soldan, St George answered in the following manner:

"Great potentate of Asia, I crave the liberty and law of arms, whereby all the kings of the earth are by oath for ever bound. First, in my native country, my descent is of royal blood, and therefore I challenge a combat; secondly, I am an ambassador from the mighty Ptolemy, king of Egypt; therefore is my person sacred: lastly, the laws of Asia, and indeed of all nations, grant me a safe conduct back; and Ptolemy is answerable for every thing I have done."

Thereupon he delivered the letter, sealed with the great seal of Egypt, which was no sooner broken open and read, than the Soldan's eyes sparkled with fire, and upon his brow sat the image of wrath and indignation.

"By the report of Ptolemy," said the Soldan, "thou art a great contemner of our holy prophet, and his laws; therefore his pleasure is, that you be put to death; which, I swear by Mohammed, shall be fulfilled."

Upon this he gave him over to the safe custody of a hundred of his guards, till the time of execution, which was ordered to be in thirty days. Hereupon they disrobed him of his rich apparel, and clothed him in base and servile weeds; his arms, that were lately employed in supporting the mighty target, and wielding the weighty battle-axe, were now strongly fettered with iron bolts; and those hands which were wont to be garnished with steel gauntlets, they bound with hempen cords, till the purple blood started from his fingers' ends; and being thus despoiled of all knightly dignity, he was conveyed to a dark dungeon where the light of heaven was never seen, nor could the glorious sun send one gladdening ray to show a difference betwixt day and night. All his comfort was to reckon up the number of Persians he had slain; sometimes his restless thoughts were pondering on ungrateful Ptolemy, and sometimes running on the charms of lovely Sabra, distracted with reflecting how she had borne his sudden departure.

Thus Sorrow was his companion, and Despair his chief solicitor, till Hyperion's golden car had rested thirty times in the purple palace of Thetis; which was the precise time allotted by the Soldan of Persia for him to live; so expecting every minute the wished-for messenger of death, he heard afar off the terrible roaring of two lions, which for the space of four days had been restrained from food and natural sustenance, that with the more eagerness and fury they might satiate their hunger with the body of the thriced-renowned English champion. The cry of these lions so terrified his mind, that the hair of his head grew stiff; on his brow were large drops of sweat, and in his soul arose such fire and rage, that with violence he broke his chains asunder, then rent his amber coloured hair from his head, with which he wrapped his arms, preparing for the assault of the lions, which he imagined were designed to be the executioners of the Soldan's sentence against him, as indeed they were; and at that instant the guards, who brought them, let them out of the dungeon upon him. But such was his invincible fortitude, and so careful was he in his defence, that when the starved lions came running on him with open jaws, he courageously thrust his sinewy arms, which were covered with the hair of his head, into their throats, whereby they were presently choked, and he then pulled out their hearts.

Which spectacle the Soldan's guards beholding, were so amazed with fear, that they ran in all haste to the palace to acquaint the Soldan with what had happened, who thereupon commanded every part of the court to be guarded with armed soldiers, supposing the English knight rather some monster, from the infernal regions, than one of the human species. And such terror seized the Soldan, when he heard that he had killed the two lions, after having slaughtered two thousand Persians with his own hands; and being likewise informed of his having destroyed the burning dragon of Egypt, that he caused the dungeon wherein he was kept, to be doubly fortified with iron bars, lest, by force or stratagem, the champion should recover his liberty, and thereby endanger the whole kingdom of Persia. Here, for the term of seven winters, he remained in the greatest want and distress, feeding upon rats, and mice, and creeping worms, which he caught in the dungeon; nor tasting, in that whole time, any bread but what was made of bran, and drinking only channel water, which was daily served him through the iron gates. Here we will now leave St George, languishing under want and oppression, and return to Egypt, where we left Sabra, the champion's betrothed lady, lamenting the absence of him whom she loved dearer than all the world besides.

Sabra was the fairest virgin that ever eye beheld. In her nature had shown the utmost perfection; her body was straighter than the stately cedar, and the tincture of her skin surpassed the beauty of the Paphian queen; but one was bending with her weight of woes, and the other tarnished with the brackish tears that daily trickled down her cheeks, whereon sat the image of discontent, and she herself seemed a mirror of patient sorrow. All company was loathsome to her sight; she shunned even the fellowship of those ladies who were once her most intimate companions, and betook herself to a solitary chamber, where, with her needle, she amused the time; and having wrought the figures of many a bleeding heart, she bathed them with the tears that fell from her eyes; then, with her auburn locks that hung in wanton ringlets down her neck, she dried them up; and thinking on the plighted promises of her dearly-loved knight, fell into these sad complainings:

"O Love!" said she, "more sharp than keenest razors, with what inequality dost thou torment my wounded heart, not linking my dear lord's in like affection with it. O Venus! whom both gods and men obey, if thou art absolute in thy power, command my wandering lord to return, or let my soul be wafted to his sweet bosom, where my bleeding heart already is enshrined. But, foolish fondling that I am! he hath rejected me, and even shuns my father's court, where he was honoured and esteemed, to wander through the world to seek another love. No, no, it cannot be; he is more constant, his mind more noble than to forget his plighted vows; and much I fear some treachery has bereft me of him, some stony prison keeps him from me, for only chains and fetters could thus long withhold him from me. If so, sweet Morpheus, god of golden dreams, reveal to me my love's abode, show me in sleep the shadow of his lovely form, give me to know the reason of his sudden departure, and of his long and painful absence."

After this exclamation, she closed her radiant eyes in sleep, when presently the very image, as she thought, of her dearly-loved knight, St George, appeared; not as he was wont, in shining arms, and with his burgonet of glittering steel, nor mounted on his stately steed, decked with a crimson plume of spangled feathers, but in worn-out and simple attire, with pale looks and emaciated body, like a ghost just risen from the silent grave, breathing, as it were, the following sad and woful expressions:

> Sabra, I am betrayed for love of thee,
>     And lodged in cave as dark as night;
> From whence I never more, ah woe is me!
>     Shall have the pleasure of thy beauteous sight:
> Remain thou true and constant for my sake,
> That of my absence none may 'vantage make.
>
> Let tyrants know, if ever I obtain
>     What now is lost by treason's faithless guile,
> False Egypt's scourge I ever will remain,
>     And turn to streaming blood Morocco's soil.

That hateful prince of Barbary shall rue
The fell revenge that is his treason's due.

The Persian towers shall smoke with fire,
    And lofty Babylon be tumbled down;
The cross of Christendom shall then aspire
    To wear the proud Egyptian triple crown.
Jerusalem and Judah shall behold
The fall of kings by Christian champions bold.

Thou maid of Egypt, still continue chaste,
    A tiger seeks thy virgin's name to spoil;
Whilst George of England is in prison placed,
    Thou shalt be forced to wed against thy will;
But after this shall happen mighty things,
For from thy self shall spring three wondrous kings.

This strange and woful speech was no sooner ended, but she awakened from her sleep, and presently stretched out her arms, thinking to embrace him, but met with nothing but empty air, which caused her to renew her former complaints.

"Oh! wherefore died I not in this my troublesome dream," said the sorrowful lady, "that my ghost might have haunted those inhuman monsters who have thus betrayed the bravest champion that the eye of heaven, or the sons of the earth, have ever beheld? For his sake will I exclaim against the ingratitude of Egypt, and fill every corner of the land with echoes of his wrongs. My woes are greater, and by far exceed the sorrows of Dido, queen of Carthage, mourning for Æneas."

At last, her father, understanding what ardent affection she bore to the English champion, spoke to her in this manner:

"Daughter, I charge thee, on the obedience and duty which thou owest to me, both as thy father and thy king, to banish from thy thoughts all fond affection for the wandering knight whom thou hast unworthily made the object of thy love, for he hath neither home nor habitation. Thou seest he has forsaken thee, and in his travels is wedded to another. Therefore, as you value my love, or dread my displeasure, I charge thee again to think no more of him; but cast your eyes on the black king of Morocco, who is deserving of thee, and whose nuptials with thee I intend to celebrate in Egypt shortly, with all the honours due to my own and his high rank."

Having said these words, he departed, without waiting for an answer; by which fair Sabra knew he was not to be thwarted in his will. Therefore she poured forth these sad words:

"O unkind father! to cross the affection of thy child, and thus force love where there is no liking; yet shall my mind continue true to my dearly-loved lord; although I be forced to obey, and marry Almidor, yet shall English George alone possess my heart."

Which words were no sooner ended, than Almidor entered her chamber, and presented her with a wedding-garment, which was of the purest Median silk, embossed with pearls and glittering gold, and perfumed with Syrian powders; it was of the colour of the lily, when Flora has bedecked the fields in May with nature's ornaments; glorious and costly were her vestures, and so stately were the nuptial rites solemnized, that Egypt admired the grandeur of her wedding, which for seven days was held in the court of Ptolemy, and afterwards at Tripoli, the chief city of Barbary, where Almidor's reluctant bride was crowned queen of Morocco; at which coronation the conduits ran with Greek wine, and the streets of Tripoli were beautified with pageants and delightful shows. The court resounded with melodious harmony, as though Apollo with his silver harp had descended from the heavens; such tilts and tournaments were performed betwixt the Egyptian knights and the knights of Barbary, that they exceeded the nuptials of Hecuba, the beauteous queen of Troy. These revellers we leave for this time to their own enjoyments, some masking, some dancing, some singing, some tilting, some banquetting. We also leave the champion of England, St George, mourning in his horrible dungeon in Persia, and return to the other six champions of Christendom, who departed from the brazen pillar, every one his several way, whose knightly and noble adventures, if the Muses grant me their assistance, I will most amply detail, to the honour of Christendom.

## CHAPTER III

*St Denis, the champion of France, lives seven year in the shape of a hart; and proud Eglantine, the king of Thessaly's daughter, is transformed into a mulberry tree; they recover their former shapes by means of St Denis's horse, and travel to the Thessalian court.*

W E NOW CALL to mind the long and weary travels of St Denis, the worthy champion of France, after his departure from the other six champions at the brazen pillar, as you heard in the beginning of the former chapter, from which he wandered through many a desolate grove and wilderness, without any adventure worth noting, till he arrived upon the borders of Thessaly, (at that time a land inhabited only by wild beasts;) wherein he endured such a scarcity of victuals, that he was forced, for the space of seven years, to feed upon the herbs of the field, and the fruits of trees, till the hairs of his head were like eagles' feathers, and the nails of his fingers like birds' claws; his drink, the dew of heaven, which he licked from the flowers of the field; his attire, the bay leaves and broad docks that grew in the wood; his shoes, in which he traveled through many a thorny brake, the bark of trees. But at last, it was his fortune, or cruel destiny, (being overprest with the extremity of hunger), to taste and feed upon the berries of an enchanted mulberry tree, whereby he lost the lively form and image of his human substance, and was transformed into the shape and likeness of a wild hart; which strange and sudden transformation, this noble champion little suspected, till he espied his misshapen form in a clear fountain, which nature had made in a cool and shady valley; but when he beheld the shadow of his deformed body, and how his head, lately honoured with a burgonet of steel, was now disgraced with a pair of sylvan horns; his countenance, which was the index of his noble mind, now covered with the likeness of a brute: and his body, which was erect, tall, smooth, and fair, now bending to earth on four feet, and clothed in a rough hairy hide of a dusky brown colour; having his reason still left, he ran again to the mulberry-tree, supposing the berries he had eaten to be the cause of his transformation, and there laying himself upon the ground, he thus began to complain:

"What magic charms, or what bewitching spells," said he, "are contained in this cursed tree, whose deceitful fruit hath confounded my future fortunes, and reduced me to this miserable condition? O thou celestial Ruler of the world! O merciful power of heaven! look down with pity on my hapless state; incline thine ears to listen to my woes; I, who was a man am now an horned beast; a soldier, once my country's champion, now a timorous deer, the prey of dogs; my glittering armour changed into a hairy hide, and my brave array, now vile as common earth; henceforth, instead of princely palaces, these shady woods must be my sole retreat, wherein my bed of down must be a heap of sun-dried moss; my sweet music, blustering winds, that with tempestuous gusts make the whole wilderness tremble; the company I am obliged henceforth to keep, must be the Sylvan Satyrs, Driads, and airy Nymphs, who never appear to human eyes, but at twilight or the midnight moon; the stars that beautify the crystal vault and wide expanse of heaven, shall hereafter serve as torches to light me to my woful bed; scowling clouds shall be my canopy; and my clock, to give me notice how the time runs stealing on, the dismal sounds of hissing snakes or croaking toads!"

Thus during many days this champion of France continued in the shape of a hart, in greater misery than the unfortunate English champion in Persia, not knowing how to recover his former shape and human substance. But one day, as he lamented the loss of his natural form, under the branches of that enchanted mulberry-tree, which was the cause of his transformation, he heard a most grievous and terrible groan, upon which, suspending his sorrows for a time, he heard a hollow voice breathe from the trunk of the tree the following words:

> Cease to lament, thou famous man of France,
>     With gentle ears come listen to my moan;
> In former time it was my fatal chance
>     To be the proudest maid that e'er was known;
> By birth I was the daughter of a king,
> Though now a breathless tree, and senseless thing.
>
> My pride was such that heaven confounded me—
>     A goddess in my own conceit I was:
> What nature lent, too base I thought to be,
>     But deemed myself all others to surpass;
> And therefore nectar and ambrosia sweet,
> The food of heaven, for me I counted meet.
>
> My pride despised the finest bread of wheat,
>     And purer food I daily sought to find!
> Refined gold was boil'd, and formed my meat,
>     Such self-conceit my senses all did blind;
> For which the gods above transformed me
> From human substance to this senseless tree.

Seven years in shape of hart thou must remain,
  And then the purple rose, by Heaven's decree,
Shall bring thee to thy former shape again,
  And end at last thy woful misery;
When this is done, be sure you cut in twain
This fatal tree wherein I do remain.

After he had heard these words he was so much amazed at the strangeness thereof, that for some moments he was deprived of speech; and the thoughts of his long-continued punishment bereaved him of his understanding; but at last, recovering his senses, he bitterly complained of his misfortunes.

"Oh! unhappy creature," said the distressed champion, "more miserable than Progne in her transformation, and more unfortunate than Actæon, whose perfect picture I am made! His misery continued but a short time; for his own dogs, the same day, tore him into a thousand pieces, and buried his transformed carcass in their hungry bowels; but mine is appointed by the angry destinies, till seven times the summer's sun shall yearly replenish its radiant brightness, and seven times the winter's rain shall wash me with the showers of heaven."

Such were the complaints of the transformed knight of France, sometimes remembering his former fortunes, how he had spent his days in the honour of his country; at other times thinking upon the place of his nativity, renowned France, the nurse and mother of his youth; and again treading with his foot (for hands he had none) in sandy ground, the print of the words which he had heard from the mulberry-tree, and often times numbering the minutes of his tedious punishment. But during the whole term of his seven years' misery, his trusty steed never once forsook him, but with all love and diligence attended on him day and night, never straying from his side; and if extreme heat in summer, or pinching cold in winter, grew troublesome to him, his horse would shelter and defend him.

At last, after the term of seven years had fully expired, when he was to recover his former substance and human shape, his good horse, which he regarded as the apple of his eye, clambered a high and steep mountain, which nature had beautified with all kinds of fragrant flowers, as odoriferous as the gardens of the Hesperides; from whence he pulled a branch of purple roses and brought it betwixt his teeth to his distressed master, still lying in the same disorder and discontent, under the mulberry-tree. The champion of France no sooner beheld this, than he remembered that by a purple rose he should recover his former shape, and so joyfully received the roses from his trusty steed; then casting his eyes up to heaven, he conveyed these consecrated flowers into his empty stomach.

After which he lay down upon the bosom of his mother earth, where he fell into such a sound sleep, that all his senses and vital spirits ceased to perform their usual offices for the space of four-and-twenty hours, in which time the windows and doors of heaven were opened, from whence descended such a shower of rain, that it washed away his hairy coat and beast-like shape; his horned head and long visage were turned again into a lively countenance; and all the rest of his members, arms, legs, hands, feet, fingers, toes, with all the rest of nature's gifts, received their former shape.

But when the good champion awakened from his sleep, and perceived the wonderful goodness of heaven, in transforming him to his human likeness, he first gave honour to Almighty God; next, blessed the ground whereon he had lived so long in misery; then beholding his armour, which lay near him, quite stained, and almost spoiled with rust; his burgonet and keen-edged sword besmeared over with dust; and lastly, pondering in his mind the faithful service his trusty steed had done him, during the time of his calamity, whose sable-coloured mane hung frizzling down his brawny neck, which before was wont to be platted curiously with artificial knots, and his forehead, which was always beautified with a tawny plume of feathers, now disfigured with overgrown hair, the good champion, St Denis of France, was so grieved, that he stroked down his jetty back till the hair of his body lay as smooth as Arabian silk; he then pulled out his trusty falchion, which in so many fierce assaults, and dangerous combats, had been bathed in the blood of his enemies, but by the long continuance of time lying idle, was now almost consumed with cankered rust, and by great labour and industry, he recovered its former beauty and brightness.

Thus both his sword and horse, his martial furniture, and all other habiliments of war, being brought to their first and proper condition, the noble champion resolved to pursue his intended adventure in cutting down the mulberry-tree; so taking his sword, which was of the purest Spanish steel, he made such a stroke at the root thereof, that at one blow he cut it quite asunder, from whence immediately flashed such a mighty flame of fire, that the mane was burnt from his horse's neck, and even the hair of his own head would have been fired had not his helmet preserved it. No sooner was the flame extinguished, but there ascended from the hollow tree a virgin, (in shape like Daphne, whom Apollo turned into a bay-tree,) fairer than Pygmalion's ivory image, or the northern snow; her eyes more clear than the icy mountains, her cheeks like roses dipped in milk, her lips more lovely than Turkish rubies, her alabaster teeth like Indian pearls, her neck seemed an ivory tower; the rest of nature's lineaments a stain to Juno, Pallas, or Venus: at whose excellent beauty, this valiant and undaunted champion was more astonished than at her wonderful transformation; for his eyes were ravished with such exceeding pleasure, that his tongue could remain no longer silent, but was forced to unfold the secrets of his heart, and in these terms he began to utter his mind:

"Thou most divine and singular ornament of nature!" said he, "fairer than the feathers of the sylvan swan that swims upon Meander's crystal streams, and far more beautiful than Aurora's morning countenance, to thee, the fairest of thy sex, most humbly, and only to thy beauty, do I here submit my affections. Also I swear, by the honour of my knighthood, and by the love of my country of France, whether thou art an angel descended from heaven, or a fury ascended from the vast dominions of Proserpine; whether thou art some fairy or sylvan nymph, which inhabits this fatal wood, or else an earthly creature, for thy sins transformed into this mulberry-tree; I cannot judge. Therefore, sweet saint, to whom my heart must pay its due devotion, unfold to me thy birth, parentage, and name, that I may the bolder presume upon thy courtesies." At which demand, this new-born virgin, with a shame-faced look, modest gesture, sober grace, and blushing countenance, began thus to reply:

"Sir knight, by whom my life, my love, and fortunes are to be commanded, and by whom my human shape and natural form are recovered, first know, that I am by birth the king of Thessaly's daughter, and my name was called for my beauty, proud Eglantine; for which contemptuous pride, I was transformed into this mulberry-tree, in which green substance I have continued fourteen years. As for my love, thou hast deserved it before all knights in the world, and to thee do I plight that true promise before the Omnipotent Judge of all things. And before that sacred promise shall be infringed, the sun shall cease to shine by day, the moon by night, and all the planets forsake their natural order."

At which words the champion gave her the courtesies of his country, and sealed her promises with a loving kiss.

After which, the beautiful Eglantine weaved herself a garment of green rushes, intermixed with such variety of flowers, that it surpassed, in workmanship, the Indian maidens' curious webs; her curling locks of hair continued still of the colour of the mulberry-tree, and made her appear like Flora in her greatest royalty, when the fields are decked with nature's tapestry.

Thus, in green vestments, she is ready, in company of her true love, the valiant knight of France, to take her journey to her father's court; where, after some few days' travel, they arrived safe, and were welcomed according to their wishes, with the most honourable entertainments. The king of Thessaly no sooner beheld his daughter, of whose strange transformation he was ignorant, than he fell into a swoon through exceeding joy, but coming to his senses, he embraced her, and proffered such courtesy to the strange knight, that St Denis accounted him the mirror of chivalry, and the pattern of true nobility.

After the champion was unarmed, his stiff and wearied limbs were bathed in new milk and white wine, he was conveyed to a sweet-smelling fire made of juniper, and the fair Eglantine conducted by the maidens of honour to a private chamber, where she was disrobed of her Sylvan attire, and apparelled in long robes of purple silk. In this court of Thessaly we will will leave our champion of France with his lady, and go forward to discourse of the other champions, relating what adventures happened to them during the seven years.

## CHAPTER IV

*How St James, the champion of Spain, continued seven years dumb for the love of a fair Jewess, and how he would have been shot to death by the maidens of Jerusalem; with other things which happened in his travels.*

NOW MUST MY MUSE speak of St James of Spain, the third champion, and what happened unto him in his seven years' travels through many a strange country by sea and land, where his honourable acts were so dangerous and wonderful, that I want skill to express, and art to describe them. Also I am forced to pass over his dangerous battle with the burning drake upon the flaming mount in Sicily, which terrible combat continued for the space of seven days and seven nights. Likewise I omit his travels in

Cappadocia, through a wilderness of monsters; his passage over the Red Sea, where his ship was devoured with worms, his mariners drowned, and himself, his horse, and furniture, safely brought to land by the sea-nymphs and mermaids; until after long travel, perils, and dangerous tempests, among the stormy billows of the raging seas, he arrived in the unhappy dominions of Judah; unhappy by reason of the long and troublesome misery he endured for the love of a fair Jewess. For coming to the beautiful city of Jerusalem, (being in that age the wonder of the world, for grand buildings, princely palaces, and wonderful temples,) he so admired its glorious situation, that he stood before the lofty walls, one while gazing upon her golden gates, glittering in the sun; another while beholding her stately pinnacles, whose lofty tops seemed to touch the clouds; another while wondering at her towers of jasper, jet, and ebony, her strong and fortified walls, glittering spires of the temple of Sion, the ancient monument of Greece, whose battlements were covered with steel, the walls burnished with silver, the ground paved with tin. Thus, as this noble and famous knight stood beholding the situation of Jerusalem, there suddenly thundered such a peal of ordnance within the city, that it seemed, in his ravished conceit, to shake the veil of heaven, and to move the deep foundations of the solid earth; whereat his horse gave such a sudden start, that he leaped ten feet from the place whereon he stood. After this, he heard the sound of drums, and the cheerful echoes of brazen trumpets, by which the valiant champion expected some honorable pastime or some great tournament to be at hand; which indeed so fell out; for no sooner did he cast his eyes towards the east side of the city, than he beheld a troop of well appointed horse come marching through the gates; after them twelve armed knights mounted on twelve warlike coursers, bearing in their hands twelve blood-red streamers, whereon was wrought in silk the picture of Adonis, wounded by a boar; after them, the king, drawn in a chariot by Spanish mares. The king's guards were a hundred Moors, with Turkish bows and darts, feathered with ravens' wings; after them came Celestine, the king of Jerusalem's fair daughter, mounted on a tame unicorn. In her hand a javelin of silver, and armed with a breast-plate of gold, artificially wrought like the scales of a porcupine; her guard was one hundred Amazonian dames clad in green silk; after them followed a number of esquires and gentlemen, some upon Barbary steeds, some upon Arabian palfreys, and some on foot, in pace more nimble than the tripping deer, and more swift than the tamest hart upon the mountains of Thessaly.

Thus Nebuzaradan, the great king of Jerusalem, (for so he was called,) solemnly hunted in the wilderness of Judah, a country very much overrun with wild beasts, as the lion, the leopard, the boar, and such like; in which exercise the king appointed, as it was proclaimed by his chief herald at arms, that whosoever slew the first wild beast in the forest should have in reward a corselet of steel, so richly engraven that it should be worth a thousand shekels of silver. Of which honourable enterprise when the champion had understanding, and with what liberal bounty the adventurous knight would be rewarded, his heart was fraught with invincible courage, thirsting after glorious attempts, not only for hope of gain, but for the desire of honour, at which his illustrious and undaunted mind aimed, to immortalise his deeds in the memorable records of fame, and to shine as a crystal mirror to all ensuing times. So closing down his beaver, and locking on his furniture, he scoured the plains before the hunters of Jerusalem, in pace more swift than the winged winds, till he approached an old unfrequented forest, wherein he espied a huge and mighty wild boar, lying before his mossy den, gnawing the mangled joints of some passenger whom he had murdered as he travelled through the forest.

This boar was of wonderful length and size, and so terrible to behold, that at first sight he almost daunted the courage of the Spanish knight: for his monstrous head seemed ugly and deformed, his eyes sparkled like a fiery furnace, his tusks more sharp than pikes of steel, and from his nostrils fumed such a violent breath, that it seemed like a tempestuous whirlwind; his bristles were harder than seven times solid brass, and his tail more loathsome than a wreath of snakes. When St James approached this huge beast, and beheld how he drank the blood of human creatures and devoured their flesh, he blew his silver horn, which hung at the pommel of his saddle by a scarf of green silk; whereat the furious monster turned himself, and most fiercely assailed the noble champion, who very nimbly leaped from his horse, and with his spear struck such a violent blow upon the breast of the boar, that it shivered into twenty pieces; then drawing his falchion from his side, he made a second encounter, but all in vain, for he struck as it were upon a rock of stone, or a pillar of iron, not hurting the boar; when at last, with staring eyes and open jaws, the greedy monster assailed the champion, intending to swallow him alive, the nimble knight trusted more to policy than fortitude, and so skipped from place to place, till on a sudden he thrust his keen-edged battle-axe down the monster's throat, and split his heart asunder. Which being accomplished, he cut off the head, and so presented the issue of the combat to the king of Jerusalem, who, with his mighty train of knights, had now entered the forest. Having graciously received the gift, and bountifully fulfilled his promises, he demanded the champion's country, his religion, and place of his nativity. But no sooner had he intelligence that he was a Christian knight, and born in the territories of Spain, than his kindness changed to a great fury, and in these words he expressed his anger to the Christian champion:

"Knowest thou not, bold knight," said the king of Jerusalem, "that it is the law of Judah to harbour no uncircumcised man, but either to banish him out of the land, or end his days by some untimely death? Thou art a Christian, and therefore shalt die: not all thy country's treasures, the wealthy Spanish mines, nor if the Alps, which divide the countries of Italy and Spain, were turned to hills of burnished gold, and made my lawful heritage, could redeem thy life. Yet for the honour thou has done in Judah I grant thee this favour by the law of arms, to choose thy death, else hadst thou suffered most grievous torment." This severe judgment so amazed the champion, that, in desperation, he would have killed himself by his own sword, but that he thought it more honour to his country to die in the defence of Christendom. So, like a truly noble knight, fearing not the threats of the Jews, he gave the sentence of his own death. First, he requested to be bound to a pine-tree, with his breast laid open naked against the sun; then to have an hour's respite to make his supplication to his Creator; and afterwards to be shot to death by a fair virgin.

Which words were no sooner pronounced, than they disarmed him, bound him to a pine-tree, and laid his breast open, ready to receive the bloody stroke of some unrelenting maiden: but such pity, meekness, mercy, and kind lenity lodged in the heart of every maiden, that none would take in hand, or be the bloody executioner of so brave a knight. At last the tyrannous Nebuzaradan gave strict commandment, upon pain of death, that lots should be cast among the maids of Judah that were there present, and she on whom the lot fell should be the executioner of the condemned Christian. But by chance the lot fell to Celestine, the king's daughter, being the fairest maid then living in Jerusalem, in whose heart no such deed of cruelty could be harboured. Instead of death's fatal instrument, she shot towards his breast a deeply-drawn sigh, the true messenger of love, and afterwards to heaven she thus made her humble supplication:

"Thou great Commander of celestial moving powers, convert the cruel motions of my father's mind into a spring of pitiful tears, that they may wash away the blood of this innocent knight from the habitation of his stained purple soul. O Judah and Jerusalem, within whose bosoms live a wilderness of tigers, more cruel than the hungry cannibals, and more obdurate than untamed lions! What merciless tigers can unrip that breast, where lives the image of true nobility, the very pattern of knighthood, and the seal of a noble mind, No, no, before my hand shall be stained with Christians' blood, I will, like Scylla, against all nature, sell my country's safety, or, like Medea, with the golden fleece, wander to unknown nations."

In such manner complained the beauteous Celestine, the king's daughter of Jerusalem, till her sighs stopped the passage of her speech, and her tears stained the natural beauty of her rosy cheeks; her hair, which glittered like golden wires, she besmeared with dust, and disrobed herself of her costly garments; and then, with a train of her Amazonian ladies, went to the king her father, where, after a long suit, she not only obtained our noble champion's life, but liberty; yet therewithal his perpetual banishment from Jerusalem, and from all the borders of Judah. So this noble and praiseworthy Celestine returned to the Christian champion, who expected every minute to be put to death; and after she had sealed two or three kisses upon his pale lips, being changed through the fear of death, cut the bands that bound his body to the tree into many pieces; and then, with a flood of tears, the emotions of true love, she thus revealed her mind:

"Most noble knight, and true champion of Christendom, thy life and liberty I have gained, but therewith thy banishment from Judah, which is a thought of horror to my soul; for in thy bosom have I built my happiness, and in thy heart I reckon the paradise of my true love; thy first sight and lovely countenance did enchant me; for when these eyes beheld thee mounted on thy princely palfrey, my heart burned in affection towards thee. Therefore, dear knight, in reward of my love, be thou my champion, and for my sake wear this ring, with this poesy engraven in it, *Ardeo affectione*." And so giving him a ring from her finger, together with a kiss from her mouth, she departed with a sorrowful sigh, in company of her father and the rest of his honourable train, back to the city of Jerusalem, being then near sunset. But now St James, having escaped the danger of death, and at full liberty to depart, fell into many cogitations, one time thinking upon the true love of Celestine, (whose name as yet he was ignorant of,) another time upon the cruelty of her father; then resolving to depart into his own country, but looking back to the towers of Jerusalem, his mind suddenly altered, for thither he made up his mind to go, hoping to have sight of his lady and mistress, and to live in some disguised form in her presence, and be his love's true champion against all comers. So gathering certain black berries from the trees, he coloured his body all over like a Blackmoor; and considering that his country's speech would betray him, determined likewise to continue dumb all the time of his residence in Jerusalem.

So, all things settled according to his desire, he took his journey to the city, where with signs he declared his intent, which was, to be entertained in the court, and to spend his time in the service of the king. When the king beheld his countenance, which seemed of the natural colour of the Moor, he little thought that he was the Christian champion, whom before he greatly envied, but accounted him one of the bravest Indian knights that ever his eye beheld; therefore he conferred on him the honour of knighthood, and appointed him to be one of his guard, and likewise his daughter's sole champion. Now when St James saw himself invested in this honourable place, his soul was ravished with such exceeding joy, that he thought no pleasure comparable to his, no Elysium but the court of Jerusalem, and no goddess but his beloved Celestine.

He long continued dumb, casting forth many a loving sigh in the presence of his lady and mistress, not knowing how to reveal the secrets of his mind.

Sometime after, there arrived in the court of Nebuzaradan, the king of Arabia, with the admiral of Babylon, both presuming upon the love of Celestine, and craving her in marriage; but she excluded all notions of love from her chaste mind, only building her thoughts upon the Spanish knight, whom she supposed to be in his own country.

Her importunate suitors, the king of Arabia, and the admiral of Babylon, marvelled at her melancholy; and therefore intended upon an evening to present her with some rare devised masque. So choosing out fit consorts for their courtly pastimes, of which number the king of Arabia was chief and first leader of the train, the great admiral of Babylon was the second, and her own champion, St James, called by the name of the "Dumb Knight," was the third. In this manner the masque was performed:

First, a most excellent concert of music; after which the aforesaid masquers in cloth of gold most curiously embroidered, danced about the hall; at the conclusion the king of Arabia presented Celestine with a costly sword, on the hilt whereof hung a silver glove, and upon the point was placed a golden crown. Then the music sounded another course, of which the admiral of Babylon was leader, who presented her with a vesture of pure silk, of the colour of the rainbow, brought in by Diana, Venus, and Juno. Which being done, the music sounded the third time; in which course, St James, though unknown, was the leader of the dance, and, at the end thereof, presented Celestine with a garland of sweet flowers, which was brought in by three Graces, and put upon her head. Afterwards the Christian champion, intending to discover himself unto his lady and mistress, took her by the hand, and led her to a stately Morisco dance, which was no sooner finished than he offered her the diamond ring which she gave him at his departure in the woods; this she presently knew by the poesy, and shortly after discovered his dumbness, his counterfeit colour, his changing of nature, and the great danger he put himself to for her sake; which caused her, with all the speed she could possibly make, to retire into a chamber which she had by, where the same evening she had a long conference with her faithful lover and adventurous champion. To conclude, they made an agreement betwixt them, and the same night, unknown to any in the court, she bade Jerusalem adieu, and by the light of Cynthia's glittering beams, stole from her father's palace, where, in the sweet company of St James, she took her journey towards the country of Spain. But this noble knight by policy prevented all likely danger, for he shod his horse backwards, whereby, when they were missed in the court, they might be followed the contrary way.

By this means the two lovers escaped from the fury of the Jews, and arrived safely in Spain, in the city of Seville, wherein the brave champion, St James, was born; where we now leave them for a time to their own contented minds. Also passing over the disturbances in Jerusalem for the loss of Celestine, the vain pursuits of adventurous knights, the preparing of fresh horses to follow them, the frantic passion of the king for his daughter, the melancholy grief of the admiral of Babylon for his mistress, and the woful lamentation of the Arabian king for his lady and love, we will return to the adventures of the other Christian champions.

17

# The Pleasant History
# Of Thomas Hic-ka-thrift,

### His Birth and Parentage, and the True Manner
### Of His Performing Many Manly Acts,
### And How He Killed a Gyant. Young Man, Here Thou Mayest
### Behold What Honour Tom Came Unto.

IN THE PEPYSIAN LIBRARY, *Cambridge, is a late seventeenth-century copy of a chapbook which tells a story of a poor lazy boy of great strength who chases a giant away with a wheel and an axletree. The tale undoubtedly had a long oral history before it was printed and still has a faint tradition in the area of Norfolk, England.*

*The story has a universal flavor, recalling many tales of strong boys who protect their parents and neighbors, from the Japanese tales of the exploits of Kintaro to the Scandinavian tales of Grettir—to which it may be related.*

*Of interest are the many games mentioned in the story, including cudgels (a boisterous fighting with short, round sticks), wrestling, hammer throwing (for distance records), football, and bear-baiting. (The latter sport, though illegal, still occurs occasionally in the Great Smokies, when men tie a bear to a tree and then sic dogs on it, taking bets as to the winner of the attack.)*

*The story no doubt appealed both to lusty young protectors and to the protected. It bears some resemblance to Tolkien's narrative of Farmer Giles of Ham.*

The Pleasant History of Thomas Hic-ka-thrift *is reprinted from* Chap-Books and Folk-Lore Tracts, *printed for the Villon Society, London, 1885.*

## THE CONTENTS

What honour Tom came unto.

How Tom Hic-ka-thrift's strength came to be known.

How Tom came to be a Brewers man, and
how he came to kill a gyant, and
at last was Mr. Hic-ka-thrift.

How Tom kept a pack of hounds and kickt
a foot-ball quite away, and how he had like to
have been robbed with four thieves, and how Tom escaped.

*And if that thou dost buy this Book,*
*Be sure that thou dost in it look,*
*And read it o're, then thou wilt say,*
*Thy money is not thrown away.*

In THE REIGN before William the conqueror, I have read in ancient histories that there dwelt a man in the marsh of the Isle of Ely, in the country of Cambridge, whose name was Thomas Hic-ka-thrift, a poor man and day labourer, yet he was a very stout man, and able to perform two days works instead of one: He having one son and no more children in the world, he called him by his own name, Thomas Hickathrift. This old man put his son to good learning, but he would take none, for he was as we call them now in this age, none of the wisest sort, but something soft, and had no docility at all in him.

God calling this old man his father out of the world, his mother being tender of him, and maintained him by her hand labour as well as she could; he being sloathful and not willing to work to get a penny for his living, but all his delight was to be in the chimney corner, and would eat as much at one time as might very well serve four or five ordinary men; for he was in length when he was but ten years of age about eight foot, and in thickness five foot, and his hand was like unto a shoulder of mutton, and in all parts from top to toe he was like a monster, and yet his great strength was not known.

### How Tom Hic-ka-thrifts strength came to be known, the which if you please but to read will give you full satisfaction.

The FIRST TIME that his strength was known was by his mothers going to a rich farmer's house (she being but a poor woman) to desire a buttle of straw to shift herself and her son Thomas. The farmer being an honest charitable man, bid her take what she would. She going home to her son Tom, said, I pray thee go to such a place and fetch me a buttle of straw, I have asked him leave. He swore a great oath he would not go: nay, prithee, Tom go, said his old mother. He swore again he would not go, unless she would borrow him a cart rope. She being willing to please him, because she would have some straw, went and borrowed him a cart rope to his desire.

He taking it went his way; so coming to the farmer's house, the master was in the barn, and two men a thrashing. Said Tom, I am come for a buttle of straw. Tom, said the master, take as much as thou canst carry. He laid down his cart rope, and began to make his buttle; but said they, Tom, thy rope is to short, and jeer'd poor Tom, but he fitted the man well for it: for he made his buttle, and when he had made it, there was supposed to be a load of straw in it, of two thousand weight. But said they, what a great fool art thou, thou canst not carry the tith on't? but Tom took the buttle and flung it on his shoulder, and made no more of it then we do of an hundred weight, to the great admiration of master and men.

Tom Hic-ka-thrift's strength being known in the town, then they would not let him any longer lie basking by the fire in the chimney corner, every one would be hiring him to work; they seeing him to have so much strength, told him that it was a shame for him to live such a lazy course of life, and to lie idle day after day, as he did. So Tom seeing them bait at him in such a manner as they did, he went first to one work then to another; but at length came a man to Tom and desired him to go with him unto the wood, for he had a tree to bring home, and he would content him. So Tom went with him, and he took with him four men beside; but when they came to the wood, they set the cart by the tree and began to draw it up with pullies; but Tom seeing them not able to lift it up, said, stand away, you fools, and takes the tree and sets it on one end, and lays it in the cart. Now, says he, see what a man can do. Marry, it is true, said they. So when they had done coming through the wood they met the woodman, Tom asked him for a stick to make his mother a fire with. I, said the wood-man, take one what thou canst carry. So Tom espyed a tree bigger then was in the cart, and lays it on his shoulder, and goes home with it as fast as the cart and six horses could draw it. This was the second time that Tom's strength was known.

So when Tom began to know that he had more strength than twenty men had, he then began to be merry with men and very tractable, and would run, or go, or jump, and took great delight to be amongst company, and to go to fairs and meetings, and to see sports and pastimes. So going to a feast, the young men were all met, some to cudgels, some to wrastling, some throwing the hammer, and the like; so Tom stood a little to see their sport, and at last goes to them that were a throwing the hammer; and standing a little by to behold their manlike sport, at last he takes the hammer in his hand to feel the weight of it, and bid them stand out of the way, for he would throw it as far as he could. I, said the smith, and jeer'd poor Tom, you'l throw it a great way I'le warrant you; but Tom took the hammer and flung it; and there was a river about five or six furlungs off, and flung it into that: so when he had done, he bid the smith go fetch his hammer again, and laught the smith to scorn; but when Tom had done that, he would go to wrastling, though he had no more skill than an ass had, but what he did by strength; yet he flung all that came, for if once he laid hold they were gone. Some he would throw over his head, some he would lay down slyly, and how he pleased; he would not lock nor strike at their heels, but flung them two or three yards from him, ready to break their necks asunder; so that none at last durst go into the ring to wrastle with him, for they took him to be some devil that was come amongst them; so Tom's fame was spread more in the country.

## *How Tom came to be a Brewer's man; and how he came to kill a Giant, and at last was Mr. Hic-ka-thrift.*

Tom's fame being spread abroad in the country, there was not a man durst give Tom an angry word for he was something foolhardy, and he did not care what he did at them; so that those that knew him would not in the least displease him. But at length there was a brewer at Lyn, that wanted a good lusty man to carry his beer in the marsh and to Wisbich; so hearing of Tom went to hire him, but Tom seemed coy and would not be his man, until his mother and friends did perswade him, and his master intreated him; and likewise promised him a new suit of clothes and cloath him from top to toe; and besides he should eat and drink of the best. So Tom at last yielded to be his man, and his master told him how far he should go; for you are to understand there was a monstrous Gyant, who kept some part of the marsh, and none durst go that way; for if they did he would keep them or kill them, or else he would make bond slaves of them.

But to come to Tom and his master, that he did more work in one day then all his men would do in three; so that his master, seeing him so tractable, and to look so well after his business, made him his head man to go into the marsh, to carry beer by himself, for he needed no man with him. So Tom went every day to Wisbich, which was a very great journey, for it was twenty mile the road way.

Tom going so long that wearisome journey, and finding that way which the Gyant kept was nearer by half, and Tom having gotten more strength by half then before by being so well kept, and drinking so much strong ale as he did; one day he was going to Wisbich, and without saying anything to his master or to any of his fellow servants, he was resolved to make the nearest way to be a road or lose his life, to win the horse, or lose the saddle; to kill or be killed; if he met with the Gyant; and with this resolution he goes the nearest way with his cart, flinging open the gates for his cart and horses to go through; but at last the Gyant spying him, and seeing him to be so bold, thought to prevent him, and came intending to take his beer for a prize, but Tom cared not a fart for him, and the Gyant he met Tom like a lyon, as though he would have swallowed him. Sirrah, said he, who gave you authority to come this way? Do you not know that I make all stand in fear of my sight, and you like a rogue must come and fling my gates open at your pleasure! How dare you presume to do this? Are you so careless of your life? Do you not care what you do? I'le make thee an example for all rogues under the sun; dost thou not see how many heads hang upon yonder tree that have offended my law! But thy head shall hang higher then all the rest for an example. But Tom made him answer, A turd in your teeth for your news, for you shall not find me like one of them. No, said the Gyant, why thou art but a fool, dost thou come to fight with such a one as I am, and bring no weapon to defend thyself withal? Said Tom, I have a weapon here will make you to know you are a traytorly rogue. I, sirrah, said the Gyant, and took that word in high disdain, that Tom should call him a traytorly rogue, and with that he ran into his cave to fetch his great club, intending to dash out Tom's brains at the first blow.

Tom knew not what to do for a weapon, for he knew his whip would do but little good against such a monstrous beast as he was, for he was in length twelve foot, and six foot about the waste; but while the Gyant went for his club, Tom bethought himself of a very good weapon, for he makes no more ado, but takes his cart and turns it upside down, and takes the axletree and the wheel for his shield and buckler, and very good weapons they were in such time of need.

The Giant coming out again, began to stare at Tom, to see him take the wheel in one hand and the axle tree in the other to defend himself with. O! said the Gyant, you are like to do great service with those weapons; I have here a twig, said the Gyant, that will beat thee and thy wheel and axle tree at once unto the ground; that which the Gyant called a twig was as thick as some mill posts are, but Tom was not daunted for all that, for he saw there was but one way to kill or be killed; so the Giant made at Tom with such a vehement force that he made Tom's wheel crack again, and Tom lent the Gyant another as good, for he took him such a weighty blow on the side of the head that he made the Gyant reel again. What, said Tom, are you drunk with my strong beer already.

The Gyant recovering laid on Tom most sad blows; but still as they came Tom kept them off with his wheel so that he had no hurt at all. Tom plyed his work so well, and laid such huge blows at the Giant, that the sweat and blood together ran down his face, and he being fat and foggy, and fighting so long, was almost tired out, asked Tom to let him drink a little, and then he would fight with him again. No, said Tom, my mother did not teach me that wit; whose a fool then? Tom seeing the Gyant begin to be weary, and finding him to fail in his blows, he thought best to make hay while the sun did shine, for he laid on so fast as though he had been mad, till he had brought the Gyant to the ground. The Gyant seeing himself down, and Tom laying so hard on him, roared in a most sad condition, and prayed him not to take away his life and he would do anything for him, and yield himself to him and be his servant; but Tom having no more mercy on him then a dog of a bear, laid still at the Gyant 'till he had laid him for dead, and when he had done he cut off his head and went into his cave, and there he found great store of silver and gold which made his heart to leap. But when he had done, he loaded his cart and went to Wisbich and delivered his beer; and coming home to his master, he told it to him; but his master was so overjoy'd at the news that he would not believe him till he had seen; and getting up the next day he and his master went to see if he spoke true or no, and most of the town of Lyn. But when they came to the place and found the Gyant dead, he shewed them where the head was, and what silver and gold there was in the cave, all of them leapt for joy, for the Gyant was a great enemy to all the country.

This news was spread all up and down the country how Tom Hic-ka thrift had kill'd the Gyant, and well was he that could run or go to see the Gyant and the cave; then all the folks made bonefires for joy; and Tom was a better man respected than before. And Tom took possession of the cave by consent of the country, and everyone said that he did deserve twice as much more. So Tom pulled down the cave and built him a brave house where the cave stood; all the ground that the Gyant kept by force and strength, some he gave to the poor for their common, and the rest he made pastures of and divided the most part into good ground to maintain him and his old mother Jane Hic-ka-thrift. And Tom's fame was spread both far and near throughout the country; and then it was no longer Tom, but Mr. Hickathrift, so that he was now the chiefest man amongst them, for the people feared Tom's anger as much as they did the Gyant before. So Tom kept men and maids, and lived most bravely; and he made him a park to keep deer in; and by his house, which is a town, he built a famous church and gave it the name of St. James' Church, because he killed the Gyant on that day, which is so to this hour and ever will be; and many more good deeds he did which is too tedious to write in this column, but to tell the chief I shall do my endeavour.

### How Tom kept a pack of Hounds; and kickt a Foot-ball quite away; and how he had like to have been robbed by Four Thieves, and how he escaped.

TOM HAVING so much about him and not used to it could hardly tell how for to dispose of it, but yet he did use a means to do it, for he kept a pack of hounds, and men to hunt with him; and who but Tom then. So he took such delight in sport that he would go far and near to any meetings, as cudgel-play, bear-baiting, football play, and the like. But as Tom was riding one day, he seeing a company at football play he lighted off his horse to see that rare sport, for they were playing for a wager; but Tom was a stranger there and none did know him there; but Tom soon spoiled their sport, for he meeting the football took it such a kick that they never found their ball no more; they could see it fly, but whither none could tell, nor to what place; they all wondered at it, and began to quarrel with Tom, but some of them got nothing by it, for Tom gets a spar which belonged to a house that was blown down and all that stood in his way he either killed or knocked down, so that all the country was up in arms to take Tom, but all in vain, for he manfully made way wherever he came. So when he was gone from them, and was going homeward, he chanced to be somewhat late in the evening. On the road there met him four lusty rogues that had been robbing of passengers that way, and none could escape them, for they robbed all they met, both rich and poor. They thought when they met Tom they should get a good prize, they perceiving he was alone, made them cocksure of his money, but they were mistaken, for he got a prize by them. When they met with Tom they straight bid him stand and deliver. What, said Tom, what should I deliver? Your money, sirrah, said they. But, said Tom, you shall give me better words for it first, and be better armed too. Come, come, said they, we do not come hither to prate, but we come for money, and money we will have before you stir from this place. I, said Tom, is it so? Nay then, said he, get it, and take it.

So one of them made at him, but he presently unarmed him, and took away his sword which was made of good trusty steel, and smote so hard at the others that they began to set spurs to their horses and begone, but he soon stayed their journey, one of them having a portmantle behind him, Tom perceiving it to be money fought with more courage than he did before, till at the last he had killed two of the four, and the other two he wounded most grievously that they cryed for quarter. So with much intreating he gave them quarter, but he took all their money which was two hundred pounds to bear his charges home. So when Tom came home he told them how he had served the football players and the four thieves which caused a laugh from his old mother, and to refresh himself went to see how all things did, and what his men had done since he went from home. And going to the forest he wandred up and down, and at last met with a lusty tinker that had a good staff on his shoulder and a great dog to carry his bag and tools. So Tom asked the tinker from whence he came, and whither he was going, for that was no highway. But the tinker being a sturdy fellow bid him go look, and what was that to him, but fools must be meddling. No, says Tom, but I'le make you to know before you and I part it is to me. I, said the tinker, I have been these three long years and have not had one combat with any man. I have challenged many a man but none durst make me answer; I think, said he, they be all cowards in this country, but I hear there is a man in this country which is called Tom Hickathrift that killed a gyant; him I would fain see, said the tinker, to have one combat with him. I, said Tom, but methinks, said he, it might be master with you; I am the man, said he, what have you to say to me? Why verily, said the tinker, I am glad we are so happily met together, that we may have one single combat. Sure, said Tom, you do but jest. Marry, said the tinker, I am in earnest. A match, said Tom. 'Tis done, said the tinker. But, said Tom, will you give me leave to get me a twig? I, said the tinker, hang him that will fight with a man unarmed, I scorn that.

So Tom steps to the gate and takes one of the rails for his staff; so to it they fell, the Tinker at Tom, and Tom at the Tinker, like two giants they laid on at each other. The Tinker had a leathern coat on, and at every blow Tom gave the Tinker, his coat roar'd again, yet the Tinker did not give way to Tom an inch. But Tom gave the Tinker a blow on the side of the head, which felled the Tinker. Now, Tinker, where are you? said Tom.

But the Tinker being a nimble fellow, leapt up again, and gave Tom a blow, made him reel again, and followed his blows, and took Tom on the other side which made Tom's neck crack again. So Tom flung down his weapon and yielded the Tinker the better on't, and took him home to his house, where I shall leave Tom and the Tinker till they be recovered of their sad wounds and bruises.

FINIS.

# 18

# The Famous and Remarkable History Of Sir Richard Whittington, Three Times Lord Mayor Of London:

### Who Lived in the Time of King Henry The Fifth In the Year 1419, with all the Remarkable Passages, And Things of Note, Which Happened in his Time: With his Life and Death.

LIKE THE TALE of *Thomas Hickathrift, this story is part history, mainly folklore. The chapbook version reprinted here belongs to the seventeenth century, and bears the initials "T.H." which may stand for the playwright and pamphleteer, Thomas Heywood (1574–1641). The story was very popular, there being a play, three ballads, and at least two chapbooks about it in the seventeenth century. On September 21, 1668, Pepys saw a puppet show about Whittington at Southwark Fair, which suggests how much it had entered the domain shared by children and adults.*

*The story is one of a poor boy, who by following instinctively certain inner directions —turning back at the sound of Bow Bells—becomes rich and much honored . . . thrice Lord Mayor of London.*

*Actually, the real Whittington did become Lord Mayor, but he was not of humble origin. Born in the late fourteenth century, a contemporary of Chaucer, he was a younger son of a Gloucestershire nobleman. Appointed mayor originally by Richard II, he continued in office, was knighted by Henry V, and in 1419, elected mayor for the fourth time. He was a good man who gave money to the poor, founded Whittington College, and contributed to the building of Guildhall Library. The following version of his story is in the Pepysian Library, Cambridge.*

*The tale also enjoyed great popularity in the eighteenth and nineteenth centuries. Families enjoyed it when it was produced as a parlor play in the toy theatre. An edition was published in Hartford by Nathaniel Patten in 1788. In 1937 a Holiday House, New York, edition was so attractively presented that it was selected by the American Institute of Graphic Arts as one of the Fifty Books of the Year.*

The Famous and Remarkable History of Sir Richard Whittington *is reprinted from* Chap-Books and Folk-Lore Tracts, *printed for the Villon Society, London, 1885.*

THE SAYING is not so old as true, He that refuseth to buy counsel cheap shall buy repentance dear; neither let any work [mock?] a man in his misery, but rather beware by him how to avoid the like misfortune; if thou intend to do any good, defer it not till the next day, for thou knowest not what may happen over night to prevent thee. Behold thyself in a looking glass, if thou appearest beautiful do such things as may become thy beauty; but if thou seem foul or deformed, let the actions of thy life make good that splendor which thy face lacketh. Tell not thy mind to every man, make thy self indebted to no man, be friend to few men, be courteous to all men, let thy wit be thy friend, thy mind thy companion, thy tongue thy servant, let vertue be thy life, valour thy love, honour thy fame and heaven thy felicity. These (Reader) be good documents for thee to follow, and I am now to present thee with a worthy president to imitate; observe his beginning, forget not the middle passage of his life, and thou wilt no question crown his head. He that made all things of nothing can of a little make much, and multiply a mite into a magazine, as will easily appear by the succeeding history.

This Richard Whittington was so obscurely born that he could scarcely give account of his parents or kindred, and being almost starved in the country, necessity compelled him up to London, hoping to find more charity in the town than in the country: to beg he was ashamed, to steal he did abhor: two days he spent in gaping upon the shops and gazing upon the buildings feeding his eyes but starving his stomach. At length meer faintness compell'd him to rest himself upon a bench before a merchant's gate, where he not long sat but the owner of the house having occasion of business into the town finding him a poor simple fellow, and thinking that he had no more within him than appeared without, demanded of him why he loytered there, and being able to work for his living did not apply himself unto some lawful calling, threatning him at the first with the stocks and the whipping-post; but the poor man, after the making of some plain leggs and courtesie, desired him to pardon him, and told him that he was a dejected man, who desired any imployment, and that no pains how mean or course (*sic*) soever could seem tedious or burthensome unto him, so he might but find some good master, by whose charity he might relieve his present necessity: for his great ambition was but to keep his body from nakedness and his stomach from hunger, and told him withal how long it was since he had tasted meat or drink.

The worthy merchant seeing him of a personable body, and an ingenious aspect howsoever both were clouded under a rustick habit, began somewhat to commiserate his estate, and knocking for a servant had him take in that fellow and give him such victuals as the house for the present afforded, and at his return he would have further conference with him. The servant did as he was commanded and took him in.

The merchant went then to the Exchange, which was then in Lumber Street, about his affairs; in which intrim (*sic*) poor Whittington was hied into the kitchin to warm himself, for faintness by reason of hunger and cold (for it was then in the winter time) had quite rob'd him of his colour. Meat was set before him in plenty, and being bred in the country, as the proverb goeth, *He fed like a farmer*, and having satisfied himself sufficiently and warm'd him to the full, a fresh colour began to come into his cheeks: at which the Merchant's daughter (hearing of a new come guest) came into the kitchin, and began to question him of divers things concerning the country, to all which he gave her such modest and sensible answers that she took a great liking unto him, and so left him.

Dinner time came, and Master Fitzwarren (for so was the merchant called) came home with a good stomach, and brought a friend or two with him from the Exchange; down they sat to meat, and had speech of many things at the table; meanwhile the servants were set also at dinner, who would needs have Whittington, though he had so lately broke his fast, to keep them company, some of them delighting in his country speech, others deriding his supposed simplicity.

But to come to the purpose, the table being withdrawn in the parlour, and the guests departed, and Master Fitzwarren and his daughter left alone, she being of a good and gentle disposition, began to commend his charity concerning the poor man whom he relieved that morning, to whom he answered, God-a-mercy daughter, thou hast done well to remember me, such a one I sent indeed, but have my servants done as I commanded them? and where is he now? who answered him, that she had given order he should stay dinner, and not depart the house till he himself had further spoken with him. At which they both went unto the Hall, and called the fellow before them; who appeared unto them with such a bashful humility that it seemed to them both to beg a charity; some language past betwixt them concerning him, which gave them content; at length they bid him retire himself.

When the father and the daughter had some private conference concerning him she urged him to entertain him into his house, and that there would be some employment for him, either to run or to go of errands or else to do some drudgery in the kitchin, as making of fires, scouring kettles, turning the spit, and the like: To whom the father reply'd that indeed his work might be worth his meat, but he had no lodging to spare, and she again answered that there were garrets in the house that were put to no use at all, and in one of them he might conveniently be lodged and put the house to no trouble at all.

Well at length he was admitted, and made a member of the family, in which he demeaned himself so well by his willingness to run or go or do any service how mean so ever that he had got the good will of all the whole household, only the kitchin maid being a curst quean, and knowing him to be an under servant to her, domineered over him and used him very coursely and roughly, of which he would never complain, though he had cause enough. The garret in which he lay, by reason it had been long unfrequented, was troubled with rats and mice, insomuch that he could not sleep in the night but they ran over his face, and much disturb'd him in his rest: to prevent which having got a penny either for going of an errand, or for making clean boots or shooes or the like, with that he bought a young cat which he kept in his garret, and whatsoever he had from the reversion of the servants table he would be sure to reserve part for her, because he had found by experience that she had rid him of the former inconveniences.

The History tells us that this merchant, Master Hugh Fitzwarren, was so generous that he never adventured any ship to sea but he would have his daughter, his cashire, and every one of his servants, whar (sic) or whatsoever, to put in something, and to adventure with him, and according to that proportion which they could spare, every one received to a token at the return of the ship. His daughter she began, the rest followed, and the servants borrowed out of their wages everyone according to their abilities, and when they all had done Whittington was remembered and called for, and his master telling him the custome of his home, asked him what he had to hazard in this adventure. who replyed again, he was a poor man, and had nothing in the world saving the cloaths upon his back, but for money he had none at all: then his daughter drew out her purse and told her father, that for his servant Whittington she would lay down whatsoever he would desire. Who answered again, that what she had spoke was nothing to the purpose; for whatsoever was ventured in that kind must be out of ones proper goods and chattels, and again demanded of him if he had anything he could call his own to put to hazard, and charged him deeply concerning that point, who making some unnecessary leggs, told him that he had nothing which he could call his saving a cat, which he had bought with his penny, which he could not spare because she had done him so many good offices, and told them every circumstance before related, which when the merchant heard he told him that he should venture that commodity and none else, and charged him to fetch her instantly (for the ship which was called the Unicorn) was fallen down as low as Blackwal and all their lading was already had aboard. Whittington although unwilling to part from so good a companion yet being forced by his masters command by whom he had his subsistence he brought her and (not without tears) delivered her to his factor who was partly glad of her, by reason they were troubled with mice and rats in the ship, which not only spoyled their victuals but damaged their wares and commodities.

I must leave the cat upon her voyage at sea and honest Whittington on land, who by that cursed quean the kitchin maid was so beaten and abused that he was as weary of his life as of his service: for she (usurping upon his plainness and modesty) would be quarrelling with him, upon every small or no occasion at all; sometimes beating him with the broom, sometimes laying him over the shoulders with a laddle, the spit or what came next to her hands, being of so dogged a disposition that she still continued her cruelty towards him, and therefore he resolved with himself to run away, and for that purpose he had bundled up those few clothes which he had, and before day broke was got as far as Bun-hill, and then he sat down to consider with himself what course he were best to take; where by chance (it being all-hallows day) a merry peal from Bow Church began to ring, and as he apprehended they were tun'd to this ditty,—

Turn again Whittington, Lord Mayor of London,
Turn again Whittington, Lord Mayor of London.

This took such a great impression in him, that finding how early it was, and that he might yet come back in his masters house before any of the family were stirring, he resolved to go back, and found every thing according to his own wishes and desires, insomuch that when the household were up none could challenge him to have been missing. And thus he continued as before in his first plainness and honesty, well beloved of all save the kitchin drudge; I come now to tell you what became of his adventure.

It so hapned that this goodly ship Unicorn was by contrary gusts and bad weather driven upon the utmost coast of Barbary, where never any Englishman (or scarce any Christian) had ever traded before, where they showed their commodities and offered them to be vended. The Moors came down in multitudes, much taken with the beauty of their ship, for they had never seen any of that bigness or burthen before, but when they had taken a serious view of their commodities as hatchets, knives and looking-glasses, fish-hooks, &c. but especially their cloth and kersies of several sizes and colours, they brought them gold in abundance for it was more plentiful with them then (*sic*) lead or copper with us.

Presently the news was carried to the king who sent some of his chief nobility to bring him some sorts of every commodity that was aboard, which when he saw they pleased him highly, sending for the master and merchants factor to court. He at their own rate bargained with them for their whole lading, nor would he suffer them to depart till he had feasted them royally.

Now the fashion of the Moors is not to sit at the table as the custom is among us, but to have a rich carpet spread upon the ground, and when the meal or banquet is served in, as well the king himself as the rest sit round about cross-legg'd as taylors commonly used to do upon their shop-boards, and in that manner our English are set at the king's banquet, but the meal was no sooner served in but swarms of rats and mice seized upon the dishes, and snatched away the meat even from the king and queen's trenchers: at which the factor being annoyed asked one of the nobility (by an interpreter) if they preserved those vermin for sport, or if they were noysome, and troublesome unto them: who answered him again, that they were the greatest vexation unto them that could be possible, and by reason. of their multitudes they could not be destroyed, but the king would willingly give half the revenue of his crown if he could but only clear the court of them, for not only his table but his very bed-chamber swarmed with them, insomuch that he durst not lay him down to rest without a watch about him, to keep them off his pillow: To whom the factor replyed, that they had a strange beast aboard which he made no doubt would rid them of these vermine: which being told the king he rose from his place and imbracing the factor told him if he could shew him such a creature he would ballast his vessel with silver and lade her with gold and pearl. Who appre-hending the occasion made very coy of the business, telling him it was a creature of great value and not common. Besides they could not spare her from the ship, in regard when they were asleep yet she was still waking in the night, not only to preserve their merchan-dise but there dyet from the like spoyl. The more dainty that he made of the matter the more earnest was the king for this beast, insomuch that he was presently sent for.

And a second feast being prepared and the rats and mice appearing as they did before, the young merchant having the cat under his cloak the king desired to see the thing which he had before so much commended; when presently he discovered her, and cast her among them; she no sooner saw these vermine but fell upon them with such a fury that here lay one panting, there another quite dead; nor left them till she had frighted and disperst the whole number, but such as she seized their carkasses lay there as witnesses of their unexpected slaughter.

Great pleasure took the king and the nobility in the sport, vowing that the hunting of the lyon (of which there was plenty in that country) was not answerable unto it. In the interim one began to praise her for her colour, another commending her for her valour, one said she had the countenance of a lyon, and every one gave his sentence. When the poor cat finding no more work for her to do, went round to the King and Queen purling and curling (as their manner is), which they apprehended to be, as if she inquired of them what she had deserved for that late service.

To cut off circumstance, no price could part them, and the rather when the factor had told the king that she was with kittens, and that her brood would in some few years, being carfully lookt into, furnish the whole kingdom, so that Whittingtons cats adventure only surmounted all the ships lading beside, with which fortune and unexpected gain we bring them safe into England; the ship lying at anchor near Blackwal, and the Pilot and Cape-merchant, with some other officers in the ship at Mr. Fitzwarrens house, which was by Leaden-Hall, to give accompt of their voyage. But these caskets of jewels and pearls, with other unvaluable (*sic*) riches which were given for the cat, they caused to be brought along, not daring, by reason of their inestimable value, to trust them in the ship. The Bills of lading and the benefit of the return of the Commodities being viewed and considered of by the owner, he praised God for so prosperous a voyage, and called all his servants and gave order that according to their adventures every one should receive his portion.

At length casting his eye upon those rich caskets and cabinets, he asked to whose share they belonged; who whispered him in the ear, and told him to his poor Whittington, relating every particular as is before discoursed. To whom Master Fitzwarren replyed, if they then be his, God forbid I should keep from him the least farthing that is his right, and presently commanded Whittington to be sent for by the name of Mr. Whittington.

The servants not knowing anything of the business, went unto him into the kitchin, where he was then rubbing the spits, scouring the kettles, and making clean the dressers, and told him he must come to his Master presently into the parlor. The poor man excused himself, that his shooes were dirty and the room was rubb'd, and if he should but touch any thing there he should spoyl and deface those things in the room. But still the master of the House called for Master Whittington, sending one servant after another till he was brought before him; and having scraped some few legs, instantly his master took him by the hand, and called for a chair for Master Whittington, his daughter, the pilot, and the factor, every one of them saluted him by the name of Mr. Whittington and forced him to sit down. He wondering what this should mean desired them not to mock a poor simple man who meant none any harm, &c. and wept (the tears dropping from his eyes), desiring them not to deride his poverty, for his ambition was never to come so high as from the kitchin to the hall much more from the hall to the parlor.

Then came his master to him seriously and said, Indeed Mr. Whittington, we are all in very good earnest, for you are at this time a better man than myself in estate, and then shewed him all those cabinets and caskets, and how richly they were lined.

When he perceived by all their earnest asserverations that all was true he first fell down upon his knees and gave God most hearty thanks, who out of his great bounty would vouchsafe to cast an eye upon so poor and wretched a creature as himself; then turning to his master he presented all his riches before him and told him that all he had was at his disposing and service, who answered him again, that for his own part God had sent him sufficient of his own, neither would he take from him the value of one Barbary ducket. He came nere and with a low leg saluted his mistris, and told her that when she pleased to make choice of a husband he would make her the richest marriage in London, because she was so willing out of her own purse (when he was altogether penniless) to lay out for his adventure. To the pilot, and master, and every officer, and common saylor he gave liberal according to their degree, even to the ship boy, and then to every servant of the house, nay to the very kitchin wench who was so churlish unto him, and had so often basted him instead of her roast meats; having caused her to be called unto him he gave her an hundred pounds towards her marriage.

This being done, taylors were sent for, sempsters and the like to put him into cloaths and linnen of the best, who were to accommodate him with all speed possible, and his lodging in the garret was chang'd into the best chamber of the house. And when the barber had been with him and the rest to make him compleat in his habit, there was a strange and sudden metamorphosis; for out of a smoky and dirty kitchin-drudge there appeared a proper and well-proportioned man, and gentile merchant, in so much that his young mistris began to cast a more amorous eye upon him than before, which not a little pleased Master Fitzwarren her father, who intended a match betwixt them.

The brute of this great adventure was presently revised through the whole city, insomuch that his master intreated his late servant to walk with him into the Exchange to see the fashion of the merchants, which he did, when all of them came about him and saluted him, some bid God give him joy of his fortune, others desired of him better and further acquaintance, and every one as his several fancy led him: some commended him for his person, others for his modest answers and discreet carriage. Indeed, wealth is able to make all these good where they are most wanting, which was not in him as appears by the sequel.

Within few weeks the match was propounded betwixt Master Whittington and Mistris Alice, and willingly entertained by both parties and not without great cost, with the invitation of the Lord Mayor and the Aldermen very nobly celebrated, and the bridegroom by this means had got acquaintances with the best.

After this his father-in-law demanded of his son what he purposed to take in hand (his freedom being offered him). Who made answer again that since God had so blest him in his small adventure he would not leave it of so, but prove his goodness in a greater, and that his purpose was to turn merchant, which reply gave him no small content in regard he knew the best among them would be glad to have the society of so hopeful a citizen, which he continued adventuring in divers bottoms with his father, and had very happy and prosperous returns.

The time being come when he was prickt for Sheriff he modestly refused it as unable to take so great a charge, and would willingly have paid his fine, which his father-in-law would not suffer, at whose persuasion he took the place upon him, in which he so well behaved himself in the management of all affairs belonging to his office that he not only left it without the least taxation, but with a general love and approbation, insomuch that the universal eye of the whole ctiy was fixt upon him in an hopeful expectation what a profitable member of that united body he might futurely prove, and this hapned in the year of our Lord 1493, Sir John Hodley grocer being mayor and Drewerie Barentine his fellow Sheriff, of the truth of which Mr. Fabian in his *Chronicle* and Mr. John Stow in his *Survey of London* can fully satisfie you.

In the year 1497 and the one and twentieth of the same Kings reign, Sir Richard Whittington was Lord Mayor of London, John Woodcok and William Askam being Sheriffs, and he held the place with great reputation and honour. In which time of his Mayoralty there was much discontent in the kingdom, by reason of many differences betwixt the King and the Commons; the circumstances whereof were here too long to relate, only one thing is worthy of observation that whether by his adventures or no may it be questioned, bringing in yearly such store of gold, silks, sattins, velvets, damasks, stones, and jewels, &c. into the kingdom might be the cause of that great pride and rioting in apparel which was used in those days. But as Harding, Fabian, and others have left to me how in that year of his Mayoralty and after there resorted to the Kings Court at their pleasures daily, at the least ten thousand persons. In his kitchin were three hundred servitors, and in every office according to that rate. Moreover of ladies, chamber-maids, and laundresses about three hundred, and they all exceeded in gorgeous and costly apparel far above their degrees; for even the yeomen and grooms were clothed in silks and velvets, damasks, and the like, with imbroydery, rich furs, and goldsmiths work, devising very strange and new fashions.

And in this year also, about the feast of St. Bartholomew, grew a great discord betwixt the Duke of Hereford and Mowbery, Duke of Norfolk, the beginning thereof being as followeth: The two Dukes riding from the Parliament towards their lodgings, the Duke of Norfolk said to the other, Sir, you see how variable the King is in his words, and (reflecting upon what had past) how without mercy he putteth his Lords and kinsfolks to death, imprisoning some and exciting others. Therefore it behoveth us not too much to trust to his fair and smooth language, for doubtless in time he will bring even to us the like death and destruction. Of which words he accused him to the King, which the other denying it was to be tryed by combate. The lists were appointed and the day of meeting the eleventh day of September, to which place and on the day assigned came both the Dukes and bravely accoutred, appeared before the King ready to enter into battel; when the King threw down his warder, and staying the combate banished the Duke of Hereford for ten years, but the Duke of Norfolk for ever, was travelling many countries, at the last came to Venice and then ended his life.

Again in 1406, and in the eighth of Henry the fourth, Sir Richard Whittington was the second time Lord Mayor, Nicholas Worton and Geffery Brook being Sheriffs. Again in the year 1409, being the seventh year of Henry the fifth, he supplyed the Pretorship, Robert Whittington (his near Kinsman) and John Butler being Sheriffs, and which is more remarkable of him then of any other that ever preceded him in that place of honour, he was once Sheriff and three times Lord Mayor of this famous and honourable City in three several Kings reigns.

Now to cut off all circumstances and come close to the matter, we may easily find what this man was, by the pious and religious acts done in his life to the Cities present grace, use and benefit, and to his own blessed memory for ever.

In the Vintry-ward he built a church and dedicated it to S. Michael calling it Pater Noster in the Royal, and added to it a Colledge founded to St. Mary, and placed therein a President and four fellows which ought to be masters of arts, besides other yearly allowance to clerks and young schollars, near which he erected an Hospital which he called God's house, for thirteen poor men, and there according to the devout superstition of those days were to pray for the souls of his father-in-law Hugh Fitzwarren and Dame Molde his wife, for whom he erected a fair tomb in the church he before built, leaving also a place for himself and Dame Alice his lady when it should please God to call them. In which place they were afterwards both of them according to their degree very honourably interred, great mourning and much lamentation being made for him by the Commons of the City in regard he was a man so remarkable for his charity.

He builded another brave structure which he called after his own name Whittington Colledge, with a perpetual allowance for Divinity Lectures to be read there for ever, leaving good land for the maintenance thereof.

And on the west side of the City he built that famous gate and prison to this day called Newgate, and thereupon caused the Merchants arms to be graven in stone. He added to St. Bartholomew's Hospital in Smithfield and was at the charge of repairing thereof.

Further at the Grey-Fryars in London he erected a Library as a testimony of the great love he had to Learning, which he began in the year of our Lord 1421 and finished it in the year following. Moreover that place which is called the Stocks to this day, betwixt Cheapside and Cornhill, a good house of stone, which for a flesh market and a fish market greatly beneficial to the City.

Besides he enlarged Guild Hall and glazed most or all of the windows at his own costs or charges, paving the Hall and contributing largely to the Library, adding to those places a conduit which yieldeth store of sweet and wholesome water to the general good and benefit of the City.

In the year 1497, when Sir Richard Whittington was first elected Lord Mayor, that rebel Sir John Oldcastle was taken in the territories of the Lord Powess, not without danger and hurt of some that took him, at which time all the States of the realm were assembled at Parliament in London, therein to provide the King of a subsidy and other aid of money and ammunition, who took great pains beyond the seas in France. These Lords and others when they heard that the publick enemy was taken they agreed all not to dissolve the Parliament, until he were examined, and heard to answer in the same. Whereupon the Lord Powess was sent for to fetch him up with power and great aid, who brought him to London in a lyter wounded very much having received seventeen wounds and also a clerk which he called his Secretary with him that was of his counsel in all his secrecy. As soon as the aforesaid Sir John Oldcastle was brought into the Parliament before the Earl of Bedford who was then left Regent and Governor of the Realm in the time of the King's absence being in France and other Lords and States, his indictment being read before him of his forcible insurrection against the King and State in St. Gyles's Fields, and other treasons and outrages by him committed, the question was asked how he could excuse himself and show why he should not be judged to dye according to the law. But he seeking other talk and discourse of the mercies of God, and that all mortal men that would be followers of God ought to prefer mercy above judgment and that vengeance pertained only to the Lord, and ought not to be practised by them that worship, but to be left to God alone, with many other words to protract the time, until the Lord Chief Justice admonished the Regent not to suffer him to spend the time so vainly, in molesting the nobles of the Realm, whereupon the Duke of Bedford, Regent, commanded him to answer formally and punctually to the matter laid to his charge.

Then said Sir John, being thus urged at last after deliberation taken, he said, It is the least thing that I account of to be judged by you as of man's judgment, and again he began to talk, but nothing to the purpose until the Chief Justice commanded him again to answer finally, and to answer them if he could, why he should not suffer death according to his desert. To which he stoutly answered that he had no judge amongst them, so long as his liege Lord King Richard was alive and in his realm of Scotland, which answer when he had made, because there needed no further witness, he was then presently censured to be drawn and hanged on a gallows and then to be burnt hanging upon the same, which judgment was executed upon him the thirtieth day of December in St.

Gyles's Fields, where many honourable persons were present, and the last words that he spake were to Sir Thomas Upingham, adjuring him that if he saw him rise from death to life again the third day he would procure that his sect which he had raised might be in peace and quiet. He was hanged by the neck in a chain of iron and after consumed by fire.

Moreover it is recorded that in the time of this worthy pretor Sir Richard Whittington the glorious city of Constantinople was taken by Mahomet the Second, Prince of the Turks, whose souldiers sacked it with all extremity and omitted no manners of cruelty by violence to either virgins, aged women, or sucking babes. This Sir Richard Whittington had traffick from thence by his factors which there abode, and were then taken prisoners, so that he lost near upon fifteen thousand pounds, which when he heard of never was so much as cast down or dismayed, but said God will send more; yea such was the incessant practice of the Turkish tyranny upon this imperial city, as it exceeded the damage, rapes and spoyls of other cities. They also beheaded at the same time Constantine, sticking his head upon a launce, and with derision caused it to be carried thorow the Turkish camp.

In the space of a week after, there hapned a horrible tempest of thunder and lightning which burned almost eight hundred houses and spoiled three thousand people at the sacking of the aforesaid city by the said Mahomet. The Turks found therein so much treasure that they wondred that the citizens would not spend it in souldiers for their own defence, but so dotingly to spare the true spending thereof to become an enticing prey for their irreconcileable enemies, for indeed it was thought that if the State would have hired souldiers, and given them good pay they might have raised the siege of the Turks. It is an old and true saying, Covetousness is the mother of ruine and mischief.

This strange thing hapned in the second time that he was elected Lord Mayor and that was upon the twenty-seventh of April, being Tuesday in Easter week: William Foxley, Pot maker for the Mint in the Tower of London, fell asleep, and so continued sleeping and snoring and could not be wakened with pricking, cramping, or otherwise burning or whatsoever till the first day of the term, which was full 14 days and 15 nights. The cause of this his sleeping could not be known though the same was diligently searched for by the King's Command of his Physicians and other learned men, yea the King himself examined the said William Foxley, who was in all points found at his awaking to be as if he had slept but one night, and yet lived 41 years after. But in length of time did call to mind how he did wish to God that he might sleep a fortnight together if it was not so and so concerning a bargain between a neighbour of his and himself.

One Thursday in Whitson week following the Duke of Somerset with Anthony Rivers and four others kept Justs and Tournament before the King and Queen and others of the nobility in the Tower of London, against three Esquires of the Queen's Bedchamber, which were performed before some of the French nobility that then were Prisoners to the King, which he took in France, to the great admiration of those strangers who never saw the like action before, being so earnestly performed. There was also Sir Richard Whittington and the two Sheriffs, and that night the King and Queen did sup with the Lord Mayor.

Those strangers which beheld those Justs were prisoners in the Tower at that time, namely, the Duke of Orleance and Burbon, brother to the Duke of Britain, the Earls of

Vaudosine, of Ewe and Richmond, and the High Marshal of France, and many other Knights and Esquires to the number of seven hundred, all which were at one time prisoners to the King, but nobly used and attended every one according to their rank and quality, who when they were ransomed made it known to their King how honourably they were attended in England, and what respect the King and our English nation shewed them being prisoners who might have taken their lives away as well as their persons prisoners.

The second thing that was remarkable in Sir Richard Whittington's year was that the King kept his Christmas at Lambeth, and at the feast of Purification seven Dolphins of the sea came up to the River of Thames and played there up and down until four of them were kill'd.

On Saturday the eve of St. Michael the Archangel the year following, in the morning before day, betwixt the hour of one and two of the Clock, began a terrible earthquake with Lightning and thunder which continued the space of six hours, and that universally through the whole world, so that most men thought the world as then would have ended. The unreasonable beasts roared and drew to the town with a hideous noise, also the fowls of the ayr cryed out, such was the work of God at that time to call his people to repentance.

The four and twentieth day of January following a battel or combat was fought in Smithfield within the lists before the King between the men of Feversham in Kent, John Upton Notary Appelant and John Down Gentleman defendant. John Upton accused John Down that he and his compiers should design the King's death on the day of his Coronation following. When they had fought somewhat long and received each of them some wounds, and still persisting in their violent action and no hopes to find out the truth, the King took up the matter and forgave both parties.

On Candlemas eve following in divers places of England was great weathering of wind, hail, snow, rain with thunder and lightning, whereby the church of Baldock in Hertfordshire and the church and part of the town of Walden in Essex, with other neighbouring villages, were sore shaken, and the steeple of St. Pauls in London about two in the afternoon was set on fire in the midst of the shaft first on the west side and then on the south, and divers people espying the fire came to quench it in the steeple, which they did with vinegar, so far as they could find, so that when the Lord Mayor with much people came to Pauls to have holpen if need had been they returned again every man to his own home, trusting in God all had been well, but anon after between eight and nine of the clock the fire burst out again afresh out of the steeple, by reason of the wind more hot and fervent than before, and did much hurt to the lead and timber thereof. Then the Lord Mayor and many people came thither again and with vinegar quenched the fire which was so violent, but no man received any hurt.

Moreover in Sir Richard Whittington's time lived one Richard Fleming, Bishop of Lincoln, in the year 1430 who founded Lincoln Colledge in Oxford, which was afterwards in Richard the third's time in the year of our Lord 1479 by Thomas Rotherham Bishop of the same sea (*sic*) much augmented and enlarged with great revenues. Likewise Magdalen Colledge in Oxford was built by William Wainfleet Bishop of Winchester, who was a loving and constant friend to Sir Richard Whittington and did much good in many parts of this kingdom, and the said Sir Richard did largely contribute to these and the like pious uses by the intreaty of this Bishop.

In the year of our Lord 1419, in which Sir Richard Whittington was the third time inaugurated into the Mayoralty as is before mentioned King Henry the fifth, who having conquered the greatest part of France and espoused Katherine sole daughter to the King and heir to the crown, taking leave of his father-in-law, embarked with his Royal bride and landed at Dover upon Candlemas Day, leaving in France for his deputy his brother the Duke of Clarence, from thence arrived in London the fourteenth day of February, and the Queen came thither the one and twentieth day of the same month, being met upon Black-Heath by the Lord Mayor and three hundred aldermen and prime citizens in gold chains and rich costly habits with other sumptuous and brave devices as pageants, speeches and shows to the great delight and content of both their Maiesties.

The four and twentieth day of February following being St. Mathew's Day her coronation was solemnized in St. Peter's Church in Westminster; which being ended, she was afterwards royally conveyed into the great hall and there under a rich canopy of State sat to dinner, upon whose right hand sate at the end of the table the Lord Archbishop's grace of Canterbury and Henry called the rich Cardinal Bishop of Winchester, upon the left hand of the Queen sat the King of Scots in a chair of State, and was served with covered dishes, as the Bishops were. But after them and upon the same side next to the Boards end were scated the Dutchess of York and Countess of Huntington, the Earl of March holding a scepter in his hand, kneeling upon the right side, the Earl Marshal in the like manner kneeled upon the left hand of the Queen: the Countess of Kent sat under the table at the right foot, and the Countess Marshal at the left foot of her Majesty.

Humphrey Duke of Glocester was that day overseer and stood before the Queen bareheaded, Sir Richard Newel was carver and the Earl of Suffolk's brother cup-bearer, Sir John Stewart, Sewer, the Lord Clifford (instead of the Earl of Warwick) Pantler, the Lord Willoby (instead of the Earl of Arundel) chief Butler, the Lord Gray Caterer, Naperer, the Lord Audley (in the stead of the Earl of Cambridge) Almner, the Earl of Worcester was Lord high Marshal, who rode about the Hall on a great courser, with many tip-staves about him to make room in the Hall. In the which Hall next after the Queen, the Barons of the Cinque Ports began the table, upon the right hand towards St. Steven's Capel (*sic*), and beneath them at the table sat the Vouchers of the Chancery, and upon the left hand next to the cupboard sat Sir Richard Whittington (now the third time Lord Mayor) and his brethren the Aldermen of London. The rest of the Bishops began the table over against the Baron of the Cinque Ports, and the ladies and chief noble-women the table against the Lord Mayor and the Aldermen, at which two tables of the Bishops the Bishop of London and the Bishop of Durham sat highest at the one and the Countess of Stafford and the Countess of March on the other. And for ordering of the service divers chief lords were appointed officers as Steward, Controuler, Surveyor, and the like, which places were supplyed by the Earls of Northumberland and Westmorland, the Lord Fizmur, the Lord Farneval, the Lord Gray of Wilton, the Lord Feres of Groby, the Lord Poynings, the Lord Harrington, the Lord Ducy, the Lord Daker, the Lord Delaware, &c.

I have shewed you onely the ordering of this rich feast, but the cost and sumptuousness of the fare would ask too long and large a circumstance to discourse; what I have hitherto done was onely to show to the world that at those high solemnities inaugurations and coronations the Lord Mayor of the City of London and the Aldermen have place,

and their presence is still required; the City being the King's Chamber and in an inter-
regnum he the first and prime officer in the kingdom. But I fear I have dwelt too long on
the premises which I hope none will hold for an unnecessary deviation. I come now to
discourse unto you of Sir Richard Whittington's invitation of the King and Queen into
the City when he bountifully feasted them in his own house at his own proper charge.

How great and magnificent the Londoners feasts be even amongst themselves especially at that high and pompous festival at Guild-Hall the day after Simon and Jude, at
the solemn inuaguration of his Lordship who but knows, as also the ordinary Tables of the
Lord Mayor and the Sheriffs where there is free and generous entertainment for all men of
fashion and quality, the like both for plenty of dishes and order of service is not elsewhere
to be or found through Europe. If then their daily provision be so curious and costly, what
may we think their variety and rarity was at the invitation and entertainment of two such
great majesties? I must therefore leave it to the Readers imagination being so far tran-
scending my expression. Let it therefore give satisfaction to any one that shall doubt
thereof, that it was performed to the everlasting reputation of the honour of the city and
great content of these royal personages invited. The bounty of the table not to be
question'd. I come now to the fire that he made in the Presence chamber where the King
and Queen then dined, which was only of sweet and odoriferious (sic) wood, far exceeding the smell of juniper, for it was mixed with mace, cinnamon, and other rare and costly
spices, which did cast such a pleasant and delightful savor through the room that it
pleased his majesty to call him unto him and say, my good Lord Mayor, though your fare
be choice, costly and abundant, yet above all things I have observed in your noble entertainment this fire which you have provided for me gives me more content. To whom Sir
Richard Whittington making a low obeysance made answer, It much rejoyceth me dread
Soveraign that any that remaineth in my power can give your highness the least cause to
be pleased, but since you praise this fire already made I purpose ere your sacred majesty
depart the house to entertain you with one (I hope) that shall content you much better.
The King not thinking it could be possible desired him to make a proof thereof, when he
(having before provided himself for that purpose) brought a great bundle of Bonds,
Indentures and Covenants under his arm, said thus to the King, Royal Soveraign to whom
I owe both my fortunes and my life, I have here a faggot of purpose left for this fire,
which I hope will smell much more sweetly than the first in your nostrils, for saith he,
here is first your Highness security for ten thousand marks, lent you for the maintainance
of your royal wars in France, by the Right Worshipful Company of the Mercers, which I
here cancel and cast into the fire, fifteen hundred lent by the City to your Majesty I
send after the former, two thousand marks borrowed of the Grocers Company, three
thousand of the Merchant Taylors, one thousand of the Drapers, one thousand of the
Skinners, one thousand of the Ironmongers, one thousand of the Merchant Staplers, of
the Goldsmiths three thousand, of the Haberdashers as much, of the Vintners, Brewers
and Brown Bakers three thousand marks. All these you see are cancl'd and burnt, saith
he, with divers other bonds for money lent by my father in law Alderman Fitzwarren for
the payment of your souldiers in France, which coming unto me by executorship I have
taken in and discharged.

Others there likewise due to me of no small sums by divers of your nobility here
present, all which with the former I have sacrificed to the love and honour of my dread
sovereign, amounting to the sum of three score thousand pounds sterling, and can your

Majesty (saith he) desire to sit by a fire of more sweet scent and savour? At this the King was much extasi'd and the rather because it came unexpectedly and from so free a spirit, and embracing him in his arms said unto him that he thought never King had such a subject, and at his departure did him all the grace and honour that could descend from a King to a subject, promising him moreover that he should ever stand in the first rank of those whom he favoured. And so the Lord Mayor bearing the sword before their two most sacred Majesties as far as Temple Bar the King for his former service and his most kind and loving entertainment at that time, and the noble men for that extraordinary courtesie offered them all unitely (*sic*) and unanimously commended his goodness, applauded his bounty and wished that he might live to perpetual memory and so bid both him and the City for that time adieu.

To omit all other circumstances having acquainted you with the poor and mean estate of this Sir Richard Whittington when he came first into the City of London, and by what means he was relieved in his miserable poverty, as also the fortunate success of his small adventure whereby he was raised unto so great honour, that he became the Cities Governour, and how discreetly and wisely he behaved in his authority and office, gaining thereby the love and probation (*sic*) of all men. And further having shewed you what goodly buildings have been raised by his great cost and charge, as one church, two colledges, and certain almshouses, with yearly means left for the maintenance of all such as shall be admitted into them, and many other charitable acts performed by him which are before related, to the great good and benefit of the City, and what things of note happened in this time, I will now conclude with Master Stow, O that London had a Park near adjoining to it, stored with such Deer (as doubtless it hath, though not easily known) for some build Alms houses, free schools, causies and Bridges in needful and necessary places, others repair ruinated and decayed churches, relieving Hospitals in a bountiful manner, and are weekly benefactors to Prisons and those performed by such agents faithfully, that the true bestowers are not publicly noted, howsoever they may be easily supposed. But the glory they seek to invade here will (no doubt) for ever shine on them elsewhere. And that great God who hath created us, and plentifully distributed in his great bounty all things to men, and yet not given all things to any one man, lest it might take away that necessary commerce and mutual society which ought to be amongst us, stir up the minds of more of them to imitate at least, though not to exceed them in their bounty and liberality.

FINIS.

# 19

# The Man in the Moone
## Telling Strange Fortunes; or
# The English Fortune Teller

So MYSTERIOUS IS THE *concept of the man in the moon, often the subject of poetry and plays in the seventeenth century, that it is not surprising to learn that on occasion, as with the work reproduced here, the concept sometimes merged with that of an equally mysterious figure, the Wandering Jew.*

*The "man in the moon" is an old and exceedingly wise philosopher figure. Like Teresias, he can reveal the future of human beings. He is aided in his observations by two assistants: Opinion, who had been so thoroughly instructed in physiognomy, or the art of telling character by physical features, that at one keen glance, he could make a full report; and Mockso, who could make a comparable analysis of a human being by studying his wearing apparel and his gestures.*

*The tobacco smoker, for instance, is described by Mockso as someone who pants and looks pale and dirties up the porch. He is found by Opinion to be "his own strength's enfeebler, his beauty's blemisher, his wit's blunter, his memory's decayer, and his appetite's abater." Besides this, his smoking is an all-absorbing habit—and he has smelly breath. The Man in the Moon, "Fido," then tells the smoker's fortune: the habit will hurt every part of his body, including his lungs, and shorten his life. Besides this, the smoke will even hurt his wife's health. Fido advises him to drop the habit.*

*It is amazing that long and costly scientific investigations have been needed in the twentieth century to arrive at the conclusions reached by* The Man in the Moone *in 1609. Of course, other writers of that period, including King James I, in his* Counterblast to Tobacco *(1604) also came to the same conclusions.*

The Man in the Moone *is reprinted from Percy Society Publications, Vol. 29 (London, 1849).*

*To his worthie friend, M. Thomas Smith of Clarkenwell, and gentleman to the Right Honorable the Lord Lesle, Lord Chamberlane to the queene's most excellent Majestie.*

GENTLE SIR, to rippe up the excellent parts abiding in you might be reputed parasiticall by many, and offensive to you, whom I know no whit vaine glorious: to disclose your kindnesse towards my weake deserving would be accounted follie, that I could not receive a benefit, but make all the world acquainted therewith: to desire you secure this poore infant of my braine with your favour, as with Ajax shield, were too trite an imitation, an apes tricke: therefore leaving fawning to flatterers, and offence to him that mindes it, bequeathing follie to such as will not keepe their owne councell, and imitation to them that cannot invent, I doe plainely present this part of my love unto you. Your ever loving.

W. M.

## TO THE READER

GOOD FORTUNE to you, for the fortune-teller meaneth so, whatsoever you thinke: if his attendant Opinion decipher you plainely, his fashion is not to make faire figures of deformed bodies: if his page, Mockso, gibe at your ill manners, it is to make you mend them; and if hee himselfe, the principall, cutteth you to the quicke, know that hee is no cogging chirurgion: what false orthographie escapeth in the print, impute to the hast of the supravisor of the proofes, for I have read the spelling booke; what blame you put on the penning lay upon mee, it will make mee wiser.

W. M.

### *The man in the moone telling strange fortunes; or, the English fortune-teller.*

TRAVELLING A long journey, and striving one day beyond my reach, the sudden approach of the night prevented me, so that being unexperienced in the way and seeing no reasonable creature to direct me, I was affrighted. The starres stared upon me, beastes looked wistly after me, battes flew about mine eares, and the owle whooted over mine head: no plow-men whistling alongst the fallowes; no shepherd singing over the downes; the partrage was not diseased by the spaniell; the hare stole his foode without feare of the hue and crie of hounds and hunters. Whistnesse had taken possession of the woods; stilnes made aboad in the fieldes, and darkenes domineered in the zodiacke; no light had I to see my footsteps; no voice heard I to make unto. Thus I wandred, I knew not where; came to a place, I knew not whether; and had a glimpse of one sitting in a porch, I knew not whom. A while I stood aloofe, leaning on my staffe like a wearied pilgrime, and meditated with myselfe whether fortunately, or unhappily, I stumbled thither. By the solitarinesse of the house I judged it a lodge in a forrest, but there was no bawling of dogges thereabout; by the multiplicity of barnes I thought it some farmer's tenement, but there was no grunting of swine neare it; by the moate about it seemed some gentleman's mannor, but I could espie no wagges watching, nor wantons wagging out to breath themselves when their maddam was covered; what it was, after I had eaten a little heart a grasse, which grew at my feete, I feared not, and who was the owner I greatly cared not, but boldly accosted him, and desired house-roome; he pried in my face, tooke me by the hand, ledde me into his house, placed me in a chaire by the fire, and without any intergatories saluted me courteously, and went into an other roome.

Strange it was, and struck me in some dumpes, but considering his gentle action and gravity I a little revived; for he was of yeares many, of stature reasonable, of complexion sanguine, no pride in his apparell, no sullennesse in his lookes, silence sate in his hall, and sobriety in his butteries, temperance in his kitchen, and chastitie in his chambers, no sculding with his cookes, nor carrousing with his serving-men. This I observed, and sat very sadly, till a striplin requested me to follow him where the old man sat at a table furnished, not superfluously, but with sufficient nourishment; downe he bad me sit and welcome. Grace he said (then thought I, there is no feare in this place if there be grace), that which stood before me I fed on, and dranke when neede required: being well refreshed, as he beganne with thanksgiving, so he ended supper, and then said thus soberly unto me. "Sonne, you might marveile at your entertainement, and repute mee mute, or simple, to use no more words nor circumstances at my first view of you, but it is my fashion, as they which know me, know. For suppose I should aske you what you are? A stranger I know you are, and being a stranger unto me you may say as well what you are not as what you are: had I demaunded whence you came, or whither you would, for the one you might have told me a contrary tale, and for the other your selfe is uncertaine: from what parentage you are descended I might question you, it is frivolous and womanish, for your qualities be degenerate; how you were educated I might examine you, it is superfluous, your demeanour will informe me: fall to your meate I might have bidden you, it is needlesse if you had a stomacke: drinke to you I might, it may be I desire no further acquaintance of you, till I knowe your conditions further; but howsoever if you be my friend to use you unkindly were ingratitude: are you mine enemy? to use you friendly is charity; if you are capable you do understand my meaning, and shall know more ere we part: if you are ignorant you may tast part of my mind by the meat, drinke, and lodging I bestowe gratis upon you." This is short and sensible, thought I, and made him this answere in his own dialect:—"Sir, if I could not gratifie your kind-nesse with loving words you might deem me rusticall: if I should not labour to repay your love with my kindest requitall you might esteeme mee unthankefull; but seeing I cannot instantly performe the one, I will remaine your debter in very deede, and in one word heartily thanke you for this unexpected courtesie, and howsoever I may seeme rude and illiterate, yet was I long trained up where good manners grew and learning flour-ished." "I was once, myselfe, a lover of the Muses too," said hee, "but I had a running head, and would take no settled course; many countries have I travelled, and beheld sundrie manners, but when age beganne to tame that never otherwise suppressable indomitam juventutem, I pent myselfe in this house, where I have long time beene resident: much preferment might I have mounted to, but I knew it troublesome, plus aloes quam mellis habens: choise of wives I might have made, but by the triall of others I perceived them but mala necessaria, inconvenient commodities: great riches could I have gathered, but I found them fuller of perturbations than pleasures: if I might live alwaies, perchance then I should make me a tabernacle upon earth, but considering how small a time I have allotted in the earth I respected riches as the sand I trample on; rejected honour as a bubble, a puffe of winde, vocem populi, a meere sound, and weighed women as lightlie as fethers. No, my sonne, that which God has bestowed upon me I am contented withall. If I am now base, my griefe is the lesse, I was never better: if I am poore, my sorrow is the fuisse fœlicem; I was never richer, yet have I that which sufficeth nature. And this is my greatest griefe, because I have separated myselfe from the world, and labour to helpe such as want, and wil take paines to come to me, aut consolando aut consilio aut re, I am accounted, amongst the silly, a cunning man, a south-sayer or deviner, one that can tell fortunes."

"Beleeve me, sir," said I, "it is so bruted here about, and that tomorrow many will resort unto you to knowe their fortunes, whereof I was one, not with purpose to know my fortune, for I thinke it proper only to the Omnipotent."

"You say well, and it is my affliction that they should attribute that to me which perteineth to my Maker: yet since I am constrained I will shew them their fortunes, and what will betide them every one: but now, seeing it waxeth late and you wearie, I referre you to your rest for this part of the night, and in the morning you shall heare more." Kindly we parted, and the next day, when I was up and ready, I found the olde man seated in a chaire: who willed me to take my place as a spectator.

He sat very soberly, like Hypocrates; his beard was reverent, and his face wrinckled, a plaine gowne, girded close about his loynes, a paire of blacke buskins upon his legges, a fur'd night-cap on his head, and a paire of thicke mittens upon his hands: on his left-side stood a pert juvinall, as readie to give the welcome to all commers as a boy in a barre, and as nimble as a parasite in an old commodie: he was called Mockso, which in mocking sort described unto Fido the fantasticallity of each man's apparell, and apishnesse of gesture, who by their apparell and gesture would give a shrewd guesse at their inclinations.

On the right-side stood another, but of riper yeares, and more stayed carriage, yet somewhat criticall and taunting: he cognominated him Opinion, whom he had so throughly instructed in phisiognomie that he would anotonize any ones condition at the first sight, and so apparently display them, that Fido, his master, would tell what would betide them: thus were these three addressed as actors: Mockso described the habite and gesture; Opinion reveiled their conditions. Fido tolde every man his fortune as he came unto him for the same intent. Long had they not seated, but one knocked at the gate, as if he meant to burst it open. "See who is there," said Fido. Mockso skipped to the doore, giving every one the fœlicem adventum, and returned, saying:

### *The description of the Drunkard comming in a merrie humour to know his fortune by Mockso.*

"Syr, I may be glad I had never a beard, hee would have singed it with his flaming nose; whatsoever he be hee is troubled with an horses disease, the staggers. I thinke your pales anger him, he doth justle them on both sides: oake, he saith, they are made of, and spitteth whole pottles against them; cheu quid faciam: what a hue is his face of? and his teeth as nastie as if they laie in a grave these seven yeres: his cloake will never hide his knaverie, it is so tattered; and his breeches will shame all if he take wide strides; hee hath no hat-band, nor girdle, they lie in trouble for two cannes; now he setteth his hat on the toe side, and commeth sailing in like a shippe in a tempestuous tide."

#### THE OPINION OF THE DRUNKARD.

"This fellow is one of the faithfull, as they prophanelie term him," said Opinion; "no

Heliogabalus at meat, but he will drinke many degrees beyond a Dutchman; if you love him, pledge that health, and if you be a good fellow, make no more such snuffes: his kingdome is an alehouse, and his scepter a can, which is seldome out of his hand: you queances, or knaves, he crieth, no attendance upon gentlemen here, though he be but a tinker: fill us the other dozen, it is but taking Ludgate one yeare sooner: then hee flingeth the glasses against the wals, as if they cost nothing, and daunceth a round about a can, as if it were a May-pole: then he doth drivell his hostesse, and will dallie with any that weareth a crosse-cloth: then hee careth not for a deare yeare, nor to pay his landlord, but all that hee can get, or borrow, goeth to the pot: to be briefe with him, hee is his master's hinderance, if he be a servant: his servants torment, if he be a master: his wife's crosse, if he be an husband: his childrens beggering, if he be a father: his owne ruine whatsoever he is, a detested drunkard."

## Fido, the Fortune-teller's oration to the Drunkard, wherein he telleth him his fortune.

TRUE IS the proverbe, though fustie to fine wits, When the drinke is in, the wit is out: but seeing you have set abroach the drinke, and drawne out all the dregs too, we may gather the wit is in; the vice you are so addicted to is drunkennesse; the mother of all mischiefe, the fewell of filthinesse, the roote of rogeries, the distemperance of the head, the subversion of the senses, the shipwracke of honestie, the losse of time, and voluntaire madnesse; an ignominious languor, the detestation of manners, the disgrace of life: abhorred of God, detested of angels, derided of men. Yet although it be thus horribly detestable and ridiculous to God, angels, and men; though it be thus prejudicial to your soule, body, and substance, yet were it a more easie matter to drawe Hercules his club out of his hand than to drive you, or any of your crew, from this filthie sinne: but you would turne like the dogge to his vomite, let me, or any other, perswade you as we can: and that which causeth me to be thus opinioned, you are so delighted therewith that you preferre the pleasure thereof before all other preferment; and now I thinke of it, I remember a prettie tale, not impertinent to the same purpose. A gentleman of good worth, as he was riding alongst the highway, mette a sturdie fellow, who requested his almes: the gentleman replied that it was shame for him to begge, being yong and lustie, he was able to worke, or fit to serve, if he were in apparell. True, sir, said the begger, but apparell is not so easily gotten by such a poore man as myselfe. Goe home with mee, said the gentleman, and I will suite thee new, and thou shalt waite upon mee. Sir, answered the begger, I have a good suite of apparell in the next village which lieth not for above eightpence, if you will helpe me to that first I shall thinke myselfe beholding unto you, and will tell you more. The gentleman rid as he ledde him: who brought him to an alehouse, and request him to alight, and enter with him. The gentleman was contented, and sat down, expecting when he would call for his apparell, that he might redeeme it, and take him along with him: the beggar called to his hostesse, saying; Hostesse, bring hither my shirt; shee brought him a black pot of ale, which he drank off: now, said he, bring my dublet, then she brought him another pot of ale, which he dranke off: now my breeches; another pot she brought him, that he dranke off: now bring my hose and shooes; then she brought him two blacke pots of ale, those he drank off: now my hat-band and cloake; then she brought him three blacke pots of ale, which he dranke off: when he had done this, he said: Gentleman, this is the suite I told you off, and now I have it I thinke I am as well apparelled as an emperour. The gentleman, smiling, paied for this ale, and departed; so some of you, might it advantage them never so much, will never forsake their drunkennesse. This, therefore, is your fortune; you shall spend all your money, and runne so long on the score that the very wind-pipe of your credite shall bee so choakt, that if you doe not drinke it out with readie pay your hostesse will kicke you out of her doores: your wife will wish you in your grave; your friendes be ashamed of you; your enemies triumph over you: sober men shall shunne your companie; boyes laugh at you as you passe by them: your bodie shall bee subject to diseases: you shall live with never a penie in your purse; never a tatter on your backe; no man will commit any matter of trust, or secresie, unto you; and, in fine, you shall lie and die in some ditch, under some staule, or in some prison. If you like your fortune, proceede as you have hithertoo: but if you abandon it, better fortune will betide you."

The drunkard began to come prettily well to himselfe, and walked somewhat soberlie aside: and then Mockso whipped to the gate.

### The Tobackonist commeth in a bravado to the Fortune-teller: Mockso describeth him as he approached.

"WHO IS THAT?" said Fido. "Sir," quoth Mockso, "I know not certainlie, but I thinke he cometh to play you a fitte of mirthe, for I behelde pipes in his pockette; now he draweth forth his tinder-boxe and his touch-wood, and falleth to his tacklings: sure his throate is on fire, the smoake flyeth so fast from his mouth: blesse his beard with a bazen of water, least he burne it: some terrible thing hee taketh, it maketh him pant and looke pale, and hath an odious taste, he spitteth so after it. A boule and a broome, some bodie! if he holdeth on thus long hee will make a puddle in your porch, and keepeth such a snuffing and puffing that he maketh all smoake again."

#### OPINION OF THE TOBACKONIST.

"O have patience, Mockso," said Opinion, "he is at his breake-fast: it is his heaven, or rather hell: I should thinke it sendeth forth such mistes, fogges, and vapours, five chimnies, well fewel'd, vent not more smoake then his mouth and nostrils: a man were better have his house situated between two brew-houses than abut upon his mansion; I had rather thrust my head into a Jakes then peepe into his chamber. And nothing so noisome were it to bee yeoman to a close stoole, as to continue within fortie foote of his breathing, yet is the causer of these inconveniences meat and drinke to him, and he loveth it above the love of women: it is his morning's draught, when he riseth; his conserves or cates, when he hath well dined; his afternoones nuncions, and when he goeth to bedde, his posset smoking-hote; hee will not walk farre, nor talke long with-out it: nay, he will lose his victuals rather then neglect it: pawne his hat-band but he will have it. To be breefe with him, he is his own strengths enfeebler, his beauties blemisher, his wittes blunter, his memories decayer, and his appetites abater;—a toyish tobackonist.

### The oration of Fido to the Tobackonist, shewing his fortune.

"SIR," SAID FIDO, "if I should extract the best counsell I coulde, being disswasive from your tobacko-taking, you would take it in snuffe, custome hath so strongly combined you thereunto, that it were too indissoluble a knot for me to untye: yet this let me tell you, that it is as an incensed Atropos to a long life, clipping off the thred before it be thoroughly spun, decaying and drying up the prolonger of breath: but you are perswaded, as others few, that it doth procure the contrary: you thinke it a medicine for every maladie; give you tobacko, and a figge for the physitian: say it were physicke, as you affirme, yet physicke is not taken at al times and seasons, continually without interim; neither is one kind of physicke administered to all bodies, constitutions, and diseases: but tobacko may bee compared to the potion which Circe gave to Ulisses souldiers, metamorphosing them into swine: so this pretious weede, as you esteeme it, doth so selfe-besot those which take it, that, like swine, they wallow in the myre of their admiring conceits; that neither reason can rule them, nor experience of others harmes, sustained thereby, make them refraine. I will not denie that conceit may worke wonders: but those wonders are onely in conceite; as I have heard of some, who through an irreformable conceit, have imagined their noses to be as bigge as pinnicles to flye in the ayre, contend and quell divels by their owne naturall strength: so you, only by conceit, thinke richly of the operation of your Indian pudding, having contrarie qualities in it, a thing repugnant to philosophy, and working miraculous matters, a quillit above nature: as if you be fat, then you take it to make you leane (against the walles I hope you meane) : if leane, then it will make you fat, put V. and S. to fat and I will beleeve you: if dull, quicke witted; if oblivious, revive your memories; doing these things and many more; and helping all manner of diseases, the poxe it will as soone. But I could easily refute these, and all your opinions, had not this text beene thoroughly traver'st and condemned, with great judgement and learning, in a solemne disputation; and in the booke entituled, *Worke for a Chimnie-sweeper:* and were there as many volumnes written concerning this subject as Didimus wrote of the *Grammer,* you would martyre them, leafe by leafe, and light your pipes at the flame. Nitimur in vetitum, that which wisedom doth forbid folly will follow. This, therefore, is your fortune; if you leave not taking your Indian stuffe betime, custome will so confirme you to it, that when you perceive the inconveniences, and feel the folly thereof, you cannot forsake it, though you will. You shall die before your date; your body shall be in subjection to sundrie sicknesse, and so sooted with the smoake thereof, that it will be as foule as hell, sending forth such a filthy scent that your breath will bee death to your wife, or any that sent it, but such as yourselfe."

Aside the tobackonist stepped, and another knocked at the gate.

### The Prodigall commeth stalking in to know his fortune: Mockso deciphering his apparrell and gate.

"WHO IS THAT?" said Fido.

Mockso answered; "Sir, I know not of what countrey, nation, sex, or fashion he is. His face is like a man's, but by the tone side of his head like a woman: some purblinde barber powled him, to cut his haire so unequally, and leave one locke a quarter of-a-yard longer than the other: by the blocke of his head (put them both together, and see what they spell) he should bee a Spaniard, but his dublet sheweth him a Frenchman; now I see his breeches made like a paire of smith's bellowes, erected with the small end upwards: he seemeth a Wolloone: marrie, there is no excesse in his cloake! he tooke the length thereof by the old apes of Paris Garden: a sweete youth, no doubt, for he hath two roses on his shoes, to qualifie the heat of his feete; he looketh very bigly, and commeth prauncing in."

#### OPINION OF THE PRODIGALL.

"This prauncer," said Opinion, "hath beene a wilde colt, and leaped thorough many honest men's gates in his dayes: he was his father's dotage, his mother's darling; he hath spent more upon his paunch then the primate of belly gods: gusled downe his throate more than Cleopatra quaffed in a bravado to Marke Anthonie: layed more gold upon his backe then that which procured passage for the asse into the castle would defray: naturall meat will not suffice him, he feedeth artificially: native apparell will not content him, he flieth for uplandish fashions: honest matrimonie is not for his loines, hee watcheth nightly, and walketh by day, to entrappe other mens wives: he is never safe but when he is in pestilent companie: never well but when he is evill employed: whores he supporteth, vintners he advanceth, tailers he maketh gentlemen, if he be not too farre in their bookes: to be briefe, he is Lecherie, Mæcenas, idlenesse patrone, Pride's founder, Gluttonies erector, Drunkennesse good god-father: an impudent prodigall."

### The Fortune-teller's oration to the Prodigall, declaring the inconveniences of dissolute living, and his fortune.

"SIR, YOU ARE generously descended, the greater is your shame to expose yourselfe to an ignoble course of living: much riches were you bequeathed, the more is the pittie you have so little grace to misemploy them; well are you featured, it is ill bestowed unlesse you would preserve your beautie better: for that which God and nature have ordeined for your good, by your ill using you turne to your owne overthrowe. Had your progenitors runne the race you doe, they had never wonne the golden ball which made you a gentleman: you assume it an eminence, to be rarely arrayed: others, being wise, are not so conceited: you suppose it a great glory to lash your coyne, you care not where, nor upon whom; though they will advance you, which receive benefits thereby, yet such as will not profite themselves by such meanes, resemble you to a candle, which wasteth itselfe to give others light: you esteeme it an extraordinarie happinesse to be in favour with many and sundry beauties: you shall feele the contrarie, pride will procure your fall, when you wot not of it; excesse devoure your riches ere you are aware; variety decay your bodie when you thinke it doth most delight it; and when your bodie is decayed, your wealth devoured, yourselfe fallen, goe to your gossips, which now will hang like goodly jewels about your necke, and come with your purse emptie: stabis, Homere, foras, you may stand like an impecunious whore-master at their doores. Come to your tradesmen, which now cappe and cringe you, and see if you shall receive any further comfort, then monefull words, alasse, it is pittie, would wee were able (good wishes for themselves) ; and last of al, frequent the ordinaries, which you have in a manner enriched, and marke how they will moane their own mischances, how they sit at an unmerciful rent; what losses they have susteined by pilfering; how many have runne away in their debts, and a thousand such circumstances, which you never heard, nor are likely, so long as you have money or meanes.

> Dum juvet et ridet vultu fortuna sereno,
>     Indelibatas cuncta sequuntur opes;
> At simul intonuit fugiunt, nec noscitur ulli
>     Agminibus comitum qui modo cinctus erat.

"Whilst you are mounted on the throne of fortune, great men will countenance you, gallants be your associates, parasites flatter you, brokers borrow for you, usurers lend you, citizens cap you, lawyers plead for you, serving-men crouch to you, wantons hang like burres upon you; but when you are dejected under the wheele of chance, great men will not greatly regard you, gallants hoist their toppes and toppe-gallants and saile from you, flatterers shun you, brokers will not brooke you, usurers use you rigorously, trades-men treade on the to side of the way, lawyers leave you, serving-men hang the head as they meete you, wantons wish, or worke your overthrowe. This, therefore, is your fortune; if you proceede as you have begunne, your full feeding wil make you leane, your drinking too many healthes will take all health from you, your leaping the pale will cause you looke pale, your too close following the fashion will bring you out of all forme and fashion, your carelesse life will lead you to a miserable death: yet you may prevent your misfortunes if now you will take opportunity: you have some wealth left, husband it carefully: of a little, well ordered, will rise more profite than much carelesly disposed: yet your wit is pregnant, by industrie you may season it with wisedome: yet your bodie is not past cure, new-bred diseases are soone remedied: if you scoffe at me for my good will, you may repent when you lie like a nutmegge in a grate, or ride post with a hempen halter out of the world; but if you accept it, much good may it doe you."

The gallant very pensively walked aside, and Mockso went to the gate.

### *The Serving-man waiting on this gallant commeth in to know his fortune, whom Mockso decyphereth.*

"WHAT IS IT?" said Fido.

"A most courteous creature," answered Mockso, "so, stroke up your fore-toppe in any case; pish, your band hangeth right enough: what, yet more crevises in your stockings? fie upon it, how complementall he is, and kisseth his hand as if he were in love with it.

### OPINION OF THE SERVING-MAN.

"This fellow," said Opinion, "though he be no drunkard, yet he is none of his owne man; he was a pretty boy, and handsome stripling, and is a proper man; peevish in his childhood, proude in his youth, prodigall now in his best yeares: he spendeth his portion in hope of preferment, wasteth his substance in liewe of advancement, consumeth quite all in expectation of some requitall; his greatest felicity is to court the chambermaides in a corner, and his chiefest exercise to make his masters friends dependants drunke; hee fawneth upon them his master favoureth, and frumpeth those his mistresse frownes on; he was trained up in some point of a joyner's trade, to make legges; and the best part of his rhetoricke is, 'I forsooth', and 'no forsooth': the injunctions he standeth bounde too is, to runne at all calles, rise at all houres, and ride in all seasons: eating that which his master left, and wearing that which his master left, if hee can get it: which sheweth that he is the ante-ambulo of a gentlewoman, the consequent of a gentleman, the antecedent of a port-mantua, or a cloke-bagge: a serving-man."

### *Fidoes oration to the Serving-man, teaching him brieflye how to behave himselfe in service, and telling him his fortune.*

"INGRATEFULL AND hard hearted are many of our age, respecting none but such as profite and pleasure them at the instant: industrious, therefore, ought you be to get your master's favour; and having gotten it, circumspect to keepe the same: and, albeit, some there are respecting their services no longer then they supplie their lustes and lucre, thrusting them out of their gates, unrewarded, for the smallest trifle and displeasure conceived against them: yet the world knoweth, and thousands will acknowledge the fluent liberality of true bred gentillity extended to their followers; who, by the raising hand of their lord's assistance, have ascended many high and loftie steppes of dignity: but such masters are not sowne everie where, neither were they swaggering drunkards or swearing Jackes, which have thus flourishingly sprowted up by service, but men of good demeanor, and well qualified: for the wise looke not only on the outsides, they prie into behaviour, integritie, and uprightnesse. It is not profound quaffing or domineering will doe you any good; roysting and ryoting wil never raise you, unlesse up to the gallowes. This, therefore, is your fortune; if you be in good service and will not with care and diligence keepe you in it, when you would have the like againe you shall goe without it: if you take time you may thrive, but, if you let him passe by, you may call your heart out, and never reclaime him; for Time, though hee be an olde man, yet he is quicke of foote, and having gotten the start of any is never overtaken: if you gather nothing in the summer of your youth, in the winter of your age you may goe begge; for hee that might doe well and would not, when hee wanteth shalbe unpittied, and when you become old, and poore too, then shall you be spurned with the heele of disdaine by every foote-boy; rejected as an old woman which spent her youth wantonly; then shall you heare of your olde vagaries, your former follies shal be laide in your dish: if in your jollity you wronged any, they will wait for revenge in the time of your want and weakenesse: when the lion was olde and toothlesse the asse revenged an inveterate injurie he had sustained long before: but now you are in place, if you demeane your-selfe honestly now you are young, preserve that you get carefully: now you are in service, performe it faithfully: you may hereafter purchase much comfort, goods, and credit."

So the creature followed his master, and another knocked at the gate.

### The lewde woman commeth to knowe her fortune, whom Mockso describeth entring.

"**W**HO IS THAT?" said Fido.

"One with a maske forsooth, because you may aske," said Mockso. "A woman of tall stature and upright bodie (it is wel if her life be like it), high forehead, round cheeks, dimpled chinne, sleeke necke, and slender waste; in a light coloured hat, light coloured fanne, light coloured gown; though she were in the darke, she would appeare a light woman."

#### OPINION ANATOMIZING THE CONDITIONS OF THE WICKED WOMAN.

"O," said Opinion, "this is one of your lazie, liquerous, lascivious, femenine ingenderers; more wavering than a wethercocke, more wanton than an ape, more wicked than an infidell, the very sinke of sensuality and poole of putrifaction; a Sylla to citizens, and Caribdis to countrie-men; a comfort for cut-purses, and a companion for cony-catchers; a factor for many taverns, and benefactor for most barber-surgeons; a palsie to the bodie, a canker to the soule, a consumption to the purse; by birth commonly a bastard, by nature a caniball, by art a Puritan; in aluring a syren, in shew a saint, in deede a divell, and, in plaine English, a whoore: of all iniquities beleeve her not, for shee liveth by lying; touch her not, for she is pitch, *inquinans omnes qui tangunt eam:* proffer her nothing, for she wil pocke-eat al. And now, sir, shee appeareth in her lightnesse before you."

### The Fortune-teller's oration to the mercinarie wicked woman; declaring the abomination of her life and fortune.

"**F**AIRE CREATURE, as I have beene effectually informed of your conditions, so would I labour to reforme them: but I might with as great hopes undertake to make a Black-More white as to change your minde, and easier raise an olde oake from the earth with my decrepit shoulders then roote out that lust which hath so long beene set in your heart; yet if you would consider the inconveniences thereof, which are to effeminate the minde, weaken the bodie, endanger the soule, it might prove a motive to disswade: you would account yourselfe madd, if knowing poison to be blended in a lumpe of sugar you should for the sweetnesse of the suger swallowe the poyson: what then can you make now of yourselfe, knowing lust a pleasant poyson; hindering your health, ingendering diseases, bringing age before his time, blemishing your beauty ere it be out of the blossome, dulling your wit before it be well grounded, and drawing your minde from all vertuous cogitations: this you know for certainty, yet you will live in sensuality, disdaining Diana, and be a votarie to Venus; contemning Vesta, and devoting yourselfe to quotidiall daliance; making a mock at marriage, you will not enter into the bondes thereof because you will live loosely, without controll or subjection of an husband: yet you are servile to all slaverie, and subject to the controlement of every swaggerer; he that hath money may command you; he that can dominere will insult over you, making you crouch and curvet when he pleaseth. But if no warning wil make you wise, this then will be your fortune. You shall be ferrited like a cony out of every burrow, baited like a beare, whipped like a jade; long shall you not dare to abide in one place, authority will so closely pursue you: what you get in a quarter you shall spend in a moneth; nothing that you get will prosper with you, and what beauty and delectation your body now containeth shall be of small continuance; your haire, which now is fast and thick, shall fall from your head like leaves in autumne; your forehead, which now is smooth, shall soone be wrinkled like parched parchment: your complexion, which now is sanguine, shall be of a saffron colour; your cheekes, thinne; your nosethrils, putrifactious; your mouth, toothlesse; your breath, noysome; your flesh, rotten; your bones, cankerous; your pleasure shall be turned into paine; your singing into sorrow: aches shall lodge in your head, anguish in your heart, diseases in every part and parcell of your body, and after all these, thy soule suffer perpetuall torments."

Aside she walked, and Mockso, without any knocking, skipped to the doore, for the wagge imagined shee could not want companions, or servants, in this age, so long as her good face lasted.

### *The Retainer which waited on the Woman entereth to know his fortune, whom Mockso describeth as hee enters.*

"Is THERE any other come?" said Fido.

"There is one comming." answered Mockso, "he will scarce see the way in, his haire hangeth so in his light: *Fatuus in facie, et leno in corpore.* He looketh fat in the face, and leane in the body: how full of choler he is! yet so long as those huge slops swagge about him, he will be in some compasse: his bootes are wrinkled, as though they were made of olde wives' faces: what! capt on the toes? sure he will not put off one of those caps to the best man that meeteth him, and in sober sadnesse his spurres have scaped a scouring, they looke so rustily; whatsoever he be, I thinke he would prove an honest man if hee would wash his face and serve God."

#### OPINION UPON THE RETAINER.

"Serve God!" said Opinion, "the devill he will as soone! hee hath not seene the insides of a church these seven years, unlesse with devotion to pick a pocket, or pervert some honest man's wife he would on purpose be pued withall: villanie is his contemplation, ribaldrie his talke, and detestation his deedes; cardes are his darlings, wherewith he playeth, and a paire of dice his onely Paradice: he will omit no villanie he can cleanly commit; he will cheat his father, cosen his mother, and cony-catch his owne sister; if he can imagine the meanes how, his owne wife he will make a prostitute for money, and hold the candle to any incarnate divell whilst he committeth the deedes of darknesse with her; sixpence will make him sweare or forsweare any thing: in a word, he is a post for puncks, an harbinger for whoremongers, a bloodhound for bawdes, a perfidious pander."

### *Fido, his speech to the Pander, shewing his lewdnesse and fortune.*

"O LAMENTABLE, THY CASE is damnable, thy trade odious, thy selfe abominable, thou art a man whose conditions I know not by experience, neither have I reade of many such as thyselfe in auncient writers; yet some of thy sect there were of whom I tooke little notice, because I never meant to have any commerse with them: notwithstanding, seeing I have heard so much, I could amply delate of thy sinne, but I know it needlesse, for my hope is, I have dejected the foundation whereon all thy practises are built, I meane the woman, thy mistresse, which was even now with me, and if shee fall from her former follie thou canst not stand, unlesse thou gettest some crooked prop to support thee, which cannot hold long; expect, therefore, no other fortune than untimely death, either by the stab in some drunken fray, managed in the defence of your maintainer, or by some disease got by her, or by the halter, if you do not alter."

Away the Pander walked after his mistresse, and another knocked at the gate.

### *The Extortioner hobleth to know his fortune, and is described by Mockso as he entereth.*

"W HO IS THAT," said Fido, "that commeth next?"

"*Vetus, vietus, veternosus senex:* a wise man ile warrant him, for he can keepe himselfe warme: no friend to the barber it should seeme by his rusticall, overgrowne, and unfinified beard: his gowne is throughly foxt, yet he is sober, for hee looketh as though he quenched his thirst with whay and water rather then with wine and stout beere, and his mandilion edged round about with the stigmaticall Latine word, fur; a ruffe about his neck, not like a ruffian, but inch broad, with small sets, as if a peece of a tobacco-pipe had beene his poking-stick; his gloves are thrust under his girdle, that you may see how he rings his fingers, blesse his worship; now he commeth coughing in."

#### OPINION OF THE EXTORTIONER COMMING TO KNOW HIS FORTUNE.

"He Is," said Opinion, "*miser qui nummos admiratur;* miserable, or an able miser, which maketh much of money, gold is his god, and silver his saint; bondes are his bibles, and obligations his horizons; scriveners are his priests, which doe his service, and cousoning brokers his Christian brethren. Security is his secretarie, and sergeants his servingmen: he liveth by use like a bawde, and dealeth deceitfully, like a cheating gamester; he is a rare alchimist, which from a little gold or silver wil abstract a million in time: better is a poore gentleman to fall into the pawes of a lion then betweene his clutches, and may with more safety escape the gripe of a she beare then to be released from his leases: to be briefe with him, he is an insatiable cormorant, or rather corne-vorant, a bottomlesse Barathrum, a mercilesse mony-monger, a filthy forty in the hundreth, and unconscionable extortioner."

## *Fido, his oration to the Extortioner, displaying his damnable dealing and Fortune.*

"FATHER, YOU ARE welcome, and without feare or flatterie I will breefely tell you my minde. You have long traffickt in a wicked and unlawfull trade; wicked, I call it, because it is repugnant to the lawes of the Highest Enacter of all decrees; unlawfull, I may avouch it, because I never knew, nor heard, of any good law maintaining it; for the former, if you run over the booke of bookes, you shall finde many fearfull judgements denounced against you, and the latter you cannot contradict it by no countrie lawes, which although they flatly denie thee to take above tenne in the hundreth, a veniall sinne in respect of thy capitall, and deadly offence, yet dooth it not authorise thee to take so much, but taxeth thee if thou usurpest any more. But what should I take this text, which hath beene throughly intreated of by better and more judicious then myselfe? or why should I wast my breath to thee, which hath neither faith, hope, nor charity? What doe I talke of these thinges to thee, whom the love of riches hath so besotted, that it is impossible to divert it? or how should I thinke to prevaile by disswading: *cum te neque fervidus æstus dimoveat lucro, neque hyemps, ignis, mare, ferrum:* when neither the parching heate, nor benumbing cold, neither fire, sword, nor sea can disswade.

> Impulit amentes aurique cupidine cæcos
> Ire super gladios, super atque cadavera patrum.

Therefore if your future fortune (that is that which shall light upon you hereafter, will not drawe you from your daily practising the same, nothing will), which is this. You shall alwaies want, though you have never so much, *semper avarus eget (Hor);* though thou art a master, thou shalt be alwaies a servant, moyling for a mite, and watching to save a pennie; thou shalt live in perpetuall terrour and feare; shee that lyeth in thy bosome shall make thee suspitious, least she steale from thee; they which were begotten of thine owne bodie will scarre thee, least they robbe thee: all that looke neere the place where thy gold lyeth thou wilt be jealous of, least they lurke to defeate thee of it: *non uxor salvum te vult, non filius, omnes vicini oderunt, noti pueri atque puellæ.* Thy wife will wish thee hanged, thou keepest her so barely; thy children pray for thine end, thou maintainest them so basely; thy neighbours and kinsfolkes speake broadly of thee, thou usest them so cruelly; and when thou art dead, divels hurry thee to perdition, wishes damme thee to everlasting torments, and cursses consort with thy funerall. Nay, thy wife shall be enamored of some *spend-all*, which shall wast all as licentiously as thou hast heaped together laboriously: thy children never thrive with ought thou diddest bequeath them, it was so vilely gotten: and thy name either utterly blotted out, or remaine infamous to posterity. If you like your forture, proceed; but if you mislike it, desist from your racking and raysing, your powling and pinching the poor; recompense them which you have wronged, or at the least injury none no more, but doe good according to the quantity of your goods, and so you may bring a blessing to yourselfe and posterity." The extortioner walked aside, and another knocked at the gate.

### The Glutton entreth to know his fortune, whom Mockso decyphereth.

"WHO IS NEXT?" said Fido.

"*Monstrum horrendum, informe, ingens:* a monstrous man," said Mockso, "your gate is too little for this Grecian horse; if you cause not part of your wall to be plucked downe, he cannot come in: God bee thanked, hee hath the witte yet to enter sideling, like a gentlewoman with an huge farthingall: how he puffeth and bloweth like a short-winded hackney: now he approacheth wallowing like a woman with childe: he might be an oxe for his joule, a bull for his necke, a cow for his belly, and a calfe for his wit, I make no question."

#### OPINION OF THE GLUTTON.

"*Bona verba*, Mockso," said Opinion, "he will hate you to death if he heare you, and worke you a mischiefe, if you misuse him; he is a great man, I can tell you, and in huge request amongst no small fooles: Puago might be his grandfather, for his full feeding; and Gargantua his sire, for his gormandizing; he is none of your ordinarie fellowes, which will suffice nature for threepence; give him an oxe roasted, with a pudding in his belly; a rabbit is but a bitte with him, and he will crunch capons as fast as a beggar will cracke lice; he is a tall man at a table, and will tosse a pike strenuously, if it be soaked in white broth: he is none of your great talkers, but will do prettie well at a dinner, if silence be a vertue; he is a vertuous gentleman, for at meate hee cannot contend to talke for eating, and between meales hee sleepeth soundly. To be briefe with him, he is a pestilence to pasties, which sweepeth many of them sheere away; a consumption to capons, chickins, and other poultry; a sepulchre to seafish and others in ponds, moates, and rivers; a sharp sheepe-biter, and a marveilous mutton monger, a gorbelly glutton.

### Fido, his oration to the Glutton, inveying against his sinne, and revealing his fortune.

"*Tantum cibi et potionis adhibendum est, ut reficiantur vires, non ut opprimantur:*

sir, I salute you with this saying of Cicero, because I perceive you ever ballace your belly, an ungratefull member, never thankefully repaying that which is done unto it, but daily calling for more then is needefull; and why should man, that hath understanding to judge, and reason to rule, be so servile to filthy appetite? a small thing will content nature, and satiety doth rather displease then pleasure her; it maketh her unfitte to performe any agill or active thing: beside, the overplus might tend to many profitable uses, but you cannot fall too unlesse your table bee fully furnished: how did they in the old time, when they were sufficed with such sustenance as the grasse and trees afforded; they lived longer and were stronger then they of this instant; they had no cookes to provide them eates; hunger was their best sawce, labour and exercise the cookes which composed that sawce; if you would feed with the like sawce, composed by the same cookes, it would take you a button lower, and cause you looke not like Boreas, as you now doe; if not, I cannot remedie it, neither will I speake to your deafe god, Bell, or rather bellie, anie longer. Your fortune will be this; manie diseases wil be ingendered in you, through your immoderat eating; fit for no countrie service will you be, neither in martiall nor domesticall affaires; a foole shall you live, and a dunce shall you die, and that sooner too then otherwise you wold, keeping a sparing and temperate diet: all the pampering of your paunch shall be to no other purpose, for you strive for all delicate creatures to feed yourselfe, and you yourselfe shall be food for the wormes."

Away the Glutton lagged, and Mockso highed to the doore, expecting, that as he was larded, so hee would be garded with some or other; for rich men have manie friends, and neede not walke alone unlesse they please.

### *The Parasite, associating the Glutton to the gate, entereth, Mockso describing him.*

"WHO IS THAT?" said Fido.

"A finicall fellow," answered Mockso, "as full of salutations as a fidler; his hat was off before I coulde aske him what he would, and his knee licked the superficies of your threshold, ere I bad him enter; a crafty fellow I feare, he is so full of courtesie, and some cousoning companion, he hath such a flearing countenance; now he eieth you, sir, his head is bare. O rare, what an excellent dumb shew is this! thrise hath he kissed his hand and made you three lowe congies in coming three strides! now he approacheth neere you; I thinke he meaneth to make a pope of you, and kiss your toes."

#### OPINION OF THE PARASITE.

"He is none of your cynicks, nor criticks, hee is no Momus, that snappeth vice by the shinnes as shee passeth by him; hee respecteth not what men be, so they be rich; he wil live when they lack: he fleareth not in your face for nothing, nor reflects his legges without some surmised reason; he will fawne on you like a spaniell, follow you like a foisting hound for his commodity; say what you wil, hee will sweare to it; doe what you delight in, hee wil encourage you: are you adicted to drink drunke, he will gibe at sobriety, and christen her with innumerable nick-names. Doe you love whores? he wil scratch where it itcheth not, and tickle your cares with a tale of variable venerie: have you one sparkle of goodnesse? he wil extoll you above measure: have you never so much ill? he will mitigate it: he is in tautologies of praising that you like, and extreame in discommending that you doe condemne, be it never so praise-worthie: he giveth nothing his due, or proper right, but either too much, or too little, he careth not for the meane: he wil pervert anie thing for his purpose; if you be a coward, hee saieth you are wise and trulie valerous: if prodigall, then generouslie liberall: are you a niggard? then frugall and provident: is your head great? a note of policie; is it little? the loftiest men are so marked: is your nose long? an excellent ornament, hee knew a great ladie that never commended other: is it short? it is the comliest: are you high-coloured? it is the soundest complexion: are you pale? it is amorous and attractive: are you tall? all that are lower than you are dwarfes: are you low? all that are taller are lubbers, or May-poles: to bee briefe with him, he wil soothe you up in anie sinne, hugge anie hainous humor in you, foster anie follie; wealthie men's wel-wisher, poverties deadlie enemie, a false-hearted, fawning parasite."

### Fido, his oration to the Parasite, revealing his faults and fortune.

"SIR," SAID FIDO, "since your disposition is so largelie described, I shall not neede much to delate on it; but to speake freelie and compendiously unto you, I holde you to be the most venemous serpent that crawleth in a common-wealth, and would advise all men that tender their owne safetie to shunne yow as an harpie, and stop their eares at your words, as the enchanting of mermaydes: *plus nocet lingua adulatoris, quam gladius persecutoris:* your tongue doth more hurt then warre or pestilence, and you are the causer of more mischiefe then any impietie whatsoever; lulling men in the sleepe of securitie, whereas if they were kept waking, and had their faults laid apparently before them, no doubt but that either shame or feare would worke a reformation in them; guiltie therefore are you of all those crimes which they commit, and accessarie to their enormities whom you secure and sooth up in follies; your fortune, therefore, will be full foule in the end, and though you may flourish for a time, and live in favour, yet when your assertions are found false, your friendship fained, your counsell hurtfull unto them, then may you give an *ultimum vale* to your happinesse: they which loved you wil loath you to death; they which credited you will not believe you for a world, though then you should tell them never so truly: they that graced you wil be the first that shal publish your disgrace, and work your ruine; because, like a trayterous person, you endeavoured theirs by your conceiling their follies, and animating them to any villanie."

Away the parasite sneaked, and another knocked at the gate.

### The Wanton Wife entreth to know her Fortune, whom Mockso describeth.

"WHO IS THAT?" said Fido

"A sweete woman, no doubt," answered Mockso, "doe you not smell her? a rowling eye, she turneth it with a trice; a faire haire, if it be her owne; an high forehead, if it be not forced: a rare face, if it be not painted; a white necke, if it be not plastered; a straight backe, if it be not bolstered; a slender wast, if it be not pinched; a prettie foote, if it be not in shooe-maker's laste; a faire and rare creature, if she be not dishonest."

### OPINION OF THE WANTON WIFE.

"*O si fas dicere*, she came naked into the cittie and shal so returne, unlesse she doe penance with a white sheete pinned about her, as she now deserveth. Her husband married her for pure love, and had nought with her, and so hee is likely to have so long as he hath her; yet shee will flaunt it with the finest, and gadde abroad with the giddiest; looking for greater attendance then an empresse, and more duty then a dutchesse; envying all that are more bravely trapped then herselfe, and confederate with few but such as are wantonly intrapped as she is ; no fashion can be extant, but she must have a fling at it; no sight to be seene, but she must view it; not a gewgaw to be heard of but she must have it; she will buy nothing that is cheape, weare nothing that is common, eate nothing that is not costly; her honest husband is her hobie-horse at home, and abroad, her foole; amongst her copesmates, wanton wenches game amongst themselves, and wagges sport to point at with two fingers: who is so terrified by her that he were better in his grave; by day he dare not meet her, she is so man'd with make-shift; by night hee feareth to lie with her, her touch is so ambiguous: with meat he cannot please her, she is so dainty; in clothes hee cannot keepe her, she is so costly; with words he cannot fit her, shee is so captious; in deede hee cannot content her, for shee is a wanton. If he endevour with good counsell to disswade her, she saith she preacheth too learnedly for her to edifie; if hee gybe and jest at her follie, then he is all wit, or a wittall; if he keepeth her short of mony, then she rappeth out an oath that she will have coyne, though she be hanged for it: if he keepe her close within doores, the next time he stirreth out a sergeant clappeth him on the shoulder for some debt shee hath entred unknowne to him for such a purpose. To be breefe, she is her husband's affliction, her children's disgrace, her friend's scandall, roysters and rake-hels randevouce; a wanton, wicked, well-favoured wife."

### *Fido, his oration to the Wanton Wife, detecting the heynousnesse of her beastly life and fortune.*

"WERE YOUR MINDE as richly beautified as your body you could not be too highly prized; but seeing the beastlinesse of your behaviour blemisheth your beautie, I cannot but condemne and contemne you; who, having plighted your faith and solemnly obliged yourselfe unto an husband, are now become most faithlesse and perfidious, leaving the fruite which was allotted you fall to the forbidden tree; which, driving you out of Paradise, will expose you to the infamie of the world; if you can delude your husband's eyes with demure carriage, and possesse him with a good conceit thereof, then you care not how you cousen him of his goods privily, deride him closely, abuse him behinde his backe, so all bee done caute it is well done: but if you consider the cause aright, it is yourselfe you wrong. There is an eie which seeth you, though never so closely cabined; there is an eare that heareth you, whisper you never so softly; there is an heart which apprehendeth you, contrive you never so cunningly, from which, if you cannot conceale your thoughts, wordes, and workes, never laugh in your sleeve how you have gulled, or bulled, your husband; nay, many are so impudent they care not who know it, they thinke it a credite to bee notorious, an honour to have gallants seeke unto them; where carrion is, it is no marvell to find kites; pleasure hath an amiable face, but a loathsome bodie; a sweete taste, but a sowre digestion; a delicious life, but a miserable death: looke upon that plot in my garden, you see it fresh and fragrant, if I should permit many of my neighbours to fling their garbidge on it, it would become a fulsome dunghil; or, behold my well, the water in it is cleere and sweete; if the sinkes here about should have passage to it, they would soone alter the clearenesse and sweetnesse of the water: so now you are sound and lovely to looke on, you may maintaine the same for a small space; but being common, ulcers, filth and blauches will breed upon [you] like frogges and toades in stinking pooles. And therefore I cannot blame those which are timerous of their wives, for their owne bodies safetie; one rotten sheepe corrupts a flocke, one measeled hogge smites an herd, one plagued person infects a people. Now to your fortune. If you once loose your good name, you will never recover it; if now in youth you forsake your husband, and play false, in your age, when none respect you, he will reject you: your children may begge, or steale, wil he toile to maintaine other men's gettings? If he decease before you, no honest man will have you, unless some of your deboshed companions, more for lucre then for love, who will never trust you, knowing you false to your former husband: and then, perchance, you would wish you had beene more constant to your first betrothed, and lesse confident to every cogging companion; but it will bee then too late. Now lament your follie, and beginne a new life, abandon lewde company and idlenesse, and you may have many a faire day, and future felicity; else expect nothing but miserie, shame, and many misfortunes in the end, which will fall heavily upon you if you doe not now labour to prevent them."

Away she walked, and another rapped at the gate.

### *The Jealous Man entereth to know his fortune, Mockso describing him.*

"WHO IS THAT?" said Fido.

"One as melancholie as a cat," answered Mockso, "and glared upon me as if he would have looked through me: sure hee lacketh something, he gazeth so about him: holde not downe thine head for shame, like a beast; but erect thy countenance, like a man. High-ho, how he sigheth, and beteth his brest, as if there were something there angering him. Why doth he feele his forehead so often? it is smooth enough he doubteth; I lay my life they wil sprowt out shortly, and shal soone become as huge-headed as was Acteon, after hee gazed on the goddesse bathing herselfe with her nymphs in the fountaine."

#### OPINION OF THE JEALOUS MAN.

"He is more afraid then hurt," said Opinion, "hee macerateth his minde without cause, and troubleth his thoughts without true reason: his wife is faire, therefore hee thinketh her false; of a wittie disposition, therefore hee deemeth her a wagge-taile: all that speake to her, hee thinketh wooe her, and every man that looketh on her, he judgeth loves her: let her speake him faire, then she faigneth: let her use him dutifully, then she doth counterfet: if she keepeth home, it is *volens nolens,* against her wil: let her goe abroad, then his head aketh, and his heart panteth: is shee neatly arraied, that is but to allure and please others: is she homely dressed, she knoweth he wil keepe house that day: goe they in the streets together, if she glanceth but aside, hee knoweth her minde for-sooth: courtesie in her is the loadstone of her lust: and affabilitie the cunning orator for her concupiscence: bringeth he any to his table, if she carve to them, it is in hope of some amorous requitall; if shee drinke to them, their pledgings are but as pledges of their concealed loves: they which proffer him kindnesse, he surmiseth it pretended, for opportunitie to his wife: and they which frequent his house, be they of his neerest alliance or kindred, he suspecteth. To be briefe with him, he is his fortunes fore-staller, his mindes miserie, his bodies bane, a rejecter of his most intimate familiars, a suspitious ill liver; for the wife would never have sought her daughter in the oven unlesse she herselfe had beene there in former times: an erronious hereticke in the opinion of his wife, an unreasonable and causelesse jealous man."

## The Fortune-teller's oration to the Jealous Man, declaring his folly and fortune.

"SIR, OF ALL MEN I holde you most senselesse, who, without certaine ground and sure experience, should misconceit that which was never meant you. Cannot your wife be faire, but lascivious? what say you to Lucretia? can you not be absent but she will play foule? how thinke you of Penelope, who, in the tenne yeares absence of her husband, lived chaste and untouched? but suppose that which you suspect were certaine, sores past cure are past care. *Quod factum est, infectum esse nequit:* that which is done can-not be undone; that which will be shall be: if she be chaste and vertuous, no beautie can tempt her, no gifts allure her, no perswasions winne her: but if she be disloyall, keepe her never so close, she will sometime or other flie out in despight of you.

Ut jam servaris bene corpus adultera mens est,
Nec custodiri ni velit ipsa potest.

"When Jupiter loved Io, a delicious damsell, his wife being mistrustfull, dogged him to finde out his dealing; who, to conceale his fault, turned the lady into an heifer, which Juno begged, and resigned to the custodie of Argus, who, although he was faigned to have an hundred eies, yet was he beguiled of the jewell he watched so narrowly: so be you never so vigilant and circumspect, if she be so disposed she will. *Non caret effectu quod voluere duo:* needlesse therefore will your care be if you have no cause; and although you have good reason, of none effect: *naturam expellas furca, licet usque re-curret.* Now to your fortune; if you be obstinate in your beleefe, and so confirme in your false faith, you will martir yourselfe most miserably; your body will be soone wasted, and your substance consumed; because, when your thoughts are destracted with such frivolous matters, you can never seriously negociate your estates concerning and supporting designes; your best way, therefore, is to thinke the best, judge the best, *et modo te sanum fingito sanis eris.*"

Away the Jealous Man departed, and another knocked at the gate.

### The Lover entering to know his fortune, Mockso describeth him.

"WHO IS THAT?" said Fido.

"I know not," said Mockso, "but he looketh very pittifully upon it, and commeth sadly in; a finicall fellow he is, and very fashionable: a stiffe necke he hath, which God hateth, and a streight dublet, which no drunkard could endure: for if he had it but one sitting, he would not leave it worth a button; sure his taylor hath not done well to make it so short wasted: crie him mercie! now I looke so low, he hath put all the waste in the knees of his breeches; currage, man! if she will not, another will."

#### OPINION OF THE LOVER.

"As simple as he standeth there," said Opinion, "hee hath let his owne arme blood himselfe instead of a barber-surgeon, and quaffed an health thereof in praise of his mistresse when he had done: hee hath kneeled oftener in the honour of his sweetheart then his Saviour: hee cruciateth himself with the thought of her, and wearieth al his friends with talking on her: he is trapt in so long contemplation of her heavenly by him surmised beauties, that sometimes missing his appointed meales, *oscula dat ligno,* he kisseth the post's most daintie face, supposing it his love, and imbraceth his pillow or the ayre in his armes circumference, her bodie being onely imagined present: he maketh her a deietie with his adoration, and extolleth the lustre of her eyes above the sun and moone: he is elivated into the third heaven when he dreameth of her, and will admit no sublunarie resemblances in his comparisons concerning her, though she have a negro's head, a Virginian nose, a Spanish face, a Flemish neck, and a Turkish stature: all the morning he wasteth in finifying his body to please her eye; all the afternoone he culleth out choice and premeditate speeches to delight her care; all supper while, if they table together, he peereth and prieth into the platters to picke out dainty morsels to content her maw; and almost all the night he watcheth and prayeth for her, sighing like a senselesse beast, and sobbing like a silly sot if he be rivald and put besides her: to be briefe, hee is his friends' pittie, his enemies' derision, his soules sorrow, his bodies decay, and his sweetheart's derision: a forsaken lover."

### Fido his oration to the Lover, revealing his fondnes and fortune.

"BY THIS IT SEEMETH you are in love; with whom? a woman: good, what woman?

beauteous, rich, or honourable? so, how doth she requite your love? with scorn, hate, derision: she is a woman the contrary to man, as one defineth the greatest pleasure that can betide a man, when he is deprived of her: witnes Galba, who, seeing his neighbour's wife hang herselfe upon a figge tree, desired a slippe thereof to graft, hoping it would beare more such fruite, meaning his wife. The toylsomest burden that combreth a man, as he certified who, when the rest of his companie cast overbord such stuffe as was most combersome unto them, being so commanded by the master of the shippe, tooke his wife in his arms with intent to fling her into the sea, had hee not beene interupted. If, then, a wife be the contrary to an husband, what concord can there be betweene them? if a pleasure to be lost, who would sigh to be deprived of one? if a burden and clogge to be kept, who would not skipp for joy to have his clogge taken from him? But she is beauteous, rich, or honourable: what is beautie with untoward conditions, but a faire flower with an ill favour,—a painted sepulchre fil'd with putrid bones? what are riches with wayward qualities, but golden mazers fraught with deadly poyson? and, as the cynick likened a rich man without knowledge, to a sheepe with a golden fleece, so you may resemble a wealthy woman with willfull manners, to a jade with golden trappings: and what is honour? a celestiall thing, a radiant starre, you will say; but those starrs are not all one; some are fixæ, some errantes, some cadentes, that is, some are fixed, some wandring, some falling starres: but she you admired was none of the fixed, as her wandring and falling from you sheweth: besides, she scorneth, hateth, and derideth you: if any of your best friends should serve you so, you will renounce them, yet you will reverence her, your worst enemie; but men of your mould are like spaniels, which will creepe neerest to them that cudgell them: so the frowarder their sweetehearts are, the frowarder are they to crouch unto them: *Quod licet ingratum est, quod non licet acrius urit,* whereas being lesse obsequious they might fare better, *novi mulierum mores; ubi velis nolunt, ubi nolis capiunt ultro.* Some reason had censorius Cato to leave this precept for future times—Trust not a woman; the dogged philosopher knew causes enough, when he said it was too late for the olde man, and too soone for the young to marrie. Yet I speake not this in disgrace of vertuous women, or to deterre you from marriage: but for a man, the king and commander of al earthly creatures, whose body is pure, whose minde more magnanimous, to be dejected in spirit, pale in physnomy, leane in his limmes, and all for a woman, nay, for such a woman as doth scorne, hate, and deride him: fie, it is intollerable. Were she true and faithfull unto you in lawfull and honest sort, I would kindle and combine you with the best counsell I could: but being otherwise, take these precepts, which, if you follow, will allay all lust and love in you: the first is, to abandon idlenesse, the nurse of wantonnes: the second, shunne solitarinesse, and bee eyther doing something, or discoursing and passing the time away in company: the third, to have a good conceit of yourselfe, to cheere up your spirits, and doubt not but to have her betters: the fourth is, to mince and extenuate any laudable part in her, but to display and augment whatsoever deformity you know by her, for love is feigned blinde, because he cannot judge aright, but maketh a mountain of a mole-hill, a saint of a sow: the best course, therefore, to banish him is, to contrarie him in all his asseverations, to prise at a low rate that he highly vallueth. As for instance, is the partie fatte? fatte meate will cloy any man: is she leane? what good stomacke careth for bones? if she be pale of complexion, she will prove but a puler: is she high-coloured? an ill cognizance: is she silent? the still sow will eat up all the draugh: dooth shee talke much?

a pratling gossip she is likely to prove, and who would be troubled with a tatling tongue, and such like? Fifthly, if shee useth you hardly either in words or deeds, or countenanceth any of your enemies or evill willers, set it downe in your table-bookes, and write it upon the wal in your bed-chamber, that you may at al times better remember them: and consider if she tendered you, she would not wrong you. Many more could I expresse, but I should be over-tedious: therefore to your fortune, which now is bad enough, neither would I wish any worse, though I should wish them hanged, for hanging is the end of care, but love the enterance: but what will be hereafter, that is as your choise is: if you be advised, hope the best, if not looke for crooked fortune, as well as some of your betters have had before you." Away the lover walked, and another came to the gate.

### The Virgin entereth to know her fortune, Mockso describing her.

"WHO IS THAT?" said Fido.

"Diana, or one of her darlings," he replied. "I am perplexed with her proportion; the very glimse of her hath amazed me. Beauty sitteth enthronized on her browes, modesty in her eies, health in her cheekes, silence on her tongue, balsamum in her breath, immaculation on her necke, temperance on her waste, comlinesse on her whole body: Cytherea may sigh at her portraiture, Delia blush at her behaviour: her lookes turne not to and fro; her speech is not obstreperous; no pride in her apparell, no affectation in her gate: the map of modestie, and picture of purenesse.

#### OPINION OF THE VIRGIN.

"*Rem tenes,*" said Opinion; "now you have laid gibing aside, you have eased me of a labour. A purblinde wit may perceive what she is: an immaculate virgin."

### The Fortune-tellers oration to the Virgine, encouraging her to chastitie, and shewing her fortune.

"AMIABLE MAID, which hitherto hast led a chast and unpolluted life, persever still as you have begun, and make no doubt but to be right happy, being enriched with so inestimable a jewell as chastitie, which is a cœlestiall beatitude, the sister of the angels, the conqueresse of concupiscence, the queene of vertues, although it vouchsafeth to inhabit the minde and body of you an earthly creature: seeing therefore it is such an inestimable jewell, how warily are you to keepe it! such a peerlesse princesse, how loyally are you to love it! such a victorious triumpher, how carefully are you to guard it! so unmatchably allied, how much are you to make of it! All which that you may the better effect, I will bestowe this flower upon you: it is a lilly, not naturall but artificially composed, like to a naturall lilly, having six silver leaves, containing six severall posies, to preserve your chastitie: the first whereof hath this posie engraven in it: *Cibi et potus sobrietas;* that is, temperance in eating and drinking, which is an efficient cause to quelle and conquer wantonnesse: whereas, exercise of both or either of them doth animate and make it rebellious, and also disfigure the party pleased with the same: for immoderate eating breedeth five blemishes in the behaviour of a virgine, which do deforme her reputation more than fifteene wheales or pimples would disgrace her face: the first is scurrility of speech, a naughtie thing in any: the second talkativeness, or much babling: the third a foolish joy or petulant kinde of gesture: the fourth vomiting, belching, or such like: the fifth, drowsinesse of body, and dulnesse of minde: which although they are slightly observed in others, yet are they sooner marked in a maiden, as blacke spots are easier espied in a white cloath, then in darke coloured vestures. Touching inordinate drinking of wine, all are forbidden it, but you especially of all others: *virgo fugiat vinum ut venenum: nam vinum in adolescentia est duplex incendium voluptatis:* that is, a virgine ought to reject wine, as poison, which is a twofold firebrand to kindle lust in youth: abstinence therefore is the first weapon to defend chastitie, and put the enemie to flight; which, as it is comely in any presence, so it is commodious for any feminine personage: keeping them from fogginesse, grosnesse, and fiery faces; as one said of virgins in his time, they pinch their bellies of meate, (a good custome,) that they might be as small as bull-rushes.

The second leafe of this lilly hath engraven in it, *Asperitas vestitus,* that is, coarseness and plainenesse of apparell: for garish and fantasticall cloathes are speechlesse reporters of wanton mindes; therefore, said one, which had some trafique with such light stuffe, that sumptuous and soft raiments were the ensignes of pride; but light and loose cloathing the index of luxurie. And as in olde time, such as solde horses were wont to put flowers or boughes upon their heads, to reveale that they were vendible: so such as trim and trick themselves with toyes and gewgawes, shew that they are willing, if any will: let therefore your apparell be plaine, yet comely, which will stop the mouth of evill report; and as course as you can indure it, if you meane to tame your lust. The third leafe is set downe, *Laboris strenuitas:* labour and exercise, for if your minde be busied about any good huswifrie, or setled seriously upon any honest exercise, lust can have no power over you; therefore wee reade . . . Penelope, a constant lady, would carde and . . . wooll herselfe, least shee should be idle, and consequently, subject to lascivious thoughts and deedes in the teene yeeres absence of her husband: and the vestals, if at any time they had let the fire on the altar goe out, they were enjoyned to kindle it againe with the beames of the sunne. In the fourth leafe, is printed *Custodia sensuum:* that is, not to give your senses any scope or liberty, especially the sight or hearing, for iniquitie through the eye-lids glideth into the heart, and many have been entrapped by giving audience to the alluring songs of the sirens. In the fifth leafe, *Modestia verborum:* modest words you must use; *qualis homo, talis oratio,* such as the woman is, such are her words; for a proud woman will be rapping arrogant words, a foolish woman fond words, a wanton woman lascivious words, but a chast woman modest words and few. Therefore, said a grave father, that the speech of a virgine ought to be wise, civill, slow, and sparing: that she might be accounted as excellent for her speech, as for her chastity: for evill words corrupt good manners. In the sixth and last leafe of this lilly, is written, *Fuga opportunitatem,* the eschewing of opportunity, to shunn the company and conversation of men: for, albeit I am a man myselfe, and shall be reputed foolish to bewray mine owne neast; yet to benefit such a goodly creature as yourselfe, whom it were villany to injure, I will display the practises of some, though all use not the same, that you may take heed of any, that would goe about to rifle you of your deerest jewell, without lawe or honestie, I meane marriage. Men, generally, are wiser then women in goodnesse, yet are they sillier in wickednesse and contriving deceit then craftie and sensuall women: and as they are more simple then craftie women, so are they subtiller then well-minded maydens, who, as they are guiltlesse of effecting deceipt, so are they innocent of suspecting deceipt.

"It is no glory, I confesse, to deceive a woman; no point of valour to overthrow the weaker vessell, yet if this weaker vessell be artificially garnished, and naturally beautified, what labour will they not take to attaine it? what watching will they omit to steale it, what wealth will they spare for to compasse it? and when they have gotten it into their custody, how do some of them esteeme it? even as children gewgaws, to dandle and play with it a while; but as soone as they eye a new devise, they cast away the olde, and never are in quiet, till they be fingering the newe, or as warriours of olde time, which did spend much cost and paines to take a citie, and when they had brought it into subjection, rifled it, and ransackt it; marched to another, and so to a thirde, etc. There was a pure virgine, as I heard, dwelling not farre from me, who had so firmely devoted herselfe to chastity, that the inhabitants thereabouts did admire her; till a lustie gallant, rich and well proportioned, wooed her, who never left battering the bulwarke of her heart with piercing oathes, vowes, and protestations, darted from his smooth tongue, till he had almost brought her to the bay. Within a while, after she had considered his actions, how hee would teare his haire, weepe in most seeming sadnesse, kisse her hand with feare and trembling, and proffer, unrequested, many servile ceremonies, fearing herselfe to breake an oath or violate a vow, trusted that hee had the same feare in him, which hee had not, condescended to his desire; which as soone as hee had accomplished, forsooke her utterly. After him another came unto her, and served her with the same sawce; then a third: at last she began to wax warie: a fourth came unto her, whose fashion was to try all, and if they agreed, left them incontinently; but hee laboured in vaine, for his gifts could prevaile nothing, nor his promises perswade her; (shee had faire warning, one would thinke); to be briefe, he liked, loved, and married her, and the second night, as they lay together, the good man said to her, 'Thou knowest, sweetheart, how often I tempted thee, and I protest, if thou haddest consented, I had forsaken thee utterly.' 'Tut, tut, husband,' said shee, (sure shee was halfe asleepe and halfe waking,) 'I trow I was a little wiser then so, for three had served me in the like sort before ever I beheld your face.'

"This I do not relate, that you should make the same experiment, but that you might avoid the like men, for he that maketh no scruple to breake the seventh commandement, will make as little conscience to keepe the third: besides, if he should keepe his promise, he would have you alwaies in jealousie; for if you feare not to displease God before you are married, who forbiddeth fornication, will not your husband be perswaded that you will have as little feare to commit adulterie when you are espoused? Take this lilly, and think upon every word and posie engraven in it; and above all, beleeve not words im . . . . ing any dishonest request. I have a picture here, to the same purpose: looke upon this lady, it was Dido, queene of Carthage, who being too credulous in beleeving a wandring prince, fell to folly with him, and after forsaken, caused a great fire to be made, and for griefe and anguish leaped into it. This other is Phillis, queene of Rodope, a virgin before she lent an attentive care to Demophoon, a man of royall race, who after he had gotten his purpose, never returned neere her againe; so that for shame, and avoiding future sorrow, she hung herselfe, as this picture lively expresseth: take it with you, and think that if these two queenes were deceaved, it were an hazard for to trust. *Fide, sed cui vide:* it is an old saying, trie before you trust: but if maydens follow that saying, they may be trust round before, and after served as these were."

Away the virgine walked, like Juno in the empire, and others were at the gate expecting entrance, but Fido beeing weake and wearie, dismissed them till some other time, and forthwith committed hisselfe to his closet.

FINIS.

🔘 20

# The Famous History
# Of Valentine and Orson,
# The Two Sons
# Of the Emperor of Greece

### SELECTIONS

A LATE MEDIEVAL *French romance,* Valentine and Orson *probably was a folk tale and a poem before it was told in prose. At the beginning of the sixteenth century, it was translated and published in English by Wynken de Worde. Traces of its influence can be found in Shakespeare, particularly in* The Winter's Tale *(II.iii.187), about bears nursing children, and in* Macbeth, *where several echoes of the romance are found, especially in the banquet scene. The flying wooden horse and the talking head in Cervantes'* Don Quixote *may have been suggested by these objects in the older romance. The chained lions and other elements in John Bunyan's* Pilgrim's Progress *have also been tracked to* Valentine and Orson. *(See for these sources the introduction by Arthur Dickson to* Valentine and Orson, *published by the Early English Text Society, London, 1937). According to Professor Dickson, at least seventy-four editions of the text have appeared since the beginning of the sixteenth century, the most recent being in 1919. Of course, many editions changed as old material was dropped and new events incorporated into the story.*

*A popular chapbook in the seventeenth century, the version used here consists of the first nine chapters from the sixteenth edition, published in 1736, and reprinted courtesy of the Special Collections Dept., University of Connecticut Library.*

# TO THE READER

Amongst many histories, as well *Antient* as *Modern*, which have in *Former Times* borrowed our *English* Phrase to speak withal, this (gentle Reader) here of *Valentine* and *Orson*, Sons to the Emperor of *Greece*, now once again Imprinted, crave a free Passage of thy Acceptance, and puts itself to the Censure of those Historiographers, who make *Invention* the eldest Daughter of the *Seven Sciences*. Therefore, considering with myself the Worthiness of the Story, with the Variety thereof, being many Years ago first written in *French* and since translated into *English*; where it hath found a favourable Welcome, as well of Superiors as Inferiors; I have now again, at my own Cost and Charge, Published it to the Eye and Ear of *Such*, to be seen or heard, as take Pleasure in those kind of Writings. It is deck'd forth with many fair Models and lively Pictures, all pertinent and agreable to the Subject of the History, which I have caused to be new cut; not only to make it carry the more Grace in Reading, but a more Lustre to *Heroick Atchievements* of Knightly Adventures: For here may the Princely Mind see his own Model; the Knightly Tilter his Martial Atchievement, and the Amorous Lady her *Dulcet Passages of Love*. Here are Countries, with Courts of Kings deciphered; the Magnitude of Honours laid open; the true Form of Turnaments described; and between Knight and Knight are here most lively Combats portrayed, to the great Content of the Reader. Let no Man think his Time ill spent, or his Labour lost, where the Matter affords such Copiousness of Pleasure. The History may well bear the Title of *Courtly Contents,* for indeed it is a Garden of *Courtly Delights,* where grow Flowers of an extraordinary Savour, that gives a Scent in the Bosoms of Nobility, Ladies, Knights, and Gentlewomen: It gives also a Working to the Minds of the dull Country-Swains; and (as it were) leads them to search out for Martial Atchievements. Herein is also contained, the true Difference betwixt Art and Nature; for in *Valentine* is comprehended the Education of *Art*, and in *Orson* the true Working of *Nature*, for being both one Emperor's Sons, the one brought up in a Prince's Palace, the other among *Savage Beasts*, now makes the Current pass with more Admiration to the Reader: Mark but the Carriage of the Wild *Orson*, and you shall find that *Nature* hath a Being above *Art*, but yet *Nature* bettered by *Art*, hath a more noble Working. The History here written was translated out of *French* into *English*, above a hundred Years ago, by one *Henry Watson*, and since that Time, it hath been by him Corrected, and put into a more *easy* Style, and so followed on to the Press, till this present Edition, which I have here Published for thy Benefit: Therefore, Gentle Reader, accept of this my Cost and Pains, who had rather prove a Loser, than so Worthy a Story as this is, should lie in Obscurity; for there are few Subjects of *Human Carriage*, but are herein handled, therefore the more fitting to be seen into. If you desire to *see* the Care and Troubles of Kings, the Battles of Martial Champions; if of Courtly Turnaments and Combats of Princes; the Travels of Knightly Adventures; the Sorrows of distrested Ladies. Of strange Births, and savage Educations. Of Friends long lost, and their joyful Meeting again. Of Charms and Enchantments. Of the Rewards of Traytors and Treasons. Of long Captivities and Imprisonments, *here they are:* Yea, here are all the *Varieties* and *Passages* that may furnish forth a History fit for a *Reader's Pleasure*; for no *unseemly Words or Speeches are herein contained,* but such as are modestly carried. Considering all which, I am now encouraged to put this old Story into a *New Livery*, and not suffer that to lie *Buried*, that a little Cost may keep *Alive*. And so, *Gentle Reader*, craving thy Acceptance, I wish *Thee* as much Pleasure in the *Reading*, as I have had in the *Translating*; and so I End.

## CHAPTER I

### *How King Pepin banished his Queen Bertha; and how he gave his Sister Bellisant in Marriage to Alexander, Emperor of Constantinople.*

WE FIND IT set down in *Antient Chronicles*, that the thrice noble and valiant *Pepin*, some time King of *France*, took to Wife *Bertha*, who was descended of no less than *Royal Race*: This Lady was exceedingly fair and wise, but wondrously cumbered with many Adversities and Troubles, enviously beset on each Side, which with great Patience she suffered. The chief Instrument of all this Mischief towards this good Queen, was plotted and effected by a cursed old Woman, who first of all brought her into Disgrace with the King her Husband, and after to be quite banishe his Bed, while she in a cunning Manner, brought in a Daughter of her own in the good Queen's stead: This old Woman having thus brought her Treachery to effect, (for her Daughter somewhat resembled *Bertha*) it so came to pass, that King *Pepin* had two Sons by this Maiden, to wit, *Haufray* and *Henry*, both which Sons so grieved the King, and wasted the Country of *France*, by their Outrages and Fury, that in the End they caused the Queen *Bertha* to be utterly banished, where she passed a great Part of her Days in doleful Lamentation, and abundance of Sorrow: She long endured those miserable Days of Sorrow, at last began to receive Comfort again; for it so chanced after at the earnest Request of divers great Peers and Lords of *France*, this good Queen began to find Favour with the King, her Husband, (who when he knew the Treachery that wicked old Woman had plotted against her) much bewailed the Miseries she had endured, and with great Honour and Triumph received her again most Kindly. The Queen being thus restored to her Bed, in short time conceived, and bare unto the King a goodly Son, called *Charlemain* the *Puissant*; but the King himself was continually hunted from place to place, by the aforesaid *Haufray* and *Henry*, and at last compelled by them to forsake his Realm, as hereafter followeth more at large in the ensuing History: My Purpose at this present, is to set down to the Reader, the whole Matter contained in this Book; and especially the valiant Acts and Deeds of *Valentine* and his Brother *Orson*: This King *Pepin* had a Sister named *Bellisant*, a Woman of great Wit, Beauty, and all the Endowments that Nature might afford, which caused her Brother's Love mightily to appear to all the World, by the ardent Love and Affection that he bare her: It chanced so, that the Fame of this lovely Personage spread itself abroad in other Regions, that at last *Alexander*, Emperor of *Constantinople*, who was much enflamed with her Beauty, came into *France*, accompanied by a gallant Troop of his Nobility, all richly set out with all manner of Pomp belonging to so great a Prince. This Emperor shortly after his Arrival, suddenly assembled all his Lords in their rich Habiliments; appointing them to take their way towards King *Pepin*'s Court; which when understood, he joyfully entertained them, and quickly granted the Emperor's Request. King *Pepin* understanding this sudden, but joyful News, made great Preparations in his Court for entertaining of this noble Emperor: All things being in Readiness, King *Pepin*, with all his Train, went to meet this Prince, whom, when they met, they entertain'd with great Joy, and conducted him to the Court of *France*, where fair *Bellisant* was, and she entertained him with no less Joy than her Brother had done before; and there they spent their Time in Joy and Triumph.

This Marriage being once publickly known among all the Inhabitants, Joy began to shew itself on every Side, for such a happy Day, that such good Alliance was knit between the Emperor *Alexander*, and King *Pepin*, that Triumphs began in every Place, against the Nuptial-Day: When the time appointed came, these two were espoused in all Honour befitting their Estates, and Largeness shewed itself on every Side. This Marriage-Feast lasted long; but at last, being ended, the Emperor (assisted by all his worthy Train) made Preparation to take leave of his new Brother-in-law, and take their Way towards *Constantinople*, with his fair Empress *Bellisant*: Being all mounted on Horse-back, King *Pepin* also set forward with his Brother, to bring him on his Way, attended on every Side with Lords, Ladies, and many other Gallants of the Court; and they that could not find Legs to go, found Eyes to weep for the Departure of their fair Lady and Mistress. These mighty Princes came near to a Port of the Sea, whereat they must needs part; there taking leave of each other, they were forced to render more Thanks in Tears than Words, the which I am not able to express: But above all, the Emperor yielded King *Pepin* worthy Thanks for his quick, and generous Consent, in giving him his fair Sister *Bellisant*, and with so free a Heart to yield him Good-will. At which Words of the Emperor unto King *Pepin*, the King embraced him in his Arms; saying, *Fair Sir, and my right loving Lord and Brother, I have not received you according as your State required, nor with such Triumphs and Magnificence as became me; but in that you have so graciously accepted my small Power. I hold myself content in that I have done, but not that I should have done; and therefore, there belongeth small Thanks to me; but from me innumerable, in that you have been pleased to accept of my Sister for your Wife; whereby (I trust) long Friendship shall be continued betwixt us: In Token whereof, I take Witness of all that are here present, that my Body, Realm and Goods, and all the Powers that I can raise in* France, *to venture for your Safety and Succour all the Days of my Life.* King *Pepin* being now departed from the Emperor, turned himself to his Sister, and in this Manner takes his leave: *Fair Sister* (quoth he) *think no longer of this Country of* France, *wherein you have spent your Infancy, but remember that you are removed to a Country of better Conditions: Also let your Behaviour be such, that I, the rest of your Friends, and the whole Company of Peers may have Honour in you. Again, as the Country where you now go is strange unto you, so be you governed by the modest Ladies of the Land, and give no Ear to wicked Counsel, or to such as would move you to Disloyalty: For you are the Creature that I love the dearest in all the World; wherefore, if I should hear Tydings other than good from you, or of you, it would be the only Cause to take away my Life.* After this, he gave to his Sister many choice Gifts, and so embracing each other, with weeping Eyes, he left her to the **Mercy** of the Waves. The young Lady, whose Heart being overcharged between Joy and Fear, was not able to answer a Word; and what with Tears and Sighs, the Passage of her

Tongue was utterly stopt. Then all the Lords and Ladies took their Leave of each other, at which was let fall many Tears, as well on their Parts of *France*, as they that were to go to *Constantinople*; but especially for the Departure of the fair Lady *Bellisant*. All Duties of Love being ended, King *Pepin* returned to *France*, and the Emperor by this Time being upon the Seas, had Wind and Tide at such Advantage, that within short Space, he with all his Train arrived with Safety at *Constantinople*; where at their Landing, they were all received with great Joy, Honour and Triumph; all which were needless to recount. But mark what hapned, not long after these Joys and Triumphs were extinguished, that were made for the Lady *Bellisant*, in Place whereof, nothing but Mournings, Lamentations and Tears were placed, and all for the poor Lady, who by Treason and false Accusations, was cast out and banished, as hereafter appears more at large.

## CHAPTER II

*How the Arch-Priest of Constantinople betrayed the Emperor,*
*his Lord and Master, in making Love to the Empress;*
*and what Evil followed thereupon. The Arch-priest having*
*received a Repulse, to save his own Honour,*
*practised Treason against the Innocent Lady.*

IN *Constantinople* lived an Arch-Priest, in whom the Emperor put such Trust, and loved so fervently, that he bestowed upon him great Riches and Possessions, and committed all his Bosom-thoughts unto his Secrecy: And in the End made sole Governor and Commander over all his House; he was also his principal Confessor, and one of his greatest Favourites, for which he had many a sorrowful Heart. This Priest forgetting all the Emperor's Favours, and great Honours done unto him, being intangled with the Beauty of the new Empress, who excelled all Mortal Creatures, *Inordinate Lust* prevailed with him so far, that there was nothing stood in his Way, only fit Time and Opportunity to settle this his Determination: At last, it chanced that he espied her all alone, sitting solitary in her Chamber, which the Arch-Priest well observing, he came in and sat down by her, At last he began to behold her with a smiling and jesting Countenance, of all which the Lady mistrusted nothing, for she very well knew the Amity between him and the Emperor, and his Familiarity in the House; and she never dream'd or had such a Thought, that he thereby would cover such a filthy Act, as to tempt her to Dishonour, especially towards his Lord and Master, who so much esteemed him. But there is never more Danger like to ensue, as when one of the same House intendeth Treason. But at last, after many Gestures of Impurity, and sitting still by this virtuous Lady, he began to utter his *Lascivious Thoughts* in this Manner.

Right dear and Sovereign Lady, I am your Servant and Chaplain; therefore I beseech you not to stop your Ears, but rather set them open to hear my rude Words; especially, for that I am burnt up in Affection towards your Person, and for whose Love I have suffered intolerable Torments in my Bosom: Know therefore, (my Redoubted Lady) that the Beauty of your admirable Person, and the *Supernal Form* wherein you are framed, hath even ravished my Spirits, broken my Heart, confounded my Senses, and quite bereft me of all Rest, both by Night and Day, only with doating on your Peerless Beauty. Again (fair Lady) my Meat, Drink, Manners, yea, my very Countenance; insomuch, that only my Request and Prayers unto the Gods, is even this, that they would so enchant that Heart of yours, that you would at length give Consent unto me, your Vassal, that I might not only serve you, but also delight you in all those Pleasures you are ordained unto. If, Lady, you refuse me, and cast me off, denying these my restless Thoughts; (than which nothing will sooner cut my Heart asunder) I can look for nothing but present Death, and rather covet therein to be locked fast, as in a Prison, than receive a Denial from your fair Lips. Alas! (fair Lady) you are renowned in all the Gifts of Nature: Fair, Amiable, Courteous, Gentle, and also Youthful; be not then the Cause that I should hazard my Life by losing your Love; but rather grant my Desire, and thereby make me forever yours in hearty Affection. But, fair Lady, perhaps you will say, *How dare you to offend the Gods in this unlawful Act?* To this, fair Lady, I answer, I am one of the Vicars of the Gods upon Earth, and therefore it wholly rests in my Power to absolve you of your Sins, and enjoin your Pennance; which, trust me Lady, shall fall out to be very easy, so you grant me your Love.

These Speeches of his being ended, the Lady, out of a grave and prudent Carriage, made unto this perjured Priest this sharp Reprimand and Answer: Ah! Thou false, unjust, disloyal and devilish Priest, Stain to all thy Profession: How darest thou open thy perjured Mouth to such a Mass of Villanies, as thereon may ensue? First, against the *Sacred Order.* Secondly, but most principally, against the Majesty of that Emperor that ever nourished thee in the Bond of tender Compassion, and hath raised thee to great Dignities, far unfit for such a Devil-incarnate: And from whom may justly proceed the Sentence of Condemnation, both on thee and me, if he should understand thy *Lascivious* and *Wicked* Practices. Thou Devil, and worse than Devil, thou that should'st be unto me Instruction, and also a Guide to my Life and Conversation; in this thou art devising my utter Ruin and Destruction, by thy evil Desire, beyond that good Expectation which the Emperor trusted in thee: O never grant (ye Gods) that the Blood of *France*, from whence I am descended, nor the Emperor, my loving Lord, should be so dishonor'd either by me in my Body, or through my Privity in any other Manner. O false accursed Man, behold whereunto thou wouldst deliver me! First unto the utter Ruin and Spoil of mine Honour; next, shut up my Body in unremovable Shame forever among Men; and lastly, bring my Soul into the Jaw of *Death* and the *Devil.* Let fall all these thy vile and devilish Provocations to *Lust,* and leave forever after to solicite me, or any other *Virtuous Creature* in this Manner, which if thou further prosecute unto me, thou can'st look for nothing but a shameful *Downfal,* and a most ignominious *Death.* Therefore with this Answer depart, and see that ye attempt me no more.

This angry Farewel of the worthy Empress, stung the Priest at the very Heart; but at that time durst make no further Reply unto the fair Lady concerning Love; but as a Man all composed of Rage and Fury, he then departed, discontent at this most unfortunate and unhappy Chance. At last, when he could hold no longer, he excused himself unto the Lady, craving Pardon for these his bold, sawcy, and rash Follies committed, but yet could find no Remedy to restore his Honour. Thus being sore troubled in Mind, divers and sundry Ways he resolved upon to revenge himself upon this Innocent, which he accordingly affected by Treason against this Lady: And seeing the Emperor knew nothing in this Matter from the Empress *Bellisant*, how the Arch-Priest would have enticed her to Dishonour, and have drawn her to Disloyalty to the Emperor, but he could not; therefore he began to accuse her to the Emperor for diverse Crimes. The Arch-Priest having now begun to set abroach his devilish Practises, began to think how he might effect what he had determined, and also preserve the Reputation of the former Honours which the Emperor had bestowed upon him; whereupon at last he resolved, that he would cunningly, under the Cloak of Dissimulation, bear fair Weather towards the Emperor, also seemed to shew how great Care he had of his Preservation, and to make known his Loyalty and watchful Care he had towards the Welfare of his Estate and Person: So it befel, that on a Day when he espied a fit Opportunity, and finding the Emperor all alone, he thus accosted him:

Right High and Mighty Emperor, and my noble Lord and Master, I cannot chuse but recount and highly esteem the inumerable Favours, and great Kindness which I have always received from your mighty Highness: Wherefore, as *Duty* doth always bind me, I am ever most watchful over the Passages of your Estate, in which I now stand by you appointed; but especially in that you have made me sole Commander in your House, and therein trusted me above all others: Therefore, it is my Duty, to reveal unto you all those Carriages that any Way concerns your Royal Person; wherefore I beseech your Highness to give Ear to what I shall now disclose unto you, for I had rather suffer all the Torments of Death, than to hide any thing from you; and the rather, for that it nearly toucheth your Person and Honour: O Emperor! thus it is. *Bellisant*, your Wife, and Sister to the King of *France*, whom you have advanced to this State and Dignity, faileth in the Duty and Loyalty which she oweth unto her Dread Lord; for she wandereth in her Love, and giveth that unto another which is proper only to your Self: To name the Person unto your Majesty I will not, for you know I am a *Sacred Priest*, and may not seek the Blood of any Man; but yet, I know for certain, that by the Way of Confession I come unto the Light thereof, yet I neither ought nor will reveal the Name of him that thus usurps your Bed: But let it suffice, there is not a more unclean and lascivious Woman liveth in your Court or Kingdom; whereby your Life is in Danger, your Honour defam'd, and my Duty towards you approved by what I have told you. My Advice therefore is, to be wary of your Person, and correct this her Folly, but yet mildly and wisely, always with the Preservation of your Honour: For will it not be a great Shame among the Princes of the Earth, that you, having taking a Wife, Sister to a great King, one who for her Beauty is incomparable, her Wisdom is not to be parellel'd by any Lady on Earth, and she to prove a *Whore?* And what is worse, one who daily desireth your Death; which grieves my Heart to think on it.

The Emperor having heard this long Accusation, little mistrusted the Treachery of the Arch-Priest, and gave Credit to all his fair but false Words, and therewith became extream pensive and sad, that his Trust in her beautious Love, had been thus deceived. At last, having spent many Days in uttering forth many discontented Gestures, Words and Sighs, and many grievous Acclamations, even in the Imperial Palace, he gave Rest a while to his discontented Passions: But wakened Revenge to wait for a fitter Opportunity: And upon a Day, entering into the Chamber of *Bellisant*, and without speaking to her one Word, in a most fierce, rude and unmannerly Order, took his Lady by the Hair of the Head, and dragged her about the Chamber, throwing her on the Ground in such a horrid Manner, that the Blood besmeared her Face in most inhumane Sort. She receiving from her Lord such unlook'd-for Welcome, cried out in a lamentable Manner, and as well as she was able began to say. *Alas! (my dear Lord) what moveth you to this unwelcome Outrage; I call the Gods to witness, I never did any thing in my Life, either against your Honour or Life, or ever prostituted my Body to any Strangers Love.* The Emperor not being satisfied, replied, thou Whore, I am too well informed of thy Proceedings; and cursed be the Day and Hour that ever I saw thy deceivable Face; and therewithal, without Pity, dashed her Head against the Ground, leaving her speechless, insomuch that all the Damsels, her Attendants, thought she had been quite bereft of Life. Upon this, there arose up in the Court a most pitiful Outcry, which the Councellors and other Attendants in the Court hearing, ran spedily to the Chamber, where they found this Lady in a Trance; at which Disaster all were amazed, some ran to take up the dead Body of the Empress, others took upon them to speak to the Emperor, thereby to stay the Fury of this undeserved Rage, whose Words unto him were as followeth: Alas! (dread Sovereign) what may be the Cause of this your sudden Passion, in delivering into Danger of *Death*, so modest, chaste, and noble a Lady? A Lady so beloved of all Degrees, and in whom was never seen the least Spark of Dishonour, neither towards you, or any in this Empire: Wherefore our Request unto you is, that you would moderate your wrong-conceiv'd Anger against this harmless Lady. The Emperor not at all relenting, answered, *Speak no more, for I know, I see, I hear how cunningly she hath deluded me; therefore move me no further, for I am fully purposed to deliver her over to Death; and he who shall here-unto gainsay, shall be a Partaker in Death with this wicked Strumpet.* These Words were no sooner uttered, but up rose a worthy, wise, couragious and bold Baron, who spake to the Emperor, after this Manner: *Right worthy Sir, I could wish you to be well advised before you proceed further against this Lady, who is your espoused Wife, Sister to a great King, namely, the King of* France, *who when he hears of this great Wrong done unto her, will out of a couragious Heart, and a Brotherly Affection, muster up all his Men of War, and suddenly surprize all our Towns, Wives and Children, forgetting Mercy, and only persuing Revenge upon us for these merciless and cruel Deeds unto his Sister. Again, consider on the other Side, the Lady is great with Child, therefore it is dangerous so rudely to Smite and Wound her at this Manner, wherein you have proceeded against her.* The worthy Baron having thus ended his Advice, the Lady suddenly fell upon her Knees before the Emperor, and in Tears very submissive and lamentable, thus she spoke.

Alass! (my Lord) take Pity on an Innocent Lady, for I am free from any evil Act, nor I never thought any Evil against your Person or Dignity: At least, my Lord, if your compassion be quite extinct from pittying me, yet pity the Fruit of my Body, for I am great with Child by you, of which the Gods grant me a joyful Delivery. If nothing can appease your Anger towards me, then let my Body be imprisoned in some strong Tower till the Time of my Delivery, and then do with my Body as you please, so the Fruit of my Body may be kept safe. In this dolorous Passion she proceeded so far, that what with her Sighs and Tears following one another, it would have grieved the stoniest Heart that ever rested in the Bosom of the vilest Tyrant that ever reigned. All this nothing moved the hard-hearted Emperor, who was so wholly bewitched with the false and traiterous Accusation of the Arch-Priest, that all Lenity set apart, he burst out in this Manner: Thou false Strumpet, the Child thou goest withal is to me no Joy, but rather

Dishonour; for thy Disloyalty hath made such a Seperation between us, that noting thy dissolute Life, thou hast made another Partner in my Love. The Courtiers perceiving nothing could mitigate the Rage of the Emperor, by a common Consent removed her out of his Presence into another Chamber, shewing unto her all the Favour they could, both in Action and Gesture, although her fair Face was sore deformed and besmeared with Blood. Having thus conveyed her away, the Ladies that were her Attendants fetched Water to wash her Face, and did all they could to revive her dying Spirits. Being thus in another Chamber, in comes *Blandiman* her 'Squire, who beholding her in this disfigured Manner, for very Pity the Water trickled down his Cheeks, and at last began his Speech in this Manner: *Ah! Madam, I plainly see that You are traiterously handled, and wish that the Gods would throw down their malignant Curses upon that Person that hath been the Cause of all your Miseries: But, gentle Lady, take Comfort unto You, and trust me, if You will be ruled by me, I will conduct you back again to* France, *to the King your Brother, who gave me and my Service unto You, to attend You in all Misfortunes; all which I will, to the utmost of my Power, undertake. Sweet Lady, follow my Counsel, and free Yourself out of Danger; for be assured, that if here you stay, the Emperor will prosecute Revenge upon you, and in the End bring You to a shameful Death.* Unto this the sorrowful Lady made this Reply: *Ah!* Blandiman, *I know thy faithful Service towards me; but yet, if I should follow thy Advice, and steal out of this Country secretly, it would make me seem guilty of all that the Emperor throweth upon me, and thereby yield me Guilty of the Deed. Believe me,* Blandiman, *I had rather die all the Deaths the World can put upon me, than to bear the Blame of that, wherein I am Innocent.* By this Time the Emperor's Choler was somewhat pacified, by Means of his Lords and Barons that attended; insomuch that he caused *Bellisant* to be quickly brought before him; when she was come, his Heart trembled and fretted for very Anger that he durst not put her to Death, fearing the great Puissance and Might of her Brother, King *Pepin*; and therefore burst forth into these Speeches: Thou false and accursed Woman, by whom mine Honour is brought in Question: I take the Gods to witness, were it not for thy Brother's Sake, the Valiant *Pepin*, King of *France*, I would make thee Fry in the Fire, as an Example to all fair Ladies; but, for his Sake, I spare thy Life; stand forth and hear thy Judgment. I Banish thee out of my Country and Empire; expressly commanding, that without any Delay, to-morrow thou depart out of this City, and if thou be seen here any more, I assure thee thou shalt suffer Death in all Extremity. Also, I charge and command, that none of my Country dare be so bold as to give Aid, or accompany You, save only Your Servant *Blandiman*, whom You brought with You out of *France*. Go, get thee presently out of my Sight, for thou shalt never more sleep in my Bosom. The Emperor having pronounced Sentence against her, the Empress *Bellisant*, accompanied with her Servant *Blandiman*, speedily hasted to Horse. Being thus mounted, and then passing thro' the fair City towards one of the Gates thereof, there met her a great Multitude of People, of all Degrees, much lamenting the Loss of so fair a Lady, and so so good an Empress. When she came to the utmost Part, even ready to go out of the Gates of the City, there was heard such a lamentable Howling of mournful Voices, that the like before was never heard in the City of *Constantinople*. When she was out of the Walls of the City, and just entred into the wide Fields, she began to fall into a Womanly Fit of bitter Weeping, to see how shameful and dishonourable she was used, she being *Innocent*: Again, to think upon her Birth, and the Imperial Dignity from whence she was fallen, as also to account the Misfortune wherein she was like to finish the rest of her Days; it drove her at last from Tears to utter her Griefs in these Words: Alass! In what unhappy Hour was I born, to fall from so high an Estate to so low an Object of Poverty as I am now in? Woe is me, the unhappiest amongst Women, now are all my Joys turned topsie-turvy, my Laughter is turned into Weeping, my Songs converted into Sighs; instead of Cloath of Gold, wherewith I was wont to be cloathed, now I am glad of all Manner of mean Attire; my Precious Stones of inestimable Value are all taken from me, and Pearls of Tears stand all over my Garments. O ye Fields and Woods, to you I make my Moan, for other Company I have none, consider my Exile, and help to bewail my Misfortune: O would the Gods had pittied my Distress, and made me the poorest among Creatures, then had not Fortune given me so foul a Fall; at least my poor Estate would never have grieved me: Wherefore doth the beautious Sun send forth his Beams on a Wretch so miserable? Why doth the Earth bear such a Creature, that is composed of Calamities? O wretched Man, (whosoever thou art) that by thy wicked Treason hath brought me to this Downfal; I may well curse thee with Bitterness of Heart, by him alone am I made thus Unfortunate. Ah! my Brother, what should thou do with such a woful Wight to thy Sister? It had been better I had never been born, than that I should prove such a Stain to thy *Princely Family*. As she was thus complaining to her sacred Heart, the Anguish thereof threw her into a Swoond as she sat on Horseback, and was like at that Instant to have fallen off her Horse, e'er her Servant could alight and recover her; but he used all the speediest Means for her Recovery; at last, she coming to herself again, he said unto her, *Alass, Madam, be not discomforted, neither let Despair so far sieze upon you, but trust to the Gods, who will keep and defend you; for they are ready to aid and assist the Innocent.* Having thus spoken, he suddenly espy'd a Fountain, towards which, he and his Lady took their Way, and being come thereunto, he sat her down thereby, to ease and refresh her overtired Senses. Here at this Spring leave we the Lady and her 'Squire, and turn we now to the traiterous Arch-Priest, who was the Cause of all these treacherous and evil Practices.

## CHAPTER III

*How the Arch-Priest put on the Habit of a Knight at Arms,
and being well mounted, followed the Empress Bellisant.
How Bellisant, in her Banishment was
delivered of two fair Sons in the Wood,
whose Names were Valentine and Orson, and how she lost them.*

T HE ARCH-PRIEST having now wrought the Banishment of fair *Bellisant*, thought now with himself he should surely accomplish his Desire; wherefore in all Hast, he changed his White Rocket into a Coat of Steel, and begirt unto him a Sword; and being thus accoutred, he presently mounted on a Milk-white Steed, the fairest that could be had in all *Constantinople:* Being thus mounted, he rode after her with all Expedition, enquiring of all he met, which Way the Lady *Bellisant* was taken, who gladly told him which Way she had passed. After a few Hours Riding, at last he came to a spacious Forest and very long, taking the direct Way towards the Lady. It chanced that as he was riding along, casting his Eye aside, he spied the Lady with her Servant *Blandiman*, sitting by a Fountain full of Heaviness, lamenting her miserable Fortunes; *Blandiman* using all the Means he could to comfort her. Now this false Priest perceived it to be the Lady; but by Reason of his Disguise, she could not imagine him to be the Arch-Priest, her Enemy, but coming nearer her, she soon descry'd him, and being struck with a sudden Fear, spake to her Servant thus: *Alass,* quoth she, *I well perceive this to be the false Arch-Priest that's coming towards us, of whom I am exceeding fearful, lest he come to do me further Villany.* Lady, (said *Blandiman*) banish Fear, for if he come after us to do you further Harm, I will encounter him Body to Body, as long as Life lasteth. By this Time that they had ended their Speech to each other, the Arch-Priest was ready to alight off his Horse to salute the Lady with a courteous Behaviour; and after he had made himself known unto her, he began to say unto her after this Manner:

Right dear Lady, and our late honoured Empress, since thy Case is so pitiful, as to suffer Banishment by Sentance given against thee by the Emperor, know this, that if thou wilt give me Entertainment in thy Love, accept me into thy Favour, and to grant me what I have long sought at thy Hands; I will bring it to pass that the Emperor shall again recal thy Banishment, and make thy Greatness shine more bright than ever. Therefore consider with yourself; for I protest, what I offer to you is only tending to your Advancement. *Ah!* quoth the Lady, *thou disloyal and traiterous Adversary, it is only thou that hast wrought my Overthrow, and makest me spend the Remainder of my Days in more Misery than any Lady is able to endure.* Lady (quoth he) utter not such Curses against me, for I am not come to vex or trouble you, but to heap upon you more Joys than ever you as yet in all your Life enjoyed. And in speaking these Words, he bended his Body to the Lady, thinking to have kissed her, but *Blandiman* perceiving his Intent, suddenly started between them, and gave the Arch-Priest such a Stroak, that he fell'd him to the Earth, and with the Violence of the Blow, broke out one of his Teeth: The Priest had no sooner recovered himself, but suddenly took to his Sword, which *Blandiman* perceiving, took a Glave that he had about him; whereupon grew a sore and dangerous Fight between them: This Encounter lasted so long, that they were both much wounded, but still they continued fighting, till at last it chanced that a Merchant came by that Way, who perceiving afar off their fierce Encounter, cry'd out with a loud Voice in this Manner: Lords (quoth he) leave off, and shew the Cause of this your Variance, and I will endeavour to end this Controversy. Sir, quoth *Blandiman*, let us first try our Right by our Weapons, and afterwards we will be ruled by Words. But the poor Lady could no longer bear Silence, but began to tell the Merchant as followeth: *Alass!* quoth she, *Sir, if you ever pittied Woman, pity my Case; for this Man whom you see armed, is the false and traiterous Arch-Priest, that hath followed me to rob me of my Honour, and force me to his wicked and unsatiable Lust; also, this is he that hath made this Separation between me and the Emperor, my Lord and Husband.* The Merchant hearing her lamentable Tale, pittied her Misery, and began thus unto the Arch-Priest; leave off your Enterprize, and dare not so much as this Innocent Lady, for if the Emperor did but understand this Villany, he would soon end thy Life in

Infamy, as thou well deserveth. As soon as the Arch-Priest had heard what the Merchant said, he forsook his Combat, and fled as fast as he could through the Wood, for fear of being further known, being prevented of his Purpose towards the Lady; but though he conveyed his Body out of Sight, yet his Villanies were afterward disclosed. After his Departure, the Lady was forced to stay in the Wood, all sorrowful with her wounded Servant. The Merchant staid with them a little Time, bewailing the hard Hap of the Lady; yet comforted her, saying, *Alass! fair Lady, I see that this Arch-Priest hath falsely betrayed you, and brought you in Hatred with the Emperor; but I promise you, that if I live, I will reveal all these Treacheries to the Emperor, and bring the Traitor to a shameful Death; and so I commend you to the Gods; wishing that in those Extremities you would be patient, and comfort yourself in all these Sorrows:* So with many Thanks for his Aid from *Blandiman*, he departed. The Merchant having left them, *Blandiman* set the Lady upon her Horse, and himself on his, so riding together, they came to an Inn, where they took Lodging, and staid their Eight Days, during which Time her Servant was recovered of his Wounds, and then set forwards towards *France*; the Lady still sorrowful and complaining in this Manner: *Alass!* Blandiman, *what may my Brother and the Peers of* France *think of this, when they shall understand that I am expelled* Greece *for such a dishonourable Deed; and as a common Harlot, banished from the Emperor of* Constantinople? *Alass! I am persuaded that the* King, *my* Brother, *will believe that I am guilty of the Deed, and in his Anger deliver me over to a shameful Death.* Lady (quoth he) be not thus discouraged, but trust in the Gods, who will revenge your Injury, and send it Home upon the Offenders Head. During the Time of these Discourses, they had passed many Countries and Regions, till at last they came into *France*, and passing by *Orleans*, they took their Way towads *Paris*, where King *Pepin* then resided. So entering into a Forest near unto *Orleans*, there hapned new Miseries unto this Empress, of which more hereafter ensueth.

*Bellisant* (as you heard) being with Child, was suddenly overtaken in the Forest; the Time of her Delivery being come, caused her to forsake her Horse, and begin to complain to her Servant in this Manner: Alass! quoth she, Help, Help I say to lay me down softly under yonder great Tree; and when I am laid, make Hast and send me the Help of Women, wheresoever thou canst get any, for I can go no farther, my Pains so much encreaseth upon me. *Blandiman*, her Servant, did as she commanded, but fearing he should not find the Place again, he set a special Mark, that he might come the readier for her; and so taking his Horse, he rode forth swiftly to seek some Women to help this distressed Lady. He being gone, the Lady was left comfortless all alone withour Succour of any Creature, so that at last she was delivered of Two fair Sons in this desolate Forest: These Children were no sooner come into the World, but a fresh Misery, worse than all the rest that she had endured, happened to this Lady; for as she lay upon the Earth under the Tree, and her Two Infants by her, suddenly came to her a huge Bear, most terrible to behold, and took up one of the Infants in her Mouth, and with great Pace hasted into the thickest Part of the Forest: This strange and unlook'd-for Accident frighted the distressed Lady to the Soul, that she cryed out most lamentably, getting up on her Hands and Feet, to hasten after the Bear, which was quickly got out of her Sight. But alass, it little availed her to make any further Pursuit, for she never came to the Sight of the Child, till by Miracle it was at length disclosed. But the Lady wandered so long up and down from Place to Place, weeping and crying

out for her Child, and being overwearied with Travail, she fell into a great Sickness, insomuch that she was thereby near deprived of her Life, and immediately fell into a Swoond upon the cold Earth, as if she had yielded up the Ghost. In this Extasie, leave we her, and now proceed to the other Child, whom she left under the Tree.

It hapned the same Day, that her Brother, King *Pepin*, had taken his Journey from *Paris*, (accompanied with divers great Lords and Barons) towards *Constantinople*, to visit his Sister *Bellisant*; and passing through *Orleans*, he made such Haste, that he entred into the same Forest, whereas his banished Sister was lately delivered of her Two Children, but knew not what had hapned. Now as the King passed through this Forest, he espied, lying under a Tree alone, the other Son of *Bellisant*, which when he saw, he said unto his Attendants: My Lords, by the Appointment of the Gods, see, I have here found a fair Encounter, even a Child. By the Gods (said they) you say Truth. Well, said the King, take it up, and it shall be brought up at my Charge, neither shall it want for any Attendance, but be used as if it were my own: And if it lives until it comes to Man's Estate, I will endow it with Lands and Possessions after the most noblest Manner. And therewith, calling one of his 'Squires, he gave him the whole Care thereof, saying, *here, take thou this Infant, carry it to* Orleans, *see it baptized, provide a good Nurse for it, and let it want nothing appertaining thereunto.* The King little suspecting the Child was his Nephew, the 'Squire did as the King had commanded him, and carried the Child to *Orleans*, caused it to be baptized, and gave it his own Name, called *Valentine*. This done, the King proceeded on his Journey towards *Constantinople*, to see his lovely and beauteous Sister *Bellisant*; but e'er he could pass through the Forest, he chanced to meet with *Blandiman*, accompanied with a Woman that he had got to assist his Lady in her great Extremity of Child-Birth. *Blandiman* espying the King, knew him, and hastily alighted from his Horse, doing his Duty to him: The King perceiving it to be

*Blandiman*, said, *What News from* Constantinople? *And above the rest, how doth our Sister* Bellisant? *Blandiman* answered, *Most Gracious Sovereign, I bring you but little Tydings, yet those I do bring are sharp and bitter; for among the rest, I must tell you strange News of your loving Sister, and how she fares; and so it is, that by Force of Treason, and false Suggestion of the cursed Arch-Priest of* Constantinople, *your Sister is banished out of the Emperor's Court and Dominions; and but for the great Mercy of the Emperor's Court, and others, she had been publickly put to Death, by being burnt to Ashes in the Sight of all the People.* King *Pepin* having heard *Blandiman's* lamentable Relation, he was exceeding outragious and fierce in Anger, yet sorrowful withal, broke out in bitter Speeches against her, in this Manner: *Now, by the Gods,* quoth he, *I hold the Emperor no upright Judge, in sparing the Life of my Sister; for I swear, that if I had her now in my Possession, I would not rest, till by Death I had made her an Example to all fair Ladies, while the World endureth.* And therewithal, commanded all his Train to stay their Journey, and return back again to *Paris:* For the grievous Offences of my Sister, stays my Journey; and so he departed, without asking any more Questions, but turning his Horse's Head, Sorrow overcame his Courage, and at last made him break forth into these Words: *Ha!* quoth he, *how many Men are deceived in Women? Now am I utterly prevented of all my Purposes, for my only Hope rested in the Modesty of my Sister* Bellisant, *yea, and in her stood all my Joys and Pleasure: Again to have had* Alexander *still my Brother, and Friend at all Attacks; but now behold, by her I am disappointed, defamed, and shut out into eternal Dishonour.* And so with a heavy Heart he returned towards *Orleans.* When *Blandiman* perceived the Courage of the King to be thus daunted, he durst relate no farther News of the Lady *Bellisant*; but leaving the King, took his Way towards the Tree where he lately left her in great Pain of Child-birth: Being come thither, he sought her every where, but could hear no Tydings of her; wherefore being sorrowful, he knew not which Way to take. Being in a Surprize, at last he tyed his Horse to a Thorn Tree, and began to make a closer Search than before; wherein he was so vigilant, that at last he espyed her lying flat upon the Earth, in a manner speechless, for Grief that she had lost her Child, which the Bear had taken away. *Blandiman* being glad that he had found her, kindly embraced her, and taking her up in his Arms from the cold Earth, set her upon her Feet, and began thus unto her: *Alass! (dear Lady and Mistress) how happened you to stray so far from the Place I left you in?*

The Lady looking upon him with a ghastly Countenance, replyed thus. *Ah,* Blandiman! *My Distresses daily increase upon me; for you was no sooner gone to get me some Help of Women-kind, but I was delivered of two Babes, when a ravenous* Bear *from the Forest assailed me, and bare one of them away: I, although weak, making what Shift I was able, followed the ravenous Beast, thinking to have recovered my Loss, but all in vain, I could not overtake the* Bear, *nor, for want of Strength, recover back again to the Tree, where I left my other Infant.* Lady, quoth he, the other Infant; why, I myself but lately came from the Tree, and I am well assured that there was no Infant there. How *(quoth the Lady)* no Child under the Tree? With these Words she was so inwardly wounded, that she fell down in a Swoond; which *Blandiman* espying, he fell into brinish Tears for Sorrow, to see his Lady so plunged and overwhelmed, and at last led her towards the Tree, where she had left the Child; but when she saw the other Child was gone, who can express the Grief this Lady endured; and in the midst of her Sorrows she thus spake: Alass, *quoth she*, can there be in the World a more desolate Wretch? on every Side encompassed with Grief, and unsupportable Sorrows. But alass, Emperor, thou art the Cause, and hast been the only Means to deliver me over to Death, and that wrongfully and only by evil Counsel hast bereft me of thy Company; but I call all the Gods to witness, that I was never faulty to thee in my Body, nor disobedient to thee in any Point; wherefore, once again I am forced to cry out for Vengeance upon the Offender's Head: First, for my Disgrace; next for my Banishment; and lastly, for the Loss of my two Babes issued from the Blood-royal of the Emperor of *Constantinople*. But seeing all these Miseries are like to lay upon my Heart, come Death, and finish my Sorrows. All this while *Blandiman* was Ear-witness of all these piteous Plaints, insomuch that he grew weary of her Wailing, and in the best Manner he could, comforted her dying Spirits, by intreating her, that she would give over Moans, and betake herself to her Feet: Whereupon she gave Consent, and he, with a Woman he had brought with him, came into a neighbouring Village, where they lodged and nourished her, till she had partly recovered her Strength, and in some Measure forgotten the Depth of her Miseries. Then *Blandiman* began to tell his Lady the following Relation: *Most honoured Lady, it was my Chance (in looking you in the Woods) to meet with your Brother, King* Pepin, *who demanded of me what Tydings? But his Brows were bent, and full of Anger against you; wherefore my Advice is, that you make not towards him, for by that Countenance I well perceive, you will have but slender Welcome: For upon further Questions demanded, and answered, as soon as he heard that the Emperor had exiled you, he gave Credit that yours was the Fault; and therefore he lays all the Blame on you.* O! (quoth the Lady) now what I most feared is come to pass; and I well perceive that I am beset with Adversaries on every Side: Well, be it as it may be; the Emperor hath exiled me without Cause: What then shall I do? I will never return again to *Paris*, but take my Way into some remote Land, where my Body with my Faults shall be smothered; for my Brother's Anger is grown so great, that he would willingly deliver me over to Death; therefore it is better to fly and save my Life, than fall into the Hands of an angry Brother. This doleful Speech she delivered in Tears; which *Blandiman* perceiving, said, *Lady, leave off your Tears, for be assured of my faithful Fidelity; and here I offer myself, Life, and all to be at your Service, go whither you please.* Why then (quoth the lady) since thou art so resolute, let us resolve upon some strange Adventure; and therewithal passed forth to expose themselves to future Dangers: Where now we shall leave them with sorrowful Hearts, and return again to speak something of the Bear, that carried away one of the Children.

# CHAPTER IV

## *Of the Bear that took away one of the Children.*

Now the bear (as you heard before) that had carried away one of the Children, all this while had offered it no Violence, but bore it unto her Cave, which was dark and obscure: In this Cave the old Bear had four young Ones, amongst whom she laid the

Child to be devoured, but mark what happened, and you'll find it strange; for all this while the young Bears did it no Harm, but with their rough Paws stroaked it softly. The old Bear perceiving they did not devour it, shewed a bearish Kind of Favour towards it; insomuch, that she kept it, and gave it suck among her young Ones, the Space of a Year. This Child, by Reason of the Nourishment it received, became rough all over like a Beast; and as he grew in Strength, began to range up and down the Woods, and when he met with other Beasts, would smite them, and got such Mastery over them, that they began to shun the Place wherein he came, he was so extream fierce against them: And in this beast-like Life, he passeth the Term of fifteen Years, growing up to such Strength, that scarce any Man or Beast dare stir abroad, fearing to fall into his Hands, lest he should put them to Death. His Name was called O R S O N, because a Bear had been his Nurse, and also was grown rough like a Bear. This Bear-man lived so long in the Forest, that none durst abide his Presence: The Renown of this wild Man grew so great, and spread so far abroad, over all the Realm of *France*, that they of the Country round about chased and hunted him, but prevailed not; for he feared no Weapons, but passed through them all, snaping them in Pieces. All this Time he abode in the Forest, he neither wore Garment, nor had any Kind of Speech.

Here we leave the Wild-man in the Forest, and relate what became of the Lady *Bellisant*, and her Servant *Blandiman*; who was travelling through divers Lands and Countries; the Lady always bearing in her Mind the Loss of her two Children; wishing that if it were possible, they might be still in Safety. But in the midst of her Sorrows, passing on their weary Journey, sometimes by Sea, sometimes by Land, till at length they came to a Port in *Portugal*, where stood an invincible Castle, kept by a Giant, called *Ferragus*, so great and of Puissance, that there was not a Horse to be found that could bear the living Trunk of this Giant. It happened so at this Castle, that every

Ship that passed by this Port, was to pay Tribute to this Giant, which he himself came daily aboard to receive. At length he came into the Ship, wherein the Lady *Bellisant* and her 'Squire was, (for she was laden with all rich Merchandize) so casting his Eyes about, he espied *Bellisant*, whom he kindly took by the Hand, and led her into the Castle to his Wife (for he was married to a beautiful Lady). *Blandiman* also followed his Lady, fearing the Giant; but he behaved himself so nobly, that he did not offer her any Violence, but presented her to his Wife, who gladly received her, and was joyful at the Sight of so beautiful a Lady. The Giant having charged his Wife to use her and *Blandiman* honourably. During her Abode in the Castle, she would often shed Tears, when she thought of the Loss of her two Children; which the Lady of the Castle perceiving, would often comfort her in the best Manner she could, and ever placed her near her own Person, for she took great Delight in her Company. Within this Castle she tarried a long Time, and here we must leave her, and return back again to tell you something of the Emperor of *Constantinople*, and the false Arch-priest.

## CHAPTER V

*How, by the Counsel of the Arch-priest, new Customs and Taxations*
*were raised in the City of Constantinople; and how*
*the Treason came to light. How the Emperor, by the*
*Advice of his Nobility, sent for King Pepin, to see*
*the Combat fought between the*
*Arch-priest and the Merchant.*

THE EMPEROR having shamefully expelled *Bellisant* his Wife, oftentimes repenting him of the Fact: But by the cursed Counsel of the Arch-priest, to whose Words he gave such Credit, that whatever he spoke, was as an Oracle in his Ears; insomuch, that he continually heaped new Honours on him, advancing him above the highest in the Empire; and whatsoever he commanded was affected. At last, having gotten all Power and Authority in his Hands, he began to enhance the Customs and Taxes of the City of *Constantinople*; which Exaction of his, against all Reason, struck to the very Hearts of the Inhabitants. Among these his forced Impositions (it happened, that according to their yearly Customs) their was held a great Mart in the City, which falls out about the Month of *September*: Hereunto resorted many People for divers Occasions, especially Merchants. The Fair, or Mart-Day being come, the Emperor gave the Charge thereof to this Arch-priest, who accordingly provided two hundred armed Men to guard his own Person: Being thus accompanied, he took his Way into the City, to effect this new Charge which the Emperor had bestowed upon him. Now it chanced, that among the rest of those that sold Wares, the Merchant was one (of whom you heard before) that came riding by the Way, where *Blandiman* and the Arch-priest were a fighting. The Arch-priest seeing the Merchant, presently knew him, but took no Notice of him, for he was very fearful, lest all his Villany should come to light. The Presence of the Merchant much troubled the Arch-priest, insomuch, that he wished his Death, and would certainly have effected the same, by the Authority that he now had in his Hands; but still he feared some great Tumult would arise thereby. But mark what followed: The Merchant, among the rest, was furnished with costly Wares, as Cloath of Gold, Silver, Silk &c. Whereby he received great Wealth, and took more Money than any five Merchants beside: The Fair being ended, the Arch-priest sent forth his Officers to demand and receive his accustomed Duties, due upon the Sale of those Merchandizes: One Officer came unto this Merchant, and said, *Sir, you must pay ten Pence for every Pound that you have taken, for so it is ordered by the great Officer to whom it belongs.* The Merchant hereat being angry, said, *Cursed be that disloyal Arch-priest, for he is the only Cause of these new-raised Exactions: It had been better for us, if he had long since had his Desert, and with Shame and Infamy had ended his Days.* At which reproachful Words against the Arch-priest, the Officer took his Staff, and smote the Merchant on the Head, that presently the Blood gushed out: The Merchant feeling the Blood run about his Ears, drew his Sword, and struck so hard upon the Officer, that he laid him at his Feet for dead. Upon this, there arose a great Outcry throughout the Fair, insomuch, that the rest of the Officers coming up to help their Fellow, took the Merchant, and brought him before the Arch-priest: The Arch-priest glad of this Opportunity, would suddenly have put him to Death; but the Merchant appealed to Justice, to have his Cause tryed by Law. The Arch-priest fearing the People, sent him away to the Emperor, for nothing could satisfie him but his Life: But in seeking the Life of the Merchant, he purchased his own Death, as hereafter followeth: The Merchant was brought into the Emperor's Palace, where he in Person sat as Judge. The Emperor being set, the Arch-priest brought his Advocate to plead his Cause, which was to this Effect: That the Merchant had committed Murther; and also had spoken opprobious Words against the said Arch-priest. The Advocate having ended his Accusation, the Merchant fell on his Knees before the Emperor, and said, Most excellent Prince, I hope out of your Goodness, that you will give me Audience to be heard, before these your Nobles here attending, and I shall unfold a Matter of so great Importance, that it touches your Person, even in the highest Degree of Treason. Say on, *said the Emperor.* Then mighty Emperor, and all ye Lords, I would advise you to make fast the Gates round about your Palace, that none depart from this Place. The Emperor did as he requested. Then said the Merchant with a loud Voice,

*Hear all ye Lords, Barons, and Knights, all you that love the Honour of the Emperor, and the triumphant Reign of his Person, attend my Words: The Time is come that the Treason of the cursed Arch-Priest will now be revealed, and come to light: Then thus great Emperor, this is that cursed Man, whom you have ever nourished, and brought to great Honour, who hath deceived your Trust; for it is he that hath wrought all the Discord betwixt you and your Virtuous Lady, whom you have banished, both from your Bed, Court, and Country, and by whom you have received more Dishonour, than ever he received Honour from you: For it had been his Part most of any, to have advanced your Renown, and preferred your Honour; but contrary he hath made my dread Lord infamous, by these his wicked Projects, and brought upon you great Scandal among all Nations; for he secretly, and underhand, made Love to the Empress, but she denied him; which he perceiving, that there was no Way to accomplish his Desire, it drove him into a thousand Fears, least this his disloyal Act should come to light; and thus devised to falsify unto your Ears, her faithless Love unto your Bed: Of all which his false*

*Accusations, I say here before you, and all your* Lords *and* Barons, *that he lieth like a* Traitor, *and for the more Approbation of what I have said, I will here unfold the Truth of what my Eyes were Witnesses:* It so happened on a Day, after the Banishment of the Empress, as I was riding about my Affairs, I chanced to travel through a Wood; at last, passing along the Way, I espyed this treacherous Priest, transformed out of the Habit of his Priest-hood, into the Shape of a Knight, armed at all Points ready for Combat with the Enemy. Drawing nearer, I beheld him in Fight with another Man unarmed, which at last I found to be *Blandiman*, 'Squire to the banished Lady, who conducted her in her Exile. I perceiving they encountred one another so fiercely, began to call unto them, to give over their Fight; but they little regarded what I said. Then I perceived the Lady piteously weeping, at last she said unto me thus: Gentle Merchant, and kind Friend, lend me thy Aid against this treacherous Arch-priest, that seeketh by Force to rob me of mine Honour. This is he, and only he, by whom I am banished from my Emperor's Bed and Country. With that I put Spurs to my Horse, and ran between them, to seperate them; which the Arch-priest perceiving, suddenly fled into the Wood, being fully assured I had the Knowledge who he was. Noble Emperor, it had been my Part to have revealed this long before, but durst not open my Mouth unto you, for fear his Greatness would have outswayed my Truth, and so have brought myself to an untimely Death.

The Emperor having heard this Tale, sighed, and at last fell into Tears, and turning to the Arch-priest, he said, Ah! thou false Servant, have I ever studied to do thee Honour, and exalt thee to high Dignities, and hast thou requited all my Love and Trust with Disloyalty and Treasons? Well, I have now seen what I always mistrusted, thou hast made me, of all Men most unhappy; but it is not so much thy Fault, as mine own; thy Treason hath bewitched me: In an evil Hour I gave Credit to thy false Tongue, and thereby deserve to carry the Brand of my own Folly. The Arch-priest hearing the King thus exasperated, began to entreat his Highness not to be so impatient, neither to give Credit to this slanderous Tale, that the Merchant had said against him: For (quoth he) he belyeth me; and I am no way Guilty of that which he accuseth me. Thou lyest falsely, *quoth the Merchant*, thou canst not excuse thyself in what I have charged thee withal: And if thou still deny it, I challenge thee by a single Combat, to maintain the Truth; and hereunto I throw down my Gage, and venture my Life to make good what I have here spoken. The Emperor seeing the Merchant so resolute, to stand to the Tryal of the Combat, he said, Arch-priest, it is Time that thou either acquit thyself, by answering this Challenge, or to yield thyself Guilty of what hath been laid to thy Charge. The Arch-priest reply'd, Mighty Emperor, I must let you understand, that to answer the Merchant's Challenge, or take up Arms, is contrary to my Place and Calling, for I am a Sacred Prelate of the *Church*, and therefore I may refuse to fight. Nay, *quoth the Emperor*, in this Case, no Excuse is to be admitted; but you must either fight, or yield yourself a Traitor to our Crown and Dignity. At these Words the Arch-priest was somewhat troubled in Mind, yet at last, he was fain to accept of the Combat, because the Emperor charged him so deeply: So the Emperor commanded them both to safe Keeping, till such Time he had sent Letters to King *Pepin* of *France*; but in the End the Traitor had his Desert, as hereafter followeth.

The Day of Combat being appointed, and the Field prepared, Tydings came to the

Emperor, that King *Pepin* was come to *Rome*, to the Aid of the Pope against the Infidels. The Emperor hearing thereof, by the Grave Counsel of the Lords, dispatched Embassadors thither, with Orders to bring King *Pepin* to *Constantinople*, meaning thereby to make him an Eye-witness of these Contentions, and of the cause of this Combat, which was to prove the Arch-priest a Traitor, and to hold the Emperor excused, in that he had, by his false Accusations banished his Empress. The Embassadors thus dispatched, after a long Journey, at last they came to *R O M E*, where they found *Pepin*, as before was told them. King *Pepin* hearing they were come, gave them Entertainment according to their several Degrees; all which being done, the Embassadors thus spake: Great Lord, we present these Letters from *Alexander*, your Brother, Emperor of *Constantinople*, our Lord and Master, of which we intreat a speedy Answer. King *Pepin* took the Letters graciously, and read them; and having thoroughly considered the Contents, with a loud Voice he said, My Lords, here's much Matter of Tydings, and also of great Admiration; the Emperor greets me well, and sends me Word that my Sister *Bellisant*, his betroathed Wife, hath been by him wrongfully banished, and by reason of a false Arch-priest, unto whom he gave too much Trust; which Priest, for these his treasonable Facts, is accused by a Merchant; and for Tryal of the Truth of this his Accusation, will put himself in Jeopardy of Life, by single Combat in open Field, Body to Body, with this treacherous Arch-Priest. Now it is so fallen out, that the Day and Place is appointed for the Tryal of his Fact, whereby I shall be fully satisfied, whether my Sister hath been guilty of that wherewith she hath been charged, and most shamefully cast into Banishment: Upon all which, I vow by my Crown and Dignity, that if the Emperor be found to have offered this Indignity, without just Cause, that I will be avenged of him in the severest Manner that War can carry on against him. Having ended his Speech unto his Lords, in Presence of the Embassadors, he commanded with Speed, that every Man should address himself to accompany him to *Constantinople*, to behold the Manner of this Fight, between the Merchant and the Arch-priest. The Day of his Departure from *Rome* being come, he takes his Way towards *Constantinople*, where, after a few Days travel, he safely arrived. The Emperor hearing of his coming, commanded all the Bells to be rang, and made Triumph to welcome him, for all were filled with Joy at his Approach. The Emperor, mounted on Horse-back, richly accompanied, marched out of the City, to meet his Brother, King *Pepin*. At last they met; but the Emperor overcome with Sorrow and Tears, at the Remembrance of *Bellisant*, could not utter a Word. On the other Side, *Pepin* being full of Anger at what had happened to his Sister, gave no Respect to the Emperor's Tears, but proudly began to salute him in this Manner: Emperor (quoth he) leave off your Lamentations, and shake off these Weeds of Sorrow, that you seem to weep for my Sister; *So he that hath a Harlot to his Wife, I account him mad to grieve for her Misbehaviour*; and since my Sister hath proved such a One, let her go and take Care of herself, she is not worthy of so much as one Tear, from an Eye of Majesty.

Nay, nay, *said the Emperor*, I speak not Evil against your Sister, for I am fully persuaded, she is composed of all Virtue and Honesty, and that against all Equity, I have banished her out of my Country. Think you so? quoth King *Pepin*, then thou art worthy of a double Shame, and do shew unto the World your Weakness, and what great Foolishness remains in you; when, as by the Report of one Man, and that a Traytor too, you would with such Rigour proceed against an innocent Lady, and (like a Harlot) throw her into Banishment, Shame, and Dishonour, being of the Blood-Royal of *France*. The Emperor hearing the King to be so bitter against him, he was very sorrowful, and said unto him thus: Alass! my Lord, do not thus upbraid me with Wrath and Anger, but rather turn your Tongue upon some milder Saying, for to that Intent have I sent for you, that your own Eyes may be Witness of the Truth. 'Tis true, quoth King *Pepin*, but what you say now is all too late, for you have banished my Sister to the World's Infamy; and (for ought I know) to Death itself; for I know not whether I shall ever behold her Face again: Fie, fie, that you being so great a Person, should be so easily wrought upon, to give such sudden Judgment against the Innocent; I do confess, one may commit a foul and dishonourable Act, but Repentance is able to make Amends, and not so suddenly to overthrow their Dignity and Renown: For that once lost, whether it be right or wrong, it is never possible to be recovered. Again, how little you have esteemed the Honour of my Kingly Office, judge you, when first without Deliberation, and next, without any Knowledge given me, you have proceeded so against my Sister? I make it plain against you, that Envy towards her and me, was the only Cause of these false and unjust Proceedings. Whilst these Words passed betwixt them, they were now entered *Constantinople*, where with great Joy and Gladness they were received of the Inhabitants. The Emperor would have had King *Pepin* to have lodged with him in his Palace, but the King denyed, and caused his Train to lodge within the City, and he himself also. Then the Emperor caused many Gifts and Presents to be offered him, but he disdainfully rejected them: For King *Pepin* thought of nothing but the Dishonour unto his Sister; for the whole City accounting her the fairest, and most virtuous, and the chastest Lady in all the World, and that by Injustice and Treason, she was banished.

# CHAPTER VI

*How the Merchant and High-priest encountred at the Place appointed,*
*about the clearing the Lady Bellisant, and what a glorious*
*Victory did betide the Merchant. How King Pepin, after the Combat,*
*returned into France; and after sailed to Rome,*
*to fight the Sarazens that had surprized the City.*

Now was the Day appointed come for the Combat, between the Arch-priest and the Merchant; wherefore every thing was made in Readiness, according to the Command of the Emperor. At last there came both the Combatants into the Field, and presented themselves before the Emperor, his Attendants, Knights, and others; and the Arch-priest armed in a most sumptuous Armour of Proof, all imboss'd with Gold and Pearl, which made such a glittering Show, that it dazzled the Eyes of the Beholders. Being thus richly armed, the Arch-priest came forth into the Field, and took his Place appointed him, at the End of the List: The Emperor beholding the glorious Shew that the Arch-priest made in his Arms, called forth the Merchant, causing him first to kneel down, and in the Presence of the Assembly, dubbed him Knight; then commanded, that a most rich Armour should be put upon him, in the Presence of King *Pepin*, who, during the Time he was arming, promised unto this Merchant, if he overcame the Arch-priest, to advance him to great Livings, and high Authority. These two Adversaries being now in Readiness, and each having their Blazon about their Necks, their Horses were brought forth, and they proudly mounted, ready to give Battle: The Emperor gave strict Charge unto all his Officers of Arms, to have a special Eye upon the Arch-priest, for fear, lest on a sudden, he should quit the Field, or run away from them, as they would answer it with their Lives. The Merchant being mounted, and his Sword girt to him, first entered the Lists, after whom came such Abundance of People, that they were numberless. Then after came the Arch-priest, sumptuously accompanied with Nobles and Knights of great Honour and Dignity. The Combatants thus both entered the Lists, ready to charge one another; King *Pepin* being there in Person, called out aloud unto the Merchant, saying, My Friend, the Gods give the Victory against this Traitor. I vow unto thee here, before this Assembly (so I may find out the Truth of my Sister *Bellisant*) notwithstanding the great Advancement that the Emperor hath promised, to take thee into *France*, and make thee Companion with the best of my Kingdom. The Merchant gave the King great Thanks, and said, Dread King, I doubt not but this Night to make the traiterous Priest confess, that he hath treacherously sought the Destruction of your Sister. Then came a Herald, administring to them an Oath; and so, clearing the Lists, left the Champions to their Fortune. Now are the Combatants ready to set forth, and the Marshals of the Field brought each of them a Spear, which they no sooner had received, but they put Spurs to their Horses, and ran with such Violence together, that their Spears were broken to their Hands; then they began to set forward to another Course, charging each other with their Swords, in such a violent Manner, that with their Fury, they rebounded from their Armour to the Ground, cutting off whole Quarters of their Corslets, and left them as Prey for those that attended the Fight. The Arch-priest finding himself so stiffly matched, gave over the Fight, till towards the Evening, for such was the Custom of the Country, that in any challenged Combat, either Party might refuse to follow the Fight so eagerly, but that they might have a breathing Time; so the Combatants were yielded vanquished before Sun-set, or else abide the Sentance of Death; thinking thereby to weary out the Merchant; which the Merchant perceiving, he prepared to receive the Arch-priest couragiously, when he encountered him; which not being long after, the Merchant so redoubled his Stroaks, that he smote off one of his Ears, and his Steel Habergion, and with the Violence of the Blow, the Merchant's Sword fell from his Hands; which the Arch-priest seeing, put Spurs to his Horse, and charged him with such Violence, that he ran against the Merchant's Horse, and thrust out one of his Eyes: The Horse feeling himself hurt, ran up and down as mad, leaping and curvetting so furiously, that he unhors'd his Rider, and so hard was the Fortune of the Merchant, that in his Fall, his Foot hung in the Stirrup, whereby he was brought into great Danger, the Horse hurrying him along the Field; that all were very sorrowful to behold this lamentable Spectacle, and with the Amazement thereof, grew desperate in their Hopes. King *Pepin* also was so discouraged at this disasterous Chance, that the Tears did even trickle down his Cheeks, uttering many silent Ejaculations, against the Unkindness of Fortune.

Now that which was most miraculous, was, all this Time, that the Merchant was

dragged up and down the Field, the Arch-priest could not force his Horse to come up to the Merchant, but fled too and fro, whereby he could not make a Prey upon him, as he intended to do. But see, at the last, the Merchant's Horse fell down, by which Means he got his Leg from forth the Stirrup, and at last, got upon his Feet like a valiant and hardy Champion: The Priest perceiving the Merchant had recovered his Legs, came running with strong Violence upon him, and thereby lent him five or six Blows upon his Shoulders, that the poor Merchant was even astonished. At last, he was forced to give back to recover Breath; and in a little Space, finding himself somewhat relieved, he subtilly gave a fresh Assault upon the Arch-priest; against whom he struck with such Violence, that the Sword fell out of his Hand; but he first so wounded him, that the Blood ran through his Armour upon the Earth. This so vexed the Priest, that he grew mad with Rage, and turned his Horse upon the Merchant, thinking to over-run him; but the Merchant observing his Drift, prepared to receive him, and drawing a long Knife, push'd it into the Belly of the Horse, so that the Horse being thus wounded, began to fling and leap; insomuch, that the Priest was in Danger to be unhorss'd, and striving to save himself, he lost his Shield: The Merchant seeing him thus unarmed, ran hastily and caught up the Shield, and threw it away, so that he could no more recover it; that done, he made again towards his Horse, and smote him in the Belly with his Sword, which brought the Horse and Rider to the Ground. The Priest being thus un-horss'd, was very nimble to recover; but the Merchant watching his Opportunity, and as he was rising, he gave him such a Blow, that laid him flat upon the Ground, and leaping on him, pulled off his Helmet, thinking to have smitten of his Head: The Arch-priest seeing himself in such Danger, said thus, Alas! my Friend, I pray thee take Pity on me, and give me leave to confess, for I yield myself vanquish'd: The Merchant hereat was very courteous, and granted him his Desire: The Priest had no sooner got on his Feet, but clasping the Merchant in his Arms, threw him on the Ground, and leap'd upon him in most sudden Outrage, saying thus to the Merchant, I have now an Advantage, and from my Hands thou shalt not escape with Life, if what I shall command thee thou do not effect. Ah! reply'd the Merchant, hast thou thus betrayed me? Well, it is so now that I stand at thy Mercy, and thou may do with me what thou please; therefore let me know what it is thou commandest, and so thou save my Life, I shall gladly do it. *Then thus, go with me before the Emperor, and King* Pepin, *and there openly, in the hearing of all Men, testifie, that thou falsely hath accused me, and thereby I may be cleared of those false Accusations, which, by thy Means, have been brought upon me; all which, if you effectually accomplish, I swear and promise to save thy Life; and besides, be a Means unto the Emperor and his Brother, and buy thee Peace, and Forgiveness of this thy foul Fact, committed both against me and them also: Nay more, I swear to thee, by the Faith of a Gentleman; and by the Order of Priest-hood, to give thee a Niece of mine in Marriage, who shall be to thee rich, fair, and of a pleasant Behaviour, and to conclude, thou shalt say more than ever any of thy Kindred ever told; thou shalt be made more honourable and wealthy. Therefore now advise thyself, whether thou wilt be made happy in an honourable Life, or miserable in an untimely Death?* The Merchant having heard the Arch-priest's Tale, was upon the sudden exceeding sorrowful, and not without Cause; but not knowing what to resolve upon, he at length thus answered: Sir Priest, your Arguments are grounded upon good Reasons; therefore I am ready to accomplish your Desires, so that you will be as mindful of your Oath and Promises. In me, quoth the Arch-priest, there shall appear no Fault. Why then (quoth the Merchant) let us set forwards to the Emperor, and there I will set you free from all those Accusations which heretofore I have exhibited against you. It is well, said the Arch-priest, wherefore rise up then, and let us go together. The Merchant had no sooner got on his Feet, but he began afresh to open all the Treason of the Arch-priest, even to his Teeth; and again he took Courage, and now would requite him in the same Sauce he had served him before; and suddenly clasping the Arch-priest in his Arms, he threw him down, and having him at Advantage, he said thus, *Arch-priest, seeing you have taught me to play my Part, think no more upon Confessions, for you shall confess to me or none.* The Arch-priest seeing himself beaten at his own Weapons, began again to intreat, but the Merchant not regarding his Words, presently put out his Eyes, and gave him so many deadly Blows, that he made sure he should not rise to do him any Harm; then the Merchant called the Marshals of the Field, and said, Lo, here you may see that I have done my best Endeavour against the Arch-priest, and if he be vanquished, say so, for I am sure I have brought him to such a Pass, that I may kill him outright, if I please; therefore my Request is now, That you conduct *Alexander* Emperor of *Constantinople*, and King *Pepin* of *France* hither to this Place, accompanied with their worthy Lords and Knights, that they may be Earwitnesses of the Confession, which the Arch-priest shall make unto them, and also to hear in what unjust Manner he waged Combat against me.

The Marshals did according to the Request of the Merchant, and then presently came the Emperor, with King *Pepin* and all the Nobles, even to the Place where the Arch-Priest lay fully vanquished. Then the Emperor demanded of him the Truth, which the Arch-Priest confessed, declaring the whole Plot of his Villanies, and how by his means the Empress had been wrongfully banished. When the Standers by heard all the whole Matter, a Multitude of Tears were shed; but especially the Emperor, for his Lamentations were so violent, that all that were about wept with great Bitterness. Now, if the Emperor were so sorrowful, what may you think of King *Pepin* her Brother? Alas! It was not without great Cause, when they saw and knew, that by too much Trust given to a treacherous Priest, they had lost the virtuous Lady *Bellisant*. Between these two great Princes there was great Joy, and great Sorrow; Joy to King *Pepin*, that his Sister was found innocent and blameless; Sorrow to the *Emperor*, that he should be the only means, by false Suggestions, of his Wife's Banishment. At last, Lamentations were laid apart; when they had heard all the Confession of the Arch-Priest's Treasons, the *Emperor* consulted with his Counsel, that the Traytor should be put into a Cauldron of hot burning Oyl, and so finish his miserable Days, as he had traiterously sought the Life of that innocent Lady. Execution was suddenly to be done, and it being done, the Assembly of People of all sorts were dismissed. Afterwards King *Pepin* withdrew himself towards his Lodging; but the *Emperor*, sorrowful for what had happened, came before King *Pepin*, and humbling himself, begun thus to say: *Alas! dear Brother, I am sorrowful for my Error, in that I have so rashly committed such a detestable Crime against my Lady, your Sister, and these great Nobles your Attendants; let it suffice, that I behold my own Folly: What shall I say? I can but crave Pardon for my Fault, and give myself into your Hand; and to do with me whatsoever pleaseth you. And for a further Satisfaction, I render up into your Hands, my Empire, with all the Regality thereunto appertaining, for I am altogether unworthy to rule an Empire, that am not Master of my own Affections. Take it, I say, for I will be no longer served; but during the rest of my Life, become a Servant unto thee, or any, for no better have I deserved.* King *Pepin* perceiving the Emperor so passionate, and so humbly minded, kindly took him from the Ground, and before all his Lords, freely forgave him all Trespasses. So that before they parted, there was a general Peace concluded? and a speedy Course taken to send to all Parts of the World, to seek the distressed Lady *Bellisant*. Thus all things settled in Order, King *Pepin* having taken his Leave of *Constantinople* (as you have heard,) after a long Journey arrived in *France*, and so to *Orleans*, to refresh his long and tired Spirits, tossed to and fro in Melancholly and heavy Cogitations for the woful Mischance befallen unto his Sister *Bellisant*. Being safely arrived, and seated at *Orleans*, the King was joyful, that he had attained the Place he so much desired, by reason that it was one of the most spacious Forests in the Realm. Being come hither, he caused great Banquets to be made for his Welcome; which was accordingly done. In the midst of these Feastings and Revellings, the 'Squire that had the Charge of the Orphan *Valentine*, took and presented him before the King, saying, Dread Sovereign, Lo, here I present before you, the poor Orphan, that your Majesty found in the Forest of *Orleans*, and the same Child which you commanded me to see brought up, not at my Expence, dread Sovereign, but at your own. My Liege, the Reason why I tender him unto you at this Time, is, because he is growing to Man's Estate; and so may it please your Majesty, it is Time to dispose of him, as you please. The King having heard the Words of the 'Squire, called this Orphan (named *Valentine*) unto him, and took him by the Hand, and moved divers Questions unto him, all which he answered with much Modesty, and great Wisdom; and being ravished therewith, commanded that all his Cupboard of Plate should be given unto him: Moreover (said the King) I command that this Orphan, *Valentine*, be dearly preserved and kept, for that you shall perceive I respect him above common Love; I will also, that this Infant shall be nourished, and kept with my Daughter *Eglantine*, she is both fair, wife, and well endowed with all the Gifts of Nature. The King having given this Command, it was accordingly accomplish'd, insomuch, that they were both under Government of one and the same Nurse, and had one and the same Attendants; yea, every Way they enjoyed one in the Company of the other, in such wise, that if one was but a little absent from the other, there was a kind of Lamentation, till they came together again; but especially the King's Daughter, who so pondered on the prudent Carriages of the Orphan, that she became in Love with him; insomuch, that his Absence brought her into a thousand Fears, and drove her melancholly and disturbed her Thoughts, into a Thousand Doubts and Jealousies.

Now *Valentine* was ever practising himself in Feats of Arms; as, Horse, Armour, Justs, and Turnaments, exposing himself to all Dangers whatsoever. The King wisely beholding the Inclination of this Youth, allotted unto him what his Heart desired, and furnished him with Armour, Horse, Lands, Revenues; and made him Lord of rich Possessions. Being thus furnished, there arose within the Court, many secret Mutterings, whereby many People fretted so sore in Envy towards him, that they uttered forth many reproachful Words against him, saying, That at the best he was but a found, stray, poor, base Child, without any known Parents or Friends; of no genteel, or noble Stock, and such-like. Which when *Valentine* heard, he could take no other Revenge, but set him down and weep; whose Tears fair *Eglantine* perceiving, would, in a tender Woman-like Affection, pour forth Tears also for Company. At length, when he saw Tears little prevailed, he began to forsake them, and taking Heart, bore himself like a Man, amongst the greatest in the Court, carrying himself in such humble and genteel Frame, that he gained the Love of all Sorts and Degrees, as well Nobles, as Inferiours. *Valentine* thus growing up in the Love of the Court, and all this while his Brother *Orson* lives in the Forest, all rough, and covered with Hair, like a Bear, leading the Life of a Beast; where we will leave him for a while, and return unto the Affairs of King *Pepin:* It so chanced, that there came into *Orleans*, diverse Embassadors from the Pope, demanding Aid against the *Sarazens*, Enemies of the *Holy Faith*, who had lately taken the City of *Rome* by Violence. King *Pepin* understanding hereof, by divers Letters received, addressed himself, and his Powers, to make his Resistance against this Common Enemy; and amongst the rest of his worthy Followers, he appointed this young *Valentine* a chief Commander. Fair *Eglantine* hearing that *Valentine* should make one, became wondrous heavy and sorrowful; for she loved him more than any other Creature, and secretly sent a Messenger unto him, to come and speak with her. And when he came, she sighing, said unto him, Alas! *Valentine*, my Love, now am I quite bereft of all my Joy, for I perceive you will betake yourself to a dangerous War: Gentle Love, leave me not so desolate; would to the Gods, that I had neither Father, nor Friend in the World, to contradict my Will, then shouldst thou soon perceive how my Affections stands to thy Person: For if Wishes might avail, I swear by the Gods, that thou art the only Man I would join myself unto, in the Bands of Marriage; and then shouldst thou be the King of *France*, and I the Queen.

The young Man hearing her idle Imaginations, said, Madam, leave these Womanish Dotages, you know I am not a Person fitting your Estate; I am a found stray, that your

Father hath caused long Time to be nourished for Charity-sake; I am no way fitting you, or the meanest Damsel attending your Person; make your Choice else-where, and join Royal Blood into yours; and so, with all my Duty, I take my leave, and commend you to the Gods. Having ended his Speech, away he goes, leaving the poor Lady all heavy, desolate, and in the midst of Mourning.

By this Time the King and all his Retinue, were in Readiness to depart, and taking their Way from *Orleans* towards *Rome*, they came to a mighty Forest; and being entered, the King called his Lords and Barons together, and said thus unto them: My Lords, it is not unknown to you, that in these Woods (as Report goeth) there liveth a strange Monster, a wild Man much feared of Passengers, which Spectacle of Man's Shape, I long to behold; before I venture out farther upon our intended Voyage to *Rome*. The Lords generally consented, and the Chase was instantly appointed. Being entred the Wood, they chased several Sorts of wild Beasts, and overcame them: But as for *Orson*, the wild Man, none durst adventure the finding of him, save only his Brother *Valentine* (but he knew nothing) and he followed still the Chase; hoping at last, both to find and fight with him also. Every Way they begirt the Wood, some one Way, some another: The King himself ventred so far, that he came before a Cave, dark and obscure, whereas the wild Man used to hide himself. *Orson* perceiving the King, rushed out upon him, caught him in his Nails (which was long and crooked) and in a rough and ravenous Manner, cast him on the Ground. The King thus suddenly surprized by a Savage, never look'd for Life, but in a piteous Manner, cried out for Help, who was seconded by a valiant Knight at Arms, who espying the King to be almost strangled, suddenly drew his Sword to have run the wild Man through. *Orson* perceiving the glittering Sword, left the King and ran furiously upon the Knight, took him in his Arms, and overthrew him, Horse and all: The Horse sore affrighted, got up again, and in a mad Fit ran up and down the Forest; but as for the Rider (though a Knight at Arms) *Orson* held him so fast with his Twangs and Talons, that at last he pulled him in Pieces. In the mean Time the King escaped, and meeting Part of his Company, related to them the great Danger he had escaped, and the fearful Death of the Knight. These Tydings much amazed the rest of the Company; yet being manfully resolved, they joyned themselves together, and marched towards the Cave, to meet with *Orson*, and either to take him alive, or put him to Death in the Cave: Being come thither, they found the Knight dead, and torn in Pieces, but *Orson* they could not find, for the Gods had reserved him him to be conquered only by his Brother *Valentine*; of whose Proceedings you shall hear more hearafter.

So the King perceiving their Labour lost, gave over the Chase, and set forwards towards *Rome*. After this, the King ranked his Forces into Battle-Array, and the great Ensign of *France* was given to one, called *Myllon Daugler*, a very valiant Prince, and a wise Leader; so that he and his two Brethren, *Gervas* and *Sampson*, had the whole Command of the Forces, that then were marching towards *Rome*. When they were come unto *Rome*, King *Pepin* desired Battle, and would fain understand the State that the City now stood in, under the Conquest of the *Sarazens*; but it was told him, *He should not be too in-quisitive about those Affairs; for the Admiral of the* Sarazens *had surprized the City, and put Multitudes to the Sword, and had spoiled and defeated all the Churches, and made them Temples fit for their heathenish Idols; and he constrained the Pope, with his Cardinals, Arch-Bishops, Bishops, Priors, Monks, Friars, and all the Ecclesiastical Persons,* for to serve at their heathenish Altars, and to sacrifice to their Devils, after the Custom of the Heathens. When King *Pepin* understood this, he was much enraged, to hear that the *Christians* were thus captivated by *Heathens*; wherefore he advanced nearer to the City, and there having assembled all his Forces, he began to draw them into several Squadrons, meaning thereby to give them a sudden Assault; for his Fury was so great against these heathenish *Sarazens*, that he vowed Revenge upon them; but taking better Advice, he reserved himself and his Army for a better Season. As will appear in the next Chapter.

## CHAPTER VII

*How King Pepin besieged Rome; and how Valentine*
*justed with the Admiral of the Sarazens, and slew him,*
*whereby the City was relieved,*
*and won again from the Sarazens.*

KING *Pepin* being thus come to *Rome*, besieged it, and after some Days spent, he called about him his Barons, Knights, and mighty Men of War, and began to speak unto them in this Manner: My Lords, and Followers, you well know that this heathenish Admiral, Enemy to the *Christian Faith*, and *Church of Rome*, hath put many *Christians* to the Sword, and violently trodden under Foot, all such as withstood his Power; therefore it is our Duties to commiserate their Estate that are thus Overthrown, and to try the Fortune of a Battle, amongst these heathenish *Pagans*; and either drive them out of the City, or leave our dead Carcasses as a Prey, as many have done before: Wherefore, I King *Pepin*, resting upon this Resolution, would find out a Man, to bear unto the proud Admiral a Letter of Defiance in my Name. King *Pepin* having finished his Speech, there was none amongst them made any Answer. At length, *Valentine*, seeing all stand mute, stepped before the King, and began to speak in this Manner: *Mighty Sovereign, so you be pleased to give me leave, I shall undertake the Message, and shall not fear to speak, neither to the* Pagan *Admiral, nor to the whole Host of* Pagans, *were their Multitude twice as many as they be; and my Return shall make Proof, that I have done my Message, both with Honour, and Advantage to your Majesty.* The King hearing *Valentine* thus forward, and of such valiant Resolution, was right joyful; and all those of his Princely Train greatly marvelled at this his magnanimous Spirit. Hereupon the King called his Secretary, and ordered him to draw a Letter of Defiance, and deliver the same to *Valentine*, which he accordingly did; and no sooner had he received the Letter, but he took his leave of the King, and all his Train, and being well mounted, he took his Way towards *Rome*, and so to the Palace where the Admiral lay: So coming thither, he came before the Admiral, and saluted him after this Manner: *The Gods preserve the Noble and Puissant King* Pepin, *my Lord and Sovereign; and* Mahomet, *whom thou servest, save and defend thee, Redoubted Admiral.* When *Valentine* had thus spoken, the Admiral rouzed from his Chair, and with a fierce and frowning Brow, replied thus unto him: Messenger, return, and get thee out of my Sight; and say thus unto King *Pepin*. Will him either to renounce his Faith, and believe on *Mahomet*, or let him look to receive no other than Sentance of Death; and so destroy him, together with all his Lords and Kingdom: Get thee gone, and make here no longer abode; go, I say, reply not a Word, for my heart is all enraged, that so long I suffer thee. Again, I tell thee, that for thy part, thou hast committed a haughty enterprize, thus to enter my Palace, to deliver any such message unto me. Wherefore I assure thee, by the height of my Majesty, that if I did assuredly know, that what thou hast done, was through pride of heart and insolency, thereby to make a mock at our Majesty, thou shouldest never return to *King Pepin*, to carry an answer to thy proud *Massters Letters*.

*Valentine* hearing these furious Words sounding from the Admiral, began to be afraid: Wherefore deliberating with himself what to reply, he mildly said, High and mighty *Emperor*, do not imagine that by pride I am come before you; for when you understand the manner of my coming, you will be astonished thereat. Why then (*quoth the Admiral*) say on, tell us how thou art come, for I swear by *Mahomet*, I shall take great pleasure in hearing thee relate thine enterprize. Then said *Valentine*, Sir, so it is, that I was accused to *King Pepin* for a Coward, and that since I came to this War, I would secretly have stolen away from the Camp, and returned again into *France*; for which Reason I came into disgrace; and the King vowed the next morning to smite off my head. Perceiving my self in this danger, I sought rather to save my life, than to lose my life and honour; and therefore gave it out throughout the Court, that I would undertake to come unto your Court, to defie you on the King's behalf, and therewithal, that I would challenge you to break three spears with you in single combat, to try your valiancy, and to win my last honour that I told unto you: Wherefore my request is, that your Greatness would grant me my Request, otherwise I dare not return again, least the King should put me to Death. The Admiral hearing this pitiful tale of *Valentine*, said unto him, Son, I do swear by *Mahomet*, that thou shalt not be refused, but at this Instant, I offer thee the Justs; and to the end that those *Frenchmen* that lye in seige before the City, may have a sight thereof, I will order the place of Justing to be without the City. *Valentine* humbly thanked him, and in token of his acceptance, and feigned love, he fell down, and kissed the Feet of the Admiral. *Valentine* grew into great favour in the Admiral's Court; but yet it often troubled his mind that he could not know who were his Parents. But while he bestowed his wandring thoughts here, the Admiral said thus unto him: Fair Son, methinks you are very pensive; 'tis true (*quoth he*) and not without cause, for I am afraid that I shall be slain in these Justs; wherefore my request is, that I may have a Confessor, to give me absolution for my Sins. Then the Admiral commanded that a Priest should be brought him: The Priest being come, said unto *Valentine*, Now Confess you unto me; *Valentine* getting the Priest aside, he said thus unto him: Sir, you are a Christian Priest, and you ought most to defend the Christian-Faith: Wherefore hearken to that I shall tell you, for it is a thing requireth the greatest secrecy. Thus it is, you know that this day I am to Just with the heathenish Admiral, the greatest Enemy of Christian People: Now I am well assured, that a great number of the Sarazens will issue forth out of the City; to be Eye-witnesses of these Justs to be held without the City. Therefore you shall give warning to all *Christians*, to keep within the Walls, arming themselves in a readiness, and closely keep it from the Ears of the Pagans; so when the Pagans are come forth to behold the Justs, the *Christians* suddenly shall surprise the Guards that keeps the Gates; and if any mutiny arise, let them keep out those that are out. And send a messenger to King *Pepin* of what is done, that he with his Army, may come unto them that are without, while those within are set on by the armed *Christians*; so by girting them on every side, that in the end we may make a slaughter of them, that the *Christians* may receive both their City in Peace, and their former liberty. So having ended his Speech, the Priest departed. The Admiral commanded *Valentine* to be led into his Chamber to dine, giving them charge he should be honourably attended at the board. Being set among so many Lords, he behaved himself gently and mildly towards all. Dinner being done, the Admiral called unto him a Nephew of his, named *Salatas*, commanding him to see *Valentine* as well armed at all points as himself; and moreover, charged his Nephew to deliver unto *Valentine* the best horse in his Stable. *Salatas* having received his command from his Uncle the Admiral, took *Valentine*, and led him into a fair hall; being come thither, he caused to be laid before him divers Armours, desiring him to make choice of the best. *Valentine* cast his Eyes upon them all, and at last appointed the Armour, wherewith he should be armed, and making himself ready as fast as he could, he approached down into the Court, where he was attended with his horse, ready to put his foot into the Stirrup. Being come down into the Hall, he presently mounted his Horse; the Admiral issuing likewise ready armed, out of a privy Palace. Being thus armed, they took their way towards the chief Gate of the City of *Rome*, for on that side King *Pepin* had laid his Siege. When they were both in the Field, *Valentine* hung his shield about his Neck, in which he wore a Hart, waving in a field of Silver, and on one side a Tree; all which did signify that he was found in a Forrest, and wore the same Arms King *Pepin* bestowed on him. The Champions being entred the Lists, great was the Clamour of the *French*, in joy of *Valentine*; the sound whereof, the Pagans hearing, suddenly issued out of the City, to behold these Triumphant Justs.

The Fryar having plaid his part among the Christians, within the City, presently after the Pagans were gone out to behold these triumphs, addressed themselves to take Possession of the Gates; which having gotten, there was entrance again to be expected. King *Pepin* being acquainted with their purpose, prepared all his Men of War ready to relieve *Valentine*, if necessity required. Having all things in readiness, the hour was at hand that the Justs should begin: So each of them prepared for the encounter, they valiantly couched their Spears, and the first course proved so valiant, that their Spears shivered all in Splinters; each combatant perceiving Valour to brandish on the top of his Helm, made out a second course, where *Valentine* got the better; for with his Spear (charged against the Admiral) he gave him such a Blow, that he forced his Spear quite through his Body; insomuch that he fell from his Horse dead, making a pitiful noise at his departure; wherefore the Pagans ran at *Valentine*, and would have killed him. *Valentine* perceiving their intent, with resolute Courage, put Spurs to his Horse, and with his Sword drawn, violently rushed through the thickest of the Pagans, and slew many of them as he passed. King *Pepin* with his Host, came up to the aid of *Valentine*, but he was so beset by the Pagans, that he was smitten off his Horse; which *Valentine* espying, came up to the Rescue of the King, so that he horsed him again. The King perceiving himself delivered out of danger, called unto *Valentine*, and said, my Child thou hast saved my Life, which if the Gods grant to spare, I will reward thee liberally. By this time the Battle grew so hot, that the Pagans were forced to retire to the City; when they came to the Gates, the Christians that were in the City issued on them, and placed the Ensigns and Standards of King *Pepin* on the Walls. The Pagans seeing King *Pepin*'s Colours displayed on the Walls, betook themselves to flight; and the Christians followed them so fast, that they soon ended their Days. In this Battle were slain a thousand Pagans, only by means of *Valentine*, who behaved himself so valiant that Day. Thus by his Prowess, the City was again restored to the Christians; for which deed there was Great Triumph in all Christendom, but especially at *Rome:* So that all the Inhabitants round about, gave immortal praise to *Pepin King of France;* and by the general applause of the People, he was created Emperor, and crowned by the Pope. King *Pepin* did many goodly Acts in his time, administring Justice to all. This happened in the Time of Pope *Clement* the Fourth.

# CHAPTER VIII

### How Haufray and Henry repined at the love the King did shew towards Valentine.

KING *Pepin* having expelled the Pagans out of *Rome*, he took his way back towards *Orleans*; and being there arrived he was joyfully welcomed by *Bertha* his Queen, and her little Son, *Charlemain*, and her fair Daughter *Eglantine*; and their joy appeared so much the more, for that *Valentine*, who accordingly came unto her; and when she saw him, she saluted him kindly, and with an Amorous Countenance, begun thus unto him: *Valentine*, you above all the rest are most welcome; and well ought it so to be, for Fame hath blown forth her Trumpet of your Triumphs, and the Report says, you are the only Champion that drove the Pagans out of *Rome. Valentine* replied, Madam, I can hinder no Man to speak what pleaseth him; but as for myself, I have done little deserving praise; but it hath pleased the King your Father, to do me that Great Honour, even so as all the Days of my Life I shall not be able to make the least part of Recompence. And as he spake these Words, *Haufray* and *Henry* (two Men composed of all Envy) entred the Chamber of *Eglantine*; and seeing him, began thus to speak: Valentine, *What have you to do here, in the Chamber of our Sister? It is no place for such Straglers as you are; this your boldness is not to be borne; no Man knows of whom you are, therefore we advise you to be warned, that you attempt not the like again, lest you dearly buy these your presumptions. Valentine* hearing these Words, answered, *Wrong me not, for I entred not the Chamber of your Sister, to her dishonour. What though I be poor, and not know of whence I am, yet I am not so base as to offer Violence unto one, descended from the blood of Kings: And further, I promise and vow never to come near her Chamber again:* And therewithal departed, leaving the Lady very pensive all alone. *Valentine* hasted to the Palace, to wait upon the King at Dinner, where was in presence *Haufray* and *Henry*, and the Duke of *Myllain Daugler*, who likewise waited upon the King, during Dinner-time. Dinner being finished, the King arose, and called to *Valentine*, and in hearing of all his Nobles, began thus to say: *My Lords, here is* Valentine, *that hath well deserved at our Hands, and that saved my Life when I was in danger; therefore to the end you may take knowledge of his good service towards me, I freely* *give him the Earldom of* Clerimont *of* Avergne; *and when I can bestow more upon him,* he *shall not* be *forgotten.* Valentine *gave him many thanks, saying, That he had heaped upon him more Honours than he could any ways deserve. *Haufray* and *Henry* hearing these Words, grew greatly Malecontent; and at last *Henry* began to talk with his Brother after this Manner. This found-fellow I perceive grows in great favour with the King, and there must be some course taken to cross his Designs, or else our overthrow will shortly follow upon it: For (quoth he) you know well, that the King hath no Sons but we two, and one little one (named *Charlemain*) which if our Father dies will contest with us in right of the Kingdom. Again, it is greatly to be feared, that this *Valentine* will support and uphold him against us: Therefore Brother, I think it good to frame some Plot against him, to bring him in displeasure with the King, and so far to prosecute your revenge against him, that if it be possible, we will not only work his downfal, but life and all; this being effected, we may at our pleasure govern the Realm without Contradiction. He having ended his speech. *Haufray* replied, Let it be as thou hast said, and that we may entrap his Life, this shall be our plot: We will both go to the King, and tell him, that this Upstart hath defloured our Sister, and that we took him in Bed with her; which, when the King heareth, will certainly put him to Death. Being thus resolved, they daily fed their Imaginations with the Death of *Valentine*; while he (nothing mistrusting) served the King daily in all Duty, insomuch, that the King's love daily increased towards him, and above all other most desirous of his Company.

Here let us leave off a little, and come to *Orson*, his *Brother*, who all this while lived in the *Forest*, so much feared of all Men, that none *durst Approach* nigh the Wood: Daily Complaints came unto the King from every side; and amongst the rest it chanced one Day, that a poor Man came unto the King all wounded, saying thus unto him. *Sir, I am come before you to make complaint against a Wild-Man in the Woods, for one Day, as I and my Wife passed through the Forest, carrying bread and other Victuals, the Wild Man came upon us, took it away, and eat it every bit: and more than that, he violently took my Wife from me, and constrained her to yield unto his Lawless Lust.* The *King* hearing out the poor Man's Tale, was disposed to make himself Merry with his ill fortune, and therefore asked the poor Man this Question, Which grieved him most, either taking away his Victuals, or his Wife? By my faith said the poor Man, at the wrong offered to my Wife. Thou hast rightly said; (quoth the King) therefore I command my Treasurer to see Restitution made unto thee for the Loss of thy Victuals; but as for thy Wife, thou must bear the Burthen thereof thy self. After this, the King caused all his Barons to Assemble, and make some order to take *Orson*; all which they did; and thereupon a Proclamation was sent unto all Parts of the Realm, that whosoever he was, that could take this Wild-man alive or dead, should have a thousand Marks for his Reward. Here assembled many worthy Knights to take this task in hand; but the King being one Day in his Palace in the midst of his Nobles, talking and debating who should be appointed to this Business, *Haufray*, Enemy unto *Valentine*, being there, said thus unto the King: Sir, here is *Valentine*, whom you have nourished, and advanced to high Dignities, and one that hath offered unlawful love to our Sister *Eglantine*: He is fittest to set forward to try his Valour, and let him be imployed to fetch in this Wild-man, that is such a Terror to the inhabitants: And if with his Valour he can vanquish him, then let him have *Eglantine* in *Marriage*, which is his desired wish. The King hearing these

Words of his Son, said, Away, for thy Speech favoureth of nothing but Envy. What though he be poor, of low Birth, and found in a Forest; yet I find him to me true and trusty, and of gentle Carriage; and to me seemeth to be Born of more noble Parentage than thou art: Leave off these thy Malicious and bitter Speeches against him; for the behaviour that dwelleth in him, shews that he is descended of more noble Lineage, than as yet to us appeareth, And I, for my part (for the divers Vertues that are daily seen in him) am willing that he go to my Daughter when ever he please, for I am well assured, that no dishonour can be offered out of a branch of such a generous Spirit.

*Haufray* hearing the King make this Apology on the behalf of *Valentine*, was sore displeased in his Heart; but setting a good Face on the Matter, Dissembles his Countenance for that time; but it seemed *Valentine* well observed him, and at last brake forth into these Words: *Haufray*, without any cause given on my Part, you have spoken ill of me, and your will it is, that I should undertake the fight and Conquest of the Wild-man, only to this end, that I might end my Days, and so your Revenge be accomplished upon me: Well, be it so, here before the King, I take solemn Oath, that I will take the enterprize upon me, and find out the Wild-man; and having found him, I will fight him, and either bring him alive or dead, or else leave my dead Carcass as a Witness in the open Field. But if I Conquer and live, I will never more be seen in this Country, till I have found the Father that begot me; as also, bring to light whether I was lawfully begotten in Wedlock, and how I came to be left an Infant in the Wood. The King understanding well what danger *Valentine* had plung'd himself into, grew exceeding angry against his two Sons, cursing them, for that they were the cause of this Enterprize; for he loved *Valentine* more than any, and at last called unto *Valentine*, and said. My Child, advise you well what you undertake; for to fight with the Wild-man, is Desperation itself; for you cannot be ignorant how many valiant Men, and worthy Champions have by him been overcome: And others likewise of valiant Account, that hath forsaken this Combat: Therefore, I say, let not the evil Words of a few malicious Men make you desperate, in losing your Life. For my Child, it is far better to endure all the bitter Words of envy (which is accounted Virtue) than to hazard ones Life against such a Monster, and no Man. *Valentine* replied, Pardon me my Liege, for I will never revoke my intended purpose: They call me found-brat, which grieveth my very Soul, for indeed I know not what I am, nor of what Place; but I rest determined, and so take my leave; for to morrow morning will I set forward to my intended enterprize. Having taken his leave, marvel not, tho' the fair Lady *Eglantine* made great Lamentation for what had happened; but the next Morning, by brake of Day, she called one of her Maidens, and said, Go to *Valentine*, and bid him come and speak with me before his departure; bid him fear no danger of Life, for I would fain take my leave of him. The Damsel did as the Lady commanded; and when she came to *Valentine*, she found him mounted on Horse-back, and she did her message unto him. He understanding her errand, said unto her, Damsel, I know the love to be great between the Lady *Eglantine* and me, yet I would not wish her to desire that which will turn to her dishonour: But envy is of so great Power, that it never leaves them whom it once possesseth. For certain it is, that *Haufray* and *Henry* (brethren to your Lady) have at me great malicious Hearts, and will pursue me, even unto Death, if it were possible; wherefore, fair Damsel, bear her this Answer, which you heard me tell, and bid her think no evil thereof; and further, that she hold me in excuse, that I refuse to come; and so farewell.

# CHAPTER IX

### *How Valentine conquered his Brother Orson,*
### *(the Wild Man, in the Forest of Orleans)*
### *and afterwards departed from the Forest,*
### *with Orson, to Orleans, where King Pepin resided.*

Now is *Valentine* upon his Journey, accompanied only with his Page; and being come to the Forest, he put his Helmet on his Head, and sent him back again: So he rode about all that Day, seeking the wild Man, but he could not find him; so the Night drawing on, he dismounted his Horse, and tied him to a Tree; having so done, he refreshed his Body with such Victuals as he had; and when he had eaten, and the Day shut in, he (for Fear) betook himself to the Top of a Tree, and there lay all that Night. In the Morning, as soon as Day appeared, he looked round about, and at last, espied his Brother *Orson* running through the Forest; at length the wild Man came to the Place where *Valentine* had tied his Horse, who much wondred at the Beauty of him, began to claw him with his long Nails, thinking thereby to rouze up the Courage of the Horse; for he had never seen the like. The Horse feeling the wild Man's Nails, began to fling and kick exceedingly. *Valentine* setting on the Top of the Tree, noted the terrible Shape of the wild Man, and began to be afraid; but calling on the Gods, he requested their Aid against this Monster. *Orson* all this while was busy in beholding the Horse, and still offered him such Injury with his Nails, that the Horse did nothing but kick and bite him: When *Orson* perceived the Horse to be too hard for him, he caught fast hold on him, and thought to have over-thrown him: *Valentine* perceiving his Horse in Danger to be slain, he cried out aloud, and said, *Wild Man, leave my Horse, and stay till I come down, and with me thou shalt have Fighting enough.* The wild Man hearing a strange Voice, looked up into the Tree, and esyping a Man there, made Signs to him, with his Hands and Head, to come down, and he would pull him in Pieces. *Valentine* making all the Haste he could, drew his Sword, and leap'd upon the Ground close by the wild Man; when *Orson* saw the Sword and that he offered to smite him therewith, he leaped back, and kept himself from the Stroke; but suddenly turned again upon *Valentine*, and threw him to the Ground: *Valentine* was very much discomfitted, and looked for nothing but present Death; for he felt the Strength of the wild Man so great, that he had no Hope of escaping. Being thus both groveling on the Ground, *Valentine* strived divers Times to have gotten *Orson* under him, but could not; when he saw, that by Strength, there was no Hope to overcome him, he drew out a sharp pointed Knife, and smote *Orson* in the Side, that the Blood issued out abundantly: *Orson* feeling himself wounded, all inraged, gave such a Shriek, that the Woods echoed again at the Sound thereof; but yet recovering himself, he so fiercely assaulted *Valentine*, with his sharp Nails, that he got him at such an Advantage, that he threw him again upon the Earth, where they fought so long together, that all the Passages would be too tedious to mention. At last, *Orson* took the Shield from about the Neck of *Valentine*, greatly admiring the same, in Regard of the divers Colours thereon emblazon'd: When he had looked his Fill, he cast it against the Ground, and suddenly returned again to *Valentine*,

and with the Violence of his Nails and Teeth, he brake in Pieces both the Ribs of his Armour, and his Habergeon also, smiting and beating him so sharply, with his Nails, that he made the Blood follow in all Places whereon he laid hold: *Valentine* feeling himself sore wounded, after some Orisons used to the Gods, he made again upon *Orson* with his Sword, thinking to have smitten him; but *Orson* recalling back, step'd unto a Tree hard by, which he pulled up, and made thereof a Club; being thus prepared, he made against *Valentine*, and striking at him, he gave him such a Blow, that he made him fall upon one Knee: *Valentine* recovering again, laid about him so fiercely, there began again another dangerous Fight between these two Brethren, not knowing they were so, nor the Cause of this their Fortunes. *Orson* was so cruel and strong, that he could oftentimes have killed *Valentine*, had it not been for his Sword; for he was sore afraid thereof, by Reason he had received a Wound before by a Knife. Long time they fought together, insomuch, that they both grew faint, and gave back, as to take Breath, and stood gaping at each other: Then *Valentine* looked wishfully upon *Orson*, and said thus: *Wild Man, wherefore dost thou not yield unto me? For here thou livest like a Beast, having no Knowledge of human Society; come thy Way with me, and I will make thee know thyself, and others; I will give thee Food of all Sorts, and also cloath thee in Apparel fitting human Shape.* *Orson* understanding by Signs he meant his Good, fell down upon his Knees, and stretched forth his Hands towards his Brother, and making Signs unto him, to forgive him, and he would submit unto his Command; and with further Signs promised, that, during his Life, he would assist him in all Enterprizes. This happening thus, it was great Joy to *Valentine*, in that he had conquered the wild Man, which so many Knights dare not meddle withal; for by this only he had won himself more Honour than any Knight that lived in *France*. *Valentine* being joyful at this unexpected Accident, took *Orson* by the Hand, and shewed him by Signs that he should go on

before him, till they were out of the Wood, for he would not trust him behind; and being out of the Wood, *Valentine* took off one of his Girts, and bound both his Hands fast to his Body, that he should not attempt again to do him any Hurt; and in this Manner he mounted on Horse-back, and led the wild-Man after him, like a Beast, who never resisted; which was a thing most of all to be wondered at.

*Valentine* took his Way towards *Orleans*; but you must imagine he could not reach there in one Day, therefore he determined to lodge at the next Town or Village: Being come thither, he thought there to take his Rest that Night, but the Inhabitants perceiving the wild Man, they all ran into their Houses, shutting up their Doors; and for Fear, durst not offer to look out on him. *Valentine* seeing them so full of Fear, cried out unto them, saying, *Open your Doors, and fear not, for we are come only for Lodging,* yet for all this, they would not give him Succour. At last, seeing that Intreating would not prevail, he swore most bitterly, *That if they would not receive him into their Houses, to rest there that Night, he would let loose the wild Man amongst them*; still he proceeded to intreat for Lodging, but none would let him in. At last, as he had threatened, so he did; and letting loose the wild Man, he made him Signs how he should run against such a Gate, which was an Inn, which he did, and wringing a Post out of the Earth, he flung them open with such Violence, that they fell off the Hooks upon the Ground. *Valentine* seeing the Gate opened in this Manner, entred the House, and the wild Man with him: But when they within saw the Gate broken down, they all forsook the House, and ran out at the Back-door, leaving all to *Valentine*, and his beastly Guest: When he perceived they were all fled, he went to the Stable, and set up his Horse, and dressed him; and *Orson* in the mean Time went into the Kitchen, where there was Capons, and divers other Provisions of *Flesh*, roasting at the Fire. *Valentine* made Signs to *Orson*, that he should turn the Spit; but as soon as *Orson* understood the Meaning, he set his Talons upon the Meat, and tore it from the Spit, devouring it as greedily as a ravenous Wolf. When he had torn the Meat in Pieces, he espied a Cauldron of Water standing by, into which he put his Head like a Horse, and drank extravagantly. *Valentine* perceiving him to be thirsty, made Signs unto him, that he should forsake the Water, and he would give him Wine; and therewithal took a Pot, and led him into the Cellar; when *Valentine* had drawn the Pot full, he gave it unto *Orson*, who set it to his Mouth, and tasting the Liquor, found it to be very good, drinking so freely thereof, that he drank out all the Wine, and afterwards threw the Pot against the Ground, making a Sign for more: *Valentine* fulfilled his Signs, and filled him the Pot again; but *Orson* espying a little Bowl-dish, he put the Wine into it, and carried it into the Stable to *Valentine's* Horse; but *Valentine* perceiving that, made signs unto him, that his Horse drank nothing but Water; yet *Orson* shewed by Signs, that Wine was a great deal better than Water. Many other Accidents happened while they were in the House, which here we will pass over; for the Night was so far spent, that Rest was fitter for them than Meat, yet *Valentine* hastened to Supper, making *Orson* bear him Company (after his Kind) but *Orson* drank so freely of the Wine, that he became drunk; and in the End got to the Fire, and fell fast asleep. *Valentine* seeing what had happened, said, *Now I perceive there is neither Strength nor Resistance in this wild Man; for if I would, I could here end his Days:* But in Regard he would make further Trial of him, he punched against him with his Foot so hard, that it awaked him: Being awaked, he made Signs unto him, that there was People about the House, with that *Orson* suddenly rose as in a Trance, and catching up a great Log within the Chimney, he ran against the Gate of the House, that he made it shake again; at which sudden Action, *Valentine* fell into a great Laughter; which *Orson* perceiving, let all alone, and betook himself to Rest again. *Valentine* made unto him another Sign, that he should fear nothing, for he would be his Watchman; but *Orson* would not sleep again, but with the Log in his Arms; and *Valentine* did as he had promised unto *Orson*, and watched all that Night, fearing the Inhabitants, lest that they should grow into an Uproar; for they were so possessed with Fear, that they forsook their Houses, and ran every one to the Church, and all that Night made such a Rattling with the Bells, that e're the Morning came, all the Village was filled with Men of War.

Now the Morning being come, *Valentine* betook him to his Horse, leading bound (as he did the Day before) towards *Orleans*, and the next Day came to the City: The Inhabitants of the City perceiving the wild Man, ran every one into his House, shutting their Doors, and getting up into their highest Rooms, gazed out of their Windows. Being entered the City, Tidings came to King *Pepin*, that *Valentine* had conquered the wild Man: The King hearing thereof, was greatly astonished, and at last said thus of *Valentine:* My Child, in a happy Hour thou wast born; blessed be the Father that got thee, and the Mother that was delivered of thee in the Wood; for now I see thou art fortunate, and by thee we are delivered of our Fears. *Valentine* rode thro' the City of *Orleans*, till he came to the Palace Gate of the King; and when the Porter saw *Orson*, he shut the Gates upon them, till *Valentine*, with a loud Voice, said, *Fear not, but go and tell the King, that I will shield him, and all his Court from the Fury of the wild Man; for I have made him so tame, that he will not hurt any one.* The Porter went and told the King what *Valentine* said, who commanded them to enter the Palace. Then he took *Orson* by the Hand, and led him into the Court. When *Bertha*, and the fair

*Eglantine* heard that the Wild-man was come, they got them to their Chambers for fear, *Valentine* went up into the great Hall, where the King sat, accompanied with his Nobles, kindly welcoming him home: Amongst the rest stood *Haufray* and *Henry*, who also made great shew of love, but in Heart wished the Wild-man had been his death. King *Pepin*, and the rest of the Lords gazed on the Wild-man, insomuch, as the King said, He is made of a proper Mould, fair of Stature; and though now he seem rough, yet if he were cloathed, he would become the shape of a right worthy Knight. Then *Valentine* said, My Liege, it were requisite he were baptised. It pleaseth me well (said the King) let it be done: So the Priest was appointed to Baptize him; these were his God-fathers, King *Pepin*, the Duke of *Millain*, and *Valentine*; and the Dutchess of *Bourbon* his God-mother: So they call'd his Name *Orson:* The Baptism being solemnized, the King sat down to Dinner, and *Valentine* waited on his Cup. Then *Orson* was commanded in the Hall to see his behaviour; and being come, the King beheld him earnestly. *Orson* seeing the Meat, took as much as he could grasp in his Hand, and devoured it; having eaten that, he espyed one of the Attendants carrying a Peacock to the Table, who coming near unto him, he snatched it, and sat him down and devoured it. *Valentine* seeing his behaviour, made Signs unto him, that he did not well; whereat *Orson* seemed ashamed; but the King bad him let him alone, for he much delighted in his Rudeness. *Orson* having devoured much Meat, got a Pot of Wine, and drank it off, throwing the Pot on the Ground. Night being come, *Valentine* and *Orson* was appointed to a fair Chamber and Bed; but as soon as *Orson* entered, he laid him down on the Ground, and so fell asleep.

*Part Five*
*Religious*
*Verse*

# A Book For Boys And Girls: or, Country Rhymes For Children

## By JOHN BUNYAN

T HOUGH OSTENSIBLY *for children, Bunyan makes clear in his introduction that his rhymes are for "Boys and Girls of all Sorts and Degrees,/From those of Age, to Children on the Knees." Bunyan observes that those of every age have their toys—a new theme as well as an old one. These toys may be real or figments of the imagination.*

*Bunyan's poetry for children of all ages resembles earlier metaphysical poetry in some respects—in its rough rhythms and in the dramatic opening lines, some of which present a paradox:*

> The Egg's no Chick by falling from the Hen.    (No. 3)
> Thou Booby, sayst thou nothing but Cuckow?    (No. 20)
> Ah, Sirrah! I perceive thou art Corn-fed.    (No. 24)
> The Thief, when he doth steal, thinks he doth gain.    (No. 30)
> What hast thou there, my pretty Boy?    (No. 47)
> Purging Physick, taken to heat or cool,/Worketh
>     by Vomit, Urine, Sweat or Stool.    (No. 62)

*Most metaphysical perhaps is "Upon a Ring of Bells" (No. 29), in which the poet enters his meditation, becomes the bell, the clappers being his passions; the ropes his promises; his body the steeple; his graces or good qualities, the ringers; and his lusts, who sometimes pull the ropes, are boys. (Freud would have a field day with the last metaphor.) Though the poetry is far less subtle, there is the same self-confession and deep religious commitment which one finds in the poetry of the Anglican preacher, George Herbert, whose poetry, was written earlier in the century.*

*What poetry of Bunyan's might still hold an interest for children? Much of the interest of any of it would depend on how effectively it was presented. Possibilities are No. 7, "Upon the Fish in the Water," No. 8, "Upon the Swallow," No. 12, "Upon over-much Niceness," No. 15, "Upon the Suns Reflection upon the Clouds in a fair Morning," No. 16, "Upon Apparel," No. 20, "Of the Cuckow," No. 21, "Of the Boy and Butter Fly," No. 31, "Of the Child with Bird at the Bush," No. 36, "Upon the Frog," No. 37, "Upon the whipping of a Top," No. 43, "Of Fowls flying in the Air," No. 47,*

*"Upon the Boy and his Paper of Plumbs," No. 49, "Upon a Lanthorn," No. 52, "On the Kackling of a Hen," No. 57, "Upon the Snail," No. 67, "Upon the Boy and his Hobby-horse," No. 68, "Upon the Image in the Eye," No. 71, "Upon the Boy dull at his Book," and No. 72, "Upon Time and Eternity."*

*Some will argue that none of these poems is appropriate for a child. It is a question of taste—and of religious convictions.*

*Historically and thematically, the poems hold great interest. Two of his poems, No. 54, "Upon the Chalk-stone," and No. 70, "Upon a Sheet of white Paper," forecast John Locke's tabula rasa theory, enunciated at the end of the century. (See also Character 1— the description of "A Childe"—in John Earle's* Microcosmographie *[London, 1628] in which Earle describes the child's soul "as yet a white paper unscribled with observations of the world.")*

*One of the most effective poems is a four-line stanza, "Upon the Image in the Eye," No. 74, which comes straight out of medieval optics, with which readers of Donne's poetry are familiar. Another ancient symbol—a mirror—is effectively used in "Upon a Looking-glass" (No. 48) to symbolize man's lack of insight into his own character. The image so popular in the Renaissance, reflected in the account in Spenser's* Mutability Cantos *of straight line (finite) and circular (eternal) motion, beautifully expressed in Henry Vaughan's poem, "The World," also is found in Bunyan's "Upon Time and Eternity" (No. 72).*

*"Upon a Stinking Breath," No. 55, is an instance of Bunyan's vigorous application of a physiological fact to religion. The poem sounds almost like an excerpt out of a brief treatise on halitosis in* The byrth of mankinde, *a late sixteenth-century obstetrical text. In No. 22, "The Fly at the Candle," the fly, regarded as a lustful insect in the Renaissance because of its rapidity of reproduction, is inevitably led to destruction by the light of the Gospel. (In James Thurber's perverse fable on a similar theme, the little moth who does not obey his parents and avoids the flame is the only one to survive.) The Post Boy in No. 27 bravely sounds his horn along the stages of his life's journey and so arrives at everlasting bliss. The sounding of the horn has always been a wonderful metaphor of man's challenge of the unknown, from the dying Roland in Charlemagne's legend, to Browning's "Childe Roland," to Edwin Arlington Robinson's "Mr. Flood," who blew a lonely horn in the face of death. In "Upon the Thief" (No. 30), the child is exposed to the important ethical truth that evil boomerangs—the same truth enunciated in the Bhagavad-Gita of the Hindus, in Emerson's "If the Red Slayer . . . ," and in other places.*

*Bunyan is well aware of the importance of music in bringing home a lesson, and poems Nos. 29, 31, 34, 40, and 51 either are about music or, in Nos. 31 and 34, have musical scores to accompany them.*

*The poems, though uneven in quality, often have a rugged beauty, particularly if one omits the Application in the second part of the poems. Meditation No. 18 which asks, "Where's he whose Golden rays/Drives night away and beautifies our days?" is quite lovely. So is No. 26: "A comely sight indeed it is to see,/A World of Blossoms on an Apple-tree." Then there is No. 31, "My little Bird, how canst thou sit/And sing amidst so many Thorns!" And the first line, at least, of No. 57: "Upon a Snail": "She goes but softly, but she goeth sure."*

*Although the rhymes are mainly iambic pentameter couplets—still not so closed as those which came later with Pope—there is considerable variety in the verse patterns, including iambic trimeter (No. 2), trimeter and iambic tetrameter (No. 10), deliberate successions of feminine endings (No. 17), smooth run-on lines (No. 27), and effective use of onomatopoeia (No. 41).*

A Book for Boys and Girls *is reprinted from a facsimile—published in London in 1889—of the first edition of 1686.*

# TO THE READER

COURTEOUS READER,

The Title-page will shew, if there thou look,
Who are the proper Subjects of this Book.
They'r Boys and Girls of all Sorts and Degrees,
From those of Age, to Children on the Knees.
Thus comprehensive am I in my Notions;
They tempt me to it by their childish Motions.
We now have Boys with Beards, and Girls that be
Big as old Women, wanting Gravity.

    Then do not blame me, cause I thus describe them;
Flatter I may not, lest thereby I bribe them
To have a better judgment of themselves,
Than wise men have of Babies on their Shelves.
Their antick Tricks, fantastick Modes, and way,
Shew they like very Boys, and Girls, do play
With all the frantick Fopp'ries of this Age;
And that in open view, as on a Stage;
Our *Bearded* men, do act like *Beardless* Boys;
Our Women please themselves with childish Toys.

    Our Ministers, long time by Word and Pen,
Dealt with them, counting them, not Boys but Men:
*Thunder-bolts* they shot at them, and their Toys:
But hit them not, 'cause they were Girls and Boys.
The better Charge, the wider still they shot,
Or else so high, these *Dwarfs* they touched not
Instead of Men, they found them Girls and Boys,
Addict to nothing as to childish Toys.

    Wherefore good Reader, that I save them may,
I now with them, the very *Dottril* play.
And since at Gravity they make a Tush,
My very Beard I cast behind the Bush.
And like a Fool stand fing'ring of their Toys;
And all to shew them, they are Girls and Boys.

Nor do I blush, although I think some may
Call me a Baby, 'cause I with them play:
I do't to shew them how each *Fingle-fangle*,
On which they doting are, their Souls entangle,
As with a Web, a Trap, a Ginn, or Snare.
And will destroy them, have they not a Care,
   *Paul* seem'd to play the Fool, that he might gain
Those that were Fools indeed, if not in Grain.
And did it by *their* things, that they might know
Their emptiness, and might be brought unto
What would them save from Sin and Vanity.
A Noble Act, and full of Honesty.
   Yet he, nor I would like them be in Vice,
While by their *Play-things*, I would them entice,
To mount their Thoughts from what are childish Toys,
To Heav'n, for that's prepar'd for Girls and Boys.
Nor do I so confine my self to these,
As to shun graver things, I seek to please,
Those more compos'd with better things than Toys:
Tho thus I would be catching Girls and Boys.
   Wherefore if Men have now a mind to look;
Perhaps their Graver Fancies may be took
With what is here; tho but in Homely Rhimes;
But he, who pleases all, must rise betimes.
Some, I perswade me, will be finding Fault,
Concluding, here I trip, and there I halt,
No doubt some could these groveling Notions raise
By fine-spun Terms that challenge might the Bays.
But should all men be forc't to lay aside
Their Brains, that cannot regulate the Tide
By this or that man's Fancy, we should have
The Wise, unto the Fool, become a Slave
What tho my Text seems mean, my Morals be
Grave, as if fetcht from a Sublimer Tree.
And if some better handle can a Fly
Then some a Text, why should we them deny
Their making Proof, or good Experiment,
Of smallest things great mischiefs to prevent?
   Wise *Solomon* did Fools to Piss-ants send,
To learn true Wisdom, and their Lives to mend.
Tea, God by Swallows, Cuckows, and the Ass;
Shews they are Fools who let that season pass,
Which he put in their hand, *that* to obtain
Which is both present, and Eternal Gain.
   I think the wiser sort my Rhimes may flight
But what care I! The foolish will delight

To read them, and the Foolish, God has chose.
And doth by Foolish Things, their minds compose,
And settle upon that which is Divine:
Great Things, by little ones, are made to shine.
　I could, were I so pleas'd, use higher Strains.
And for Applause, on Tenters, stretch my Brains,
But what needs that? The Arrow out of Sight,
Does not the Sleeper, nor the Watchman fright.
To shoot too high doth but make Children gaze,
Tis that which hits the man, doth him amaze.
　And for the Inconsiderableness
Of things, by which I do my mind express;
May I by them bring some good thing to pass,
As *Sampson*, with the Jaw-bone of an Ass;
Or as Brave *Shamgar* with his Oxe's Goad,
(Both things not manly, nor for War in Mode
I have my end, tho I my self expose
To scorn; God will have Glory in the close.
　Thus much for artificial Babes; and now
To those who are in years but such, I bow
　My Pen to teach them what the Letters be,
And how they may improve their *A, B, C*.
Nor let my pretty Children them despise;
All, needs must there begin, that would be wise
　Nor let *them* fall under Discouragement,
Who at their Horn-book stick, and time hath spent
Upon that A, B, C. while others do
Into their Primer, or their Psalter go.
Some Boys with difficulty do begin,
Who in the end, the Bays, and Lawrel win.

*J. B.*

## *An help to Children to learn to read Eng-lish.*

In order to the at-tain-ing of which, they must first be taught the Let-ters, which be these that fol-low

A B C D E F G H I J K L M N O P Q R S T U V W X Y Z
a b c d e f g h i j k l m n o p q r s t u v w x y z

A B C D E F G H I J K L M N O P Q R S T U V W X Y Z
a b c d e f g h i j k l m n o p q r s t u v w x y z

*A B C D E F G H I J K L M N O P Q R S T U V W X Y Z*
*a b c d e f g h i j k l m n o p q r s t u v w x y z*

The Vowels are these, a, e, i, o, u.

As there are vow-els, so are there Con-so-nants, and they are these.
b c d f g h k l m n p q r s t v w x y z

There are also dou-ble Let-ters, and they are these.
ct ss si ssi fl fi ffi st sh

Af-ter these are known, then set your Child to spel-ling, Thus T-o, to. T-h-e, the, O-r, or, I-f, if, I-n, in, M-e, me, y-o-u, you; f-i-n-d, find, S-i-n, sin: In C-h-r-i-s-t, Christ, i-s, is, R-i-g-h-t-e-o-u-s-n-e-s-s, Right-te-ous-ness.

And ob-serve that e-ve-ry word or syl-la-ble (tho ne-ver so small) must have one vow-el or more right-ly pla-ced in it.

For instances, These are no words nor Syl-la-bles, be-cause they have no vow-els in them, namely, sl, gld, strnght, spll, drll, fll.

Words made of two Letters are these, and such-like, If, it, is, so, do, we, see, he, is, in, my.

Words con-sist-ing of three Letters.

But, for, her, she, did, doe, all, his, way, you, may, say, nay.

## To learn Chil-dren to spell a-right their names.

### NAMES OF BOYS.

| | | |
|---|---|---|
| Tho-mas. | Ja-cob. | Ralph. |
| James. | A-bra-ham. | Ste-phen. |
| Si-mon. | Mo-ses. | Je-re-mi-ah. |
| Ed-ward. | Aa-ron. | Pe-ter. |
| John. | Phi-lip. | George. |
| Ro-bert. | Mat-thew. | Jo-nas. |
| Ri-chard. | Bar-tho-lo-mew. | A-mos. |
| Ad-am. | Wil-li-am. | Ni-cho-las. |
| Ti-mo-thy. | Hen-ry. | Job. |
| | | Da-vid. |

### NAMES OF GIRLS.

| | | |
|---|---|---|
| An-na. | Re-be-kah. | E-li-za-beth. |
| Su-san-na. | Mag-da-lene. | Sa-rah. |

| | | |
|---|---|---|
| Ma-ry. | Da-ma-ris. | Ju-dith. |
| Jane. | A-bi-gail. | Joan. |
| Dor-cas. | Mi-chal. | Alice. |
| Ra-chel. | Han-nah. | Phe-be. |
| Di-nah. | Ruth. | Grace. |
| Do-ro-thy. | Mar-tha. | Chris-ti-a-na. |
| Joanna. | Ag-nis. | Ka-the-rine. |
| Ly-di-a. | Mar-ga-ret. | Fran-ces. |

## *To learn Children to know Figures, and Numeral Letters.*

| FIGURES. | NUMERAL LETTERS. |
|---|---|
| 1. One. | I. One. |
| 2. Two. | II. Two. |
| 3. Three. | III. Three. |
| 4. Four. | IV. Four. |
| 5. Five. | V. Five. |
| 6. Six. | VI. Six. |
| 7. Seven. | VII. Seven. |
| 8. Eight. | VIII. Eight. |
| 9. Nine. | IX. Nine. |
| 10. Ten. | X. Ten. |
| 11. Eleven. | XI. Eleven. |
| 12. Twelve. | XII. Twelve. |
| 13. Thirteen. | XIII. Thirteen. |
| 14. Fourteen. | XIV. Fourteen. |
| 15. Fifteen. | XV. Fifteen. |
| 16. Sixteen. | XVI. Sixteen. |
| 17. Seventeen. | XVII. Seventeen. |
| 18. Eighteen. | XVIII. Eighteen. |
| 19. Nineteen. | XIX. Nineteen. |
| 20. Twenty. | XX. Twenty. |
| 30. Thirty. | XXX. Thirty. |
| 40. Forty. | XL. Forty. |
| 50. Fifty. | L. Fifty. |
| 60. Sixty. | LX. Sixty. |
| 70. Seventy. | LXX. Seventy. |
| 80. Eighty. | LXXX. Eighty. |
| 90. Ninety. | XC. Ninety. |
| 100. a Hundred. | C. a Hundred. |
| 500. Five hundred. | D. Five hundred. |
| 1000. a Thousand. | M. a Thousand. |

I shall forbear to add more, being perswaded this is enough for little Children to prepare themselves for Psalter, or Bible.

I

## *Upon the Ten Commandments.*

1.  THOU SHALT not have another God than me:.
2.  Thou shalt not to an Image bow thy Knee.
3.  Thou shalt not take the Name of God in vain:
4.  See that the Sabbath thou do not profain.
5.  Honour thy Father and thy Mother to:
6.  In Act or Thought see thou no Murder do.
7.  From Fornication keep thy body clean:
8.  Thou shalt not steal, though thou be very mean.
9.  Bear no false Witness, keep thee without Spot:
10. What is thy Neighbours see thou Covet not.

I I

## *The awakened Childs Lamentation.*

**1.**

WHEN *Adam* was deceived,
I was of Life bereaved;
Of late (too) I perceived,
I was in sin conceived.

**2.**

And as I was born naked,
I was with filth bespaked,
At which when I awaked,
My Soul and Spirit shaked.

**3.**

My Filth grew strong, and boyled,
And me throughout defiled,
Its pleasures me beguiled,
My Soul! how art thou spoyled!

**4.**

My Joys with sin were painted,
My mind with sin is tainted,
My heart with Guilt is fainted,
I wa'nt with God acquainted.

**5.**

I have in sin abounded,
My heart therewith is wounded,
With fears I am surrounded,
My Spirit is confounded.

**6.**

I have been often called,
By sin as oft enthralled,
Pleasures hath me fore-stalled.
How is my Spirit gauled!

**7.**

As sin has me infected,
I am thereof detected:
Mercy I have neglected,
I fear I am rejected.

**8.**

The Word I have mis-used
Good Council too refused;
Thus I my Self abused;
How can I be excused?

9.
When other Children prayed,
That work I then delayed,
Ran up and down and played,
And thus from God have strayed.

10.
Had I in God delighted,
And my wrong doings righted;
I had not thus been frighted,
Nor as I am benighted.

11.
O! That God would be pleased,
T'wards me to be appeased;
And heal me thus diseased,
How should I then be eased!

12.
But Truth I have despised,
My follies idolized,
Saints with Reproach disguised,
Salvation nothing prized.

13.
O Lord! I am ashamed,
When I do hear thee named;
'Cause thee I have defamed,
And liv'd like Beasts untamed!

14.
Would God I might be saved,
Might have an heart like *David*;
This I have sometimes craved,
Yet am by sin enslaved!

15.
Vanity I have loved,
My heart from God removed;
And not, as me behoved,
The means of Grace improved.

16.
O Lord! if I had cryed
(When I told tales and lyed)

For Mercy, and denyed
My Lusts, I had not died!

17.
But Mercies-Gate is locked,
Yea, up that way is blocked;
Yea some that there have knocked,
God at their cryes hath mocked.

18.
'Cause him they had disdained,
Their wicked ways maintained,
From Godliness refrained,
And on his word complained.

19.
I would I were converted
Would sin and I were parted,
For folly I have smarted;
God make me honest-hearted!

20.
I have to Grace appealed,
Would 'twere to me revealed,
And Pardon to me sealed,
Then should I soon be healed!

21.
Whose Nature God hath mended,
Whose sinful course is ended,
Who is to life ascended,
Of God is much befriended.

22.
Oh! Were I reconciled
To God, I, tho defiled,
Should be as one that smiled,
To think my death was spoiled.

23.
Lord! thou wast crucified
For Sinners, bled and dyed,
I have for Mercy cryed,
Let me not be denyed.

24.

I have thy Spirit grieved;
Yet is my life reprieved,
Would I in thee believed,
Then I should be relieved.

25.

Were but Repentance gained,
And had I Faith unfeigned,
Then Joy would be maintained
In me, and sin restrained.

26.

But this is to be noted,
I have on Folly doted,
My Vanities promoted,
My self to them devoted.

27.

Thus I have sin committed,
And so my self out-witted;
Yea, and my Soul unfitted,
To be to Heaven admitted.

28.

But God has condescended,
And pardon has extended,
To such as have offended,
Before their lives were ended.

29.

O Lord! do not disdain me,
But kindly entertain me;
Yea in thy Faith maintain me,
And let thy Love constrain me!

I I I

## *Meditations upon an Egg.*

1.

THE EGG's no Chick by falling from the Hen;
Nor man a Christian, till he's born agen.
The Egg's at first contained in the Shell;
Men afore Grace, in sins, and darkness dwell.
The Egg when laid, by Warmth is made a Chicken;
And Christ, by Grace, those dead in sin doth quicken.
The Egg, when first a Chick, the shell's its Prison;
So's flesh to th'Soul, who yet with Christ is risen.
The Shell doth crack, the Chick doth chirp and peep;
The flesh decays, as men do pray and weep.
The Shell doth break, the Chick's at liberty;
The flesh falls off, the Soul mounts up on high.
But both do not enjoy the self-same plight;
The Soul is safe, the Chick now fears the Kite.

2.

But Chick's from rotten Eggs do not proceed;
Nor is an Hypocrite a Saint indeed.
The rotten Egg, though underneath the Hen,
If crack'd, stinks, and is loathsome unto men.
Nor doth her Warmth make what is rotten sound,

What's rotten, rotten will at last be found.
　The Hyppocrite, sin has him in Possession,
He is a rotten Egg under Profession.

### 3.

　Some Eggs bring Cockatrices; and some men
Seem hatcht and brooded in the Vipers Den.
　Some Eggs bring wild-Fowls; and some men there be
As wild as ate the wildest Fowls that flee.
　Some Eggs bring Spiders; and some men appear
More venom than the worst of Spiders are.
　Some Eggs bring Piss ants; and some seem to me
As much for trifles as the Piss-ants be.
　Thus divers Eggs do produce divers shapes,
As like some Men as Monkeys are like Apes.
But this is but an Egg, were it a Chick,
Here had been Legs, and Wings, and Bones to pick.


I V

### *Upon the Lord's Prayer.*

OUR FATHER which in Heaven art;
Thy name be always hallowed;
Thy Kingdom come, thy Will be done;
Thy Heav'nly path be followed.
　By us on Earth as 'tis with thee,
　We humbly pray;
　And let our Bread us given be
　From day to day.
　Forgive our debts, as we forgive
Those that to us indebted are:
Into temptation lead us not;
But save us from the wicked's Snare.
　The Kingdom's thine, the Power too,
　We thee adore,
　The Glory also shall be thine
　For evermore.


V

### *Meditation upon Peep of Day.*

I OFT, though it be peep of day, do'nt
　know,
Whether 'tis Night, whether 'tis Day
　or no.
I fancy that I see a little light;
But cannot yet distinguish day from night.
I hope, I doubt, but steddy yet I be not,
I am not at a point, the Sun I see not.
　Thus 'tis with such, who Grace but now
　　possest,
They know not yet, if they are curst or
　blest.


V I

### *Upon the Flint in the Water.*

THIS FLINT, time out of mind, has there abode,
Where Chrystal Streams make their continual Road,

Yet it abides a Flint as much as 'twere,
Before it touch'd the Water, or came there.
   Its hard obdurateness is not abated,
Tis not at all by water penetrated.
Though water hath a softning vertue in't,
This Stone it can't dissolve, 'cause 'tis a Flint
   Yea though it in the water doth remain;
It doth it's fiery nature still retain.
If you oppose it with it's Opposit,
At you, yea, in your face it's fire 'twill spit.

COMPARISON.

This Flint an Emblem is of those that lye,
   Like stones, under the World, until they dye.
It's Chrystal Streams hath not their nature changed
They are not from their Lusts by Grace estranged.

# VII

## *Upon the Fish in the Water.*

### 1.

THE WATER is the Fishes Element:
Take her from thence, none can her death prevent
And some have said, who have Transgressors been,
As good not be, as to be kept from sin.

### 2.

The water is the Fishes Element:
Leave her but there, and she is well content.
So's he who in the path of Life doth plod,
Take all, says he, let me but have my God.

### 3.

The water is the Fishes Element:
Her sportings there to her are excellent.
So is God's Service unto Holy men,
They are not in their Element till then.

# VIII

## *Upon the Swallow.*

THIS PRETTY Bird, oh! how she flies and sings!

But could she do so if she had not Wings?
Her Wings, bespeak my Faith, her Songs my Peace,
When I believe and sing, my Doubtings cease.

I X

*Upon the Bee.*

T HE BEE goes out and Honey home doth bring;
And some who seek that Hony find a sting.
Now wouldst thou have the Hony and be free
From stinging; in the first place kill the Bee.

COMPARISON.

This Bee an Emblem truly is of sin
Whose Sweet unto a many death hath been.
Now would'st have Sweet from sin, and yet not dye,
Do thou it in the first place mortifie.

X

*Upon the Creed.*

I DO BELIEVE in God;
And in his only Son;
Born of a Woman, yet* begot

Before the World begun.
   I also do believe
That he was crucifi'd,
Was dead and buried; and yet
Believe he** never dy'd.

   The Third day I believe
He did rise from the dead;
Went up to Heav'n, and is of God
Of all things made the Head.
   Also I do believe,
That he from thence shall come,
To judge the quick, the dead, and to

---

\* as to his Godhead.
\*\* as to his Godhead.

Give unto all just Doom.
　　Moreover I believe
In God the Holy Ghost;
And that there is an Holy Church,
An universal Host.
　　Also I do believe,
That sin shall be forgiven;
And that the dead shall rise; and that
The Saints shall dwell in Heaven.

## X I

### *Upon a low'ring Morning.*

WELL, WITH the day, I see, the Clouds appear,
And mix the light with darkness every where:
This threatning is to Travellers, that go.
Long Journeys, slabby Rain, they'l have or Snow,
　Else while I gaze, the Sun doth with his beams
Belace the Clouds, as 'twere with bloody Streams;
This done, they suddenly do watry grow,
And weep, and pour their tears out where they go.

COMPARISON.
Thus 'tis when Gospel-light doth usher in
To us, both sense of Grace, and sense of Sin;
Yea when it makes sin red with Christ's blood,
Then we can weep, till weeping does us good.

## X I I

### *Upon over-much Niceness.*

T IS MUCH to see how over-Nice some are,
About the Body, and Houshold Affair:
While what's of Worth, they slightly pass it by,
Not doing, or doing it slovenly.
Their house must be well furnished, be in print;
Mean while their Soul lies ley, has no good in't.
Its outside also they must beautifie,
When in it there's scarce common Honesty.
　Their Bodies they must have trick'd up, and trim
Their inside full of Filth up to the brim.

Upon their cloths there must not be a spot,
But is their lives more then one common Blot?
   How nice, how coy are some about their Diet,
That can their crying Souls with Hogs-meat quiet.
All drest must to an hair be, else 'tis naught,
While of the living bread they have no thought.
Thus for their Outside they are clean and nice,
While their poor Inside stinks with sin and vice.

## XIII

## *Meditations upon the Candle.*

Man's like a Candle in a Candlestick,
Made up of Tallow, and a little Wick;
   And as the Candle is when 'tis not lighted,
So is he who is in his sins benighted.
Nor can a man his Soul with Grace inspire,
More than can Candles set themselves on fire.
   Candles receive their light from what they are not,
Men Grace from him, for whom at first they care not,
   We manage Candles when they take the fire;
God men, when he with Grace doth them inspire.
   And biggest Candles give the better light,
As Grace on biggest Sinners shines most.
   The Candle shines to make another
A Saint unto his Neighbour light should
   The blinking Candle we do much despise,
Saints dim of light are high in no mans eyes.
   Again, though it may seem to some a Riddle,
We use to light our Candle at the middle:
True, light doth at the Candles end appear,
And Grace the heart first reaches by the Ear.
But 'tis the Wick the fire doth kindle on,
As 'tis the heart that Grace first works upon.
Thus both doth fasten upon what's the main,
And so their Life and Vigour do maintain.
   The Tallow makes the Wick yield to the fire;
And sinful Flesh doth make the Soul desire,
That Grace may kindle on it, in it burn;
So Evil makes the Soul from Evil turn.
   But Candles in the wind are apt to flare;
And Christ'ans in a Tempest to despair.
   The flame also with Smoak attended is;

And in our holy lives there's much amiss.
   Sometimes a Thief will candle-light annoy;
And lusts do seek our Graces to destroy.
   What brackish is will make a Candle sputter;
T'wixt sin and Grace there's oft a heavy clutter.
   Sometimes the light burns dim, 'cause of the snuff,
Sometimes it is blown quite out with a puff;
   But Watchfulness preventeth both these evils,
Keeps Candles light and Grace in spight of Devils.
   Nor let not snuffs nor puffs make us to doubt;
Our Candles may be lighted, though pufft out.
   The Candle in the night doth all excel.
Nor Sun, nor Moon, nor Stars, then shine so well.
So is the Christian in our Hemisphere,
Whose light shews others how their course to steer.
   When Candles are put out, all's in confusion;
Where Christians are not, Devils make Intrusion.
Then happy are they who such Candles have,
All others dwell in darkness and the Grave.
   But Candles that do blink within the Socket,
And Saints whose heads are always in their pocket,
Are much alike; such Candles make us fumble,
And at such Saints, good men and bad do stumble.
   Good Candles do'nt offend, except sore eyes,
Nor hurt unless it be the silly Flies:
Thus none like burning Candles in the night,
Nor ought to holy living for delight.
   But let us draw towards the Candles end,
The fire, you see, doth Wick and Tallow spend.
As Grace mans life, until his Glass is run,
And so the Candle and the Man is done.
   The man now lays him down upon his Bed;
The Wick yields up its fire; and so is dead.
The Candle now extinct is, but the man,
By Grace mounts up to Glory, there to stand.

### X I V

### *Upon the Sacraments.*

TWO SACRAMENTS I do believe there be,
Baptism and the Supper of the Lord:
Both Mysteries divine, which do to me,
By Gods appointment, benefit afford:

But shall they be my God? or shall I have
Of them so foul and impious a Thought,
To think that from the Curse they can
    me save?
Bread, Wine, nor Water me no ramsom
    bought.


## X V

## *Upon the Suns Reflection upon the Clouds in a fair Morning.*

Look yonder, ah! Methinks mine eyes do see,
Clouds edg'd with silver, as fine Garments be!
They look as if they saw that Golden face,
That makes black Clouds most beautiful with Grace.
   Unto the Saints sweet incense or their Prayer,
These Smoaky curdled Clouds I do compare.
For as these Clouds seem edg'd or lac'd with Gold,
Their Prayers return with Blessings manifold.


## X V I

## *Upon Apparel.*

God gave us Cloaths to hide our *Nakedness*,
And we by *them*, do *it* expose to View.
Our Pride, and unclean Minds, *to an excess*,
By our Apparel we to others shew.


## X V I I

## *The Sinner and the Spider.*

SINNER.

What black? what ugly crawling thing art thou?
SPIDER.
I am a Spider —— ——
SINNER.
*A Spider, Ay, also a filthy Creature.*
SPIDER.
  Not filthy as thy self, in Name or Feature:

My Name intailed is to my Creation;
My Feature's from the God of thy Salvation.
SINNER.

   *I am a Man, and in God's Image made,*
*I have a Soul shall neither dye nor fade:*
*God has possessed me with humane Reason,*
*Speak not against me, lest thou speakest Treason.*
*For if I am the Image of my Maker,*
*Of Slanders laid on me he is Partaker.*
SPIDER.

   I know thou art a Creature far above me,
Therefore I shun, I fear, and also love thee.
But tho thy God hath made thee such a Creature,
Thou hast against him often play'd the Traitor.
Thy sin has fetcht thee down: Leave off to boast;
Nature thou hast defil'd, God's Image lost.
Yea thou, thy self a very Beast hast made,
And art become like Grass, which soon doth fade.
Thy Soul, thy Reason, yea thy spotless State,
Sin has subjected to th' most dreadful fate.
But I retain my primitive condition,
I've all, but what I lost by thy Ambition.
SINNER.

   *Thou venom'd thing, I know not what to call thee,*
*The Dregs of Nature surely did befal thee;*
*Thou wast made of the Dross, and Scum of all;*
*Man hates thee, doth in scorn thee* Spider *call.*
SPIDER.

   My Venom's good for something, 'cause God made it;
Thy Sin has spoilt thy Nature, doth degrade it
Of humane Vertues; therefore tho I fear thee,
I will not, tho I might, despise and jear thee.
Thou sayst I am the very Dregs of Nature,
Thy Sin's the spawn of Devils, 'tis no Creature.
Thou sayst man hates me, 'cause I am a Spider,
Poor man, thou at thy God art a Derider:
My venom tendeth to my Preservation;
Thy pleasing Follies work out thy Damnation.
Poor man, I keep the rules of my Creation;
Thy sin has cast thee headlong from thy Station.
I hurt no body willingly; but thou
Art a self-Murderer: Thou knowst not how
To do what good is, no thou lovest evil;
Thou fly'st God's Law, adherest to the Devil.
SINNER.

   *Ill-shaped Creature there's Antipathy*

*'Twixt Men and Spiders, 'tis in vain to lie,*
*I hate thee, stand off, if thou dost come nigh me,*
*I'll crush thee with my foot; I do defie thee.*
SPIDER.

They are ill shap't, who warped are by sin;
Antipathy in thee hath long time bin
To God. No marvel then, if me his Creature
Thou dost defie, pretending Name and Feature.
But why stand off? My Presence shall not throng thee,
'Tis not my venom, but thy sin doth wrong thee.
Come I will teach thee Wisdom, do but hear me,
I was made for thy profit, do not feer me.
But if thy God thou wilt not hearken to,
What can the Swallow, Ant, or Spider do?
Yet I will speak, I can but be rejected;
Sometimes great things, by small means are effected.
Hark then; tho man is noble by Creation,
He's lapsed now to such Degeneration;
Is so besotted, and so careless grown,
As not to grieve, though he has overthrown
Himself, and brought to Bondage every thing
Created, from the Spider to the King.
This we poor Sensitives do feel and see;
For subject to the Curse you made us be.
Tread not upon me, neither from me go;
'Tis man which has brought all the world to Wo.
The Law of my Creation bids me teach thee,
I will not for thy Pride to God impeach thee.
I spin, I weave, and all to let thee see,
Thy best performances but Cob-webs be.
Thy Glory now is brought to such an Ebb,
It doth not much excel the Spider's Web.
My Webs becoming snares aud traps for Flies,
Do set the wiles of Hell before thine eyes.
Their tangling nature is to let thee see,
Thy sins (too) of a tangling nature be.
My Den, or Hole, for that 'tis bottomless,
Doth of Damnation shew the Lastingness.
My lying quat, until the Fly is catcht,
Shews, secretly Hell hath thy ruin hatcht.
In that I on her seize, when she is taken,
I shew who gathers whom God hath forsaken.
The Fly lies buzzing in my Web to tell
Thee, how the Sinners roar and howl in Hell.
Now since I shew thee all these Mysteries,
How canst thou hate me; or me Scandalize?

SINNER.

*Well, well, I no more will be a Derider;*
*I did not look for such things from a Spider.*

SPIDER.

Come, hold thy peace, what I have yet to say,
If heeded, help thee may another day.
Since I an ugly ven'mous Creature be,
There is some Semblance 'twixt vile Man and Me.
My wild and heedless Runnings, are like those
Whose ways to ruin do their Souls expose.
Day-light is not my time, I work i'th' night,
To shew, they are like me who hate the Light.
The slightest Brush will overthrow my house,
To shew false Pleasures are not worse a Louse.
The Maid sweeps one Web down, I make another,
To shew how heedless ones Convictions smother.
My Web is no defence at all to me,
Nor will false Hopes at Judgment be to thee.

SINNER.

*O Spider I have heard thee, and do wonder,*
*A Spider should thus lighten, and thus thunder!*

SPIDER.

Do but hold still, and I will let thee see,
Yet in my ways more Mysteries there be.
Shall not I do thee good, if I thee tell,
I shew to thee a four-fold way to Hell.
For since I set my Webs in sundry places,
I shew men go to Hell in divers traces
  One I set in the window, that I might
Shew, some go down to Hell with Gospel-light.
  One I set in a Corner, as you see,
To shew, how some in secret snared be.
  Gross Webs great store I set in darksome places,
To shew, how many sin with brazen faces.
  Another Web I set aloft on high,
To shew, there's some professing men must dye.
Thus in my Ways, God Wisdom doth conceal;
And by my ways, that Wisdom doth reveal.
  I hide my self, when I for Flies do wait,
So doth the Devil, when he lays his bait.
If I do fear the losing of my prey,
I stir me, and more snares upon her lay.
This way, and that, her Wings and Legs I tye,
That sure as she is catcht, so she must dye.
But if I see she's like to get away,
Then with my Venom, I her Journey stay.

All which my ways, the Devil imitates,
To catch men 'cause he their Salvation hates.
SINNER.

   *O Spider, thou delight'st me with thy Skill,*
*I prethee spit this Venom at me still.*
SPIDER.

   I am a Spider, yet I can possess
The Palace of a King, where Happiness
So much abounds. Nor when I do go thither,
Do they ask what, or whence I come, or whether
I make my hasty Travels, no not they;
They let me pass, and I go on my way.
I seize the Palace, do with hands take hold
Of Doors, of locks, or bolts; yea I am bold.
   When in, to Clamber up unto the Throne,
And to possess it, as if 'twere mine own.
Nor is there any Law forbidding me
Here to abide, or in this Palace be.
   Yea. If I please I do the highest Stories
Asoond, there sit, and so behold the Glories
My self is compast with, as if I were
One of the chiefest Courtiers that be there.
   Here Lords and Ladies do come round about me,
With grave Demeanor: Nor do any flout me,
For this my brave Adventure, no not they;
They come, they go, but leave me there to stay.
   Now, my Reproacher, I do by all this
Shew how thou may'st possess thy self of Bliss:
Thou art worse than a Spider, but take hold
On Christ the Door, thou shalt not be controul'd.
By him do thou the Heavenly Palace enter,
None chide thee will for this thy brave Adventure.
   Approach thou then unto the very Throne,
There speak thy mind, fear not, the Day's thine own.
Nor Saint nor Angel will thee stop or stay;
But rather tumble blocks out of thy way.
My Venom stops not me, let not thy Vice
Stop thee; possess thy self of Paradice.
   Go on, I say, although thou be a Sinner,
Learn to be bold in Faith of me a Spinner.
This is the way the Glories to possess,
And to enjoy what no man can express.
   Sometimes I find the Palace door up lock't;
And so my entrance thither as up blockt.
But am I daunted? No. I here and there
Do feel, and search; so, if I any where,

At any chink or crevise find my way,
I could, I press for passage, make no stay;
And so, tho difficultly, I attain
The Palace, yea the Throne where Princes reign.
I croud sometimes, as if I'd burnt in sunder;
And art thou crush't with striving do not wonder.
Some scarce get in, and yet indeed they enter;
Knook, for they nothing have that nothing venture.

    Nor will the King himself throw dirt on thee,
As thou hast cast Reproaches upon me.
He will not hate thee, O thou foul Backslider!
As thou didst me, because I am a Spider.

    Now, to conclude; since I such Doctrine bring,
Slight me no more, call me not ugly thing.
God wisdom hath unto the *Piss-ant* given,
And *Spiders* may teach men the way to Heaven.
SINNER.

    *Well, my good Spider, I my Errors see,*
*I was a fool for railing upon thee.*
*Thy Nature, Venom, and thy fearful Hue,*
*Both shew what Sinners are, and what they do.*

    *Thy way and works do also darkly tell.*
*How some men go to Heaven, and some to Hell.*
*Thou art my Monitor, I am a Fool;*
*They learn may, that to Spiders go to School.*


## XVIII

### *Meditatiens upon day before Sun-rising.*

But all this while, where's he whose Golden rays
Drives night away, and beautifies our days?
Where's he whose goodly face doth warm and heal,
And shew us what the darksome nights conceal?
Where's he that thaws our Ice, drives Cold away?
Let's have him, or we care not for the day.

    Thus 'tis with who partakers are of Grace,
There's nought to them like their Redeemers face.


## XIX

### *Of the Mole in the Ground.*

The mole's a Creature very smooth and slick,

She digs i'th'dirt, but 'twill not on her stick.
So's he who counts this world his greatest gains,
Yet nothing gets but's labour for his pains.
Earth's the Mole's Element, she can't abide
To be above ground, dirt heaps are her pride;
And he is like her, who the Wordling plays,
He imitates her in her works, and ways.

   Poor silly Mole, that thou shouldst love to be,
Where thou, nor Sun, nor Moon, nor Stars can see.
But oh! How silly's he, who doth not care,
So he gets Earth, to have of Heaven a share.


## X X

### *Of the Cuckow.*

THOU BOOBY, sayst thou nothing but *Cuckow*?
The *Robin* and the *Wren* can thee out do.
They to us play thorow their little throats,
Not one, but sundry pretty taking Notes.
   *But thou hast Fellows, some like thee can do*
*Little but suck our Eggs, and sing Cuckow.*

   Thy notes do not *First* welcome in our Spring,
Nor dost thou it's first Tokens to us bring.
Birds less then thee by far, like Prophets, do
Tell us 'tis coming, tho not by Cuckow.

   Nor dost thou Summer have away with thee,
Though thou a yauling, bauling Cuckow be.
When thou dost cease among us to appear,
Then doth our Harvest bravely crown our year.
   *But thou hast fellows, some like thee can do*
*Little but suck our Eggs, and sing Cuckow.*

   Since Cuckows forward not our early Spring,
Nor help with notes to bring our Harvest in:
And since while here, she only makes a noise,
So pleasing unto none as Girls and Boys;
The Formalist we may compare her to,
For he doth suck our Eggs and sing Cuckow.


## X X I

### *Of the Boy and Butter Fly.*

BEHOLD how eager this our little Boy,

Is of this Butter Fly, as if all Joy,
All Profits, Honours, yea and lasting Pleasures,
Were wrapt up in her, or the richest Treasures,
Found in her would be bundled up together,
When all her all is lighter than a feather.
    He hollo's, runs, and cries out here Boys, here,
Nor doth he Brambles or the Nettles fear:
He stumbles at the Mole-Hills, up he gets,
And runs again, as one bereft of wits;
And all this labour and this large Out-cry,
Is only for a silly Butter fly.

### COMPARISON.

This little Boy an Emblem is of those,
Whose hearts are wholly at the World's dispose.
The Butter-fly doth represent to me,
The Worlds best things at best but fading be.
All are but painted Nothings and false Joys,
Like this poor Butter-fly to these our Boys.
    His running thorough Nettles, Thorns and Bryers,
To gratifie his boyish fond desires,
His tumbling over Mole-hills to attain
His end, namely, his Butter-fly to gain;
Doth plainly shew, what hazards some men run,
To get what will be lost as soon as won.
Men seem in Choice, then children far more wise,
Because they run not after Butter-flies:
When yet alas! for what are empty Toys
They follow Children, like to beardless Boys.

## XXII

### Of the Fly at the Candle.

WHAT AILS this Fly thus desperately to enter
A Combat with the Candle? will she venture
To clash at light? Away thou silly fly;
Thus doing, thou wilt burn thy wings and dye.
    But 'tis a folly her advice to give,
She'l kill the Candle, or she will not live.
    Slap, says she, at it; then she makes retreat.
So wheels about and doth her blows repeat.
    Nor doth the Candle let her quite escape,
But gives some little check unto the Ape:

Throws up her heels it doth, so down she falls,
Where she lies sprawling, and for succor calls.
    When she recovers, up she gets again,
And at the Candle comes with might and main
But now behold, the Candle takes the Fly,
And holds her till she doth by burning dye.

### COMPARISON.

This Candle is an Emblem of that Light,
Our Gospel gives in this our darksome night.
The Fly a lively Picture is of those
That hate, and do this Gospel light oppose.
At last the Gospel doth become their snare,
Doth them with burning hands in peices tear.

## XXIII

### *Upon the Lark and the Fowler.*

THOU SIMPLE BIRD what mak'st thou here to play!
Look, there's the Fowler, prethee come away.
Dost not behold the Net? Look there 'tis spread,
Venture a little further thou art dead.
    Is there not room enough in all the Field
For thee to play in, but thou needs must yield
To the deceitful glitt'ring of a Glass,
Plac'd betwixt Nets to bring thy death to pass?
    Bird, if thou art so much for dazling light,
Look, there's the Sun above thee, dart upright?
Thy nature is to soar up to the Sky,
Why wilt thou come down to the nets, and dye?
    Take no heed to the Fowler's tempting Call;
This whistle he enchanteth Birds withal.
Or if thou seest a live Bird in his net,
Believe she's there 'cause thence she cannot get.
    Look how he tempteth thee with his Decoy,
That he may rob thee of thy Life, thy Joy.
Come, prethee Bird, I prethee come away,
Why should this net thee take, when 'scape thou may?
    Hadst thou not Wings, or were thy feathers pull'd,
Or wast thou blind or fast asleep wer't lull'd:
The case would somewhat alter, but for thee,
Thy eyes are ope, and thou hast Wings to see.
    Remember that thy Song is in thy Rise,

Not in thy Fall, Earth's not thy Paradise.
Keep up aloft then, let thy circuits be
Above, where Birds from Fowlers nets are free.

COMPARISON.

This Fowler is an Emblem of the Devil,
His Nets and Whistle, Figures of all evil.
His Glass an Emblem is of sinful Pleasure,
And his Decoy, of who counts sin a Treasure.
   This simple Lark's a shadow of a Saint,
Under allurings, ready now to faint.
   This admonisher a true Teacher is,
Whose work's to shew the Soul the snare and bliss,
And how it may this Fowler's net escape,
And not commit upon itself this Rape.


# X X I V

## *Of the fatted Swine.*

AH, SIRRAH! I perceive thou art Corn-fed,
With best of Hoggs-meat thou art pampered.
Thou wallow'st in thy fat, up thou art stal'd,
Art not as heretofore to Hogs-wash call'd.
   Thine Orts lean Pigs would leap at, might they have it.
One may see by their whining how they crave it.
But Hogg, why look'st so big? Why dost so flounce,
So snort, and fling away, dost now renounce
Subjection to thy Lord, 'cause he has fed thee?
Thou art yet but a Hogg, of such he bred thee.
Lay by thy snorting, do not look so big,
What was thy Predecessor but a Pig.
   But come my gruntling, when thou art full fed,
Forth to the Butchers Stall thou must be led.
Then will an end be put unto thy snortings,
Unto thy boarish Looks and hoggish Sportings;
Then thy shrill crys will eccho in the air;
Thus will my Pig for all his Greatness fare.

COMPARISON.

This Emblem shews, some men are in this life,
Like full-fed Hoggs prepared for the Knife.
It likewise shews some can take no Reproof,
More than the fatted Hogg, who stands aloof.
Yea; that they never will for mercy cry,
Till time is past, and they for sin must dye.

X X V

## On the rising of the Sun.

LOOK, LOOK, brave *Sol* doth peep up from beneath,
Shews us his golden face, doth on us breath.
He also doth compass us round with Glories,
Whilst he ascends up to his higher Stories.
Where he his Banner over us displays,
And gives us light to see our Works and Ways.
   Nor are we now, as at the peep of light,
To question, Is it day, or is it night?
The night is gone, the shadow's fled away;
And we now most sure are that it is day.
Our Eyes behold it, and our Hearts believe it,
Nor can the wit of man in this deceive it.
   And thus it is when Jesus shews his face,
And doth assure us of his Love and Grace.

X X V I

## Upon the promising Fruitfulness of a Tree.

A COMELY SIGHT indeed it is to see,
A World of Blossoms on an Apple-tree.
Yet far more comely would this Tree appear,
If all its dainty blooms young Apples were.
But how much more might one upon it see,
If all would hang there till they ripe should be.
But most of all in Beauty 'twould abound,
If then none worm-eaten could there be found.
   But we, alas! Do commonly behold
Blooms fall apace, if mornings be but cold.
They (too) which hang till they young Apples are,
By blasting Winds and Vermine take despair.
Store that do hang, while almost ripe, we see
By blustring Winds are shaken from the Tree.
So that of many only some there be,
That grow till they come to Maturity.

COMPARISON.

This Tree a perfect Emblem is of those,
Which God doth plant, which in his Garden grows.

It's blasted Blooms are *Motions* unto Good,
Which chill Affections do nip in the bud.
  Those little Apples which yet blasted are,
Shew, some good *Purposes*, no good Fruits bare.
  Those spoilt by Vermin are to let us see,
How good *Attempts* by bad Thoughts ruin'd be.
  Those which the Wind blows down, while they are green,
Shew, good *Works* have by Tryal spoyled been:
  Those that abide, while ripe, upon the Tree,
Shew, in a good man *some* ripe Fruit *will* be.
  Behold then how abortive some Fruits are,
Which at the first most promising appear.
The Frost, the Wind, the Worm with time doth shew,
There flows from much Appearance, works but few.


## XXVII

### On the Post-boy.

BEHOLD THIS Post-boy, with what haste and speed
He travels on the Road; and there is need
That he so does, his Business call for haste.
For should he in his Journey now be cast,
His Life for that default might hap to go;
Yea, and the Kingdom come to ruin too.
  Stages are for him fixt, his hour is set,
He has a Horn to sound, that none may let
Him in his haste, or give him stop or stay.
Then Post-boy blow thy horn, and go thy way.

#### COMPARISON.

This Post-boy in this haste an Emblem is,
Of those that are set out for lasting Bliss.
Nor Posts that glide the road from day to day,
Have so much business, nor concerns as they.
Make clear the road then, Post-boy sound thy horn,
Miscarry here, and better n'ere been born.


## XXVIII

### Upon the Horse in the Mill.

HORSES THAT work i'th'Mill must hood-wink't be;
For they'l be sick or giddy, if they see.

But keep them blind enough, and they will go
That way which would a seeing Horse undo.

### COMPARISON.

Thus 'tis with those that do go *Satan's* Round,
No seeing man can live upon his ground.
Then let us count those unto sin inclin'd,
Either besides their wits, bewitch'd or blind.

# XXIX

## Upon a Ring of Bells.

BELLS HAVE wide mouths and tongues, but are too weak,
Have they not help, to sing, or talk, or speak
But if you move them they will mak't appear,
By speaking they'l make all the Town to hear.
  When Ringers handle them with Art and Skill,
They then the ears of their Observers fill,
With such brave Notes, they ting and tang so well
As to out strip all with their ding, dong, Bell.

### COMPARISON.

These Bells are like the Powers of my Soul;
Their Clappers to the Passions of my mind:
The Ropes by which my Bells are made to tole,
Are Promises (I by experience find.)
  My body is the Steeple, where they hang,
My Graces they which do ring ev'ry Bell:
Nor is there any thing gives such a tang,
When by these Ropes these Ringers ring them well.
  Let not my Bells these Ringers want, nor Ropes;
Yea let them have room for to swing and sway:
To toss themselves deny them not their Scopes.
Lord! in my Steeple give them room to play.
If they do tole, ring out, or chime all in,
They drown the tempting tinckling Voice of Vice:
Lord! when my Bells have gone, my Soul has bin
As 'twere a tumbling in this Paradice!
  Or if these Ringers do the Changes ring,
Upon my Bells, they do such Musick make,
My Soul then (Lord) cannot but bounce and sing,
So greatly her they with their Musick take.
But Boys (my Lusts) into my Belfry go,

And pull these Ropes, but do no Musick make
They rather turn my Bells by what they do,
Or by disorder make my Steeple shake.
   Then, Lord! I pray thee keep my Belfry Key,
Let none but Graces meddle with these Ropes:
And when these naughty Boys come, say them Nay,
From such Ringers of Musick there's no hopes.
   O Lord! If thy poor Child might have his will,
And might his meaning freely to thee tell;
He never of this Musick has his fill,
There's nothing to him like thy ding, dong, Bell.

## X X X

### *Upon the Thief.*

THE THIEF, when he doth steal, thinks he doth gain;
Yet then the greatest Loss he doth sustain.
Come Thief, tell me thy Gains, but do not falter
When sum'd what comes it to more than the Halter?
   Perhaps, thoul't say, the Halter I defie;
So thou mayst say, yet by the Halter dye.
Thoul't say, then there's an end; no, prethee hold,
He was no Friend of thine that thee so told.
   Hear thou the Word of God, that will thee tell,
Without Repentance Thieves must go to Hell.
But should it be as thy false Prophet says,
Yet nought but Loss doth come by Thievish ways.
   All honest men will flee thy Company,
Thou liv'st a Rogue, and so a Rogue wilt dye.
Innocent boldness thou hast none at all,
Thy inward thoughts do thee a Villain call.
   Sometimes when thou ly'st warmly on thy Bed,
Thou art like one unto the Gallows led.
Fear, as a Constable, breaks in upon thee;
Thou art as if the Town was up to stone thee.
   If Hogs do grunt, or silly Rats do rusle,
Thou art in consternations, think'st a busle
By men about the door is made to take thee
And all because good Conscience doth forsake thee.
   Thy case is most deplorably bad;
Thou shun'st to think on't, lest thou shouldst be mad.
Thou art beset with mischiefs ev'ry way,
The Gallows groaneth for thee ev'ry day.

Wherefore, I prethee Thief, thy Theft forbear,
Consult thy safety, prethee have a care.
If once thy Head be got within the Noose,
'Twill be too late a longer Life to chuse.
  As to the Penitent thou readest of,
What's that to them who at Repentance scoff.
Nor is that Grace at thy Command or Pow'r,
That thou shouldst put it off till the last hour.
  I prethee Thief think on't, and turn betime;
Few go to Life who do the Gallows clime.

## XXXI

### *Of the Child with the Bird at the Bush.*

**M**Y LITTLE BIRD, how canst thou sit;
And sing amidst so many Thorns!
Let me but hold upon thee get;
My Love with Honour thee adorns.
  Thou art at present little worth;
Five farthings none will give for thee.
But prethee little Bird come forth,
Thou of more value art to me.
  'Tis true, it is Sun-shine to day,
To morrow Birds will have a Storm;
My pretty one, come thou away,
My Bosom then shall keep thee warm.
  Thou subject art to cold o'nights,
When darkness is thy covering,
At day's thy dangers great by Kites,
How canst thou then sit there and sing?
  Thy food is scarce and scanty too,
'Tis Worms and Trash which thou dost eat;
Thy present state I pity do,
Come, I'll provide thee better meat.

I'll feed thee with white Bread and Milk,
And Suger-plumbs, if them thou crave;
I'll cover thee with finest Silk,
That from the cold I may thee save.
  My Father's Palace shall be thine,
Yea in it thou shalt sit and sing;
My little Bird, if thoul't be mine,
The whole year round shall be thy Spring.
  I'll teach thee all the Notes at Court;
Unthought of Musick thou shalt play;
And all that thither do resort,
Shall praise thee for it ev'ry day.
  I'll keep thee safe from Cat and Cur,
No manner o'harm shall come to thee;
Yea, I will be thy Succourer,
My Bosom shall thy Cabbin be.
But lo, behold, the Bird is gone;
These Charmings would not make her yield:
The Child's left at the Bush alone,
The Bird flies yonder o'er the Field.

#### COMPARISON.

This Child of Christ an Emblem is;
The Bird to Sinners I compare:
The Thorns are like those Sins of his,
Which do surround him ev'ry where.
  Her Songs, her Food, and Sun-shine day,
An Emblem's of those foolish Toys,
Which to Destruction lead the way,
The fruit of worldly, empty Joys.
  The Arguments this Child doth chuse,
To draw to him a Bird thus wild,
Shews Christ familiar Speech doth use,
To make's to him be reconciled.
  The Bird in that she takes her Wing,
To speed her from him after all:
Shews us, vain Man loves any thing,
Much better than the Heav'nly Call.

## XXXII

### Of Moses and his Wife.

THIS *Moses* was a fair and comely man;

His wife a swarthy Ethiopian:
Nor did his Milk-white Bosom change her Skin;
She came out thence as black as she went in.
Now *Moses* was a type of *Moses* Law,
His Wife likewise of one that never saw
Another way unto eternal Life;
There's Myst'ry then in *Moses* and his Wife.

   The Law is very Holy, Just and good,
And to it is espous'd all Flesh and Blood:
But this its Goodness it cannot bestow,
On any that are wedded thereunto.

   Therefore as *Moses* Wife came swarthy in,
And went out from him without change of Skin:
So he that doth the Law for Life adore,
Shall yet by it be left a Black-a-more.


## XXXIII

### *Upon the barren Fig-tree in God's Vineyard.*

WHAT BARREN, here! in this, so good a soyl?
The sight of this doth make God's heart recoyl
From giving thee his Blessing. Barren Tree,
Bear Fruit, else thine end will cursed be!

   Art thou not planted by the water side?
Know'st not thy Lord by Fruit is glorifi'd?
The Sentence is, cut down the barren Tree:
Bear Fruit, or else thine End will cursed be!

   Hast not been dig'd about, and dunged too,
Will neither Patience, nor yet Dressing do?
The Executioner is come, O Tree,
Bear Fruit, or else thine End will cursed be!

   He that about thy Roots takes pains to dig,
Would if on thee were found but one good Fig,
Preserve thee from the Axe: But barren Tree,
Bear Fruit, or else thy End will cursed be!

   The utmost end of Patience is at hand,
'Tis much if thou much longer here doth stand.
O Cumber-ground, thou art a barren Tree,
Bear Fruit, or else thine End will cursed be!

   Thy standing nor thy name will help at all,
When fruitful Trees are spared thou must fall.
The Axe is laid unto thy Roots, O Tree!
Bear fruit, or else thine End will cursed be!

## XXXIV

### *Of the Rose-bush.*

This homely Bush doth to mine eyes expose,
A very fair, yea comely, ruddy, *Rose.*
   This *Rose* doth also bow its head to me,
Saying, come, pluck me, I thy Rose will be.
Yet offer I to gather Rose or Bud,
Ten to one but the Bush will have my Blood.
   This looks like a Trappan, or a Decoy,
To offer, and yet snap who would enjoy.
Yea, the more eager on't, the more in danger,
Be he the Master of it, or a Stranger.
   Bush, why dost bear a Rose? If none must have it,
Why dost expose it, yet claw those that crave it?
Art become freakish? Dost the Wanton play,
Or doth thy testy humour tend this way?

#### COMPARISON.

This Rose God's Son is, with his ruddy Looks.
But what's the *Bush?* Whose pricks, like Tenterhooks,
Do scratch and claw the finest Ladies hands,
Or rent her Cloths, if she too near it stands.
   This *Bush* an Emblem is of *Adam's* race
Of which Christ came, when he his Father's Grace
Commended to us in his crimson Blood,
While he in Sinners stead and Nature stood.
   Thus *Adam's* Race did bear this dainty Rose,
And doth the same to *Adam's* Race expose:
But those of *Adam's* Race which at it catch,
*Adam's* Race will them prick and claw and scratch.

## X X X V

### *Of the going down of the Sun.*

WHAT, HAST thou run thy Race? Art going down?
Thou seemest angry, why dost on us frown?
Yea wrap thy head with Clouds, and hide thy face,
As threatning to withdraw from us thy Grace?
Oh leave us not! When once thou hid'st thy head,
Our Horizon with darkness will be spread.
Tell's, who hath thee offended? Turn again:
Alas! too late Entreaties are in vain!

#### COMPARISON.

Our Gospel has had here a Summers day;
But in its Sun-shine we, like Fools, did play.
Or else fall out, and with each other wrangle,
And did instead of work not much but jangle.
    And if our Sun seems angry, hides his face,
Shall it go down, shall Night possess this place?
Let not the voice of night-Birds us afflict,
And of our mis-spent Summer us convict.

## X X X V I

### *Upon the Frog.*

THE FROG by Nature is both damp and cold,
Her Mouth is large, her Belly much will hold:
She sits somewhat ascending, loves to be
Croaking in Gardens, tho unpleasantly.

#### COMPARISON.

The Hyppocrite is like unto this Frog;
As like as is the Puppy to the Dog.
His is of nature cold, his Mouth is wide,
To prate, and at true Goodness to deride.
He mounts his Head, as if he was above
The World, when yet 'tis that which has his Love.
And though he seeks in Churches for to croak,
He neither loveth Jesus, nor his Yoak.

## X X X V I I

### *Upon the whipping of a Top.*

T IS WITH the Whip the Boy sets up the Top,
The Whip makes it run round upon it's Toe;
The Whip makes it hither and thither hop:
Tis with the Whip, the Top is made to go.

COMPARISON.

Our Legalist is like unto this Top,
Without a Whip, he doth not Duty do.
Let *Moses* whip him, he will skip and hop;
Forbear to whip, he'l neither stand nor go.

## X X X V I I I

### *Upon the Pismire.*

M UST WE unto the Pis-mire go to School,
To learn of her, in Summer to provide
For Winter next ensuing; Man's a Fool,
Or silly Ants would not be made his Guide.
    But Sluggard, is not a shame for thee,
To be out-done by Pis-mires? Prethee hear:
Their Works (too) will thy Condemnation be,
When at the Judgment Seat thou shalt appear.
    But since thy God doth bid thee to her go,
Obey, her ways consider, and be wise.
The Piss-ants tell thee will what thou must do,
And set the way to Life before thine eyes.

## X X X I X

### *Upon the Beggar.*

H E WANTS, he asks, he pleads his Poverty,
They within doors do him an Alms deny.
He doth repeat and aggravate his Grief;
But they repulse him, give him no relief.
He begs, they say, be gone; he will not hear,

But coughs, sighs and make signs, he still is there
They disregard him, he repeats his groans;
They still say nay, and he himself bemoans.
They grow more rugged, they call him Vagrant;
He cries the shriller, trumpets out his want.
At last when they perceive he'll take no Nay,
An Alms they give him without more delay.

##### COMPARISON.

This Beggar doth resemble them that pray.
To God for Mercy, and will take no Nay.
But wait, and count that all his hard Gain-says,
Are nothing else, but fatherly Delays.
Then imitate him, praying Souls, and cry:
There's nothing like to Importunity.

### X L

## *Upon an Instrument of Musick in an unskilful Hand.*

Suppose a Viol, Cittern, Lute, or Harp,
Committed unto him that wanteth Skill;
Can he by Strokes, suppose them flat or sharp,
The Ear of him that hears with Musick fill?
    No, no, he can do little else then scrape,
Or put all out of tune, or break a string:
Or make thereon a mutt'ring like an Ape,
Or like one which can neither say nor sing.

##### COMPARISON.

The unlearn'd Novices in things Divine,
With this unskill'd Musician I compare.
For such, instead of making Truth to shine,
Abuse the Bible, and unsavoury are.

### X L I

## *Upon the Horse and his Rider.*

There's one rides very sagely on the Road,
Shewing that he affects the gravest Mode.
Another rides Tantivy, or full Trot,

To shew, much Gravity he matters not.
   Lo, here comes one amain, he rides full speed,
Hedge, Ditch, nor Myry Bog, he doth not heed.
   One claws it up Hill without stop or check,
Another down, as if he'd break his Neck.
   Now ev'ry Horse has his especial Guider;
Then by his going you may know the Rider.


COMPARISON.

Now let us turn our Horse into a Man,
His Rider to a Spirit, if we can:
Then let us by the Methods of the Guider,
Tell ev'ry Horse how he should know his Rider.


   Some go as Men direct in a right way,
Nor are they suffered to go astray:
As with a Bridle they are governed,
And kept from Paths, which lead unto the dead.
   *Now this good man has his especial Guider;*
   *Then by his going let him know his Rider.*


   Some go as if they did not greatly care,
Whether of Heaven or Hell they should be Heir.
The Rein it seems as laid upon their Neck,
They seem to go their way without a check.
   *Now this man too has his especial Guider;*
   *And by his going he may know his Rider.*


   Some again run, as if resolv'd to dye,
Body and Soul to all Eternity:
Good Counsel they by no means can abide;
They'l have their course, whatever them betide.
   *Now these poor Men have their especial Guider;*
   *Were they not Fools they soon might know their Rider.*


   There's one makes head against all Godliness,
Those (too) that do profess it he'l distress:
He'l taunt and flout, if Goodness doth appear,
And at its Countenancers mock and jear.
   *Now this man (too) has his especial Guider;*
   *And by his going he might know his Rider.*

## XLII

### *Upon the Sight of a Pound of Candles falling to the Ground.*

BUT BE THE Candles down, and scatt'red too,
Some lying here, some there? What shall we do?
Hold, light the Candle there that stands on high,
It you may find the other Candles by.
Light that, I say, and so take up the Pound,
You did let fall, and scatter on the Ground.

#### COMPARISON.

The fallen Candles to us intimate,
The bulk of God's Elect in their lapst State.
Their lying scatt'red in the dark may be,
To shew by Man's lapst State his Misery,
  The Candle that was taken down, and lighted,
Thereby to find them fallen, and benighted,
Is Jesus Christ: God by his Light doth gather
Who he will save, and be unto a Father.

## XLIII

### *Of Fowls flying in the Air.*

METHINKS I SEE a Sight most excellent,
All Sorts of Birds fly in the Firmament:
Some great, some small, all of a divers kind,
Mine Eye affecting, pleasant to my Mind.
Look how they tumble in the wholesom Air,
Above the World of Wordlings, and their care.
  And as they divers are in Bulk and Hue,
So are they in their way of flying too.
  So many Birds, so many various things,
Tumbling i'th'Element upon their Wings.

#### COMPARISON.

These Birds are Emblems of those men, that shall
Ere long possess the Heavens, their All in All.
  They are each of a divers shape, and kind;
To teach, we of all Nations there shall find.
  They are some great, some little, as we see;
To shew, some great, some small, in Glory be.

Their flying diversly, as we behold;
Do shew Saints Joys will there be manifold.
    Some glide, some mount, some flutter, and some do,
In a mixt way of flying, glory too.
And all to shew each Saint, to his content,
Shall roul and tumble in that Firmament.

## XLIV

### Upon a Penny Loaf.

T HY PRICE one Penny is, in time of Plenty;
In Famine doubled 'tis, from one to twenty.
Yea, no man knows what Price on thee to set,
When there is but one Penny Loaf to get.

#### COMPARISON.

This Loaf's an Emblem of the Word of God,
A thing of low Esteem, before the Rod
Of Famine smites the Soul with Fear of Death:
But then it is our All, our Life, our Breath.

## XLV

### Upon the Vine-tree.

W HAT IS THE Vine, more than another Tree,
Nay most, than it, more tall, more comly be?
What Work-man thence will take a Beam or Pin,
To make ought which may be delighted in?
    *It's Excellency in it's Fruit doth lie.*
    *A fruitless Vine! It is not worth a Fly.*

#### COMPARISON.

What are Professors more than other men?
Nothing at all. Nay, there's not one in ten,
Either for Wealth, or Wit, that may compare,
In many things, with some that Carnal are.
Good are they, if they mortifie their Sin;
But without that they are not worth a Pin.

## X L V I

### *The Boy and Watch-maker.*

THIS WATCH my Father did on me bestow,
A Golden one it is, but 'twill not go,
Unless it be at an Uncertainty;
But as good none, as one to tell a Lye.
   When 'tis high Day, my Hand will stand at nine;
I think there's no man's Watch so bad as mine.
Sometimes 'tis sullen, 'twill not go at all,
And yet 'twas never broke, nor had a Fall.

WATCH-MAKER.

   Your Watch, tho it be good, through want of skill,
May fail to do according to your will.
Suppose the Ballance, Wheels, and Spring be good,
And all things else, unless you understood
To manage it, as Watches ought to be,
Your Watch will still be at Uncertainty.
Come, tell me, do you keep it from the Dust?
Yea wind it also duly up you must.
Take heed (too) that you do not strain the String;
You must be circumspect in ev'ry thing.
Or else your Watch, were it as good again,
Would not with Time, and Tide you entertain.

COMPARISON.

This Boy an Emblem is of a Convert;
His Watch of th'work of Grace within his heart.
The Watch-maker is Jesus Christ our Lord,
His Counsel, the Directions of his Word.
Then Convert, if thy heart be out of frame,
Of this Watch-maker learn to mend the same.
   Do not lay ope'thy heart to Worldly Dust,
Nor let thy Graces over-grow with Rust.
Be oft renew'd in th' Spirit of thy mind,
Or else uncertain thou thy Watch wilt find.

## X L V I I

### *Upon the Boy and his Paper of Plumbs.*

WHAT HAST THOU there, my pretty Boy?

Plumbs? How? Yes, Sir, a Paper full.
I thought 'twas so, because with Joy
Thou didst them out thy Paper pull.
   The Boy goes from me, eats his Plumbs,
Which he counts better of than Bread:
But by and by he to me comes,
With nought but Paper and the Thread.

### COMPARISON.

This Boy an Emblem is of such,
Whose Lot in worldly things doth lie:
Glory they in them ne'er so much,
Their pleasant Springs will soon be dry.
   Their Wealth, their Health, Honours and Life,
Will quickly to a period come;
If for these, is their only Strife,
They soon will not be worth a Plumb.

## X L V I I I

## *Upon a Looking-glass.*

In THIS, see thou thy Beauty, hast thou any:
Or thy defects, should they be few or many.
Thou mayst (too) here thy Spots and Freckles see,
Hast thou but Eyes, and what their Numbers be.
But art thou Blind, there is no Looking Glass,
Can shew thee thy defects, thy Spots, or Face.

### COMPARISON.

Unto this Glass we may compare the Word,
For that to man advantage doth afford,
(Has he a Mind to know himself and State;)
To see what will be his Eternal Fate.
   But without Eyes, alas! How can he see?
Many that seem to look here, blind Men be.
This is the Reason, they so often read,
Their Judgment there, and do it nothing dread.

## X L I X

## *Upon a Lanthorn.*

The LANTHORN is to keep the Candle Light,

When it is windy, and a darksome Night.
Ordain'd it also was, that men might see
By Night their Day, and so in safety be.

COMPARISON.

Compare we now our Lanthorn to the man,
That has within his heart a Work of Grace.
As for another let him, if he can,
Do as this Lanthorn, in its time and place:
   Profess the Faith, and thou a Lanthorn art:
But yet if Grace has not possessed thee:
Thou want'st this Candle Light within thy heart,
And art none other, than dark Lanthorns be.

L

## *Of the Love of Christ.*

THE LOVE OF Christ, poor I! may touch upon
But 'tis unsearchable. Oh! There is none
It's large Dimensions can comprehend,
Should they dilate thereon, World without end.
   When we had sinned, in his Zeal he sware,
That he upon his back our Sins would bear.
And since unto Sin is entailed Death,
He vowed, for our Sins he'd lose his Breath.
   He did not only say, vow, or resolve,
But to Astonishment did so involve
Himself, in man's distress and misery,
As for, and with him, both to live and dye.
   To his eternal Fame, in Sacred Story,
We find that he did lay aside his Glory.
Step'd from the Throne of highest Dignity;
Become poor Man, did in a Manger lie;
Yea was beholding unto his for Bread;
Had, of his own, not where to lay his Head.
Tho rich, he did, for us, become thus poor,
That he might make us rich for evermore.
   Nor was this but the least of what he did,
But the outside of what he suffered
God made his Blessed Son under the Law;
Under the Curse, which, like the Lyon's Paw,
Did rent and tear his Soul, for mankinds Sin,
More than if we for it in Hell had bin.

His Crys, his Tears, and Bloody Agony,
The nature of his Death, doth testify.
     Nor did he of Constraint himself thus give,
For Sin, to death, that man might with him live.
He did do what he did most willingly,
He sung, and gave God Thanks, that he must dye.
     But do Kings use to dye for Captive Slaves?
Yet we were such, when Jesus dy'd to save's.
     Yea, when he made himself a Sacrifice,
It was that he might save his Enemies.
     And, tho he was provoked to retract
His blest Resolves, for such, so good an Act,
By the abusive Carriages of those
That did both him, his Love, and Grace oppose:
Yet he, as unconcerned with such-things,
Goes on, determines to make Captives Kings.
Yea, many of his Murderers he takes
Into his Favour, and them Princes makes.


## L I

### *Of the Horse and Drum.*

Some horses will, some can't endure the Drum,
But snort and flounce, if it doth near them come.
They will, nor Bridle nor Rider obey,
But head strong be, and fly out of the way.
     These skittish Jades, that can't this noise abide,
Nor will be rul'd by him that doth them ride;
I do compare those our Professors to,
Which start from Godliness in Tryals do.
To these, the threats that are against them made,
Are like this Drum to this our starting Jade.
They are offended at them and forsake
Christ, of whose ways they did Profession make.
     But, as I said, there other Horses be,
That from a Drum will neither start, nor flee.
Let Drummers beat a Charge, or what they will,
They'l nose them, face them, keep their places still.
They fly not when they to those rattlings come,
But like War-Horses do endure the Drum.

### L I I

## On the Kackling of a Hen.

THE HEN so soon as she an Egg doth lay,
(Spreads the Fame of her doing what she may.)
  About the Yard she kackling now doth go,
To tell what 'twas she at her Nest did do.

  Just thus it is with some Professing men,
If they do ought that good is, like our Hen,
They can't but kackle on't, where 'ere they go,
What their right hand doth, their left hand must know.

### L I I I

## Upon an Hour-Glass.

THIS GLASS when made, was by the Work mans Skill,
The Sum of sixty minutes to fulfill.
Time more, nor less, by it will out be spun,
But just an Hour, and then the Glass is run.

  Man's Life, we will compare unto this Glass,
The Number of his Months he cannot pass;
But when he has accomplished his day,
He, like a Vapour, vanisheth away.

### L I V

## Upon the Chalk-stone.

THIS STONE is white, yea, warm, and also soft,
Easie to work upon, unless 'tis naught.
It leaves a white Impression upon those,
Whom it doth touch, be they it's Friends or Foes.

  The Child of God, is like to this Chalk-stone,
White in his Life, easily wrought upon:
Warm in Affections, apt to leave impress,
On whom he deals with, of true Godliness.

He is no sulling Coal, nor daubing Pitch,
Nor one of whom men catch the Scab, or Itch;
But such who in the Law of God doth walk,
Tender of heart, in Life whiter than Chalk.

## L V

### Upon a Stinking Breath.

DOTH THIS proceed from an infected Air?
Or from a man's common, sweet and wholesome Fare?
It comes from a foul Stomack, or what's worse,
Ulcerous Lungs, Teeth, or a private Curse.

To this, I some mens Notions do Compare,
Who seem to breathe in none but Scripture Air.
They suck it in, but breathe it out again,
So putrified, that it doth scarce retain
Any thing of its native Excellence.
It only serves to fix the Pestilence
Of their delusive Notions, in the mind
Of the next foolish Proselyte they find.

## L V I

### Upon Death.

DEATH'S A COLD Comforter to Girls and Boys,
Who wedded are unto their Childish Toys:
More Grim he looks upon our lustful Youth,
    Who, against Knowledge, slight God's saving Truth:
But most of all, he dismal is to those,
Who once profess'd the Truth, they now oppose.
    Death has a Dart, a Sting, which Poyson is,
As all will find, who do of Glory miss.
This Sting is Sin, the Laws it's Strength, and he,
Or they, will find it so, who damned be.
    True, Jesus Christ, indeed, did Death destroy,
For those who worthy are, him to enjoy.
He washes them in's Blood from ev'ry Sin
They'r guilty of, or subject to hath bin.
So here's, nor Sting, nor Law, nor Death to kill,

And yet Death always, some men torment will.
    But this seems Het'rodox or Mystery,
For Death to live to some, to some to dye;
Yet 'tis so, when God doth man's Sin forgive,
Death dies, but where 'tis charged, Death doth live.


## LVII

### *Upon the Snail.*

SHE GOES BUT softly, but she goeth sure,
She stumbles not, as stronger Creatures do:
IIer Journeys shorter, so she may endure,
Better than they which do much further go.
    She makes no noise, but stilly seizeth on
The Flow'r or Herb, appointed for her food
The which she quietly doth feed upon,
While others range, and gare, but find no good.
    And tho she doth but very softly go,
How ever 'tis not fast, nor slow but sure;
And certainly they that do travel so,
The prize they do aim at, they do procure.

#### COMPARISON.

Although they seem not much to stir, less go,
For Christ that hunger, or from Wrath, that flee;
Yet what they seek for, quickly thy come to,
Tho it doth seem the farthest off to be.
    One Act of Faith doth bring them to that Flow'r,
They so long for, that they may eat and live;
Which to attain is not in others Pow'r.
Tho for it a King's Ransom they would give.
    Then let none faint, nor be at all dismaid,
That Life by Christ do seek, they shall not fail
To have it, let them nothing be afraid;
The Herb, and Flow'r is eaten by the Snail.


## LVIII

### *Of the Spouse of Christ.*

WHO'S THIS that cometh from the Wilderness,
Like Smoaky Pillars, thus perfumed with Myrrhe

Leaning upon her dearest in Distress,
Led into's Bosom, by the Comforter?
   She's clothed with the Sun, crown'd with twelve Stars,
The spotted Moon her Footstool he hath made.
The Dragon her assaults, fills her with Jarrs,
Yet rests she under her Beloved's Shade.
   But whence was she? What is her Pedigree?
Was not her Father, a poor *Amorite*?
What was her Mother, but as others be,
A poor, a wretched and sinful *Hittite*!
   Yea, as for her, the day that she was born,
As loathsome, out of doors, they did her cast;
Naked, and Filthy, Stinking, and forlorn:
This was her Pedigree from first to last.
   Nor was she pittied in this Estate;
All let her lie polluted in her Blood:
None her Condition did commiserate,
Their was no Heart that sought to do her good.
   Yet she unto these Ornaments is come,
Her Breasts are fashioned, her Hair is grown;
She is made Heiress of the best Kingdom;
All her Indignities away are blown.
   Cast out she was, but now she home is taken,
Naked (sometimes) but now you see she's clo'd;
Now made the Darling, though before forsaken,
Bare-foot, but now, as Princes Daughters, shod.
   Instead of Filth, she now has her Perfumes,
Instead of Ignominy, her Chains of Gold:
Instead of what the Beauty most consumes,
Her Beauty's perfect, lovely to behold.
   Those that attend, and wait upon her, be
Princes of Honour, cloth'd in white Aray,
Upon her Head's a Crown of Gold, and she
Eats Wheat, Honey, and Oil, from day to day.
   For her Beloved, he's the High'st of all,
The only Potentate, the King of Kings:
Angels, and Men, do him *Jehovah* call,
And from him, Life, and Glory, always springs.
   He's white, and ruddy, and of all the Chief;
His Head, his Locks, his Eyes, his Hands, and Feet,
Do for Compleatness out-go all Belief;
His checks like Flowers are, his Mouth's most sweet.
   As for his Wealth he is made Heir of all,
What is in Heav'n, what is on Earth, is his:
And he this Lady, his Joynt-Heir, doth call,
Of all that shall be, or at present is.

Well Lady, well, God has been good to thee,
Thou, of an Out-cast, now art made a Queen.
Few or none may with thee compared be;
A Beggar made thus high is seldome seen.
Take heed of Pride, remember what thou art,
By Nature, tho thou hast in Grace a share:
Thou in thy self doth yet retain a part
Of thine own Filthiness, wherefore beware.


## L I X

### *Upon a Skilful Player on an Instrument.*

He that can play well on an Instrument,
Will take the Ear, and captivate the Mind,
With Mirth, or Sadness: For that *it* is bent
Thereto as Musick, in it, place doth find.
    But if one hears that hath therein no skill,
(As often Musick lights of such a chance)
Of its brave Notes, they soon be weary will;
And there are some can neither sing nor dance.


COMPARISON.

Unto him that thus skilfully doth play,
God doth compare a Gospel-Minister,
That rightly preacheth (and doth Godly pray)
Applying truly what doth thence infer.
    This man, whether of Wrath or Grace he preach,
So skilfully doth handle ev'ry Word;
And by his Saying, doth the heart so reach,
That it doth joy or sigh before the Lord.
    But some there be, which, as the Bruit, doth lie
Under the Word, without the least advance
God-ward: Such do despise the Ministry,
They weep not at it, neither to it dance.


## L X

### *Upon Fly-blows.*

There is good Meat provided for man's Health.
To this the Flesh fly comes, as twere by Stealth

Bloweth thereon, and so *Be-maggots* it,
As that it is, tho wholsome, quite unfit
For queazy Stomachs, they must pass it by:
Now is not this a prejudicial Fly?

### COMPARISON.

Let this good Meat, good Doctrine signify,
And call him which reproaches it, this Fly.
For as this Flesh-fly blows this wholsome meat,
That it the queazy Stomach cannot eat:
So they which do good Doctrine scandalize,
Present it unto some in such Disguize;
That they cannot accept, nor with it close,
But slight it, and themselves to Death expose.
Reproach it then, thou art a mauling Club,
This Fly, yea, and the Son of *Belzebub*.

## L X I

### *Of Man by Nature.*

FROM GOD he's a Back slider,
Of Ways, he loves the wider;
With Wickedness a Sider,
More Venom than a Spider.
   In Sin he's a Confider,
A Make-bate, and Divider;
Blind Reason is his Guider,
The Devil is his Rider.

## L X I I

### *Of Physick.*

PURGING PHYSICK, taken to heat or cool.
Worketh by Vomit, Urine, Sweat or Stool;
But if it worketh not, then we do fear
The danger's great, the Person's Death is near.
If more be added, and it worketh not;

And more, and yet the same's the Patients Lot.
All hope of Life from Standers-by is fled,
The Party sick is counted now as dead.

## COMPARISON.

Count ye the Sick, one that's not yet converted,
Impenitent, Incredulous, Hard hearted:
In whom vile Sin is so predominant,
And the Soul in it's Acts so conversant;
That like one with Diseases over-run,
This man with it at present is undone.
   Now let the Physick be the Holy Word,
(The Blessed Doctrine of our Dearest Lord.)
And let the Doses to the Patient given
Be, by Directions of the God of Heaven.
Convincing Sermons, sharp and sound Rebukes,
Let them be Beggars, Knights, Lords, Earls or Dukes:
You must not spare them, Life doth lie at Stake,
And dye they will, if Physick they don't take.
   If these do finely work, then let them have
Directions unto him that can them save.
Lay open then the Riches of his Grace,
And Merits of his Blood before their Face.
Shew them likewise, how free he is to give
His Justice unto them, that they may live.
If they will doubt, and not your Word believe,
Shew them, at present they have a Reprieve;
On purpose they might out their Pardon sue,
And have the Glory of it in their view.
   Instances of this Goodness set before,
Their Eyes, that they this Mercy may adore.
And if this Physick taken worketh well,
Fear not a Cure, you save a Soul from Hell.
   But if these Doses do not kindly work,
If the Disease still in their Mind doth lurk:
If they instead of throwing up their Vice,
Do vomit up the Word, loath Paradice:
Repeat the Potion, them new Doses give,
Which are much stronger, perhaps they may live:
But if they serve these as they serv'd the rest,
And thou perceiv'st it is not to them Blest:
If they remain incorrigible still,
And will the Number of their Sins fulfill;
The Holy Text doth say that they must dye;
Yea, and be damned without Remedy.

## LXIII

### *Upon a Pair of Spectacles.*

SPECTACLES ARE for Sight, and not for Shew,
Necessity doth Spectacles commend;
Was't not for need, there is but very few,
That would for wearing Spectacles contend.
    We use to count them very dark indeed,
Whose Eyes so dim are, that they cannot be
Helped by Spectacles; such men have need
A Miracle be wrought to make them see.


#### COMPARISON.

Compare Spectacles to God's Ordinances,
For they present us with his Heav'nly Things;
Which else we could not see for hinderances,
That from our dark and foolish Nature springs.
    If this be so, what shall we say of them,
Who at God's Ordinances scoff and jear?
They do those Blessed Spectacles condemn,
By which Divine Things are made to appear.


## LXIV

### *Upon our being so afraid of small Creatures.*

MAN BY CREATION was made Lord of all,
But now he is become an Underling;
He thought he should a gained by his Fall,
But lost his Head-ship over ev'ry thing.
    What! What! A humane Creature and afraid
Of Frogs, Dogs, Cats, Rats, Mice, or such like Creature?
This fear of thine has fully thee betraid,
Thou art Back-slid from God, to him a Traytor.
    How by his Fall is stately Man decay'd?
Nor is it in his hand now to renew him,
Of things dismaid, at him, he is afraid;
Worms, Lice, Flies, Mice; Yea Vanities subdue him.

## L X V

### *Upon our being afraid of the Apparition of Evil Spirits.*

SOME FEAR MORE the Appearance of the Devil,
Than the Commission of the greatest Evil.
They start, they tremble, if they think he's near,
But can't be pleased unless Sin appear.
These Birds, the Fowler's Presence doth afright,
To be among his Lime twigs, they delight.
But, just men who have with the Devil bin.
Have been more safe, than some in Heav'n with Sin.

## L X V I

### *Upon the Disobedient Child.*

CHILDREN BECOME, while little, our delights,
When they grow bigger, they begin to fright's
Their sinful Nature prompts them to rebel,
And to delight in Paths that lead to Hell.
Their Parents Love, and Care, they overlook,
As if Relation had them quite forsook.
They take the Counsels of the Wanton's rather,
Then the most grave Instructions of a Father.
They reckon Parents ought to do for them,
Tho they the Fifth Commandment contemn.
They snap, and snarl, if Parents them controul,
Tho but in things, most hurtful to the Soul.
They reckon they are Masters, and that we,
Who Parents are, should to them Subject be!
If Parents fain would have a hand in chusing,
The Children have a heart will in refusing.
They'l by wrong doings, under Parents, gather
And say, it is no Sin to rob a Father.
They'l jostle Parents out of place and Pow'r,
They'l make themselves the Head, and them devour.
How many Children, by becoming Head,
Have brought their Parents to a peice of Bread?
Thus they who at the first were Parents Joy,
Turn that to Bitterness, themselves destroy.
  But Wretched Child, how canst thou thus requite

Thy Aged Parents, for that great delight
They took in thee, when thou, as helpless lay
In their Indulgent Bosoms day by day?
Thy Mother, long before she brought thee forth,
Took care thou should'st want, neither Food, nor Cloth.
Thy Father glad was at his very heart,
Had he, to thee, a Portion to impart.
Comfort they promised themselves in thee,
But thou, it seems, to them a Grief wil't be.
How oft! How willingly brake they their Sleep,
If thou, their Bantling, didst but whinch or weep.
Their Love to thee was such, they could have giv'n,
That thou might'st live, almost, their part of Heav'n.
  But now, behold, how they rewarded are!
For their Indulgent Love, and tender Care,
All is forgot, this Love he doth despise,
They brought this Bird up to pick out their Eyes.


## L X V I I

### Upon the Boy on his Hobby-horse.

Look how he swaggers, cocks his Hat and rides,
How on his Hobby-horse, himself he prides:
He looketh grim, and up his Head doth toss,
Says he'l ride over's with his Hobby-horse.

#### COMPARISON.

Some we see mounted upon the *Conceit*
That their Wit, Wealth, or Beauty is so great:
But few their Equals may with them compare,
Who yet more Godly, Wise, and Honest are.
Behold how *huff*, how big they look; how high
They lift their heads, as if they'd touch the Skie:
Nor will they count these things, for Christ, a loss
So long as they do ride *this* Hobby-horse.


## L X V I I I

### Upon the Image in the Eye.

Who looks upon another stedfastly,
Shall forthwith have his Image in his eye.

Dost thou believe in Jesus? (Hast that Art?)
Thy Faith will place his Image in thy heart.


## L X I X

### *Upon the Weather cock.*

Brave, weather-cock, I see thou't set thy Nose,
Against the Wind, which way so 'ere it blows:
So let a Christian in any wise,
Face it with Antichrist in each disguize.


## L X X

### *Upon a Sheet of white Paper.*

This subject is unto the foulest Pen,
Or fairest, handled by the Sons of Men.
'Twill also shew what is upon it writ,
Be't wisely, or non-sence, for want of wit.
Each blot, and blur, it also will expose,
To thy next Readers, be they Friends, or Foes.

#### COMPARISON.
Some Souls are like unto this Blank or Sheet,
 (Tho not in Whiteness:)  the next man they meet;
If wise, or Fool, debauched, or Deluder,
Or what you will, the dangerous Intruder
May write thereon, to cause that man to err,
In Doctrine, or in Life, with blot and blur.
   Nor will that Soul conceal from who observes,
But shew how foul it is, wherein it swerves:
A reading man may know who was the Writer,
And by the Hellish Non-sence, the Inditer.


## L X X I

### *Upon the Boy dull at his Book.*

Some boys have Wit enough to sport and play,
Who at their Books are Block-heads day by day.

Some men are arch enough at any Vice,
But Dunces in the way to Paradice.


## LXXII

### Upon Time and Eternity.

ETERNITY IS like unto a Ring.
Time, like to Measure, doth it self extend;
Measure commences, is a finite thing,
The Ring has no beginning, middle, end.


## LXXIII

### Upon Fire.

WHO FALLS into the Fire shall burn with heat;
While those remote scorn from it to retreat.
Yea while those in it, cry out, oh! I burn,
Some farther off those crys to Laughter turn.

COMPARISON.
While some tormented are in Hell for sin;
On Earth some greatly do delight therein.
Yea while some make it eccho with their Cry,
Others count it a Fable and a Lye.


## LXXIV

### Of Beauty.

BEAUTY, AT BEST is but as fading Flow'rs,
Bright now, anon with darksome Clouds it low'rs.
'Tis but skin-deep, and therefore must decay;
Times blowing on it, sends it quite away.
    Then why should it be, as it is, admired,
By one and to'ther, and so much desired.
Things flitting we should moderately use,
Or we by them our selves shall much abuse.

# THE CONTENTS

44. *Upon a Penny Loaf.*
45. *Upon the Vine-tree.*
46. *The Boy and Watch-maker.*
47. *Upon the Boy and his Paper of Plumbs.*
48. *Upon a Looking-glass.*
49. *Upon a Lanthorn.*
50. *Of the Love of Christ.*
51. *Of the Horse and Drum.*
52. *On the Kackling of a Hen.*
53. *Upon an Hour Glass.*
54. *Upon the Chalk-stone.*
55. *Upon a Stinking Breath.*
56. *Upon Death.*
57. *Upon the Snail.*
58. *Of the Spouse of Christ.*
59. *Upon a Skilful Player on an Instrument.*
60. *Upon Fly-blows.*
61. *Of Man by Nature.*
62. *Of Physick.*
63. *Upon a Pair of Spectacles.*
64. *Upon our being afraid of small Creatures.*
65. *Upon our being afraid of the Apparition of Evil Spirits.*
66. *Upon the Disobedient Child.*
67. *Upon the Boy on his Hobby-horse.*
68. *Upon the Image in the Eye.*
69. *Upon the Weather-cock.*
70. *Upon a Sheet of white Paper.*
71. *Upon the Boy dull at his Book.*
72. *Upon Time and Eternity.*
73. *Upon Fire.*
74. *Of Beauty.*

FINIS.

# "A Hymm Sung as by the Shepherds"
## From In the Holy Nativity Of Our Lord God
### By RICHARD CRASHAW

RICHARD CRASHAW *(1612–1649) was an Anglican who turned Roman Catholic. He was exiled from England for his beliefs and died a priest at the shrine of Loretto in Italy. His poetry is sensuous and mystical—in it he evokes his intense love for Heaven, St. Theresa, and all beings in the spiritual world. Below is reprinted the chorus—"A Hymn Sung as by the Shepherds"—from the poem, "In the Holy Nativity of Our Lord God." Two shepherds are singing with child-like piety of the birth of Jesus.*

## THE HYMN

**CHORUS.**

COME WE shepherds whose blest Sight
Hath met love's Noon in Nature's night;
   Come lift up our loftier Song
And wake the *Sun* that lies too long.

To all our world of well-stoll'n joy
   He slept; and dreamt of no such thing.
While we found out Heav'n's fairer eye
   And Kist the Cradle of our *King.*
Tell him He rises now, too late
To show us aught worth looking at.

Tell him we now can show Him more
   Then He e'er show'd to mortal Sight;
Then he Himself e'er saw before;
   Which to be seen needs not His light.
Tell him, Tityrus, where th'hast been
Tell him, Thyrsis, what th'hast seen.

**TITYRUS.**

Gloomy night embrac't the Place
   Where The Noble Infant lay.
The *Babe* look't up and show'd his Face;
   In spite of Darkness, it was *Day.*
It was *Thy* day, *Sweet!* and did rise
Not from the *East,* but from thine *Eyes.*

**CHORUS.**

It was *Thy* day, *Sweet,* &c.

**THYRSIS.**

*Winter* chid aloud; and sent
   The angry North to wage his wars.
The North forgot his fierce Intent;
   And left perfumes instead of scars.
By those sweet eyes' persuasive pow'rs
Where he meant frost, he scatter'd flow'rs.

315

CHORUS.

By those sweet eyes', &c.

BOTH.

We saw thee in thy balmy Nest,
     Young dawn of our eternal *Day!*
We saw thine eyes break from their *East*
     And chase the trembling shades away.
We saw thee; and we blest the sight
We saw thee by thine own sweet light.

TITYRUS.

Poor *World* (said I.) what wilt thou do
     To entertain this starry *Stranger?*
Is this the best thou canst bestow?
     A cold, and not too cleanly, manger?
Contend, ye powers of heav'n and earth
To fit a bed for this huge birth.

CHORUS.

Contend, ye powers, &c.

THYRSIS.

Proud world, said I; cease your contest
     And let the *Mighty Babe* alone.
The Phœnix builds the Phœnix' nest.
     Love's architecture is his own.
The *Babe* whose birth embraves this morn,
Made his own bed ere he was born.

CHORUS.

The *Babe* whose, &c.

TITYRUS.

I saw the curl'd drops, soft and slow,
     Come hovering o'er the place's head;
Offring their whitest sheets of snow
     To furnish the fair *Infant's* bed:
Forbear, said I; be not too bold.

Your fleece is white But 'tis too cold.

CHORUS.

Forbear, said we, &c.

THYRSIS.

I saw the obsequious *Seraphims*
     Their rosy fleece of fire bestow.
For well they now can spare their wings
     Since *Heav'n* itself lies here below.
Well done, said I: but are you sure
Your down so warm, will pass for pure?

CHORUS.

Well done, said we, &c.

TITYRUS.

No no, your *King's* not yet to seek
     Where to repose his Royal *Head.*
See see, how soon his new bloom'd *Cheek*
     Twixt's mother's breasts is gone to bed.
Sweet choice, said I! no way but so
Not to lie cold, yet sleep in snow.

CHORUS.

Sweet choice, said we, &c.

BOTH.

We saw thee in thy balmy nest,
     Bright dawn of our eternal Day!
We saw thine eyes break from their *East*
     And chase the trembling shades away.
We saw thee: and we blest the sight.
We saw thee, by thine own sweet light.

CHORUS.

We saw thee, &c.

# FULL CHORUS

Welcome, all *Wonders* in one sight!
  Eternity shut in a span.
Summer in Winter. Day in Night.
  Heaven in earth, and *God* in *Man*.
Great little one! whose all-embracing birth
Lifts earth to heaven, stoops heav'n to
    earth.

*Welcome.* Though not to gold nor silk,
  To more than Cæsar's birthright is;
Two sister-seas of Virgin-Milk,
  With many a rarely-temper'd kiss
That breathes at once both *Maid* and
    *Mother,*
Warms in the one, cools in the other.

*Welcome.* Though not to those gay flies,
  Guided i'th' Beams of earthly kings;
Slippery souls in smiling eyes;
  But to poor Shepherds, home-spun
      things:
Whose Wealth's their flock; whose wit,
    to be
  Well read in their simplicity.
Yet when young April's husband show'rs
  Shall bless the fruitful Maia's bed
We'll bring the First-born of her flow'rs
  To kiss thy *Feet* and crown thy *Head.*
To thee, dread lamb! whose love must
    keep
  The shepherds, more than they the
      sheep.
To *Thee*, meek Majesty! soft *King*
  Of simple *Graces* and sweet *Loves.*
Each of us his lamb will bring
  Each his pair of silver Doves;
Till burnt at last in fire of Thy fair eyes,
  Ourselves become our own best
      *Sacrifice.*

# The Holy Bible;
# Containing, The Old and New
# Testaments, With The Apocrypha

## Done into Verse by B. H. for the Benefit of Weak Memories

T HIS CHARMING—*and extremely rare—little book was prepared and published by Benjamin Harris in London in 1698. According to Wilbur Macey Stone (Library Journal, March 1, 1938), this Benjamin Harris is believed to be the same man who compiled and published* The New England Primer, *so influential in establishing strong moral attitudes among American children of the eighteenth and nineteenth centuries.*

*Miniature Bibles were popular in the seventeenth, eighteenth, and early nineteenth centuries. The copy reproduced in this volume is in the possession of the Ross County Historical Society Museum, Chillicothe, Ohio.*

*Aside from instances where the poet falters, the entire book is in rhymed tetrameter couplets. The miracle lies in how the poet manages to squeeze both the Old and New Testament into so small a space and yet retain so much of the essence and flavor of the larger work. Lacking the dignity, inevitably, of the King James version, still a certain wholesome meekness and absolute faith sustain it.*

*Because of the tight binding, it is difficult at times to see words in the gutters of pages, but much of the text can be followed fairly easily.*

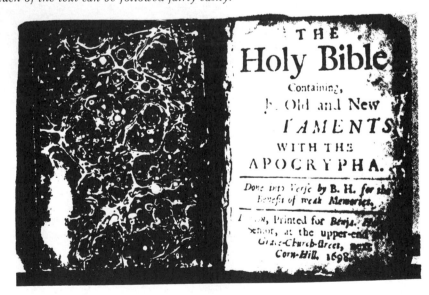

## The Introduction.

OH! Holy *Trinity*, afford
  *Grace* to *epitomize* thy *Word*;
Else, Lord, at best, 'twill only be
A *Blot* on thy *Divinity*.
  Oh! blessed Father, God of might,
Be thou the *Pen*, the same to *Write*;
The *stand-dish*, Lord, be thou, the which
Contains a *Crimson-Ink*, more rich
Than *Kedar*'s *Tents* of *Solomon*,
Even the *blood* of God's *dear Son*.
The *Paper* let thy *Spirit* be;
Which *Ink* will bear t'Eternity.
Now, that the *Reader*'s Soul may find
*Health* in Body, *Peace* in Mind;
Lord! let no *Unbelief* deter it,
From closing with thy *blessed Spirit*.
  Which is the hearty Desire
          and Prayer of *E. H.*
                              The

## Christian Reader.

WHoe'er thou art, of what Per-
  *suasion* soever, surely thou hast
*some secret Respect* for any thing which
*favours of the Oracles of God*. Lo!
here thou hast a Smell of that Garden
of *Spices*; would to God it may Ra-
vish thy Heart so far, as to drive thee
ev'ry Morning to pluck a Flower
therefrom. Christian, Read it with
*gravity*, and you'll find it an excellent *Antidote* for a weak Memory.
And that it may make thee turn Be-
rean, and drive thee the more to its
*Sacred Original*, that thy Name may
be *Writ* in the *Lamb's Book of Life*,
is the Sincere Prayer of thine,

              B. Harris, *Junior*.
                          *Genesis*

### The Holy Bible.

How *Paradise* is planted, and
*Adam* is made t'enjoy the Land;
And God, because he was alone,
Makes him a *Help-meet of his Bone*
Who is deceiv'd, oh! worst of all!
From whence derives Man's shameful
But yet, by Heaven, 'tis decreed (fall.
That *Christ* shall pay for Man's misdeed.
  *Cain* Murders *Abel*, and his blood
To God for Vengeance cries aloud.
Man's wickedness is very great,
For which a Deluge God does threat;
The *Deluge* comes, and all are drown'd
Save only Eight, who *Mercy* found.
God's Covenant with *Noah*, and
How he replenisheth the Land.
*Noah* is drunk, and naked lies;
Which shameless *Ham*, his *Son* espies;
                              His

### The Holy Bible.

His Father's Nakedness discovers,
Immediately unto his Brothers;
*For which he's Curst, his Brothers Bless*
Old *Noah* dies, and goes to rest.
*Abra'm* for *Sodom* doth intercede
Five times with God, yet cannot speed;
Angels of Righteous *Lot* take care
Who with his *Daughters* saved are,
*His Wife turns back, and for that fault*
A Pillar she is made of Salt.
  *Joseph* is sold to *Egypt*, and
By *Pharaoh* he's made Lord o'th' Land.
*Israel* goes down with's Family,
To see his Son, and there doth dye.
*Joseph* grows old, and also dy'd.

### Exodus.

Then *Israel's* Children multiply'd
                    A 4              So.

### The Holy Bible.

So fast that *Pharaoh's* heart's on fire,
Who does command to drown the Male
But *Moses* God preserves, that he
From Bondage should all *Israel* free,
And *Pharaoh's* heart God hardens so;
That he'll not let his People go.
Then Plagues from Heav'n in number
Destroy'd a multitude of Men: (ten,
The *Israelites* are freed at last.
And o'er the *Red Sea* safely past.
But *Pharaoh* thinking to surround
Them, he, and's host, are therein drown'd.
The Holy Law is writ in Stone;
To guide Men to the *great Three-one.*
The Ceremonies in this Word,
Are Types of Jesus Christ our *Lord.*

### The Holy Bible.
### Leviticus.

This *Book* contains th'*Almighty's will*,
To love what's *good*, and punish *ill*;
*And 'cause that Men are apt to stray,*
It tells them how their God t'obey.
The Levites are appointed; who
Must Preach *the Word his Flock unto.*

### Numbers.

*Moses* the People numbers so,
That every Tribe to War must go.
The *Israelites* to murm'ring take;
Which does *Jehovah* angry make;
*Korah, Abiram,* and proud *Dathan,*
Are swallow'd up for Recantation,
And *Og,* and *Sihon's* Faithless King,
The *Israelites* to ruin bring.
An Ass doth *Balaam* here detain,
From being by an Angel slain.

## The Holy Bible.

The *Israelites* are strong in might,
And with five *Million Monarchs* fight.
They kill them all, and have access
Unto the Land of Blessedness.

## Deuteronomy.

The Law of God repeated i,
That Men no more may do amiss
Then Heav'n born *Moses* meekly di.
And in a Tomb unknown he lies.

## Joshua.

Next *Joshua* the Son of Nun
Immediately supplies his room:
Who does obtain from *Heaven high*,
Th' Instructions of God's Majesty.
Then *Joshua* with Courage great,
O'er *Jordan*'s River goeth strait:
The City *Jericho* they all
Encompass, till down falls the Wall.

Next

## The Holy Bible.

Next *Israel* doth lose the Day,
And *Achan* steals the Wedge away.
*Five Kings are hang'd, the Sun stands*
'Till Joshua he his Foes does kill. (still
*And one and thirty Kings were slain,*
'Fore *Israel* did in Peace obtain
*Their Land: and then their peace drew*
*In which blest* Joshua *does die. (nigh,*

## Judges.

But then the *Israelites* Rebel,
For which God's Judgments on them fell.
And *Deborah* (with *Barak*) does
Deliver *Israel* from its Foes : (*Jael,*
*And Heber*'s Wife, who nam'd was
Thro *Sisera*'s *Temple* drove a Nail.
*Jephtha* does make a Vow to God,
And offers up his *Daughters blood.*

Samp-

## The Holy Bible.

*Sampson* is born, a Man of might,
And with a Lyon he does fight ;
He Marries, and a Riddle's told,
For the Philistines to unfold:
He by his *Dalilah*'s betray'd,
And so the Riddle known is made.
*Sampson* to *Askelon* down goes,
And killeth *Thirty* of his Foes.
Three Hundred *Foxes*, tail to tail,
With *Fire* does their *Corn* assail ;
And with an *Asses* Jaw-bone then,
He slew compleat a Thousand men.
*Sampson* to *Geza* quick escapes,
And carries thence away the *Gates,*
The *Philistines* with's Wife devise,
To take him, and put out his Eyes :
Which Cruel act he did repay,
For he *Three Thousand* more did slay.

Ruth.

## The Holy Bible.
## Ruth.

*Ruth* tho' she is a *Moabite,*
Yet constant is in doing right ;
Serving the *Lord*, who makes her life
Happy, in being *Boaz*'s Wife.

## Samuel I.

*Hannah* does bear a Prophet, who
She Dedicates, the Lord unto :
But *Eli*'s Sons, they do Transgress,
By acting grievous Wickedness ;
Cause *Isra'l* doth their God forsake,
The *Philistines* the *Ark* do take.
And *Saul* in seeking *Asses*, sped
Far better by a Crowned Head.
The Lord did *Samuel* appoint,
*David*, the Son of *Jesse* t' Anoint.
*Goliah* with a mighty Host,
Over the *Israelites* do Boast :

## The Holy Bible

But *David* with a Sling and Stone,
Made great *Goliah* tumble down.
*Saul* envieth *David*, and his will
With fury seeks his Blood to spill.
*Sauls* hatred now comes on apace,
And *David's* Glory does encreafe.
*David* has power in the *Cave*,
To kill K. *Saul* but does him fave.
The *Philiftines* obtain the Day,
And *Saul* and's Sons in Battle flay.

### Samuel II.

*David* a Lamentation
Doth make o'er, *Saul* and *Jonathan*,
He's Crowned King, and up he goes
To *Hebron*, there to fight with's foes.
The *Philiftines*, and *Moabites*
He does fubdue; and *Syria* fmites.
                                                      On

---

## The Holy Bible.

On *Bathsheba* he casts his Eyes,
And she to Luft's a Sacrifice.
At which th' *Almighty Nathan* fent,
In order that he might Repent.
And *Abfalom* doth *Amnon* kill,
For forcing *Tamar* 'gainft her Will.
For which Offence *Joab* does bring,
The Murderer before the King,
Where all is hufh'd, yet *Abfalom*,
Does at his Fathers Kingdom aim.
But as he hung i'th' *Oak* by's Hair,
He killed was with *Joab's* fpear :
The News was foon to *David* fent,
And bitterly he does Lament.
*David* the People Numbreth ; and
The Plague increafeth in the Land.

### Kings,

---

## The Holy Bible.

### Kings I.

King *David* dyes, and leaves the
Unto the wife K. *Solomon* ; (Throne,
Who fends for Workmen from afar,
The *Temple* of the Lord to Rear :
Before, (nor after) found was one.
That e'er fo wifely Rul'd the *Throne*
Yet he neglects his God (Oh worft
Of all !) to Idolize his Luft.
He dyes, and by his Father's laid,
And *Reboboam* does fucceed.

### Kings II.

*Ahaziah* 'gainft God Rebels,
And *Elijah* his Death foretells :
He does confume by Fire, then,
Two Captains, with a Hundred men
                                                      *Elijah*

---

## The Holy Bible.

*Elijah* up to Heaven is ta'en,
But here *Elifha* does remain ;
At whom the wicked Children jeer
Who all by *Bears* devoured are,
*Elifha* many wonders, by
God's Spirit works, and fo doth dye.
This Book ( in General ) doth tell,
Some Kings act Ill, & fome act well.

### Chronicles I.

        ( came,
The *Tribes*, which from Old *Adam*
Are numbred ; (to Immortal *Fame*)
And *David's* Acts recorded are,
That mifled men may take more care.

### Chronicles II.

This *Book* unto *remembrance* brings
The ftate of *Ifrael's*, Judah's Kings.
     B         And

## The Holy Bible.

And how *Mannasseh* in difpair,
Finds Mercy by a hearty Prayer,

### Ezra.

*Cyrus* the *Perfian* granteth leave,
The *Jews* their Freedom fhould re-
And to the people does Proclaim, ceive
The *Temple* of the Lord to Frame.
But yet, thofe hinder'd are that build
By wicked men with anger fill'd;
Till God gives leave, they fhall obtain,
Their *Church* & *Commonwealth again*

### Nehemiah.

TheNews is brought by *Hanani*,
Of *Jerufalem's* Mifery;
WhichHoly *Nehemiah* hears;
And prays to God with many Tears
　　　　　　　　　　　　　Then

## The Holy Bible.

Then quickly after he begins,
For to Reform abufive Sins.

### Efter.

*Ahafruerus* men doth fend,
That *Vafoti* may on him attend;
But fhe refufes to be feen;
And *Efter* thereupon's made Queen;
A Plot's Contriv'd againft the King
Which *Mordica* to Light doth bring
But *Haman*, by the King's advanc'd
Who feeks *Revenge* the Jews againft
And for which end he does obtain
The K's Decree to have them flain,
Yet *Mordicai* to *Efther* fues,
Who begs the K. to fave the Jews.
At which proud *Haman's* bafe de-
Reverfed is immediately. 　(cree.
　　　B 2　　　　　　　　 And

## The Holy Bible.

And *Haman's* hang'd, whilft *Mor-*
Is cloathed in the Kings array. *dica*

### Job.

This *Book* doth holy *Job* fet forth,
In his Religious Care, and Worth:
How *Satan* does through *Calumny*,
Indeavour him to *Vilifie*;
His Cattel he doth take away;
And all his Children likewife Slay:
But yet he cann't obtain his Will,
For God, by *Job*, is Bleffed ftill.
The *Devil* Tempts him yet *once more*,
By fmiting him with *Boils moft fore*;
And makes his Wife (O wickedly!)
To bid him *Curfe his God*, and dye:
Whom he Reproveth without Sin,
Though fhe a FoolifhWife hadbeen.
　　　　　　　　　　　　　His

## The Holy Bible.

His *Three Friends* they in Silence do
Condole his Mifery and Woe.
*Job* Curfing then the *Day of's Birth*,
Hates *Life*, & longs to taft of *Death*:
But God, who did his *Patience* try,
With Bleffings him doth magnify:
His Cattel ftrangely doth increafe,
And *Wealth* upon him comes apace.
Sev'n *Sons* to him the *Lord doth rear*,
And Daughters three, who Beauties are.
For which *Job* bleffeth God always,
So *Dyes*, b'ing *Old* and full of *Days.*

### Pfalms.

Here Royal *David* doth Rejoice
With *Harp*, with *Timbrel*, & with *Voice*.
Harmoniously he Chants the Praife
Of *Jah*, with various Notes & Lays.
　　　B 3　　　　　　　　[ *Ob*

### The Holy Bible.

[ Oh blessed Chorister, which Sings
Eternally Jehovah's Hymns ! ]
This Book, in gen'ral, doth discover
God's Justice, Mercy, Favor, Power.

### Proverbs.

The Proverbs of VVise Solomon,
(Who was King David's only Son)
Before our Eyes like Pearls appear,
Exhorting us the Lord to fear.
He bids his Son, with Care, avoid
The subtle, cunning Harlot's Fraud,
And Precepts lays before our Eyes,
That to our Souls we may be wise.

### Ecclesiastes.

The Preacher here all things doth try,
And calls them worse than Vanity.

He,

### The Holy Bible.

He, in an ample manner, brings
Both Times and Seasons for all things.
And all which Man doth here inherit,
Will only serve to Vex his Spirit.
He bids the Youth Rejoice, but know
To Judgment he must come also:
And in Conclusion, bids Man to
Fear God, and his Commandments do.

### Solomon's Song.

This Love-sick Song of Solomon's,
To Jesus and his Church belongs :
And, in this blessed Song, we read
How Christ and's Church are Married.
[ O God, my soul desires to be
Wedded unto thy Church and Thee! ]
This Song a Myst'ry is, therefore
Who Reads it, let him Grace implore.

B 4     Isaiah.

### The Holy Bible.
### Isaiah.

Isaiah here doth Prophesie, (be
That Death and Hell shall conquer'd
By Christ ; whose blessed Kingdom
A Sanctuary be to all. ( shall
God's Woes herein denounced are
'Gainst all things which impious were.
The Godly will Rewarded be,
But th' Wicked shall have Misery.

### Jeremiah.

This blessed Prophet Prophesies
Of Jerusalem's Miseries ;
For which the Priests do him arraign,
But he in Judgment's free'd again:
Yet Jeremiah's beat, and cast
In Prison, where he's shut up fast ;

From

### The Holy Bible.

From thence, into the Durgeon, he
Is thrown, t'indure more Misery ;
Till Ebed-Melech maketh Suit .
Unto the King, and gets him out.
But now proud Babylon doth take
Their City, and all Captives make,
King Hezekiah's Son's are slain,
And he himself's a Pris'ner ta'en ;
Losing his Eyes, & Chained strong,
To Babylon he's led along.
The rest Contains, in general,
How Babylon at last will fall.

### Lamentations.

The Prophet Jeremiah, here
Wisheth his Head a Fountain were,
That he might weep Sufficiently,
For Jerusalem's Misery :

This

## The Holy Bible.

This Book may Exhortation bring,
To all, to have a Care of sin;
Which did provoke the *jealous* God,
To Scourge them with a heavy Rod.

### Ezekiel.

Ezekiel is in *Babylon*,
A Captive made; who calls upon
The Lord his God, and Prophesies
Of Woes, and blest Felicities,
He many Visions hath, wherein
The *Jews* Reproved are for Sin,
And by dry Bones b'ing made alive
The *hope* of *Israel* does revive. (in all
Chrift's Kingdom's Promis'd where-
pon the Lord their God will call;
*Israel* o'er *Gog* obtains the Day,
And *Princes* are to Bird's a Prey.

God's

## The Holy Bible.

God's Glory in the *Temple* ftays.
*Whilft Priefts therein do give him*
(*praife*)

### Daniel.

This Prophet worfhips God before
He Superftition will adore;
*Nebuchadnezzar* Dreameth, and
His meaning he doth underftand,
Which to the King he does relate,
And for the fame's made very great
The King an Image, makes that all
The People may before it fall:
But *Shadrach* with his Brethren two
Nam'd *Meshach* and *Abednego*, (turn
Before they would from Heaven
Refolved in the Flames to burn;
And by the K's Command all *Three*
Were flung therein Immediately:
But

## The Holy Bible.

But by the power of God's arm,
They walkt about and felt no harm
For which the King doth magnify
God's *Kingdoms* in the *Heavens* high
He Dreams again, and *Daniel* fays,
That he with Beafts i'th field fhall
*Daniel* unto his God doth call (graze
'T' unfold the writing on the wall.
For which he by the King is prais'd
And thereupon to Honour's rais'd.
But yet he's flung by wicked men,
Into the Roaring Lyons Den.
But *Daniel* on his God doth call,
Who faves him out of Dangers all.
But thofe mifchievous evil men,
Were all devoured in the Den.
Whilft K. *Darius* makes Decree,
That *Daniel*'s God fhall worfhipt be
The

## The Holy Bible.

The other Chapters do contain (*reign*
(I think) the time when Chrift will
[*Lord let thy Spirit o're me spread,*
*When e're this Miftery I read?*
*But never let me in it pry,*
*Without thy blessed Majefty.*]

### Hosea.

The bleffed Prophet's Prophecy,
Gainft *Whoredom* and *Idolatry*;
Briefly to *Israel* doth declare, (*are*
Gods *Judgments, which moft righteous*
Exhorts them with a good intent,
To leave off Sinning, and Repent.

### Joel.

And *Joel* tells the Jews withall,
That Heaven's wrath will on'em fall
With-

### The Holy Bible.

VVithout Repentance which will be
A stop unto their Misery.

### Amos.

The Israelites are wanton grown,
At which Jehovahs brow doth frown
And then God threatens Israel, (dwell
That Fire and Plague shall with'em
But by the Prophet Amos prayer (were
Those Judgments then diverted

### Obadiah.

And now for Edom's Ruin look,
I'th' Prophet Obadiah's Book.
For pride and wrong to Jacob, they
Justly become blest Israel's prey.

### Jonah.

Jonah to Nineveh is sent,
But he to Joppah straitways went;

---

### The Holy Bible.

And, in a Ship, to'ards Tarshish, he
From God Almighty's Face doth flee;
A Storm ariseth, and they all,
(Each to his God) for help do call:
But all will not appease the Sea,
Till ev'ry one, by Lots, agree,
The Evil person for to tell;
And lo! the Lot on Jonah fell.
They over-board do Jonah hale,
Where he is swallow'd by a Whale.
Three Days and Nights he doth remain
Therein, till he is freed again,
And then to Nineveh he went,
Where, at his word, they all repent
[ If this thy Prophet must, O Lord !
To do thy will, be thereto Spur'd ;
What will become of Stubborn me,
Who's ten times far more dull than he?
Spur

---

### The Holy Bible.

Spur me, O Lord ! but let me find,
As thou art Just, thou'rt also Kind.

### Micha.

In Micha's prophecy we see,
God's wrath against Idolatry,
Princes are Cruel, Prophets all,
To vanity and falshood fall :
The Birth of Christ is prophecy'd
His Kingdom, Conquest, over Pride.

### Nahum.

The blessed Majesty of God,
Unto his people's very good ;
But full of just Severities,
Against his sinfull Enemies.
And God's victorious Armies fights,
VVith the rebellious Ninevites.

Hab.

---

### The Holy Bible:
### Habakkuk.

The Land's full of Iniquity,
Which makes the Prophet loudly cry
The whole in general contains,
How th'land is plagu'd by Caldeans
And Wees 'gainst sins denounced are
Concluding with the prophet's prayer
Who doth therein submissively,
Tremble before God's Majesty.

### Zephaniah.  (here,

God's Judgments by the Prophet
'Gainst Judah still denounced are.
Jerusalem's reprov'd and, then,
It's Restauration comes again.

### Haggai.

The people by this Prophet are,
Incouraged God's House to rear.

C                      And

## The Holy Bible.

*And God, that man will kep from's foe*
*Nam'd Zerubbabel, whom he'ath chof*

### Zachariah.

By Types good *Zachariah* here,
Foretells *Jerusalem's* welfare.
Chrift's coming to deftroy likewife
Bleft *Jerusalem's* Enemies :
The Kingdom of his Majefty,
Adorned will with Graces be.

### Malachy.

Good *Malachi* doth here *complai*
That *Ifrael's* grown unkind again
*The Priefts by him are fharply checkt*
'Caufe they their Covenant negle&
The people, for *Idolatry,*
Reprov'd are with Severity,

H

---

## The Holy Bible.

He fhoweth that the Wicked will;
With *Judgments* be attended ftill
And in God's Ire be burnt to duft,
Whilft ever bleffed are the Juft.
And of *Elijah's* coming, and
His Office, doth this Prophet end

*The end of the Prophets.*

---

### Apocripha.

Th' *Apocripha* doth feem to carry,
A Senfe from *Scripture* contrary :
*Which makes it thus by Church decree*
From Sacred *Scripture* placed be.
It tells how *Tobit* being *Blind.*
Did by his Son recov'ry find.
And how that woman Judith did
Cut of Proud *Holifornes* head;

C 2                And

---

## The Holy Bible.

And that two *Elders* Luftfull are;
Who for *Sufannah* lay a fnare :
And 'caufe fhe keeps her Chaftit,
Condemn'd fhe's for Adultery :
But *Daniel* in the matter prye,
And finds the Judges falfities ;
Whereon *Sufannah* Freedom hath.
And both the *Elders* put to Death.
*And next th' Fraud of the Priefts o*
Difcovered is by *Daniel.*        ( bel,
The *Maccabees* do moft contain.
How many Jews in *War* are Slain.
*How Seven Brethren with their Mother*
*All in one Day the Flames do fmother*
And how for all the tyrants Threat,
*Thofe Martyrs did no Swines flefh eat.*

*The End of the Apocripha.*

---

# The New

# Testament.

## In *VERSE*;

---

### By *B. H.*

---

*London,* Printed for *B. Harris* Senior, at the upper-end of *Grace-Church-Street,* next *Corn-hill,* 1698.

LO! From the *Law*, by *Gospel* he
    Relates *Christ's Genealogy*.
*How by Old, Faithful* Abram's *Root,*
*From* Joseph's *Virgin-wife does sprout*

### The Holy Bible.

*Jesus*, God-man ( Conceived by
The *Holy Ghost* ) for Sin to Dye)
*Wise Men from th' East directed are,*
*To find Christ* Jesus *by a Star.*
Joseph *and* Mary *with their Son,*
*Into the Land of* Egypt *run.*
*Where they do live till* Herod's *Death.*
*And back they come to* Nazareth.
*Then* John *Repentance Preacheth, and*
*Tells all* God's *Kingdom is at hand :*
*Jesus* doth come from Galilee,
*To* Jordan *there of* John *to be*
*Baptiz'd, at which Gods Spirit bright*
*Like to a Dove on him doth Light ;*
*And lo ! whilest open'd was the Frame*
*Of Heav'n, a Voice from thence down*
This my belov'd Son is, in (came,
    whom well pleas'd I am.

                                *Christ*

### The Holy Bible.

*Christ* Fasteth in the VVilderness,
And by the *Devil* Tempted is.
He leaves him, and the *Angels* they
In Ministration him Obey.
Jesus *Repentance* Preacheth then,
To Turn the Hearts of Sinful men ;
And after him, at's word doth run,
Both *Peter, Andrew,* James and John.
*Christ* healeth all diseas'd and lame
*Which throughout Siry a spreads bis fame*
*And then i'th' Mount be doth declare*
*Who all those be which blessed are.*
*Expounds the Law, of Alms, of Prayer,*
*Of Fasting, and of worldly Care.*
*The Leeper by Christ's touch is heal'd*
*And by his word the Tempest's still'd.*
And *Devils* by his Power Divine,
*From Men run in a Herd of Swine.*

                                Dead

## The Holy Bible.

Dead People by him Life do find;
And Sights reftor'd unto the *Blind.*
Chrift his Apoftles fends out, who
Have Power Miracles to do. (*reach,*
*And with bleft Comfort doth them*
*How, and to whom they ought to Preach*
Chrift then upbraids thofe *Cities, in*
*The which his Miracles have been.*
For not Repenting, feeing all
*His mighty works on them did fall.*
To weary Sinners, Come (faith he)
For I your refting place will be.
Chrift many Parables doth fhow,
*Whereby we good from bad may know*
But then his Faithlefs Country-men
Their Lord & Saviour do contemn
*John Baptift* in a Prifon laid,
By *Herods* Oath doth lofe his Head
An I

## The Holy Bible.

And Chrift being in the *Defert* then
*Was with him full Five Thoufand Men,*
*Who all were with Five Loaves of Bread*
*And Fifhes two, by him there Fed.*
Then walks upon the Sea by Night
VVhich doth the *Mariners* affright:
He many *Miracles* does do, (fhew.
And then his Death he doth Fore-
*Judas* his Lord betrays to thofe
*Who were their own Salvations-Foes :*
Before high Priefts he's led away,
And cloathed in a Mock array.
*Peter* three times his Lord denies,
*With Oaths, with Curfes, and with Crys*
*And then Repents :* But *Judas,* he
Doth hang himfelf upon a Tree.
*Jefus* i'th' Judgment Hall's abus'd
By *Jews,* and Cruelly mifus'd.
But

## The Holy Bible.

But *Pilate* warned by his VVife,
Is free to fave our Saviours Life.
At which a Multitude arofe :
And *Barnabas* the Murderer chofe,
And lifting up their Voices cry'd
*Let him, Let him be Crucified.*
Then *Pilate* taking water, ftands
Before 'um, wafhing of his Hands
Freeing himfelf therefrom, *when a*
*The wicked Jews* aloud do *Baul ;*
*His Blood on us, and on our Children fa*
Lo then deliver'd up, he's ftript,
*Of's Robes, then mocked at and whipt.*
And after they do him deride,
At *Golgotha* he's Crucify'd *ftretch*
Nail'd to the Crofs *his arms out-*
Thro' Agony a Sigh he fetch't ;
*Whofe Voice all Thunders did out-do,*
Rending the *Temples Vail* in two.

## The Holy Bible.

Making the Earth to fhake, & thefe
VVho flept in *Graves* forthwith arofe
And after he aloud had cry'd,
Gave up the Ghoft thus Crucify'd
Buried he is by *Jofeph,* who,
The *Tomb* out of a *Rock* did hew ;
But by his power in three days,
His body from the *Grave* doth raife
And in the Mount of *Galilee,*
His own *Difciples* do him fee,
*Where they do worfhip him ; but yet,*
Some doubted of the Truth of it.
He then Commands them all to go,
*And Preach his word the World unto*

### Mark.

*The Evangelift doth here declare,*
*John Baptift's Office, what and where.*
Jefus

## The Holy Bible.

Jesus Baptized is of John,
And casts a *Devil* out of one ;
Cleanseth the *Leper*, and doth sit
Down with the *Publicans* to Eat,
*The Twelve Apostles Christ doth choose,*
*And who his Brethren are he shews,*
By Parables he much doth Teach;
And of the *Sower* he doth Preach.
And in a *Ship* he entreth then,
Expounding it to many men.
The roaring winds his Voice obeys
And with his word the *Storm* allays
*The Fruitless* Fig-tree *Christ doth see*
And Cursed 'tis imediately.
The force of Faith he sheweth too,
And how to *Cæsar* Tribute's due.
The *Temples* Lofty Buildings, he
Foretells will Ruinated be,

                 Falſe

## The Holy Bible.

*Falſe Chriſts will come, and wars will*
*With Famines, Plagues, and Miſery.( be*
Brother, his Brother shall betray,
*And Children shall their Parents slay*
The Sun & Moon be darkned shall,
And all the Stars from *Heaven* fall,
*The Powers thereof shall shaken be,*
And then the Son of Man they'l see
*Come down in Clouds by powerful*
*With Majeſty and Glory bright( Might*
*Therefore take heed, Watch ye and Pray*
*For none there is which knows the day.*
Soon after this the *Jews* agree,
'Gainst Jeſus by Conſpiracy.
The reſt I think doth moſt contain
How wickedly our Lord is slain,
Likewiſe his Reſurrection, and
How he to *Heaven* doth aſcend.

                 Luke

## The Holy Bible.
## Luke.

St. *Luke* tells how *Elizabeth,*
Of *John* the *Baptiſt* Conceiveth.
And how the Son *of God comes down*
To take abode in *Mary's* VVomb.
*John's* birth, at which good *Zachari*
Lifts up his Praiſe to God on high ;
And at our Saviours *Birth* likewiſe
Old Father *Simeon* Propheſies,
*Depart,? let thy Servant Lord!*
In Peace according to thy word.
*Chriſt's Tempting, Victory & Preaching*
*Parables, Wonders, Meekneſs, Teaching,*
Diſputing with the Doctors, and
*How th' sick are healed by his hand,*
Are all related in this *Book,*
Of the Evangeliſt St. *Luke.*

             John.

## The Holy Bible.
## John.

John the Evangiliſt doth treat,
Of Chriſt's Divinity moſt great.
*In the Begining was the Word,( Lord*
*Which Word was then with God the*
His Office and Humanity.
*John Baptiſt* here doth Teſtify.
The *Temple* by Chriſts power divine
*Is purg'd ; and Water's turn'd to Wine*
He shews th' *Samaritans* his Zeal,
And then the Ruler's Son doth heal
Th' Impotent on the Sabbath day,
*He bids Riſe, Walk and go his way.*
*I am the Bread of Life (ſaith he)*
VVho Eats shall live t'Eternity.
Rebukes the boaſting of the *Jews,*
And many Miracles he shews.

     D            Chriſt

## The Holy Bible.

Christ is the Door, and Shepherd go..
And proves himself the Son of Go..
And Lazarus to Life doth raise,
Who in the Grave had lain four d..
Mary Anoints our Saviours Feet
VVith Ointment as he sat at mea..
A new Commandment Christ do..
That we in Unity may live. (giv..
To his Disciples he doth say,
I am the true and living way;
Therefore let Comfort you atten..
For I the Holy-Ghost will send.
Then Prays to's Father heartily,
To keep them all in Unity.
And then by Judas he's betray'd..
And to the Judgment-Hall is lea..
Where they him Mock, and do Devid..
And then with Thieves he's Crucif..
                                    Acts.

## The Holy Bible.
### Acts.

In Judas Room the Apostles they,
To choose another do agree;
And as they Pray the Lord to show
Who 'tis h'ath chosen of the Two,
The Lot on Matthias doth fall,
Who numbred is among them all,
They being all, with one accord,
Together, praising of the Lord,
Were filled with the Holy-Ghost,
Upon the Day of Pentecost;
The cloven Tongues of Fire fall
From high, and they're inspired all.
Peter, by's Sermon doth Convert
Many from Sin, and Satan's smart.
Peter and John, by heav'nly Pow'r.
Of Lameness doth a Man restore.
                                    Fq

## The Holy Bible.

For preaching in Christs name they,
And of the same they are forbid. (chi..
Stephen is stoned, and doth ...,
Lord Jesus let my Spirit Fly
To the, the Eunuch strait believes,
And then Baptism he receives.
Saul in his Persecution Road,
Converted's to the Word of God.
James killed is by Herod's Sword;
And Peter he is kept in ward.
But he is Freed an Angel by,
And Worms proud Herod do destroy
Lydia and the Jaylor do receive,
Conversion, and in Christ Believe
Paul earnestly the Gospel then,
Doth Preach to turn the hearts of me..
He's put in Prison, and the Jews
Maliciously do him accuse,
                                    To..

## The Holy Bible.

To Cæsar he appeals, to whom,
By Festus, he is sent to Rome,
Which he at last doth safely see,
Thro Shipwracks, Dangers, storms at Sea

### Romans.

Paul to the Romans writeth, and
Therein his Calling doth commend
Tells who Justification hath,
None by the Law, but purely Faith
And who from Condemnation's free,
And how th' Elect shall saved be.
With Zeal their hearts he seems to move
To'ards Faith, Hope, Chairty and Love
Advising, with a good Intention,
His Brethren to avoid Dissention.

                D 3        Cor-

### The Holy Bible.
### Corinthians, I.

Th' *Corinthians* are exhorted by
The *Apostle Paul* to Unity.
Chrift *Crucified* he doth Preach,
Not feeking Flourishes of Speech,
Of many things he doth them tell,
In which they never can act well

### Corinthians II.

*Paul* the *Corinthians* fortifies,
'Gainft Troubles and Adverfities.
His Faithfulnefs in Miniftry ;
And bids them flee Idolatry :
And *Precepts* lays for *each Condition*
Exhorting all unto Contrition.
He glories in *Afflictions*, and
Wifhes their *Faith may ftedfaft ftand.*
            Gala-

### The Holy Bible.
### Galatians.

*Paul* ftands *amaz'd* at them, to fee
*How foon they from the Gofpel flee.*
He asketh them the Reafon why
*From Faith* unto the *Law* they fly.
And telleth them, when Jefus came
*They then were freed from the fame.*
And in Conclufion endeth thus ;
*'Tis beft to Glory in Chrift's Crofs.*

### Ephefians.

Herein he fhows us what we were
By *Nature* ; what by *Grace* we are
Exhorts to Unity ; and then
Saith angry be, but do not fin.

### Philippians.

*Paul prays to God for them , that they
In Grace, increafe may every Day.*
         D 4         And

### The Holy Bible.

*And bids them from falfe Teachers fly,
And Cloath'd be with Humility.
Then tells them all is Dung, and Drofs,
Unto bleft Jefus and his Crofs.*

### Coloffians,

*He thanks th' Almighty for their faith
And for increafe in Grace he prayeth,
And that they fafe to Heaven may go
Their Duties he doth plainly fhow.*

### Theffalonians I, II.

*Paul fhews in mind he doth them bear
Both by Thanksgiving, and in Prayer
Defiring alfo them to fee ;
To whom he fends young Timothy.
And how we muft for th' Dead lament
And of Chrift's coming to Judgment.*
           Then

### The Holy Bible.

*Then Prays to God for them, that they*
May firm be in the truth alway.

### Timothy I, II.

And in thefe Books we have at large
How *Paul* to *Timothy* gives Charge
*That Prayers and thanks for all Men*
            ( muft,
Be made, and *Bifhops* fhould be Juft
And in the latter days, he faith,
That men *depart* fhall from the *faith*
*Paul* biddeth *Timothy* beware,
And in Gods Grace to perfevere.
He of's own Death doth Prophefie
And takes his leave of *Timothy.*

### Titus.

In many things *Paul* him directs,
How he muft deal with *Hereticks*
           T-

### The Holy Bible.

The Aged, Young, and Servants, he
Exhorteth to Sobriety.

### Philemon.

*Paul's joy for th' Faith of* Philemon,
And begs him to receive his Son
*Onesimus* ; and saith, that he
Will Satisfy, if Ought there be.

### Hebrews.

The *Jews* admonished are here,
*Their Saviour Jesus Christ to fear* :
And tells them, *the Old Law is gone*
Thro Jesus Christ, God's only Son.

### James.

*It is not well.(saith James therefore)*
To *love* the Rich, & *hate* the Poor.

### Peter.

---

### The Holy Bible

### Peter I, II.

He them exhorts the Lord to *fear,*
And saith, the *judgment-day is near.*

### John I, II, III.

Chrifts *person* he defcribes, & fhows
His *Death, & how therefrom he rose.*
Exhorts to perfevere in Love,
Commending them to God above.

### Jude.

Jude doth the fame, & *saysthey muft*
Be punifhed, who teach unjuft,

### Revelations.

Divine S. John, revealeth when
The Lord of life will come agen :
How glorioufly he'l come *from high*
With Power and great Majefty,

*To*

---

### The Holy Bible.

*judge the World, & burn up those*
Who are his difobedient Foes.
He fhews how *Antichrift* will be
Confumed by his Majefty,
And how for ever bleffed fhall
Those be who on his Name do call

F I N I S.

$$24$$

# "Apples of Gold
# In Pictures of Silver"
## From
## The Key of Knowledg

### Opening the Principles of Religion and the Path of Life

**B**Y FAR THE MOST *delightful and intelligent portion of* The Key of Knowledg *is the section added at the end, entitled,* "Apples of Gold in Pictures of Silver, For The Use and Delight of Children and Servants." *This section consists of a collection of thirty-four poems, most of them by major seventeenth-century poets, loyal subjects of the King, some high church if not secretly Catholic. Seven of the poems are by the major metaphysical poet, George Herbert; one is by the metaphysical poet who turned Roman Catholic priest, Richard Crashaw; two are by the best-known metaphysical poet, John Donne; two are by Abraham Cowley, who antedates Pope in his use of the closed couplet (and who also developed a form of Pindaric ode); one by Giles Fletcher (whose poem, "Heaven," is in Spenserian stanzas, an eight-line adaptation of the* Faerie Queene's *ababbccC, which is characteristic of Fletcher's verse). Ten are by one of the most popular poets of the seventeenth century, the emblem writer, Francis Quarles, and, eight are by George Sandys, who is especially interesting to Americans because he not only was well known in England, but also served as Treasurer of the Virginia Company in Jamestown. His translation of Ovid's* Metamorphoses *may well be the first literary work of English settlers in America.\* Three poets are not named, but only the initials given. One of them, however, is the Jesuit martyr, Robert Southwell, who was dragged to his death on a hurdle through London in winter. Southwell had been arrested in 1592 for preaching and giving Holy Communion to Catholics and, after extreme tortures, was executed in 1595. He was then only about thirty years old. (He was beatified by Pope Pius XI in 1929.) His identity is hidden in Willis' work not because he was obscure, as Willis suggests in the introduction, but because the book came out at a time when a strong Protestant undercurrent was developing in England—in six years there would be a Protestant monarch.*

*For those unfamiliar with earlier poetic forms, it might be helpful to add that metaphysical poetry, to follow Samuel Johnson's definition, consists of heterogeneous ideas yoked by violence together. It was preceded by emblematic verse in the sixteenth century—a picture illustrating some moral or divine truth followed by a quotation from the Bible, then a poem commenting on the picture, and then a final epigram. One can*

---

\* See R. B. Davis, "Early Editions of George Sandys's *Ovid," Papers, Bibliographical Society of America,* xxxv (1941), 255–276.

see the relationship between emblematic poetry, fashionable in the early seventeenth century, and metaphysical poetry, which, if well done, operates simultaneously on at least two levels. It was easier to write at a time when everyone simultaneously led two or three lives: the doctrine of correspondences equated all things in man with all things on earth or in heaven. Thus a walnut could be equated with the human brain because of its segments and its convolutions—and was sometimes taken for a headache. Sparkling eyes were related to diamonds and to stars. One's father was to be obeyed, as one's father obeyed the King as the King obeyed God, the ultimate Father. All things had their relative place on the great Chain of Being, which stretched from heaven to earth.

Herbert's poetry is generally the most subtle and difficult metaphysical poetry, though the poems selected by the anthologizer, Willis, are comparatively easy to follow. The first poem selected has been cut down by Willis to less than a third of its original seventy-seven stanzas to focus more nearly on advice to young men. Certain interesting changes have been made in what Herbert wrote, possibly to accommodate the verse to a more morally accommodating age. For instance, Herbert wrote, "Restore to God his due in tithe and time:/A tithe purloin'd cankers the whole estate." In Willis ("Counsel to Young men," stanza 18), the lines appear as, "Render to God his due, part of thy time:/Treasure purloin'd cankers the whole Estate."

The next poem by Herbert selected by Willis, "Charms and Knots," has the same didactic manner as the first, and is also fairly simple. "The Quip" is somewhat more difficult, more personal. It has to do with the many worldly temptations offered to the handsome, brilliant, and aristocratic young Herbert, who gave them all up to become a simple country preacher. In mentioning the "Oration" (next to last stanza) Herbert may be thinking of his honorary position, while a young scholar, as Public Orator at Cambridge.

"Sunday," in which Sundays and weekdays are seen as God's garden, is very beautiful. "The Sundays of man's Life/Threaded together, on time's string,/Make bracelets to adorn the wife,/Of the Eternal Glorious King." The collapse of the temple when Samson tore it down is compared with the earthquake at the crucifixion.

In Herbert's poem, "Grace," there is a play on the words "Grace" and "grass." Just as water bedews the grass, so God's mercy quenches the thirst of those who seek grace. In "Paradise," Herbert prunes his poem in an amusing reduction of letters—like Christ, the divine gardener, who prunes our souls. His poem, "Paradise," is not difficult—especially for youngsters—to understand. In fact, adults should be able to follow the rest of the poems themselves with a little help from the children.

Robert Southwell's poem beginning "I dwell in Grace's Court," has been cut from its original seventeen stanzas to six. Here again there are changes to make the lines more sectarian. Thus, Southwell's lines in stanza two, "My seely shrowde true honor bringes,/My poore estate is rich," are changed by Willis to "My honest meanness Honour bringes,/My poor Estate is rich." Southwell's "seely shrowde" (simple clothing) may suggest death too nearly. At any rate, the word "seely" was not yet archaic in the sense in which it is used here.

Willis did not hesitate to edit poetry—even to change lines—to suit his purposes. Thus, of Sandys' poetic versions of the Psalms, he used three stanzas of the five in Part I and the first stanza of Psalm 51; Parts II and III of Psalm 119; sections of Parts I and II of

I Samuel 2; *all of* Psalm 8; *part of* Psalm 131; *but of* Psalm 19, *in Sandys' version, only sections of Parts I and II. Part of* Psalm 84 *was omitted and, of* Psalm 127, *he used only the first two stanzas. Willis' purposes seem primarily to make the poetry shorter and more appealing to youthful readers.*

*Francis Quarles was a Protestant who lost his property for siding with Charles I and never regained it. His divided loyalties earned him enemies both with Protestants and Catholics, and his life was hard. Though not reproduced in Willis' text, the illustrations which accompanied Quarles' Emblems help to clarify the poems and four of them are reproduced here. These include Emblem IV in Book I, which accompanies Quarles' "O What a Crocodilian world is this" (actually stanza 6 of Quarles' entire poem); Emblem VI, Book I, to accompany "How is the anxious Soul of man befool'd" (again not all of the poem is reprinted by Willis, but only stanzas 1, 3, and 4); Emblem XIII, Book I, to accompany "Lord, when we leave the world, and come to thee," which Willis telescoped considerably, and he made up the last two lines; and Emblem VI, Book V: "I love, and have some cause to love the earth."\**

*"Apples of Gold in Pictures of Silver" is reprinted from a 1682 edition of* The Key of Knowledg, *printed for Tho. Parkhurst, London, England. The illustrations seen here are reproduced from Francis Quarles'* Emblems, Divine and Moral *(London: William Tegg, 1866).* This fresh transcription of the above seventeenth century edition of Willis' book follows the original in spelling and punctuation.

---

* SUGGESTED READING:
Josephine Bennett, *Four Metaphysical Poets* (New York, 1953).
Rosemary Freeman, *English Emblem Books* (London, 1948).
Louis L. Martz, *The Poetry of Meditation* (New Haven, 1954).
E. M. W. Tillyard, *The Elizabethan World Picture* (New York, 1959) .

# The Key of Knowledg,

Opening

## The PRINCIPLES of RELIGION;

And

# The Path of Life,

Directing

## The PRACTICE of true PIETIE :

Defign'd

For the Conduct of *Children* and *Servants*, in the right way to Heaven and Happinefs.

By         D. D.

Prov. 22. 6.

*Train up* [ *or,* Chatechize ] *a Child in the way he fhould go : and when he is Old he will not depart from it.*

Pfal. 119. 9.

*VVherewith fhall a Young man cleanfe his way ? By taking heed thereto according to thy VVord.*

LONDON. Printed for *Tho. Parkhurft,* at the Bible and three Crowns, at the lower end of *Cheap-fide,* near *Mercers Chappel.* 1682.

# A Collection of certain Verses, from some of our Divine Poems, more fit to be Imprinted on the Memories of Young People, than Prophane Songs.

## THE PREFACE.

F OR *the* close of your entertainment, *I here present you with a* Delicate Dish. *'T is* choice Fruit, *which grew in a* Rich Soil. *'T is as the Fruit of* Eden,

*Gen. 3. 6.*

*that Tempted* Eve, good for Food, pleasant to the Eyes, and desirable to make one Wise. *Only here is the difference; She could not eat of that without* Sin *against God, and* Hurt *to her self: your eating of this may keep you from* Sin, *and prove the* Health *of your Soul. Freely feed then on this Fruit; 'tis not less wholesome than pleasant. 'Tis not as the Banquet of* Midas *or* \* Pythes, *a* Mock-Feast; *'tis* Gold *for worth, but* Food *for use. A*

*Prov. 25. 11:*

Word fitly spoken (*saith* Solomon) is like Apples of Gold in Pictures of Silver. *And* instruction in virtue, *to Persons in the* Flower of their Age, is a word fitly spoken. *Such are these pieces of Divine Poesie, wherewith I here present you, Read, Remember and Practise them: so shall you learn that* Knowledge and Wisdom, *which is better than* Silver and Gold; *seeing it will*

*Prov. 3. 18.*

*at once make you* Rich and Happy. *For* Wisdom is a Tree of Life (*saith* Solomon) to them that lay hold upon her; and Happy is every one that retaineth her. *And therefore*, Receive my Instruction, (*saith He*) and not Silver, and Knowledge rather than choice Gold. For Wisdom is better than Rubies; and all the things that may be desired are not to be compared to it. *Here you have the* Words of Wisdom, *which are* Golden Apples, *by the curious Art of Divine Poesy, set in* Silver Frames. *Take and eat: for here you have both* Food and Treasure. *What can you desire more than what is here offer'd to your Acceptance? Accept and Improve, and you shall not fail at once, to find both* Profit and Delight.

> And Profit with Delight combin'd,
> Is Meat and Musick to the Mind.

---

\* *Plut. Mor.*

## The Names of the Authors, from whose Poems the following Verses are Collected.

*G. H.* Mr. *George Herbert*'s Sacred Poems, called the Temple.
*R. C.* Mr. *Richard Crashaw*'s steps to the Temple.
*F. Q.* Mr. *Francis Quarles,* his Emblems and Divine Fancies.
*J. D.* Dr. *Donne*'s Poems.
*G. F.* Mr. *Giles Fletcher*'s, Christ's Victory and Triumph.
*G. S.* Mr. *George Sandy's,* his Paraphrase of the Psalms and Scripture Hymns.
*A. C.* Mr. *Abraham Cowley's* Sacred Poems.

Some few others of less note, are signified by the first Letters of their Names.

## *Counsel to Young men.*   G. H.

THOU, WHOSE sweet youth, and early hopes inhance
Thy rate and price, and mark thee for a Treasure;
Hearken unto a Verser, who may chance
Rhyme thee to good, and make a bait of Pleasure.
   A Verse may find him, who a Sermon flies,
   And turn Delight into a Sacrifice,

Beware of Lust: it doth pollute and foul
Whom God in Baptism washt with his own Blood
It blots the Lesson written in thy Soul;
The Holy Lines cannot be understood.
   How dare those eyes upon a Bible look,
   Much less towards God, whose Lust is all their Book?

Drink not the third glass, which thou canst not tame,
When once it is within thee; but before
Mayst rule it, as thou list: and pour the shame,
Which it would pour on thee, upon the Floor.
   It is most just to throw that on the ground,
   Which would throw me there, if I keep the round.

He that is drunken, may his Mother kill
Big with his Sister: he hath lost the Reins,
Is out-law'd by himself: all kind of ill
Did with his Liquor slide into his Veins.
   The Drunkard forfeits man, and doth divest
   All worldly Right save what he hath by Beast.

Take not his name, who made thy mouth, in vain:
It gets thee nothing, and hath no excuse.
Lust and Wine plead a pleasure, Avarice gain:
But the cheap swearer through his open sluce
   Lets his Soul run for nought, as little fearing:
   Were I an *Epicure*, I could bate swearing.

When thou dost tell anothers Jest, therein
Omit the Oaths, which true wit cannot need:
Pick out of Tales the Mirth, but not the sin.
He pares his Apple, that will cleanly feed.
   Play not away the virtue of that name,
   Which is thy best Stake when griefs make thee tame.

Lie not; but let thy heart be true to God,
Thy mouth to it, thy actions to them both:
Cowards tell Lies, and those that fear the Rod;
The stormy working Soul spits Lies and Froth.
   Dare to be true. Nothing can need a Lye,
   A fault, which needs it most, grows two thereby.

Fly Idleness; which yet thou canst not fly
By Dressing, Mistressing and Complement.
If those take up thy day, the Sun will cry
Against thee: for his light was only lent.
   God gave thy Soul brave wings: put not those feathers
   Into a Bed, to sleep out all ill weathers.

When thou dost purpose ought (within thy power)
Be sure to do it, though it be but small.
Constancy knits the bones, and makes us stowre,
When wanton pleasures becken us to thrall.
   Who breaks his own Bond, forfeiteth himself:
   What nature made a Ship, he makes a shelf.

Do all things like a man, not sneakingly:
Think the King sees thee still; for his King does.
Simpring is but a Lay-hypocrisie:
Give it a corner, and the Clew undoes:
   Who fears to do ill, sets himself to task:
   Who fears to do well sure should wear a Mask.

Look to thy Mouth: Diseases enter there.
Thou hast two Sconces, if thy Stomach call;
Carve, or discourse, do not a Famine fear.

Who carves is kind to two; who talks to all.
 Look on Meat, think it dirt, then eat a bit;
 And say with all; *Earth to Earth I commit.*

By all means use sometimes to be alone.
Salute thy self: see what thy soul doth wear.
Dare to look in thy Chest; for 'tis thine own:
And tumble up and down what thou findest there.
 Who cannot rest till he good fellowes find,
 He breaks up house, turns out of doors his mind.

In Conversation boldness now bears sway.
But know that nothing can so foolish be,
As empty boldness: therefore first assay
To stuff thy mind with solid bravery;
 Then march on gallant: get substantial worth,
 Boldness gilds finely, and will set it forth.

Laugh not too much: the witty man laughs least:
For wit is Newes only to Ignorance.
Less at thine own things laugh; lest in the jest
Thy person share, and the conceit advance.
 Make not thy sport abuses: for the Fly
 That feeds on Dung, is coloured thereby.

Pick out of Mirth, like stones out of thy ground,
Profaneness, Filthyness, Abusiveness.
These are the scum, with which course wits abound:
The fine may spare these well, yet not go less.
 All things are big with Jest: nothing that's plain
 But may be witty, if thou hast the vein.

Towards great persons use respective boldness:
That temper gives them theirs, and yet doth take
Nothing from thine, in service, care or coldness
Doth ratably thy Fortunes marr or make.
 Feed no man in his sins: for Adulation
 Doth make thee parcel-Devil in Damnation.

Scorn no man's Love, though of a mean degree;
(Love is a Present for a Mighty King)
Much less make any one thine Enemy.
As Guns destroy, so may a little sling.
 The cunning workman never doth refuse
 The meanest tool, that he may chance to use.

Render to God his due, *part of thy* time:
*Treasure* purloin'd cankers the whole Estate.
Sundays observe: think, when the Bells do chime,
'Tis Angels Musick; therefore come not late.
    God then deals Blessings: If a King did so,
    Who would not hast, nay give, to see the show.

Let vain or busie thoughts have there no part:
Bring not thy Plough, thy Plots, thy Pleasures thither
Christ purg'd his Temple, so must thou thy heart.
All worldly thoughts are but thieves met together
    To cozen thee. Look to thy Actions well:
    For Churches are either our Heav'n or Hell.

Judge not the Preacher; for he is thy Judge:
If thou mislike him, thou conceiv'st him not.
God calleth Preaching Folly. Do not grudge
To pick out treasures from an Earthen pot.
    The worst speak something good: if all want Sense,
    God takes a Text, and Preacheth Patience.

He that gets Patience, and the Blessing which
Preachers conclude with, hath not lost his pains.
He that by being at Church escapes the ditch,
Which he might fall in by Companions, gains.
    He that loves God's abode, and to combine
    With Saints on Earth, shall one day with them shine.

In brief, acquit thee bravely, play the man.
Look not on pleasures as they come, but go.
Defer not the least virtue: life's poor span.
Make not an Ell, by trifling in thy wo.
    If thou do ill, the Joy fades, not the pains:
    If well, the pain doth fade, the joy remains.

## *The Confession.* G. S. in Psal. 51.

Lord, to a sinner Mercy show:
    Which since in thee so infinite;
Let all thy streames of Mercy flow,
    And purifie me in thy sight.

My sins unmaskt, before thee lye;
    Who have deserv'd thy wrath alone:

Which I confess, to testifie
   Thy truth, and make thy Justice known.

In sin conceiv'd, brought forth in sin;
   Sin suckt I from my Mothers Breast:
Thou lov'st a heart sincere within,
   Where wisdom is a constant guest.

Blot out my crimes; O separate
   My trembling guilt far from thy view!
A clean Heart in my Breast Create;
   A Mind, to thee confirm'd, renew.

Nor cast me from thy Presence, Lord;
   Nor, O! Thy Holy Spirit withdraw:
But thy Life-quickning Grace afford;
   Inlarge my will, t' embrace thy Law.

## *The Resolution.* G. S. in Psal. 119.

Y OUNG MAN thine Actions by God's Precepts guide:
From these let not thy zealous servant slide.
Thy word, writ in my heart, shall curb my will.
Lord, teach me how I may thy laws fulfil.
Those by thy tongue pronounc't I will unfold.
Thy Testaments by me more priz'd than Gold.
On these I meditate, admire; there set
My Souls delight: these never will forget.
O let me live, t' observe thy laws: mine eyes
Illuminate to view those Mysteries.
Me, a poor Pilgrim, with thy truth inspire:
For which my Soul even fainteth with desire.
The proud is curst, who from thy Precepts straies,
Bless and preserve my soul, which them obeyes.
No hate of Princes from thy law deters:
My Study, my Delight, my Counsellers.

## *The Bible.* A. C.

T HIS HOLY BOOK, like *Heaven it self*, doth shine,
   With thousand lights of truth Divine.
So numberless the Stars, that *well they may*

*To Heaven's Gate make a Milky way.*
Yet reason must assist too; for in Seas
   So vast and dangerous as these,
Our course by Stars above we cannot know,
   Without the compass too below.

Tho *Reason* cannot through *Faith's Mysteries* see,
   It sees that there, and such they be;
Leads to *Heav'n's Door*, and there does humbly keep
   And there through chinks and key-holes peep.
Though it like *Moses*, by a sad command,
   Must not come into th' *Holy Land*;
Yet thither it infallibly does guide,
   And from a far 'tis all descry'd.


## *Charms and Knots.*  G. H.

W HO READ a Chapter when they rise,
Shall ne're be troubled with ill eyes.

A poor man's Rod, when thou dost ride,
Is both a weapon and a guide.

Who shuts his hand hath lost his Gold:
Who opens it, hath it twice told.

Who goes to Bed, and doth not pray,
Maketh two nights to ev'ry day.

Who by aspersions throw a stone
At th' head of others, hit their own.

Who looks on ground with humble eyes,
Finds himself there, and seeks to rise.

When th' hair is sweet, through Pride or lust,
The Powder doth forget the dust.

Take one from ten, and what remains?
Ten still, if Sermons go for gains.

In shallow waters Heaven doth show:
But who drinks on, to Hell may go.

### God's Greatness. G. S. in I Sam. 2.

GOD OUR secret thoughts displayes;
All our works his balance weighs;
Giants bows his Forces break;
He with strength invests the weak.
Who were full, now serve for bread;
Those who serv'd, infranchised.
Barren wombs with children flow;
Fruitful Mothers Childless grow.
God frail man of life deprives:
Those who sleep in death revives:
Leads us to our silent Tombs;
Brings us from those horrid Rooms:
Riches sends, sends Poverty:
Casteth down, lifts up on high.
He from the despised dust,
From the dunghil takes the just;
To the height of honour brings;
Plants them in the Thrones of Kings.

### Man's Meanness. G. S. Psal. 8.

LORD, HOW illustrious is thy Name!
Whose power both Heav'n and Earth proclaim!
Thy Glory thou hast set on high,
Above the Marble-arched Sky.
The wonders of thy power thou hast
In mouths of Babes, and Sucklings plac't;
That so thou might'st thy Foes confound,
And who in Malice most abound:
When I pure Heaven, thy Fabrick see,
The Moon and Stars dispos'd by thee;
O what is man, or his frail Race,
That thou should'st such a shadow Grace!
Next to thy Angels most renown'd,
With Majesty and Glory Crown'd;
The King of all thy Creatures made;
That all beneath his feet hast laid:
And that on Dales or Mountains feed;
That shady woods or deserts breed;
What in the Aery Region glide,
Or through the rowling Ocean slide.
Lord, how illustrious is thy Name,
Whose Pow'r both Heav'n and Earth proclaim!

### *Humility.* G. S. Psal. 131.

THOU LORD, my witness art:
I am not proud of heart;
Nor look with lofty eyes;
Nor envy, nor despise;
Nor to vain pomp apply
My thoughts, nor soar too high:
But in behaviour mild;
And as a tender child,
Wean'd from his Mothers Breast
On thee alone I rest.

### *The word of God.* G. S. in Psal. 19.

GOD'S LAWS are perfect, and restore
The Soul to life, even dead before.
His Testimonies, firmly true,
With wisdom simple men indue.
The Lord's Commandments are upright,
And feast the Soul with sweet delight.
His Precepts are all purity,
Such as illuminate the eye.
The fear of God, soil'd with no stain,
Shall Everlastingly remain.
*Jehovah's* Judgments are Divine,
With Judgment he doth Justice join.
Which men should more than Gold desire,
Than heaps of Gold refin'd by fire:
More sweet than honey of the Hive,
Or Cels, where Bees their treasure stive.
Thy servant is inform'd from thence,
They their observers recompence.

### *The World.* F. Q.

O WHAT A Crocodilian world is this,
   Compos'd of treacheries and insnaring wiles!

She cloaths destruction in a formal kiss,
    And lodges death in her deceitful smiles;
        She hugs the Soul she hates, and there does prove,
        The veryest tyrant, where she vowes to love:
And is a Serpent most, when most she seems a Dove.

Thrice happy he, whose nobler thoughts despise
    To make an object of so easie gains;
Thrice happy he, who scorns so poor a prize
    Should be the Crown of his heroick pains;
        Thrice happy he that ne'er was born to try,
        Her frowns or smiles, or being born did lye
In his sad Nurses Arms an hour or two, and dye.

## *The Quip.* G. H.

THE MERRY world did on a day,
    With his Train-bands and Mates agree
To meet together where I lay,
    And all in sport to jeer at me.

First, Beauty crept into a Rose,
    Which when I pluckt not, Sir said she,
Tell me I pray, whose hands are those?
    *But thou shalt answer, Lord, for me.*

Then Money came, and chinking still,
    What tune is this, poor man? said he:

I heard in Musick you had skill;
   *But thou shalt answer, Lord for me.*

Then came brave Glory puffing by,
   In Silks that whistled, who but he?
He scarce allow'd me half an eye.
   *But thou shalt answer, Lord, for me.*

Then came quick wit and Conversation,
   And he would needs a comfort be,
And to be short, make an Oration.
   *But thou shalt answer, Lord, for me.*

Yet when the hour of thy design,
   To answer these fine things shall come;
Speak not at large, say, I am thine:
   *And then they have their Answer home.*

## The Rest.   F. Q.

How is the anxious Soul of man befool'd
    In his desire,
That thinks a Hectick Fever may be cool'd
    In flames of Fire;
Or hopes to rake full heaps of burnisht Gold
    From nasty Mire!
  A whining Lover may as well request
    A scornful Breast,
To melt in gentle tears, as woe the world for rest:

Whose Gold is double with a careful hand,
　　　　His cares are double;
The Pleasure, Honour, Wealth of Sea and Land
　　　　Bring but a trouble;
The world it self, and all the world's command
　　　　Is but a bubble:
　The strong desires of man's insatiate breast
　　　　May stand possest
Of all that earth can give, but earth can give no rest.

The world's a seeming Paradise, but her own
　　　　And man's Tormenter;
Appearing fixt, but yet a rowling-stone:
　　　　Without a tenter
It is a vast circumference, where none
　　　　Can find a Centre:
　Of more than earth can earth make none possest;
　　　　And he that least
Regards this restless world, shall in this world find rest.

## The Retreat, Return.  F. Q.

Lord, when we leave the world, and come to thee,
　　　　How dull, how slug are we!
But when at earth we dart our wing'd desire,
　　　　We burn, we burn like Fire.
If pleasure becken with her balmy hand,
　　　　Her beck's a strong command.

If honour call us with her Courtly breath,
  An hours delay is death.
If Profits Golden finger'd-charms inveigle's,
  We clip more swift than Eagles.
*Lord, stop our Flight, and turn our Course, that we*
  *May fly as fast to thee.*

### *Sunday.*   G. H.

O DAY MOST calm, most bright;
The Fruit of this, the next world's Bud;
 Th' Indorsment of supreme delight,
Writ by a Friend, and with his Blood;
 The Couch of time, cares Balm and Bay;
The week were dark but for thy light:
  Thy torch doth show the way.

 The other dayes, and thou
 Make up one man, whose face thou art,
Knocking at Heaven with thy brow:
 The worky dayes are the back part;
The burden of the week lies there,
 Making the whole to stoop and bow
  Till thy release appear.

 Man had straight forward gone
 To endless death: but thou dost pull
And turn us round to look on one,
 Whom, if we were not very dull
We could not choose but look on still;
 Since there is no place so alone,
  The which he doth not fill.

 Sundayes the Pillars are,
 On which Heaven's Palace arched lies:
The other dayes fill up the spare
 And hollow room with vanities.
They are the fruitful Beds and Borders
 In God's rich Garden: that is bare
  Which parts their ranks and orders:

 The Sundayes of man's Life
 Threaded together, on time's string,
Make bracelets to adorn the wife,

Of the Eternal Glorious King.
On Sunday Heaven's Gate stands ope;
  Blessings are plentiful and rife,
    More plentiful than hope.


    This day my Saviour rose,
    And did inclose this Light for his:
That as each Beast his Manger knowes,
    Man might not of his Fodder miss.
Christ hath took in this piece of ground;
    And made a Garden there for those
      Who want Herbs for their wound.


    The Rest of our Creation
    Our great Redeemer did remove
With the same shake, which at his Passion
    Did earth, and all things with it move.
As *Sampson* bore the doors away,
    Christ's hands though nailed, wrought our Salvation,
      And did unhinge that day.


    The brightness of that day
    We sullied by our foul offence:
Wherefore that Robe we cast away,
    Having a new at his expence,
Whose Drops of Blood paid the full price,
    That was required to make us gay,
      And fit for Paradise.


    Thou art a day of Mirth:
    And where the week dayes trail on ground,
Thy Flight is higher as thy Birth.
    O let me take thee at the bound,
Leaping with thee from seven to seven,
    Till that we both, being toss'd from Earth,
      Fly hand in hand to Heaven.


## *The Church*  G. s. in Psal. 84.

O HOW amiable are
Thy abodes, great God of war!
Happy men who spend their dayes
In thy Courts, there sing thy praise.
Happy, who on thee depend;

Thine their way, and thou their end.
One day in thy Courts alone,
Far exceeds a Million.
In thy house contemn'd and poor,
I had rather keep a door,
Than with wicked men possess,
All that they call happiness.
O thou Shield of our defence!
O thou Sun, whose influence
Sweetly glides into our hearts!
Thou, who all to thine imparts!
Happy! O thrice happy he,
Who alone depends on thee.


### The Young Man's Mirth.   F. Q. *Eccl. 11. 9.

*Young man Rejoyce: what jolly mirth is here?
*Let thy heart chear thee*: what delicious chear?
*In thy Young dayes:* thy cates will relish sweeter.
*Walk thy own wayes:* thy cares will pass the fleeter.
*Please thine own heart:* carve where it likes thee best.
*Delight thine Eyes*: and be a joyful Guest.
*But know withall, the day will come, whereon*
*Thy Judge will doom thee for the deeds th'hast done.*
O what a Feast! O what a reckoning's here!
Thy cates are sweet; the shot's extreamly dear.


### Grace.   G. H.

My stock lies dead, and no increase
    Doth my dull Husbandry improve:
O let thy Graces without cease
        Drop from above.

If still the Sun should hide his Face,
    Thy house would but a Dungeon prove,
Thy works nights Captives; O let Grace
        Drop from above.

The Dew doth every Morning fall;
    And shall the Dew out-strip thy Dove?

The Dew, for which Grass cannot call,
        Drop from above.

Death is still working like a Mole,
   And digs my Grave at each remove:
Let Grace work too, and on my Soul
        Drop from above.

Sin is still hammering my heart
   Unto a hardness, void of love:
Let suppling Grace, to cross his Art,
        Drop from above.

O come! for thou dost know the way:
   Or if to me thou wilt not move,
Remove me where I need not say,
        Drop from above.

## *Contentment.* R. S.

I DWELL in Grace's Court,
   Enricht with Virtue's rights:
Faith guides my wit, Love leads my will;
   Hope all my mind's delights.

In lowly vales I mount
   To pleasure's highest pitch:
My honest meanness Honour brings,
   My poor Estate is rich.

My Conscience is my Crown,
   Contented thoughts my rest.
My heart is happy in it self;
   My Bliss is in my Breast.

Enough, I reckon wealth;
   A mean, the surest Lot;
That lies too high for base contempt,
   Too low for envies shot.

My wishes are but few;
   All easie to fulfil:
I make the limits of my power,
   The bounds unto my will.

I feel no care of Coin;
   Well-doing is my wealth:
My mind to me an Empire is,
   While Grace affordeth health.


## Prosperity. F. Q.

TAKE HEED, thou prosperous sinner, how thou liv'st
   In sin, and thriv'st.
Thou that dost flourish in thy heaps of Gold,
   And Sums untold.
Thou, that hadst never reason to complain
   Of Cross or Pain:
Whose unafflicted Conscience never found
   Nor check, nor wound.
Believe it, *Prosper*, thy deceitful lease
Affords thee neither wealth, nor joy, nor peace.

Thy Golden heaps are nothing but the price
   Of Paradise:
Thy flatt'ring pleasures, and thy aery joyes,
   But painted toyes:
Thy peaceful Conscience is but like a dog,
   Ty'd in a clog.
Believe it, *Prosper* thy deceitful Lease
Allows thee neither wealth, nor joy, nor peace.

Thy heaps of Gold will stand thee in no steed.
   At greatest need:
Thy empty pleasure will convert thy laughter
   To groans hereafter.
Thy silent Conscience when inlarg'd, will roar,
   And rage the more.
Believe it, *Prosper* thy deceitful lease
Affords thee neither wealth, nor joy, nor peace.


## Paradise. G. H.

I BLESS THEE Lord, because I *GROW*
Among thy trees, which in a *ROW*,
To thee both Fruit and Order *OW*.

What open Force, or hidden *CHARM*

Can blast my Fruit, or bring me *HARM*,
While the inclosure is thine *ARM*.

Inclose me still for fear I *START*,
Be to me rather sharp and *TART*
Then let me want thy hand and *ART*.

When thou dost greater Judgments *SPARE*,
And with thy knife but prune and *PARE*.
Ev'n fruitful trees more fruitful *ARE*.

Such sharpness showes the sweetest *FREND*:
Such cuttings rather heal then *REND*:
And such beginnings touch their *END*.

## *Several sins.* F. Q.

*Drunkenness.*

I T IS A Thief, that oft before his face,
Steals man away, and layes a beast in's place.
*Gross sin.*
It is a show'r, which e're we can get in,
*And find a shelter,* wets us to the skin.
*Sin of Infirmity.*
Is like the falling of an *April*-show'r:
'Tis often rain, and sun-shine in an hour.
*Sin of Custom,*
Is a long show'r beginning with the light;
Oft-times continuing till the dead of night.
*Sin of Ignorance,*
It is a hideous mist, that wets amain,
Though it appears not in the form of rain.
*Crying sin.*
It is a sudden show'r that tears in sunder,
The cope of Heaven, and always comes with thunder.
*Sin of Delight.*
Is like a feather'd show'r of snow, not felt,
But soaks to th' very skin when e're it melt.
*Sin of Presumption,*
Does like a show'r of hail, both wet and wound
With sudden death, or strikes us to the ground.
*The sin of Sins.*
It is a sulph'rous show'r, like that which fell.

On *Sodom*, strikes, and strikes to th' pit of Hell.

*Lord, let thy saving Grace thy servants shrow'd,*
*Till we arrive where's neither show'r nor cloud.*


### *Repentance.*  F. Q.

'T IS NOT to cry God mercy, or to sit
    And droop; or to confess that thou hast fail'd:
'Tis to bewail the sins thou didst commit,
    And not commit those sins thou hast bewail'd.
He that bewails, and not forsakes them too,
Confesses rather what he means to do.


### *Praise.*  G. H.

KING OF Glory, King of Peace!
        I will love thee:
And that love may never cease,
        I will move thee.

Thou hast granted my request,
        Thou hast heard me:
Thou did'st note my working breast;
        Thou hast spar'd me.

Therefore with my utmost art,
        I will sing thee:
And the cream of all my heart
        I will bring thee.

Though my sins against me cry'd,
        Thou didst clear me:
And alone, when they reply'd,
        Thou did'st hear me.


#### *The Offering.* [G. H.]

        Since my sadness
        Into Gladness
    Lord thou dost convert,
        O accept

What thou hast kept
As thy due desert.
Had I many,
Had I any,
(For this heart is none)
All were thine,
And none of mine,
Surely thine alone.
Yet thy favour
May give savour
To this poor Oblation;
And it raise
To be thy praise,
And be my Salvation.


## *Light.* A. C.

HAIL ACTIVE nature's watchful life and health!
Her joy, her ornament and wealth!
Hail to thy Husband heat, and thee*!*
Thou the world's beauteous Bride, the lustry Bridegroom he.

Say from what Golden quivers of the Sky,
Do all thy winged arrows fly?
Swiftness and Power by Birth are thine:
From thy great Sire they came, thy Sire the word Divine.

'Tis I believe, thine archery to show,
That so much cost in colours thou,
And skill in painting dost bestow
Upon thine antient arms, the gaudy Heavenly bow.

Swift as wing'd thoughts their light carrier do run
Thy race is finisht when begun*:*
Let a Post-Angel start with thee,
And thou the Goal of earth shalt reach as soon as he.

Thou in the Moons bright chariot proud and gay,
Dost thy bright world of Stars survey;
And all the year doth with thee bring
A thousand flowry lights, thine own Nocturnal spring.

Thou *Scythian* like dost round thy lands above
The Suns gilt tent for ever move;

And still as thou in pomp dost go,
The shining Pageants of the world attend thy show.

Nor amidst all these triumphs dost thou scorn
   The humble glow-worms to adorn,
   And with those living spangles gild
(O greatness without pride) the bushes of the field.

Night, and her ugly subjects thou dost fright;
   And sleep, the lazy Owl of night:
   Asham'd, and fearful to appear
They skreen their horrid shapes with the black Hemisphere.

At thy appearance fear itself growes bold;
   Thy sun-shine melts away his cold:
   Encourag'd at the sight of thee,
To the Cheek colour comes, and firmness to the Knee.

Ev'n lust, the master of a harden'd face,
   Blushes, if thou be'st in the place;
   To darkness Curtains he retires,
In sympathising night he rowls his smoaky fires.

When *Queen of Beauties*, thou lift'st up thy head,
   Out of the Mornings purple bed,
   The quire of birds about thee play,
And all the joyful world salutes the rising day.

All the worlds brav'ry that delights our eyes,
   Is but thy several liveries;
   Thou the rich dye on them bestow'st,
Thy nimble pencil paints this landshape as thou go'st.

A crimson garment in the rose thou wear'st:
   A Crown of studded Gold thou bear'st;
   The Virgin-lillies in their white,
Are clad but with the lawn of almost naked light.

The Violet like a little Infant stands,
   Girt in thy purple swadling bands:
   On the fair Tulip thou dost dote:
Thou cloth'st it in a gay, and party colour'd coat.

But when firm bodies thy free course oppose,
   Gently thy source the Land o're flows;

Takes there possession, and does make
Of colours mingled, light, a thick and standing lake.

But the vast Ocean of unbounded day,
In th' Empyræan Heaven does stay:
Thy Rivers, Lakes and Springs below
From thence took first their rise, thither at last must flow.

## *Success.* G. S. Psal. 127.

UNLESS THE LORD the house sustain,
They build in vain,
In vain they watch unless the Lord,
The City Guard.
In vain ye rise before the light,
And break the slumbers of the night:

In vain the bread of sorrows eat,
Got by your sweat;
Unless the Lord with good success
Your labours bless:
For he all good on his bestows.
And crowns their eyes with sweet repose.

## *Hope.* A. C.

HOPE OF ALL ills that men endure,
The only cheap and universal cure!
Thou captives freedom, and thou sick mans health!
Thou loosers vict'ry, and thou beggars wealth!
Thou Manna, which from Heav'n we eat,
To ev'ry tast a several Meat!
Thou strong retreat! thou sure intail'd Estate,
Which nought has power to alienate!
Thou pleasant, honest flatterer! For none
Flatter unhappy men but thou alone.

Hope, thou first fruits of happiness!
Thou gentle dawning of a bright success!
Thou good preparative, without which our joy
Does work too strong and whilst it cures destroy;

Who out of tortures reach dost stand,
    And art a Blessing still in hand!
Whilst thee, her *Earnest-money* we retain,
    We certain are to gain,
Whether she her bargain break, or else fulfil,
Thou only good, not worse for ending ill.

    Brother of Faith, 'twixt whom and thee
The joyes of Heaven and Earth divided be!
Though faith be Heir, and have the first Estate,
Thy portion yet in moveables is great.
    Happiness it self's all one
    In thee, or in Possession:
Only the future's thine, and present his:
    Thine's the more hard and noble bliss.
Best Apprehender of our joyes which hast
So long a reach, and yet canst hold so fast.


### *Good Conscience.* Q.

A CONSCIENCE pure, unstain'd by sin,
Is Brass without, and Gold within.


### *The Holy Heart.* F. Q.

THE ROYAL Off-spring of a second Birth,
Sets ope to Heaven, and shuts the doors to Earth.
If Earth (Heavens Rival) dart her idle Ray,
To Heaven 'tis wax, and to the world 'tis Clay.
If earth present delights, it scorns to draw;
But, like the Jet unrubb'd, disdains that straw.
No hope deceives it, and no doubt divides it;
No grief disturbs it, and no errour guides it.
No fear distracts it, and no rage inflames it;
No guilt condemns it, and no folly shames it.
No sloth besots it, and no lust inthrals it;
No scorn afflicts it, and no passion galls it.
It is a Carknet of immortal Life;
An Ark of Peace; the lists of sacred strife;
A purer piece of endless transitory;
A shrine of Grace, a little Throne of Glory.
A Heaven born Off-spring of a new born Birth;
An earthly Heaven, an ounce of Heavenly earth.

## Man's Life.  F. Q.

Our life is nothing but a winters day:
Some only break their fast, and so away:
Others stay dinner, and depart full fed;
The deepest age but sups, and goes to bed.
He's most in debt that lingers out the day:
Who dies betime has less, and less to pay.

## Man's Folly.  I. C.

Lord, what a foolish thing is man!
  How fond is he of toyes!
How does he spend that little span
  Of his in empty joyes!

But for that precious soul of his,
  He takes no further care
To fit it for immortal bliss
  Such thoughts too serious are.

Himself to every pleasure gives,
  And drowns his soul in lust:
In all destructive sins he lives;
  'Till levell'd with the dust.

Give me, O Lord, that pious care,
  And that obsequious love;
That all my actions may declare,
  I seek that place above.

Where we from sin exempt shall be;
  From sorrow and from tears:
And where no trouble we shall see,
  Nor be disturb'd with fears.

## Christ Crucified.  R. F.

Behold and see, if ever any pain
Did match his sorrow who for us was slain!
Lo, God bleeds on the Cross! high Heav'n descends

In blood to make man and his Maker friends.
When guilty man lay doom'd Eternally
To Death and Hell, ev'n God himself could dye,
And smile upon those wounds, that spear, that grave,
Which our Rebellion merited and gave.
This love exceeds all height: yet I confess
'Twas God that did it, how could it be less?

## *Death.* J. D.

Death, be not proud, though some have called thee
　　Mighty and dreadful: for thou art not so.
　　For those, whom thou think'st thou dost overthrow,
Die not, poor death; nor yet canst thou kill me.
From rest and sleep, which but thy picture be,
　　Much pleasure, then from thee much more must flow:
　　And soonest our best men with thee do go,
Rest of their bones, and souls delivery;
　　Th' art slave to fate, chance, Kings and desperate men;
　　　And dost with poyson, war and sickness dwell:
　　　Hard pains or poppy make us sleep as well,
　　And better then thy stroke: why swell'st thou then
One short sleep past, we wake Eternally;
And death shall be no more, death, thou shalt dye.

## *The Resurrection.* J. D.

At the round earth's imagin'd corners blow
　　Your trumpets, Angels: men arise, arise
　　From death; you numberless infinities
Of souls unto your scatter'd bodies go;
All whom one floud did, and fire shall or'ethrow;
　　All whom war, death, age, agues, tyrannies,
　　Despair, law, chance hath slain, and you whose eyes
Shall behold God, and never tast death's wo.
But let them sleep, Lord, and me mourn a space,
　　For if above all these my sins abound,
'Tis late to ask abundance of thy Grace,
　　When we are there. Here on this lowly ground
Teach me how to repent: for that's as good
As if th' 'adst seal'd my pardon with thy blood.

## *The Judgment-Day.* R. C.

Hear'st thou my Soul, what serious things,
*The Prophets say*, the Psalmist sings
Of a strict Judge from whose sharp ray,
The world in flames shall fly away.

O that fire! before whose face
Heav'n and Earth shall find no place.
O those eyes! whose angry light
Must be the day of that dread night.

O that trump! whose blast shall run,
An even round with th' circling sun,
And urge the murm'ring graves to bring
Pale Mankind forth to meet their King.

Horrour of nature, Hell and Death!
When a deep groan shall from beneath
Cry out, *We come, we come*; and all
The caves of night answer one call.

O that book! whose leaves so bright
Will set the world in severe light:
O the Judge! whose Hand, whose Eye,
None can endure, yet none can fly.

Yet thou giv'st leave, dread Lord, that we
Take shelter from thy self in thee;
And with the wings of thine own Dove
Fly to thy Sceptre of soft love.

Mercy, my Judge, mercy I cry,
With blushing cheek, and bleeding eye:
The conscious colours of my sin
Are red without, and pale within.

O let thine own soft bowels pay
Thy self, and so discharge that day.
If sin can sigh, love can forgive:
O say the word, my soul shall live.

O when thy last frown shall proclaim
The flocks of goats to folds of flame;
And all thy lost sheep found shall be,
Let *come ye blessed* then call me.

## *Heaven.*  G. F.

Behold this house where man doth now reside.
 The flow'rs pour out their odours in his way:
To serve him all the creatures take a pride:
 The winds do sweep his chambers ev'ry day,
 And clouds do wash his rooms: the ceiling gay
Starred aloft the gilded knobs imbrave.
 If such a house God to another gave,
How shine those glitt'ring Courts he for himself will have?

And if a sullen cloud, as sad as night,
 In which the Sun may seem imbodied,
Depur'd of all his dross we see so white,
 Burning in melted Gold his watry head.
 Or round with Ivory edges silvered,
What Lustre super-excellent will he
Lighten on those that shall his sun-shine see,
In that all glorious Court, in which all glories be.

If but one Sun with his diffusive fires,
 Can paint the Stars, and the whole world with light;
And joy and life into each heart inspires;
 And ev'ry Saint shall shine in Heaven as bright
 As doth the Sun in his transcendent might,
(As faith may well believe what truth once sayes)
What shall so many Suns united Rayes
But dazle all the eyes, that now in Heav'n we praise?

Here that bright band, that now in triumph shines,
 And that (before they were invested thus)
In earthly bodies carried Heavenly minds,
 Pitch, round about a Throne most glorious,
 Their sunny tents, and houses luminous;
All their Eternal day in Songs employing,
Joying their end, without end of their joying,
While their Almighty Prince, destruction is destroying.

Full, but yet never cloy'd with what might whet
 And dull the keenest craving Appetite:
Where never Sun did rise, nor ever set;
 But one Eternal day, and endless light
 Gives time to those, whose time is infinite:

Speaking with thought, obtaining without fee;
Beholding him whom never eye could see,
And magnifying him, that cannot greater be.

How can such joy as this want words to speak?
   And yet what words can speak such joy as this?
Far from the world that might their quiet break,
   Here the glad souls the face of beauty kiss,
   Pour'd out in pleasure on their beds of bliss:
And drunk with Nectar-Torrents, ever hold
Their eyes on him, whose Graces manifold,
The more they do behold, the more they would behold.


## *Happiness.* F. Q.

I LOVE, AND HAVE some cause to love the earth:
   She is my Makers creature; therefore good:
She is my Mother; for she gave me birth:
   She is my tender Nurse; she gives me food.
But what's a creature, Lord, compar'd with thee?
Or what's my Mother, or my Nurse to me?

I love the Air; her dainty sweets refresh
   My drooping soul, and to new sweets invite me:
Her shrill-mouth'd quire sustain me with their flesh,
   And with their *Polyphonian* notes delight me.
But what's the air, or all the sweets that she
Can bless my Soul withal, compar'd to thee?

I love the Sea; she is my fellow-creature,
   My careful Purveyor; she provides me store;
She walls me round; she makes my diet greater;
   She wafts my treasure from a forreign shore.
But Lord of Oceans, when compar'd with thee,
What is the Ocean, or her wealth to me?

To Heaven's high City I direct my Journey,
   Whose spangled Suburbs entertain mine eye;
Mine eye, by contemplations great attorney,
   Transcends the Crystal pavement of the Sky.
But what is Heav'n great God, compar'd to thee?
Without thy presence Heav'n's no Heaven to me.

Without thy presence earth gives no refection;
   Without thy presence sea affords no treasure;
Without thy presence air's a rank infection;
   Without thy presence Heav'n it self's no pleasure.
If not possest, if not enjoy'd in thee,
What's earth, or sea, or air, or Heav'n to me?

The highest honours that the world can boast,
   Are Subjects far too low for my desire: ·
The brightest beams of Glory are  (at most)
   But dying sparkles of thy living fire.
The proudest flames that earth can kindle, be
But nightly Glow-worms, if compar'd to thee.

Without thy presence, wealth are bags of cares;
   Wisdom, but folly; joy, disquiet sadness:
Friendship is treason, and delights are snares;
   Pleasures but pain, and mirth, but pleasant madness.
Without thee, Lord, things be not what they be;
Nor have they being when compar'd with thee.

In having all things, and not thee, what have I?
   Not having thee, what have my labours got?
Let me enjoy but thee, what farther crave I?
   And having thee alone, what have I not?
I wish nor Sea, nor Land, nor would I be
Possest of Heav'n, Heav'n unpossest of thee.

*FINIS.*

# Divine and Moral Songs

### Attempted in Easy Language,
### For the Use of Children

## By ISAAC WATTS

**M**ORE INFLUENTIAL THAN BUNYAN'S *poems for children have been Watts'* Divine and Moral Songs, *cautionary poems more severe in their warnings against evil than those of Bunyan. In* The New England Primer, *where some of the more stringent were repeated in many editions, and in imitations which appeared in nineteenth-century newspapers and Sunday School tracts, these poems helped to shape the life of English-speaking children during the eighteenth and nineteenth centuries. (They were published in 1715, or some twenty-five years after Bunyan's.)*

*Typical of the Divine Songs is No. 2, with its stately measures and eighteenth-century world view, in which the beauties of the earth are praised and man's indebtedness to God acknowledged. Song No. 11, with its grim warnings, is reprinted in editions of* The New England Primer *in the eighteenth and nineteenth centuries. Song No. 12 sounds Horatian in its beginning: "Happy's the child, whose youngest years," but then it goes on to rhyme receiving instructions well with avoiding the road to hell. Song No. 13, which begins, "Why should I say—'Tis yet too soon/To seek for heav'n, or think of death?" was reprinted in Sunday School pamphlets which flooded the American market in the nineteenth century.*

*Still famous for its opening sentence is Song No. 16, which begins, "Let dogs delight to bark and bite." Song No. 17 is remembered for the line, "Birds in their little nests agree," often repeated orally and sometimes in literature in the nineteenth century, as in Louisa May Alcott's* Little Women, *where it is quoted by Beth. "How doth the little busy bee" (No. 20) became famous, not only because it was reprinted in pamphlets for children issued in the nineteenth century by* The American Tract Society *but because Lewis Carroll chose it as one of the poems which he parodied ("How doth the little crocodile") in* Alice in Wonderland. *Pious industry, the Protestant work ethic, was here inverted by Carroll, as he inverted many other social values. Song No. 23 invokes the ten commandments to enforce obedience: those who give their parents "honour due,/Here on this earth they long shall live,/And live hereafter too."*

*Among the Moral Songs, the first is interesting because Carroll also chose to parody it in* Alice: *"'Tis the voice of a sluggard, I heard him complain . . ." The most famous song is undoubtedly No. 8, "Cradle Hymn," often sung still. It appeared in editions of* The New England Primer.

*Some of the Moral Songs suggest Blake, who seems to have agreed with them, com-*

367

*pressed them, refuted them, or extended them, but in all cases, transformed them. Song No. 2, "Innocent Play," uses lambs as a learning experience just as Blake does, but Blake directs his attention to one lamb and asks the lamb if he is aware of his own divine origin. Watts' Song No. 6, "A Summer's Evening," compares the course of a day with the life of "A Christian." In "Nurse's Song" and "The Ecchoing Green," Blake treats the same subject, but his treatment is universal. He does not limit the life cycle to Christians. One notable difference between the Cradle Hymn of Watts and the Cradle Song of Blake is that Blake leaves out invidious comparisons. That is, Blake concentrates only on love between mother and child as it reflects love between God and man, whereas Watts includes a diatribe against sinful man.*

*It is interesting to contrast Watts' treatment of "The Rose" in his Moral Songs with Blake's poem on the rose in "Songs of Experience." While Watts, in the persona of a youth, promises to "gain a good name by well doing my duty,/This will scent like a rose when I'm dead," Blake concentrates on the "invisible worm," or conventional morality, within the rose, which creates possessive jealousy and brings about the true death of the human spirit.*

*Both writers use simple rhythms and objects from nature, but Watts concentrates on moral strictures and Blake swings free, makes profound statements about the nature of human life.*

*Simple songs which children—or some children—might still enjoy are (The Divine Songs): 2, 4, 7, 16, 17, 20, and 22; and (Moral Songs): 1, 2, 3, 5, 7, and 8.*

Divine and Moral Songs, attempted in easy language for the Use of Children *is reprinted from a nineteenth-century copy of the original edition in the British Library.*

## SONG I

### *General Song of Praise to God.*

How GLORIOUS is our Heav'nly King,
  Who reigns above the sky!
How shall a child presume to sing
  His dreadful majesty!

How great his pow'r is none can tell,
  Nor think how large his grace;
Not men below, nor saints that dwell
  On high before his face.

Not angels that stand round the Lord
  Can search his secret will;

But they perform his heav'nly word,
  And sing his praises still.

Then let me join this holy train,
  And my first off'rings bring;
Th' eternal God will not disdain
  To hear an infant sing.

My heart resolves, my tongue obeys,
  And angels shall rejoice,
To hear their mighty Maker's praise
  Sound from a feeble voice.

## SONG II

### *Praise for Creation and Providence.*

I SING THE almighty pow'r of God,
    That made the mountains rise;
That spread the flowing seas abroad,
    And built the lofty skies.

I sing the wisdom that ordain'd
    The sun to rule the day;
The moon shines full at his command,
    And all the stars obey.

I sing the goodness of the Lord,
    That fill'd the earth with food;
He form'd the creatures with his word,
    And then pronounced them good.

Lord, how thy wonders are display'd
    Where'er I turn mine eye;
If I survey the ground I tread,
    Or gaze upon the sky.

There's not a plant or flow'r below
    But makes thy glories known;
And clouds arise, and tempests blow,
    By order from thy throne.

Creatures (as numerous as they be)
    Are subject to thy care;
There's not a place where we can flee,
    But God is present there.

In heav'n he shines with beams of love,
    With wrath in hell beneath:
'Tis on his earth I stand or move,
    And 'tis his air I breathe.

His hand is my perpetual guard,
    He keeps me with his eye;
Why should I then forget the Lord,
    Who is for ever nigh?

## SONG III

### *Praise to God for our Redemption.*

BLEST BE THE wisdom and the pow'r,
    The justice and the grace,
That join'd in counsel to restore
    And save our ruin'd race.

Our father ate forbidden fruit,
    And from his glory fell;
And we, his children, thus were brought
    To death, and near to hell.

Blest be the Lord, that sent his Son
    To take our flesh and blood;
He for our lives gave up his own,
    To make our peace with God.

He honor'd all his Father's laws,
    Which we have disobey'd;
He bore our sins upon the cross,
    And our full ransom paid.

Behold him rising from the grave,
    Behold him rais'd on high;
He pleads his merit there, to save
    Transgressors doom'd to die.

There, on a glorious throne, he reigns,
    And, by his power divine,
Redeems us from the slavish chains
    Of Satan and of Sin.

Thence shall the Lord to judgment come,
    And with a sov'reign voice,
Shall call, and break up ev'ry tomb,
    While waking saints rejoice.

O may I then with joy appear
    Before the Judge's face,
And, with the bless'd assembly there,
    Sing his redeeming grace.


## SONG IV

### *Praise for Mercies, Spiritual and Temporal.*

WHENE'ER I TAKE my walks abroad,
    How many poor I see!
What shall I render to my God,
    For all his gifts to me?

Not more than others I deserve,
    Yet God has giv'n me more;
For I have food, while others starve,
    Or beg from door to door.

How many children in the street
    Half naked I behold!
While I am cloth'd from head to feet,
    And cover'd from the cold.

While some poor wretches scarce can tell
    Where they may lay their head,
I have a home wherein to dwell,
    And rest upon my bed.

While others early learn to swear,
    And curse, and lie, and steal,
Lord, I am taught thy name to fear,
    And do thy holy will.

Are these thy favours day by day
    To me above the rest?
Then let me love thee more than they,
    And strive to serve thee best.


## SONG V

### *Praise for Birth and Education in a Christian Land.*

GREAT GOD! to thee my voice I raise,
    To thee my youngest hours belong;
I would begin my life with praise,
    'Till growing years improve the song.

'Tis to thy sov'reign grace I owe,
    That I was born on British ground,
Where streams of heav'nly mercy flow,
    And words of sweet salvation sound.

I would not change my native land
    For rich Peru, with all her gold;
A nobler prize lies in my hand
    Than East or Western Indies hold.

How do I pity those that dwell
    Where ignorance and darkness reigns;
They know no heav'n, they fear no hell,
    Those endless joys, those endless pains.

Thy glorious promises, O Lord!
    Kindle my hopes and my desire;
While all the preachers of thy word
    Warn me to 'scape eternal fire.

Thy praise shall still employ my breath,
    Since thou hast mark'd my way to
        heav'n;
Nor will I run the road to death,
    And waste the blessings thou hast giv'n.

# SONG VI

## *Praise for the Gospel.*

Lord, I ascribe it to thy grace,
  And not to chance, as others do,
That I was born of Christian race,
  And not a Heathen or a Jew.

What would the ancient Jewish kings,
  And Jewish prophets, once have giv'n!
Could they have heard these glorious
    things
  Which Christ reveal'd, and brought
    from heav'n.

How glad the heathens would have been,
  That worshipp'd idols, wood, and
    stone,
If they the book of God had seen,
  Or Jesus and his Gospel known.

Then if this gospel I refuse,
  How shall I e'er lift up mine eyes,
For all the Gentiles and the Jews
  Against me will in judgment rise.

# SONG VII

## *Excellency of the Bible.*

Great God, with wonder and with
    praise,
  On all thy works I look;
But still thy wisdom, pow'r, and grace,
  Shine brighter in thy book.

The stars, that in their courses roll,
  Have much instruction giv'n;
But thy good word informs my soul
  How I may climb to heav'n.

The fields provide me food, and show
  The goodness of the Lord:
But fruits of life and glory grow
  In thy most holy word.

Here are my choicest treasures hid,
  Here my best comfort lies;

Here my desires are satisfied,
  And hence my hopes arise.

Lord, make me understand thy law,
  Show what my faults have been;
And from thy gospel let me draw
  Pardon for all my sin.

Here would I learn how Christ has died
  To save my soul from hell:
Not all the books on earth beside
  Such heavenly wonders tell.

Then let me love my Bible more,
  And take a fresh delight,
By day to read thy wonders o'er,
  And meditate by night.

# SONG VIII

## *Praise to God for Learning to Read.*

The praises of my tongue
  I offer to the Lord,

That I was taught and learnt so young
  To read his holy word.

That I am brought to know
  The danger I was in,
By nature and by practice too,
  A wretched slave to sin.

That I am led to see
  I can do nothing well;
And whither shall a sinner flee
  To save himself from hell?

Dear Lord, this book of thine
  Informs me where to go,
For grace to pardon all my sin,
  And make me holy too.

Here I can read and learn
  How Christ, the Son of God,

Has undertook our great concern;
  Our ransom cost his blood.

And now he reigns above,
  He sends his spirit down,
To show the wonders of his love,
  And make his gospel known.

O may that spirit teach,
  And make my heart receive,
Those truths which all thy servants
    preach,
  And all thy saints believe.

Then shall I praise the Lord
  In a more cheerful strain,
That I was taught to read his word,
  And have not learnt in vain.

## SONG IX

### *The All-seeing God.*

Almighty god! thy piercing eye
  Strikes through the shades of night,
And our most secret actions lie
  All open to thy sight.

There's not a sin that we commit,
  Nor wicked word we say,
But in thy dreadful book 'tis writ,
  Against the Judgment Day.

And must the crimes that I have done
  Be read and published there?
Be all expos'd before the sun,
  While men and angels hear?

Lord! at thy foot asham'd I lie,
  Upward I dare not look;
Pardon my sins before I die,
  And blot them from thy book.

Remember all the dying pains
  That my Redeemer felt,
And let his blood wash out my stains,
  And answer for my guilt.

O may I now for ever fear
  T' indulge a sinful thought,
Since the great God can see and hear,
  And writes down ev'ry fault.

## SONG X

### *Solemn Thoughts of God and Death.*

There is a God that reigns above,

Lord of the heav'ns, and earth, and seas;

I fear his wrath, I ask his love,
    And with my lips I sing his praise.

There is a law which he has writ,
    To teach us all what we must do,
My soul to his commands submit,
    For they are holy, just, and true.

There is a gospel of rich grace,
    Whence sinners all their comforts draw:
Lord, I repent, and seek thy face,
    For I have often broke thy law.

There is an hour when I must die,

Nor do I know how soon 'twill come;
A thousand children, young as I,
    Are call'd by Death to hear their doom.

Let me improve the hours I have,
    Before the day of grace is fled;
There's no repentance in the grave,
    Nor pardons offer'd to the dead.

Just as the tree's cut down, that fell
    To north or southward, there it lies;
So man departs to heav'n or hell,
    Fix'd in the state wherein he dies.

# SONG XI

## *Heaven and Hell.*

THERE IS beyond the sky
    A heav'n of joy and love;
And holy children, when they die,
    Go to that world above.

There is a dreadful hell,
    And everlasting pains!
There sinners must with devils dwell,
    In darkness, fire, and chains.

Can such a wretch as I
    Escape this cursed end?
And may I hope, whene'er I die,
    I shall to heav'n ascend?

Then will I read and pray,
    While I have life and breath,
Lest I should be cut off to-day,
    And sent to eternal death.

# SONG XII

## *The Advantages of early Religion.*

HAPPY'S THE CHILD, whose youngest
        years
    Receive instructions well;
Who hates the sinner's path, and fears
    The road that leads to hell.

When we devote our youth to God,
    'Tis pleasing in his eyes;
A flower, when offer'd in the bud,
    Is no vain sacrifice.

'Tis easier work if we begin
    To fear the Lord betimes;
While sinners that grow old in sin
    Are harden'd in their crimes.

'Twill save us from a thousand snares
    To mind religion young;
Grace will preserve our following years,
    And make our virtue strong.

To thee, Almighty God! to thee
  Our childhood we resign;
'Twill please us to look back and see
  That our whole lives were thine.

Let the sweet work of pray'r and praise
  Employ my youngest breath;
Thus I'm prepar'd for longer days,
  Or fit for early death.

## SONG XIII

### *The Danger of Delay.*

WHY SHOULD I say—" 'Tis yet too soon
  To seek for heav'n, or think of death?"
A flow'r may fade before 'tis noon,
  And I this day may lose my breath.

If this rebellious heart of mine.
  Despise the gracious calls of heav'n,
I may be harden'd in my sin,
  And never have repentance giv'n.

What if the Lord grow wrath and swear,
  While I refuse to read and pray,
That he'll refuse to lend an ear
  To all my groans another day?

What if his dreadful anger burn,
  While I refuse his offer'd grace,
And all his love to fury turn,
  And strike me dead upon the place?

'Tis dangerous to provoke a God;
  His pow'r and vengeance none can tell;
One stroke of his almighty rod
  Shall send young sinners quick to hell.

Then 'twill for ever be in vain
  To cry for pardon and for grace,
To wish I had my time again,
  Or hope to see my Maker's face.

## SONG XIV

### *Examples of Early Piety.*

WHAT BLEST examples do I find
  Writ in the word of truth,
Of children that began to mind
  Religion in their youth.

Jesus, who reigns above the sky,
  And keeps the world in awe,
Was once a child as young as I,
  And kept his Father's law.

At twelve years' old he talk'd with men,
  (The Jews all wond'ring stand)
Yet he obey'd his mother then,
  And came at her command.

Children a sweet Hosanna sung,
  And blest their Saviour's name;
They gave him honour with their tongue,
  While scribes and priests blaspheme.

Samuel the child was wean'd, and brought
  To wait upon the Lord;
Young Timothy betimes was taught
  To know his holy word.

Then why should I so long delay
  What others learn so soon?
I would not pass another day
  Without this work begun.

## SONG XV

### *Against Lying.*

O'TIS A LOVELY thing for youth
　To walk betimes in wisdom's way;
To fear a lie, to speak the truth,
　That we may trust to all they say.

But liars we can never trust,
　Tho' they should speak the thing
　　that's true;
And he that does one fault at first,
　And lies to hide it, makes it two.

Have we not known, nor heard, nor read,
　How God abhors deceit and wrong?
How Ananias was struck dead,
　Caught with a lie upon his tongue?

So did his wife, Sapphira, die,
　When she came in, and grew so bold,
As to confirm that wicked lie
　Which just before her husband told.

The Lord delights in them that speak
　The words of truth; but ev'ry liar
Must have his portion in the lake
　That burns with brimstone and with
　　fire.

Then let me always watch my lips,
　Lest I be struck to death and hell;
Since God a book of reck'ning keeps
　For ev'ry lie that children tell.

## SONG XVI

### *Against Quarrelling and Fighting.*

LET DOGS DELIGHT to bark and bite,
　For God hath made them so;
Let bears and lions growl and fight,
　For 'tis their nature too.

But, children, you should never let
　Such angry passions rise;
Your little hands were never made
　To tear each other's eyes.

Let love thro' all your actions run,
　And all your words be mild:

Live like the blessed Virgin's son—
　That sweet and lovely child.

His soul was gentle as a lamb;
　And, as his stature grew,
He grew in favour both with man,
　And God, his Father, too.

Now Lord of all he reigns above,
　And, from his heav'nly throne,
He sees what children dwell in love,
　And marks them for his own.

## SONG XVII

### *Love between Brothers and Sisters.*

WHATEVER BRAWLS disturb the street,
　There should be peace at home;

Where sisters dwell, and brothers meet,
　Quarrels should never come.

Birds in their little nests agree;
  And 'tis a shameful sight,
When children of one family
  Fall out, and chide, and fight.

Hard names at first, and threat'ning
    words,
  That are but noisy breath,
May grow to clubs and naked swords,
  To murder and to death.

The devil tempts one mother's son
  To rage against another;

So wicked Cain was hurry'd on,
  Till he had kill'd his brother.

The wise will make their anger cool,
  At least before 'tis night;
But in the bosom of a fool
  It burns till morning light.

Pardon, O Lord! our childish rage,
  Our little brawls remove;
That, as we grow to riper age,
  Our hearts may all be love.

## SONG XVIII

### *Against Scoffing and Calling Names.*

OUR TONGUES WERE made to bless the
    Lord,
  And not speak ill of men;
When others give a railing word,
  We must not rail again.

Cross words and angry names require
  To be chastis'd at school;
And he's in danger of hell fire
  That calls his brother fool.

But lips that dare be so profane,
  To mock, and jeer, and scoff,
At holy things, or holy men,
  The Lord shall cut them off.

When children, in their wanton play,
  Serv'd old Elisha so,
And bid the prophet go his way,
  "Go up, thou bald head, go!"

God quickly stopp'd their wicked breath,
  And sent two raging bears,
That tore them limb from limb to death,
  With blood, and groans, and tears.

Great God! how terrible art thou
  To sinners e'er so young;
Grant me thy grace, and teach me how
  To tame and rule my tongue.

## SONG XIX

### *Against Swearing and Cursing, and taking God's Name in Vain.*

ANGELS THAT high in glory dwell,
  Adore thy name, Almighty God!
And devils tremble down in hell,
  Beneath the terrors of thy rod.

And yet how wicked children dare
  Abuse thy dreadful, glorious name;
And when they're angry, how they swear,
  And curse their fellows, and blaspheme!

How will they stand before thy face,
  Who treated thee with such disdain,
While thou shalt doom them to the place
  Of everlasting fire and pain!

Then never shall one cooling drop
  To quench their burning tongues
    be giv'n;
But I will praise thee here, and hope
  Thus to employ my tongue in heav'n.

My heart shall be in pain to hear
  Wretches affront the Lord above;
'Tis that great God whose pow'r I fear—
  That heav'nly Father whom I love.

If my companions grow profane,
  I'll leave their friendship when I hear
Young sinners take thy name in vain,
  And learn to curse, and learn to swear.

## SONG XX

### *Against Idleness and Mischief.*

How DOTH THE little busy bee
  Improve each shining hour!
And gather honey all the day
  From ev'ry op'ning flow'r!

How skilfully she builds her cell,
  How neat she spreads the wax!
And labours hard to store it well
  With the sweet food she makes!

In works of labour, or of skill,
  I would be busy too,
For Satan finds some mischief still
  For idle hands to do.

In books, or works, or healthful play,
  Let my first years be past;
That I may give for ev'ry day
  Some good account at last.

## SONG XXI

### *Against Evil Company.*

Why SHOULD I join with those in play
  In whom I've no delight?
Who curse and swear, but never pray
  Who call ill names and fight.

I hate to hear a wanton song,
  Their words offend my ears;
I should not dare defile my tongue
  With language such as their's.

Away from fools I'll turn my eyes,
  Nor with the scoffers go;

I would be walking with the wise,
  That wiser I may grow.

From one rude boy that us'd to mock,
  They learn the wicked jest;
One sickly sheep infects the flock,
  And poisons all the rest.

My God, I hate to walk or dwell
  With sinful children here;
Then let me not be sent to hell,
  Where none but sinners are.

## SONG XXII

### *Against Pride in Clothes.*

WHY SHOULD our garments, made to
    hide
Our parents' shame, provoke our pride?
The art of dress did ne'er begin
Till Eve our mother learnt to sin.

When first she put the cov'ring on,
Her robe of innocence was gone;
And yet her children vainly boast
In the sad marks of glory lost.

How proud we are; how fond to shew
Our clothes, and call them rich and new!
When the poor sheep and silk-worm
    wore
That very clothing long before.

The tulip and the butterfly
Appear in gayer coats than I;
Let me be drest fine as I will,
Flies, worms, and flow'rs exceed me still.

Then will I set my heart to find
Inward adornings of the mind;
Knowledge of virtue, truth and grace,
These are the robes of richest dress.

No more shall worms with me compare,
This is the raiment angels wear:
The Son of God, when here below,
Put on this blest apparel too.

It never fades, it ne'er grows old,
Nor fears the rain, nor moth, nor mould;
It takes no spot, but still refines—
The more 'tis worn, the more it shines!

In this on earth would I appear,
Then go to heav'n, and wear it there;
God will approve it in his sight,
'Tis his own work, and his delight.

## SONG XXIII

### *Obedience to Parents.*

LET CHILDREN that would fear the Lord,
  Hear what their teachers say;
With rev'rence meet their parents' word,
  And with delight obey.

Have you not heard what dreadful
    plagues
  Are threaten'd by the Lord,
To him that breaks his father's law,
  Or mocks his mother's word?

What heavy guilt upon him lies,
  How cursed is his name!
The ravens shall pick out his eyes,
  And eagles eat the same.

But those who worship God, and give
  Their parents honour due,
Here on this earth they long shall live,
  And live hereafter too.

## SONG XXIV

### *The Child's Complaint.*

WHY SHOULD I love my sport so well,
  So constant at my play,
And lose the thoughts of heaven and hell,
  And then forget to pray?

What do I read my Bible for,
  But, Lord, to learn thy will?
And shall I daily know thee more,
  And less obey thee still?

How senseless is my heart, and wild!
  How vain are all my thoughts!
Pity the weakness of a child,
  And pardon all my faults.

Make me thy heav'nly voice to hear,
  And let me love to pray;
Since God will lend a gracious ear
  To what a child can say.

## SONG XXV

### *A Morning Song.*

MY GOD, who makes the Sun to know
  His proper hour to rise,
And to give light to all below,
  Doth send him round the skies.

When from the chambers of the east
  His morning race begins,
He never tires, nor stops to rest,
  But round the world he shines.

So like the sun would I fulfil
  The business of the day;
Begin my work betimes, and still
  March on my heavenly way.

Give me, O Lord, thy early grace,
  Nor let my soul complain,
That the young morning of my days
  Has all been spent in vain.

## SONG XXVI

### *An Evening Song.*

AND NOW another day is gone,
  I'll sing my Maker's praise;
My comforts ev'ry hour make known.
  His providence and grace.

But how my childhood runs to waste!
  My sins how great their sum!
Lord, give me pardon for the past,
  And strength for days to come.

I lay my body down to sleep,
  Let angels guard my head;
And thro' the hours of darkness keep
  Their watch around my bed.

With cheerful heart I close my eyes,
  Since thou wilt not remove;
And in the morning let me rise,
  Rejoicing in thy love.

## SONG XXVII

### *For the Lord's Day Morning.*

THIS IS THE day when Christ arose
  So early from the dead;
Why should I keep my eyelids clos'd,
  And waste my hours in bed?

This is the day when Jesus broke
  The pow'rs of death and hell;
And shall I still wear Satan's yoke,
  And love my sins so well.

To day with pleasure Christians meet,
  To pray and hear the word;
And I would go with cheerful feet
  To learn thy will, O Lord!

I'll leave my sport to read and pray,
  And so prepare for Heav'n;
O! may I love this blessed day,
  The best of all the seven.

## SONG XXVIII

### *For the Lord's Day Evening.*

LORD! how delightful 'tis to see
A whole assembly worship thee!
At once they sing, at once they pray,
They hear of Heav'n, and learn the way.

I have been there, and still would go,
'Tis like a little Heav'n below;
Not all my pleasure and my play
Shall tempt me to forget this day.

O write upon my mem'ry, Lord,
The text and doctrines of thy word;
That I may break thy laws no more,
But love thee better than before.

With thoughts of Christ and things divine,
Fill up this foolish heart of mine,
That hoping pardon through his blood,
I may lie down and wake with God.

A FEW SLIGHT

# SPECIMENS

OF

## Dr. WATTS's MORAL SONGS.

## SONG I

### *The Sluggard.*

'TIS THE VOICE of a sluggard, I heard him complain,
"You've wak'd me too soon, I must slumber again;"
As the door on its hinges, so he on his bed
Turns his sides and his shoulders, and his heavy head.

"A little more sleep and a little more slumber;"
Thus he wastes half his days—and his hours without number;
And when he gets up he sits folding his hands,
Or walks about saunt'ring, or trifling he stands.

I pass'd by his garden, and saw the wild briar,
The thorn and the thistle grow broader and higher;
The clothes that hang on him are turning to rags,
And his money still wastes, till he starves or he begs.

I made him a visit, still hoping to find
He had taken more care in improving his mind;
He told me his dreams, talk'd of eating and drinking;
But he scarce reads his Bible, and never loves thinking.

Said I then to my heart, "Here's a lesson for me,
That man's but a picture of what I might be;
But thanks to my friends for their care in my breeding,
Who taught me betimes to love working and reading."

# SONG II

## *Innocent Play.*

ABROAD IN THE meadows to see the young lambs,
Run sporting about, by the side of their dams,
    With fleeces so clean and so white;
Or a nest of young doves in a large open cage,
When they play all in love, without anger or rage,
    How much we may learn from the sight!

If we had been ducks, we might dabble in mud,
Or dogs, we might play till it ended in blood,
    So foul and so fierce are their natures;
But Thomas, and William, and such pretty names,
Should be cleanly and harmless as doves or as lambs,
    Those lovely sweet innocent creatures.

Not a thing that we do, nor a word that we say,
Should injure another in jesting or play,
    For he's still in earnest that's hurt;
How rude are the boys that throw pebbles and mire,
There's none but a madman will fling about fire,
    And tell you 'tis all but in sport.

## SONG III

### *The Rose.*

How fair is the rose! what a beautiful flower!
　　The glory of June and of May;
But the leaves are beginning to fade in an hour,
　　And they wither and die in a day.

Yet the rose has one powerful virtue to boast
　　Above all the flowers of the field;
When its leaves are all dead, and fine colours are lost,
　　Still how sweet a perfume it will yield.

So frail is the youth and the beauty of men,
　　Though they bloom and look gay like the rose;
Yet all our fond care to preserve them is vain,
　　Time kills them as fast as he goes.

Then I'll not be proud of my youth or my beauty,
　　Since both of them wither and fade;
But gain a good name by well doing my duty,
　　This will scent like a rose when I'm dead.

## SONG IV

### *The Thief.*

Why should I deprive my neighbour
　　Of his goods against his will?
Hands were made for honest labour,
　　Not to plunder or to steal.

'Tis a foolish self-deceiving
　　By such tricks to hope for gain;
All that's ever got by thieving
　　Turns to sorrow, shame, and pain.

Have not Eve and Adam taught us,
　　Their sad profit to compute?
To what dismal state they brought us
　　When they stole forbidden fruit?

Oft we see a young beginner
　　Practise little pilfering ways,
Till, grown up a harden'd sinner,
　　Then the gallows ends his days.

Theft will not be always hidden,
　　Though we fancy none can spy;
When we take a thing forbidden,
　　God beholds it with his eye.

Guard my heart, O God of Heaven,
　　Lest I covet what's not mine;
Lest I steal what is not given,
　　Guard my heart and hands from sin.

# SONG V

## *The Ant or Emmet.*

THESE EMMETS, how little they are in our eyes,
We tread them to dust, and a troop of them dies,
    Without our regard or concern;
Yet as wise as we are, if we went to their school,
There's many a sluggard and many a fool
    Some lessons of wisdom might learn.

They don't wear their time out in sleeping or play,
But gather up corn in a sunshiny day,
    And for winter they lay up their stores;
They manage their work in such regular forms,
One would think they foresaw all the frosts and the storms,
    And so brought their food within doors.

But I have less sense than a poor creeping ant,
If I take no due care for the things that I want,
    Nor provide against dangers in time;
When death or old age shall stare me in the face,
What a wretch shall I be in the end of my days,
    If I trifle away all their prime.

Now, now, while my strength and my youth are in bloom,
Let me think what will serve me when sickness shall come,
    And pray that my sins be forgiven:
Let me read in good books, and believe and obey,
That when death turns me out of this cottage of clay,
    I may dwell in a palace in heav'n.

# SONG VI

## *A Summer's Evening.*

How FINE HAS the day been, how bright was the sun,
How lovely and joyful the course that he run,
Though he rose in a mist when his race he begun,
    And there followed some droppings of rain:
But now the fair traveller's come to the west,
His rays are all gold, and his beauties are best,
He paints the skies gay as he sinks to his rest,
    And foretells a bright rising again.

Just such is the Christian: his course he begins,
Like the sun in a mist, while he mourns for his sins,
And melts into tears; then he breaks out and shines,
    And travels his heavenly way:
But when he comes nearer to finish his race,
Like a fine setting sun he looks richer in grace,
And gives a sure hope, at the end of his days,
    Of rising in brighter array.

# SONG VII

## *Good Resolutions.*

THOUGH I AM now in younger days,
  Nor can tell what shall befal me,
I'll prepare for ev'ry place
  Where my growing age shall call me.

Should I e'er be rich or great,
  Others shall partake my goodness;
I'll supply the poor with meat,
  Never showing scorn nor rudeness.

Where I see the blind or lame,
  Deaf or dumb, I'll kindly treat them;
I deserve to feel the same,
  If I mock, or hurt, or cheat them.

If I meet with railing tongues,
  Why should I return them railing?
Since I best revenge my wrongs,
  By my patience never failing.

When I hear them telling lies,
  Talking foolish, cursing, swearing;
First I'll try to make them wise,
  Or I'll soon go out of hearing.

What though I be low and mean,
  I'll engage the rich to love me,
While I'm modest, neat, and clean,
  And submit when they reprove me.

If I should be poor and sick,
  I shall meet, I hope, with pity;
Since I love to help the weak,
  Though they're neither fair or witty.

I'll not willingly offend,
  Nor be easily offended;
What's amiss I'll strive to mend,
  And endure what can't be mended.

May I be so watchful still
  O'er my humours and my passion,
As to speak and do no ill,
  Though it should be all the fashion.

Wicked fashions lead to hell;
  Ne'er may I be found complying;
But in life behave so well,
  Not to be afraid of dying.

# SONG VIII

## *A Cradle Hymn.*

Hush! my dear, lie still and slumber,
  Holy angels guard thy bed!
Heav'nly blessings without number
  Gently falling on thy head.

Sleep, my babe; thy food and raiment,
  House and home thy friends provide,
All without thy care or payment,
  All thy wants are well supplied.

How much better thou'rt attended,
  Than the Son of God could be,
When from heaven he descended,
  And became a child like thee.

Soft and easy is thy cradle;
  Coarse and hard thy Saviour lay,
When his birth-place was a stable,
  And his softest bed was hay.

Blessed babe! what glorious features,
  Spotless fair, divinely bright!
Must he dwell with brutal creatures?
  How could angels bear the sight?

Was there nothing but a manger
  Cursed sinners could afford,
To receive the heav'nly stranger?
  Did they thus affront their Lord?

Soft, my child, I did not chide thee,
  Though my song might sound too hard;
'Tis thy mother* sits beside thee,
  And her arms shall be thy guard.

Yet to read the shameful story
  How the Jews abused their King,
How they serv'd the Lord of Glory,
  Makes me angry while I sing.

See the kinder shepherds round him,
  Telling wonders from the sky!
There they sought him, there they found
    him,
  With his virgin mother by.

See the lovely babe a dressing;
  Lovely infant, how he smil'd!
When he wept, the mother's blessing
  Sooth'd and hush'd the holy child.

Lo! he slumbers in a manger,
  Where the horned oxen fed;
Peace, my darling, here's no danger,
  Here's no ox anear thy head.

'Twas to save thee, child, from dying,
  Save my dear from burning flame,
Bitter groans and endless crying,
  That thy blest Redeemer came.

May'st thou live to know and fear him,
  Trust and love him all thy days,
Then go dwell for ever near him,
  See his face and sing his praise.

I could give thee thousand kisses,
  Hoping what I most desire;
Not a mother's fondest wishes
  Can to greater joys aspire.

## THE END.

---

* Here you may use the words brother, sister, friend, &c.